Ferenc Z. Váradi

Comrades, Mistakes Were Made

To Denis Curtán

Pete Varadi

June 19, 2012

Ferenc Z. Váradi

Comrades, Mistakes Were Made

Published by

P/ V Enterprises Inc.
4620 N. Park Ave #1606W
Chevy Chase, MD 20815
USA

Comrades, Mistakes Were Made

by

Ferenc Z. Váradi

First printing in Hungarian "Rések a bástyán" 2010
Móra Publishing Company, Budapest, Hungary
The cover page was designed by the author with the help of Tom Bornstein and receiving permission to use the illustration by Jenő Dallos

To be, or not to be, that is the question:
Or to take Arms against a Sea of troubles
And by opposing end them:

Shakespeare: *Hamlet*

INTRODUCTION

1949 – 1956 was one of the saddest periods in the history of Hungary. The state machinery of terror functioned perfectly but the introduced incredibly bad functioning Soviet communist economic system and its details, which had to be used in Hungary, did not. The communist party functionaries explained this: 'Comrades, on the socialist road to communism mistakes were made.'

Today, in retrospect, more than 50 years later, that system could be found amusing, but for whoever was there those years were not only nightmares but everyday's reality including mine. This book describe real stories which at that time were horrible but many of them today are quite amusing.

Winston S. Churchill in his speech on March 5, 1946 foresaw the history[1]:
"From Stettin in the Baltic to Trieste in the Adriatic an iron curtain has descended across the Continent. Behind that line lie all the capitals of the ancient states of Central and Eastern Europe. Warsaw, Berlin, Prague, Vienna, Budapest, Belgrade, Bucharest and Sofia; all these famous cities and the populations around them lie in what I must call the Soviet sphere, and all are subject, in one form or another, not only to Soviet influence but to a very high and in some cases increasing measure of control from Moscow. The Communist parties, which were very small in all these Eastern States of Europe, have been raised to pre-eminence and power far beyond their numbers and are seeking everywhere to obtain totalitarian control.

---

[1] Winston S. Churchill speech March 5, 1946, Westminster College, Fulton, Missouri

"In these States control is enforced upon the common people by various kinds of all-embracing police governments. The power of the State is exercised without restraint, either by dictators or by compact oligarchies operating through a privileged party and a political police."

Churchill precisely predicted in 1946 how the Soviet would shape the countries in Central- and Eastern Europe which at the 1945 Yalta Conference with Roosevelt, Stralin and Churchill was decided to become its 'sphere of influence'.

The majority of us living there simply did not realize what was going on around us. Not only us, but also the majority of the world did not realize it[2]. Stalin with his pipe projected to the world the image of a nice and understanding father and friend, while millions of people disappeared. I did not know anything about them and I assume the entire population of Hungary - except probably a few of the communist bosses – knew nothing, and these facts were not known to the world either.

There were many similarities between the Nazi and the Soviet communist dictatorships. One of these was that in both ideologies people were singled out to be persecuted by people who were the persecutors. The big difference between the two was, that while in the Nazi system in the population there was 'only' (please excuse the use of the word 'only') one group, which was branded, persecuted and destined for extinction, in the Soviet communist ideology there were severale group branded and destined for extinction. Stalin developed this further that not only the

---

[2] Peter Kenez: The Journal of Modern History 75 (December 2003) 864-869

groups branded by the communist ideology, but the entire population of the country should be exposed to persecution, could be accused, mostly without merit, brought to a show trial, or without a trial, condemned and annihilated.

Mátyás Rákosi, 'the best Hungarian disciple of Stalin' introduced the terror system developed by Stalin in Hungary. In the Hungarian communist terror participated those who adopted the Stalinist ideology, carried it out and executed it, who were steeling under the cover of this ideology, who were living out their cruel nature, and who exploited the opportunity to accuse others and to get ahead in life as a result of that. As of the large group who did not participate in this, they saw many examples of what the system of terror is capable to do, and lived in the uncertainty of what was going to happen to them?

In Hungary the terror touched everybody, indiscriminately even also those who were part of the apparatus of terror. As an example was Lászlo Rajk, who established in Hungary the 'Secret Police' (Államvedelmi Osztály – AVO), the army of terror of the communist system, which later detained Rajk and executed him. The cruel odd thing about this is that people seemed to be in a big kaleidoscope, which was from time to time shaken and whoever was down went to the top and who was on top tumbled down, people, forms, patterns and colors changed.

In the Nazi system the persecuted, persecutors and people who tried to save the persecuted existed. In the Hungarian Stalinist system of Rákosi nobody tried to save the persecuted, because everybody could be persecuted. On the other hand the interesting thing was in these fearful and for everybody insecure times of 1949 – 1956, that Oases existed in the midst of the terror. Oases were those places, smaller or larger, which consisted of party members and no party members, where everybody preserved its human dignity, where the managers and the subordinates were not vying for the other's job, they were not involved to accuse one to have his job, but they were helping each other and facing the terror around them and they stayed united. These Oases probably existed because they were not detected by the terror system, or the system needed the people working in the Oasis as Stalin said: 'Leave them in peace we can always shoot them later'[3].

This book is about such Oases, the 'Távkozlesi Kutató Intézet' (TKI) and the 'Tungsram Research Laboratories' in Újpest in the suburbs of Budapest.

At the end of the war Stalin directed Rákosi and his comrades to change Hungary to the Soviet system step by step[4] as he did not want to openly provoke his western 'allies'. Accordingly, between 1945 and 1948 the conversion of Hungary by Rákosi to a Stalinist communist system was done in slices using the 'Salami Tactic', but in 1948 he could declare that this is the 'Year of Change' [5].

The story in this book starts at that time.

---

[3] Ethan Pollock: Stalin and the Soviet Science Wars – Princeton University Press – 2006; P. 91

[4] http://countrystudies.us/hungary/36. htm

[5] Mátyás Rákosi used this wording in his speech on May 23, 1948

1. The "Year of Change"

I accompanied Jóska Fényes to the railroad station of Szeged. He was dressed very elegantly. In spite that it was a late fall day, but not a cold day, he had a winter coat. He carried a small suitcase and he was wearing a nice gray hat matching his winter coat. When we arrived at the tram station at the 'Great railroad station' of Szeged (it was called the 'Great station', because Szeged had another railroad station, called 'Rókus station', which was smaller), we disembarked and I asked him casually:

"Jóska, I never have seen you wearing a hat, not even during the coldest winter days, why did you buy a hat for this trip? Why the hell do you need a hat?"

"Idiot – he whispered –my Dollars are in the hat. I am going to deposit my hat in the train's luggage rack, if by chance they find the Dollars in the hat, I can say it is not mine, and everybody can testify that I never had a hat, as nobody has ever seen me wearing a hat. I lose the Dollars, but I will not be jailed for possessing foreign currency, especially Dollars."

I admitted, that was a well thought out scheme, because if somebody were caught having Dollars, the person would for sure be jailed.

We went up the stairs to the platform and Jóska boarded the train to Budapest. He put his suitcase in the luggage compartment above his head and the hat on the opposite side. The train was quite empty there was nobody else in the compartment he was in. He opened the window, leaned out. The train started to move I wished him a good trip and told him to write when he could. The train started to accelerate and as it departed, I waived my handkerchief, waited until the train left the station, turned around and descended the stairs and walked back towards the city. I was sad, because during the last half-year many of my good friends and relatives had left Hungary and now Jóska was also leaving.

Jóska was from the town of Gyöngyös, in the northern part of Hungary. His family was killed during the war. He came to Szeged in 1945 to attend the University to study chemistry and he was my classmate. Jóska[6] was going now to Budapest and he planned to go from there somehow to Vienna. Jóska, who was uninterested in politics and spent his time studying or with girls, told me already in September, that he sooner or later had to leave Hungary, because our Commies colleagues did not like him, because sometimes he would say something, which they did not like and he gathered from their remarks, that sooner or later he was going to have 'problems'.

He left at the end of November 1948. By that time, what the 'problems' were, everybody knew. In that scare, Jóska was not alone in Hungary.

One could give lots of examples of what had started to happen in Hungary. For me for example, which touched me closely, was when at the end of June 1948 I learned that Dr. Ödön Lénárd, who was my homeroom teacher at the Piarist high school in Szeged, and after the war in 1948 he became the cultural secretary of the Actio Catholica in

[6] Joseph (Jóska) Fényes after leaving Hungary attended the University of Montreal and received a Ph.D. in Chemistry.

Budapest was arrested by the Hungarian Secret Police AVO. According to the newspapers[7] he was accused of recommending to his students for home reading, books against the Soviet Union and gave lectures in which he vilified the Soviet system. His trial was July 19 –21, 1948[8]. I liked 'Dönci' – as we called him –and as he was my homeroom teacher for four years, from 1940 until the end of the school year in 1944, I knew personally that this was absolutely not true. This untrue issue was one of the accusations he was tried for in July 1948 and sentenced to prison, and it made me think, what one could expect in the future.

By the fall of 1948, even for me, who did not care about politics, it became clear, that in Hungary we were at the beginning of a horrible communist dictatorship. At that time one could still escape from Hungary across the Hungarian – Austrian border. For this reason during the late fall, besides of Jóska, several of my acquaintances, high school classmates, university colleagues, and many others left the country. A few of my relatives living in Budapest

[7] Magyar Nemzet July 15,1948

[8] Dr Ödön Lénárd was jailed during the communist times three times for a total of 17 months. He was the last Catholic priest who was in jail during the Kádár regime. He was released from jail when he received an amnesty in 1977, when the Pope *asked* personally the release of Dr. Lenard (Hetényi Varga Károly: Elfelejtett Hitvallónk, Pro Domo, Pécs, 2001) When I was in 1987 (since 1956 the first time) in Budapest, I made an effort to find my teacher, Dr. Lánárd and whenever I was in Hungary we always had lunch together. This was during a time, when his pupils living in Hungary still did not dare to meet him. He made a very thorough research about the behavior of the priests of the Catholic Church under the communist system. (Ödön Lénárd: Erő az erőtlenségben: Marton Áron Kiadó – 1994)

were already in Austria and I knew that one of my cousins from Budapest was planning to leave by the end of December. I wanted to go with him and I wanted to get my diploma in chemistry by that time.

In 1948 I was completing my doctoral thesis under the leadership of Árpád Kiss, who was a great scholar and was the Professor at the University of Szeged's Physical Chemistry Institute. By the end of the first semester of the 1948/49 academic year I had actually completed my thesis[9], and since I started my studies in September 1945 at the University of Szeged, every year with a special permission I was able to attend 55 hours/week of lectures and laboratory studies and therefore I was able to complete all the other requirements to get my diploma earlier, such as at the end of the 1948/49 first semester, but I needed a permission for this. I understood that I had to ask the Dean of the Faculty of Mathematics and Science for such a permit.

In the 1948/49 school year Professor Bruckner was the Dean of the University's Faculty of Mathematics and Science and I had to ask him to obtain the permit. Győző Bruckner was a world-famous Professor of Organic Chemistry at the University. He had this standing in organic chemistry, because he was able to achieve his results based on his predictions and foresight. Unfortunately, the only prediction in which he failed strongly influenced my future.

---

[9] Acta Chemica et Physica Universitatis Szegediensis: Tom III. Faso. 1 1950, pp 62; P.F. Varadi: The $CoCl_2 - H_2O$ – HCL system

At the beginning of December, before the end of the first semester of the 1948/49 school year, I visited Professor Bruckner. By that time I had been his student for four years. He received me in his office and as I knew him quite well I started immediately with my problem and told him that I completed all of the requirements, including that my Dissertation was also completed and accepted by Professor Kiss and I asked Professor Bruckner to give me permission to receive my Diploma at the end of the first semester of 1948/49.

Professor Bruckner was a very tall lanky, very friendly person, who in spite of being a world famous organic chemist dealt with his students like he would be only a young assistant professor. He listened to me patiently, but at the end of my story he told me, that unfortunately, he could not fulfill my request. He asked me, why on earth I want to hurry, if I completed everything, I could have a very comfortable half a year and go to movies, theatre, opera and see girls, and so on.

As I knew him quite well and I also knew that he was a very decent and good individual, I laid out my problem. I told him, that a part of my family, many of my friends and colleagues wanted to flee from the obviously developing communist dictatorship, which at that time was relatively easy, and I would like to follow them and go to the West. But very likely what would happen was that the western borders of Hungary would be guarded more seriously and one would not be able to escape from the country. He just waved his hand and smiled:

“I am sure that such a long border between Hungary and Austria cannot be closed so that one could not escape. I suggest you complete the second semester and you are going to receive your Diploma during the school year's closing ceremony during the end of June or the beginning of July and after that you will be able to go to the West following your family and friends."

I tried to convince him, but he said that in this issue he could not do anything, and assured me again that in his opinion they were not going to be able to establish in a half a year an airtight closing of the border. I asked the Professor to keep this discussion to himself, because if it would leak out I would have serious problems. He never mentioned this discussion to anybody. Unfortunately this prediction of Professor Bruckner that the long Hungarian – Austrian border could not be closed in a half a year did not prove right.

The closing of the borders between Stettin and Triest – what Winston Churchill in his 1946 speech called 'Iron curtain', - on which at the Hungarian – Austrian border were still big gaps – by July 1949 became closed, airtight. It was practically impossible to cross the border. On the Hungarian side of the Hungarian – Austrian border land mines were laid, barbed wire fences and watchtowers were built and armed border guards with dogs patrolled continuously. It was impossible to cross this, but if somebody miraculously would have been able to cross it, the person arrived in the Austrian Russian zone, which was patrolled by the armed Russian military and somehow they also had to cross this 30 – 50 mile zone successfully.

In June 1949, a few weeks before I received my Ph.D., I encountered Professor Kiss in the corridor of the Physical Chemical Institute. He asked me to go with him to his office. When we arrived, he asked me to sit down. After we both were seated, he lit a cigarette. He knew that I was not smoking and therefore he did not offer me one. He said that after I received my Diploma I should stay working in his Institute and offered me a position as "assistant lecturer". I was very glad to receive this offer and I thanked him. He said that if I accepted it, he would submit to the University a request, that I should be employed starting with the school year of September 1. I told him that I was very happy he selected me to be suitable to work for him in his Institute, and that besides the job I would be able to continue my research work under his guidance. We shook hands and I went home and told my mother about the news of this job offer, which was a very great honor and opportunity.

A week later, Professor Kiss's secretary was looking for me and asked me to meet him in his office. When I arrived in his office he told me, that he submitted his request to the University to appoint me as his 'assistant lecturer', but the DISZ (Kommunista Diák Ifjusági Szövetség = Communist Student Union), i.e. my classmates protested against my appointment to the University as an assistant lecturer, saying that I am not a party member and if I would stay at the University I would "corrupt the youth". He also told me, they would have no objection if I could get a job anywhere else, but not at the University. Prof. Kiss said that this was an incredible thing and he was not going to let it happen this way. I indicated that in view of this I should maybe look for a job somewhere else. He said he did not think this would be necessary, he was going to straighten this out.

It was probably characteristic of my and Professor Kiss's naivety and also that we were not being well informed, that at that time neither he nor I believed that the communist organizations had so much influence in the University issues. I could not believe that my Commies colleagues, with whom I had good relations, would do something like this, but it is possible that something else lay behind this. I could not sort out the events. Tito, whose empire was 15 kilometers from Szeged and who was until now the "socialism leading fighter" lately was named to be the "chained dog of the imperialists". László Rajk was imprisoned by the dreadful Secret Police (ÁVO), which he established. After I thought everything over, I decided to look for a job, because who knew what could happen.

In Hungary in those days only very few state owned research laboratories existed. Research was conducted mainly in University laboratories, but it seemed evident, that for me it was unlikely I could work in a University research lab and if I wanted to work in research then I would have to get a job in one of the very few laboratories which were a part of a manufacturing organization. If I would look for a not research oriented position I had to seek a job in a factory. Among the very few research laboratories, which were a part of a manufacturing organization, was the world famous 'Tungsram Research Laboratory' belonging to the 'United Incandescent Lamp' factory (Tungsram), located in Újpest, which is in the outskirts of Budapest.

At the beginning of July, at the year closing celebration of the University I received my Ph.D. Diploma. In our class, only Pista Halász and I received the Diploma, he also received it for his thesis made under Professor Kiss. Pista was a good friend of mine. He worked on a similar subject as I did. In the Physical Chemical Institute we worked many times in the same laboratory as we both used the now obsolete, but at that time very up to date König Martens type spectrophotometer and played bridge at nights. Pista said that after graduation he would like to get a job in Budapest at the Technical University in the institute of Professor Géza Schay. He was surprised when I told him, that our DISZ colleagues did not agree I should get a job as an assistant lecturer in Prof. Kiss's Institute, because I could 'corrupt the youth'. He was surprised and told me that he did not know who would have been responsible for this. As he could not imagine either, he found it a good idea that I should try to contact Tungsram's Research laboratory to find out if they would employ me.

Lipot Aschner[10] under whom the 'United Incandescent Lamp' factory obtained an excellent worldwide reputation established the Tungsram Research Laboratory in 1921. The first Director of the Laboratory was Professor Ignácz Pfeiffer under whom several world reputed researchers achieved advances in the quality of the incandescent lamps and later also of the electron tubes, used for radios. These were Tivadar Millner who developed the utilization and production of tungsten wires used as the light source of the lamps, Imre Brody who initiated the use of the krypton lamps, and Ernő Winter who achieved success in the field of electron tubes.

The lead of the Laboratory was taken over in 1936 by Zoltán Bay, who in 1946 with the help of his excellent

---

[10] Lipót Aschner (1872 – 1952) started to work in 1896 at a company, which became 'United Incandescent Lamp', which he renamed as 'Tungsram'. He became its President and CEO in 1921 and built it to become one of the six largest Incandescent lamp and radio tube factory in the world.

research team made experiments and confirmed that radio waves were reflected by the moon and with this he introduced the utilization of radar in astronomy. This secured the worldwide acknowledgement of Tungsram Research Laboratory. Professor Bay, the legendary boss of Tungsram Research laboratory, was in 1949 already in the West, out of Hungary.

I got in touch with Tungsram Research Lab. and was invited to go to Budapest to be interviewed. Before I left, I asked Prof. Kiss what the situation was. He said that in his opinion I was going to be appointed to the job, but no final decision had been made.

As the decision of my job at the University dragged on and I knew nothing about those who opposed my acceptance, when I thought the matter over I realized that my friends, acquaintances, many of my family had left Hungary, as they foresaw that the matter would develop the way it was happening with me. I unfortunately made a bad decision and now unknown people were directing my life, my fate. After my discussion with Prof. Kiss I went home and after having lunch with my mother, I laid down for a half hour. I was dreaming that I was walking in Paris or London – I never had been in either of these cities, and during my walk I remembered those days when unknown DISZ colleagues of mine kept me from getting a job at the University in Szeged. I was dreaming, and realized that these colleagues had no say in what I can do here and what I can decide about my own future. I woke up with these positive thoughts, when I heard the sound of an organ concert on the radio, which somehow was connected to my dream and became unforgettable. When the organ music stopped, there was silence and the announcer said that we were listening to the 'Toccata of Léon Boëllmann's Suite gothique'[11]. I was affected by this imposing music and decided, that I was going to seriously prepare myself for the interview at Tungsram Research Laboratory to get there a job, because this would not be the "last battle" but only the beginning. As I survived the Nazi times, I was going to survive the present ones too.

I prepared a list of my 'Scientific achievements', of which I had never made a list before, and I was surprised that it really looked very impressive, given that I had just received my Ph.D. The University's Faculty of Mathematics and Science every year announced a competition for certain subjects, so the students as well as the teaching staff could submit a work which the professors evaluated and decided which they found the best to receive a diploma and a prize. During my years at the University I submitted five works and received the prize for each of them, three from Mineralogy, one for Theoretical Physics and one for Physical Chemistry. I believed that very few students had such results. My Doctoral thesis was accepted and papers, which I wrote as a result of two of these works, were submitted to Hungarian scientific magazines and were accepted and going to be published shortly. After this preparation in the middle of July I went to Budapest and visited Tungsram Research Laboratory in Újpest. In the invitation letter I was informed which day and when I should arrive and report to the Director of the Laboratory, Dr. György Szigeti.

The United Incandescent Lamp (Tungsram) factory, where the Research Laboratory was also located, was in Budapest's Újpest district on the outer Váci Blvd. When I

[11] Léon Boëllmann (1862 – 1897)

arrived at the entrance of the factory and told the guards where I was going, they gave me instructions how to get there. When I neared the dark brown-red brick building of the Research Laboratory I saw on the roof the huge radio antenna. This was the famous antenna, which was used in February 1946 for Professor Bay's and his groups experiment to establish and prove that radio waves were reflected from the Moon[12]. When I saw this antenna, I realized, that I was coming now to a world famous Research Laboratory, in which I was maybe going to get a job. This would have been a marvelous thing for me, but my confidence dropped to a low point, considering would I be suitable to become a member of such a famous Research establishment?

Tungsram Research Laboratory – On top: Professor Z. Bay's experimental antenna

[12] Lajos Takács: Fizikai Szemle 1997/1 pp 20

I arrived at Dr. Szigeti's office, where his secretary told me shortly after my arrival that Dr. Szigeti was waiting for me and I should go to his office. I introduced myself, told him that I received my Ph.D. recently and gave him a copy of my 'scientific work', which I recently assembled. He reviewed them and praised me, how much work I did during my years of studying. He had a long discussion with me about my studies and my scientific work. He called in one of his coworkers to escort me to the office of Dr. Tivadar Millner, that he should interview me also. I knew Dr. Millner's name well, as he was the one who developed the production of the large crystal size Tungsten fiber, which made the long lasting and good quality Incandescent Lamp possible. I met also other members of the Research team, including Dr. András Dallos, whom I knew well from Szeged. It seems that my interview was successful, because at the end of the day, which for me lasted a very long time, I was informed that they were going to hire me as a chemist and I was going to work in the field of "oxide cathodes". I had absolutely no idea what an 'oxide cathode' was, but I tried to look very knowledgeable. Dr. Szigeti told me, the project was very important and it would be best if I would start to work as soon as possible.

This was naturally a problem, because I already assured Professor Kiss that I would work with him as assistant lecturer if he succeeded to secure my appointment, about which I was not very sure. I managed to come up with the idea that I had to finish my work, the studies of the 'magnetic susceptibility' of materials (this was true and sounded very convincing) and therefore I suggested starting on September 1. I proposed September 1, because by that time my University appointment had to be decided and I did not want to miss the summer season on the river Tisza. It seems that my interview made them interested in me and they accepted for me to start work on September 1.

On the train back to Szeged I had time to compare the situation between the University of Szeged and the Tungsram Research Laboratory. At the University of Szeged the DISZ that is my Commies colleagues could interfere and deny me obtaining even a relatively low level University job. In the Tungsram Research Laboratory, it seemed that the technical people made the decision, because I did not have to talk with a party functionary. The question whether I was a communist party member was never asked. I received a job offer without the opinion of a party functionary or asking for my background – so called 'cadre' - file. In general I had a very good opinion about the people I had contact with, who took into their consideration only my technical knowledge and my scientific achievements and not whether I was going to 'corrupt my surroundings'. Reflecting on the experiences of my short life, I knew that during the Nazi times the fate of one depended whether one got to deal with good or evil people. It seemed that this was true in communist times too. I came to the conclusion that it would be better for me to accept the job at Tungsram and not to stay in Szeged even if I got the assistant lecturer job there.

Finally, I did not have to make this decision, because after my return to Szeged Professor Kiss told me that because of my DISZ colleagues I would not be able to receive the appointment. He was very sorry for this and he could not understand how the communists had so much influence. As of today I know who were those colleagues who opposed my appointment as assistant lecturer to the University of Szeged, and at this time I would like to thank them, because if they would have let me have that job, there would have been a very great probability that I would have been removed from it when a suitable "cadre" would have needed it, or if that would not have happened I would still live in Szeged as a retired University Professor. At that time I was very sorry to leave Professor Kiss, he was a great scientist and I was eager to work with him to learn more. But in Tungsram Research Lab they were also great scientists and I was offered to start working in an extremely interesting field and to learn new scientific areas.

I was born in Szeged and until then I spent all my life in Szeged. I attended there all of my schools, including the University. My parents lived in Szeged, at that time only my Mother was alive. We lived in the same building in Báró Jósika Street (at that time only Jósika Street) and I planned to continue to work in the University located on the beautiful Dom place. But my fate did not allow for this to happen. 1949 became the 'year of change' for me and at the end of August I moved to Budapest, to start my job on the first of September in Tungsram's 'Imre Brody' Research Laboratory.

2. Budapest

On August 22, 1949, Monday after the Saint Steven day's weekend I traveled to Budapest. Two of my uncles lived there and therefore I had no problem to start to organize my life. As I had my Ph.D. in chemistry, and I was starting a relatively good job on September 1, I decided to become independent from my family and rent a room. As I knew Budapest quite well, it was easy to define the area where I would be looking for a room. It should be in the middle of the city from where I could go relatively easily to Tungsram, which was on the outer Váci Blvd. I also wanted to live near the Danube with a good view of the mountains of Buda. My first thought was to look for a room in the 'new Lipót' district in the vicinity of Saint Steven Park, which is located, adjacent to the river. I started by looking up advertisements in the newspapers for rooms to rent. What I experienced during this process one could write a study about, but after I visited at least ten rooms to be rented I narrowed down to two rooms and was deciding which I should select. Both of these were located in Saint Steven Park.

Early afternoon I visited one of these two apartments, which was located on Pozsonyi Ave side of St Steven Park. The owner who greeted me was a woman 10 – 15 years older than I. She was a very good looking, well-dressed lady, had lively green eyes and black hair. At every interview when I was looking for a room they wanted to know who I was, why did I want to rent the room and how I was going to be able to pay? This lady when she invited me to her apartment, asked me to sit down at her dining room table, offered me coffee and put out a tray with some small cookies. After these preliminaries she asked me also some relevant questions. Naturally I was also interested to know how many renters she had and what were the rules of the house? She showed me her apartment which was a two bedroom small apartment, had a corridor, which was the entrance from the staircase, and a dining room. There was one bathroom, which served both bedrooms. When she showed her apartment she mentioned, that the room, which she going to rent is the larger bedroom with a big French bed and she is going to live in the smaller bedroom. I learned from our discussion that she was divorced and had no children. Her husband moved out because of a woman and was living in the vicinity of Gellért Mountain in another part of the city. The room offered to me had a very nice view. One could not see the Danube, but one could see a part of the Buda Mountains. The rent she asked was an amount I believed I could pay from my salary. When she escorted me through her apartment and showed the kitchen, she indicated that she would be glad to provide me breakfast and she could assure me about any other comfort. The offer was very interesting and this was a place I really liked.

The other apartment was located on the first floor of a building, the address of which was St Steven Park 10. I visited this apartment the same afternoon. This was on the narrow part of St Steven Park, close to the river. When I entered the apartment the owners, an elderly couple, greeted me. Again first they asked about me: who I was, why did I want to rent the room and how I was going to be able to pay? After this they showed me their apartment. This apartment had also two bedrooms. Both of these bedrooms overlooked the Danube. One of the rooms had a small balcony the other room had no balcony, but a big window overlooking the Danube and the Buda mountains. One could see Margaret Island and the ships going up and down on the river. The apartment had two bathrooms. They were using one attached to their room, the other was attached to the room I was offered. This bathroom had another entrance also. They told me that the apartment had a small room for the maid, which they were also renting and whoever rented that small room was also going to use the bathroom. The use of the kitchen and any other “comforts” were not mentioned. The rent was about the same as for the other apartment.

My selection was narrowed down and the problem remained which one should I choose from the two candidates? I realized that I could not procrastinate, because both of these apartments were very good for me and if I waited too long they could be rented to some other people, furthermore they were available immediately and I had to go to work in a few days so I had to make an immediate decision.

Not far from these two apartments I found a small coffee shop and ordered an espresso, and started to consider the pluses and minuses of the two rooms. One of them was located on the Pozsonyi Ave side of St Steven Park, where the furniture was much nicer than in the one which was in St Steven Park near the Danube, furthermore I would have received breakfast and also other ‘comfort’. The disadvantage was what my mother, my relatives in Budapest and my friends in Szeged or Budapest say if I practically moved in with such a good looking and relatively young woman.

For the apartment next to the Danube, except for its location I was not able to find any other good features. The breakfast would be my problem, but it was true that in my entire life I only had coffee, cocoa or tea for breakfast. The bathroom situation was not very clear about to whom they rented, or were going to rent, the maid's room. At the end I came to the same conclusion as I learned many years later to evaluate any real estate where one should move, that there are three important factors to consider: 'location', 'location' and the third is 'location'. These were in favor of the room near the Danube. I went back and rented the room immediately and the next day, August 27, Saturday I moved in. I looked out from my window and stared at the old Danube, across from me Margaret Island and the ship traffic on the river and on the other side of the Danube the mountains of Buda.

Not long after I moved in, I got acquainted with the renter who also used the bathroom. This happened on one evening when I went into the bathroom and the other door of the bathroom opened. When I turned on the light I saw that the person who opened the other door was a very good-looking, pretty girl with brown hair, about my age, in a pink nightgown. I was in my pajamas. After our first surprise was gone, I told her that my name was Ferenc. She said that her name was Ida. I suggested that it would be good if we could discuss who was using the bathroom and at what time. She agreed that this would be important. I suggested that we should sit down, maybe in my room. She agreed, saying that her room was very small and she had only one chair. We went to my room and got acquainted. I told her what I was doing and she told me that she was working in the circus. Her brother, who was several years older than she, worked as a magician in the circus and Ida was his helper. Therefore she only came home in the evening at 11 o'clock and got up late in the morning. With this the utilization of the bathroom and the comfort of my room with the magnificent view from my window were solved.

My main project for the weekend was to find out how could I get from St Steven Park to Tungsram where I had to start to work on September 1. It was evident that I had to leave from near the West Railroad station on the #3 or #55 streetcars and on Váci Blvd travel to its terminus at the railroad bridge of Újpest and transfer there to the #87 streetcar, which went on the outer Váci Blvd and which stopped at the entrance of the Tungsram factory. The #3 and #55 streetcars station was in Visegrádi Street, which could be reached from St Steven Park by foot in less than 10 minutes. I collected all of this information and on September 1, which was a Thursday, early morning shortly after 7 o'clock, I left the house to start the second job in my life –in 1945 I worked for a month at the 'Commission of Abandoned Properties' – but this was my first serious job.

When shortly after 7 o'clock I arrived in Visegrádi Street my heart almost stopped. People were hanging in bunches from the streetcar which was just leaving the station. Passengers were standing on the bumpers, between two cars and everywhere where one could stand and hang on to something. I had not seen anything like that before, because in Szeged many people walked or used bicycles and in Budapest since I arrived I did not go on streetcars during rush hours. After the streetcar left, large amounts of people were left on the sidewalk, not able to get in or on the previous car and waited for the next one which had not arrived yet. When the next one arrived and slowly turned from the Váci Blvd to reach the station in Visegrádi Street, people were waiting on it already when it slowly turned and jumped on the still moving streetcar. When finally it stopped by a miracle I was swept up by the crowd to one of the cars and wound up in the center of the car. In a sardine box there is more empty space than it was on this streetcar. Finally the streetcar left. One could not hang on to anything, because the car was so crowded that it was no need for it. The streetcar consisting of two cars, slowly turned into Váci Blvd, started to speed up and I started for my work place. The streetcar stopped at stations, where a few people disembarked. I could not imagine how anybody could get off the streetcar, stuck in the center of the car, like I was. When we arrived at the Railroad bridge of Újpest, which was the terminus of the #3 line, everybody had to disembark.

Whoever disembarked started to run in the direction where the #87 line station was. The #87 was an older type streetcar consisting of only one car and all of the passengers from the two cars #3 tried to get on. When the #87 left it was as, or more, crowded than the #3 when it left Visegrádi Street, and people were hanging from it in bunches.

Because I was in the center of the incoming streetcar, by the time I reached the #87 it was already moving. Several of us could not get on and we waited until the next one came, which was not a long wait. We could get on comfortably, but then another # 3 or #55 arrived and the one I was on got converted into an overfilled sardine can.

The #87 stopped at the station in front of the entrance to Tungsram, where the majority of the passengers, including me, disembarked. When I was on the street and looked at the #87 leaving I was shocked to realize that from now on I was going to make this trip daily and six times a week, on sunny days, in rain, snow, in daylight or in darkness. My fellow passengers God knows since how long they had been doing it and for how many more years they were going to do it every morning and I was also going to start my days this way for years and years. I became very depressed from these thoughts

When the streetcar left with the remaining passengers, I crossed Váci Blvd and went through the entrance door of Tungsram.

3. Every beginning is hard

At Tungsram Research Laboratory the working hours started exactly at 8 o'clock in the morning and were strictly enforced. Without exception everybody had to comply. School children had to be at the exact time in school, every worker had to be at the work place at the exact time. The reason this was unusual for me, because at the University I worked on research projects and that required flexible time adjusting our work hours to the time needed for experiments. As I was used to this flexible time at the University, I had to adjust to the Research Laboratory's strictly enforced time in the morning. At the end of the workday everybody left on time, but if the research work required, the person could leave only whenever he or she finished the work. As everybody, factory and research workers had to arrive exactly at the same time, personal automobiles did not exist, everybody used public transportation and the 'rush hour' was unbelievable.

Right on my first working day on September 1, I experienced the quality or rather the inferior quality of Budapest's public transportation system. The public transportation in the morning, when everybody had to arrive at the same time, was really bad in early September, but later in the fall, when the days became shorter and cooler, it deteriorated further. That pleasant walk in the morning, from St. Steven Park to Visegrádi street, during the early fall, under the trees with green foliage lining the streets, became a fast march during late fall. During the pitch black winter mornings when the streets were illuminated by street lights, fighting with the elements, heavily dressed, with galoshes to avoid being soaked through my shoes, my cap pulled down over my ears, arriving at the station the fight started to board the overcrowded tram. When it rained or there was a cold wind and not talking about the days when it snowed, to be on the tram's stairs or hanging in bunches was extremely unpleasant. The weather in Budapest during winter could be very cold, rainy and snowy.

When on the first of September I reported at the Imre Bródy Research Laboratory in Tungsram, I had to go through a number of formalities at the Personnel Department. After filling out many papers I received Identification with my picture, which certified that I was working in the Tungsram Research Laboratory. This was a very important document. It was always needed to prove that the person was working, because if there was a police raid and if somebody could not prove he or she was working somewhere, the police arrested that person.
Dr. Szigeti, who was the Head[13] of the Research Lab. had a long discussion with me and told me that I was going to work on the chemical problems of the electron tubes utilized in radio systems. He suggested I should settle down first in the Library of the Research Lab. and study the literature concerning this work. He immediately came with me to the Library and introduced me to Mrs. Törzs, the Librarian. He pointed out that I should study the relevant literature for a few weeks especially on the subject of the oxide cathodes, which he mentioned also when he hired me. He also suggested I should visit the electron tube production.

---

[13] Dr. György Gergely: Life's work of György Szigeti; Hungarian Academy of Science, 2005/2 pp 239

After Dr. Szigeti wished me success and left, Mrs. Törzs started to arrange my plans. There was a desk in the Library and she told me I should use that. She also gave me a tour of the Library and showed me where I could find the magazines and the register of the books. She also said she would come with me to have lunch in Tungsram's cafeteria. After this I settled down at 'my desk'.

At noon we went over to a building where Tungsram's dining hall was. This building was built before the war by Mr. Aschner, providing the best for the employees. The dining hall was on the first floor and above it, on the second floor, was an indoor tennis court. The food was still served in porcelain dishes that could be picked up next to the buffet tables. When served, the next dish could be put in a second porcelain container. These porcelain containers then could be put one on top of the other and carried to the table. Mrs. Törzs explained everything and also told me where I could find things I would need. After lunch I visited Dr. András Dallos, who was one of the people who interviewed me when I came to look for a job and who was also from Szeged. After that I returned to the Library and started to look for what I needed in the magazines.

Early afternoon Dr. Ernö Winter – of whom I heard quite a bit – came to visit me in the Library. He joined the Tungsram Research Lab immediately after he received his Diploma of Chemical engineering in 1925. He was working primarily with the development of electron tubes. He had a big part in Tungsram to become one of the world leaders in producing the electron tubes which were used in the new product just started, the radios. He was the big Hungarian expert and scientist of cathodes[14], because during 1927 – 1928 he developed an electron tube having a 'metallic barium' cathode, which received worldwide acknowledgement. We introduced ourselves He sat down at my desk and we spent the entire afternoon discussing issues related to the chemistry needed for the electron tubes used in radios. Naturally during August I frequently went to the Library of the University in Szeged and became familiar with the oxide cathodes and the inside of the electron tubes, therefore during this discussion I was not a novice, as I was when I got the job offer. At the end, Dr. Winter agreed that I should continue for a few weeks studying the literature in the Library but I should also visit the production and talk there with the engineers. After a few weeks I should try to assemble a program for my research, which we should discuss and finalize.

The next day Dr. György (Gyurka) Gergely came to the Library. We got acquainted and he suggested that he would escort me around the Lab. and introduce me to some of the colleagues. Gyurka was a mechanical engineer graduated from the Technical University of Budapest. He joined Tungsram Research Laboratory at the beginning of 1948 where he completed his studies to obtain a Doctorate. We made a tour in the Laboratory and he introduced me to several of our colleagues.

---

[14] The "cathode" provides the electrons needed for the operation of the "electron tube". The quality and efficiency of the cathode determines the usefulness of the electron tube.

Dr. György Gergely

The next day Mrs. Törzs informed me that she had arranged for me to visit the electron tube factory and visit first Dr. Zoltán (Zoli) László who was an engineer in that department. I found Dr. László, who was a tall, lanky, blonde, blue-eyed man. He was a few years older than I. He asked me to sit down, and outlined the various departments in the factory, which he was planning to show me. He took me on a tour and subsequently we visited the dining room to have lunch.

After lunch we went back to Dr. László's office. He turned out to be a very intelligent, sympathetic and well-learned person, who dressed very elegantly. It was evident from our discussion that he did not like the communist system. During our first meeting I felt we were going to be good friends.

Mrs. Törzs was a great help to me. She valued very much that my knowledge of the German and English languages was fairly good and I needed no help reading magazines and books in those languages. I asked her to order for me a book: 'Die Oxydkathoden' by Hermann and Wagener, which was published a year before in the DDR (Deutsche Demokratishe Republik), and therefore we received it without any difficulty. This book was the Bible of the work I was going to be involved in, in my research.

Based on my studies I assembled a research program, which was reviewed and accepted by Dr. Winter. To start this program I would need laboratory space where I could set up the required equipment. Somehow they could not find a laboratory space for me where I could start my work and my time I was spending in the Library got more and more extended. Furthermore I had to find and acquire the equipment, and I also needed a technician to assemble and build the experimental electron tubes for my planned research work.

Finally everything started to move forward. I was provided in the basement of one of the laboratories a desk and space where I could assemble the planned equipment. The laboratory space which was assigned for me was in the basement, a part of 'Uncle'[15] Toni Horváth's laboratory. He was called 'Uncle' because he was about 15 – 20 years older than I. Uncle Toni at that time was developing a furnace which was planned to be used in the semiconductor research – specifically germanium – which research was in the initial phases at that time. 'Uncle' Toni became a very good colleague, he was an engineer with much experience and was always ready to help, which I, as a beginner, needed very badly.

Around Christmas of 1949 I was informed that Mrs. Szremcsevics 'Gizike' would become my Laboratory

---

[15] In Hungarian younger persons address a middle age man as 'bácsi' instead of Mister. This word has no equivalent in English. It is translted as 'Uncle' but it does not represent a famly connection. With woman is the same 'néni' it is translated as 'aunt'.

Technician. Gizike was a very good-looking woman with brown hair, maybe one or two years older than I. By that time she had worked about eight years in Tungsram in various positions, therefore she knew practically everybody. When we started to work together I told her what type of experiments I was planning to do and what kind of equipment and materials we would need. She said that it would be no problem to obtain them. I received some of my needed equipment from Zoli László, and Gizike obtained the additional equipment from 'somewhere' and managed to get it also installed. Finally we found out that we needed more space than I had been given, and she somehow arranged that Uncle Toni came to me and offered to provide me with more area in his part of the Lab.

Mrs. Sándor Szremcsevics – "Gizike"

Finally my small laboratory was reasonably well equipped and included a vacuum pump system. The acquisition of the vacuum pump system was the biggest problem. I needed a mechanical vacuum pump and the entire system had to be built by using glass tubes. With the help of Zoli

László I got a small brand new mechanical vacuum pump. The only problem was that when after the war the Russians removed everything from the factory, this pump was hidden underground. This hidden pump was obviously not taken away and somehow it surfaced now and I received it. The problem was that the pump, which just appeared, had no inventory number. After I got the pump and transported it to my laboratory, where I cleaned it and started to operate it, took Gizike only a very short time to obtain a valid inventory number. Besides of the mechanical pump we needed a glass tube system, a part of which was a complicated so-called 'diffusion pump'. The purpose of the diffusion pump was to remove most of the gases, which the mechanical pump was not able to remove. The Laboratory had excellent glass blowers to build it, but they were extremely busy. In spite of this, when Gizike asked them to construct the entire glass system for us, they made, assembled and started to operate the entire system in a few days. We established a small laboratory where I could start my work in the field of 'oxide cathodes' [16].

By the end of 1949 I got used to the early morning wake up, to the moving sardine cans, which in Budapest were called street cars and I was able with the help of my bosses, colleagues and technicians to initiate my scientific work in a new field. From this enumeration one may find missing the communist party organization or maybe the

---

[16] The 'oxide cathode' was started to be used around 1930. It was able to supply the electrons needed for the operation of the electron tubes in larger quantities than the 'metal' or 'film' cathodes used at that time. The research of the oxide cathode was important, because the quality of the cathodes and how many electrons they were able to produce determined the quality, durability and usefulness of the electron tubes.

DISZ, but at that time in Tungsram Research Laboratory – in our oasis – the influence of these were negligible.

In the evening the commute to go 'home' from the Laboratory was much better. One did not have to leave at an exact time. If I had something to work on, I left later, by that time the street cars were not so crowded and therefore the traveling, one could not say was pleasant, but at least it was not extremely unpleasant, like it was in the morning. In general, I arrived between 6 and 7 o'clock in the evening at the terminus of the #3 streetcar and before I went "home" to my rented room at St Steven Park, I proceeded to the nearby Váci Avenue where I discovered a very nice restaurant opposite the side of the West railroad station. I had dinner there many times. Ilike, the good looking red haired waitress, knew me very well. For no specific reason my eating habit was such that I ate only a very limited selection and was never a gourmet as the French would say, or as in German 'Feinschmecker' or in Hungarian simply 'inyenc'. When I ate in this restaurant, to simplify my life, I always ordered a cup of bouillon and Wiener Schnitzel with boiled potatoes. Therefore when I entered the restaurant and as soon as I sat down, Ilike, without asking me any question, arrived with the soup, which according to the custom in Budapest was served in a metal cup. When she got to my table, she greeted me with a smile and poured the content of the metal cup into my soup plate. When I finished the soup, Ilike picked up the now empty plate and spoon carried them away and within a minute came from the kitchen with a plate on which was the Wiener Schnitzel and the boiled potato, with green parsley sprinkled over it.

As most of my family, three of my cousins, my uncle with his wife left Hungary in 1948 and by now they were in the United States, I had only two uncles in Budapest. I visited them regularly. A few of my University colleagues from Szeged were now working in Budapest, and I met them too. Among those I met regularly was István (Pista) Halász, who received his Ph.D. at the same time I did, and who as he planned was working in the Chemistry Institute of Professor Géza Schay at the Technical University in Budapest. He started to work in a new field of analytical chemistry, called 'gas chromatography'. Pista with the blessing of Professor Schay established a 'refugee center', and provided jobs for several of our very talented colleagues, for example Katalin Balázs and Sacy Reitzer, because they had difficulty finding jobs, as the communists considered them 'class-aliens'. I also made new friends in Budapest, some were my coworkers in Tungsram, some not in Tungsram. There were several in the Research Lab close to my age and I became good friends with them too.

My life in Budapest started to be established, but it was hard to totally divorce myself from Szeged. My mother was left alone, many of my friends and colleagues were still there. After I moved to Budapest, during the fall of 1949 on several weekends I went back to Szeged. At that time there was an airplane connection from Budapest to Szeged. The Russian copy of the American DC-3, the Li-2 was in service. It was an airplane with two engines and its third wheel was under the tail of the airplane. The plane was usually full and many times the corridor between the passengers was filled up with some merchandise, which made the trip very interesting when the ride was somewhat turbulent. The airport of Szeged was a grass strip with a little house, which was the terminal building and used also as the waiting room. The return flight to Budapest, which I used, was early Monday morning. A contraption attached to the top of a flatbed truck cranked the engines of the airplane. The crank was somehow connected to the propeller. When the engine came alive, the crank somehow got disconnected from the turning propeller. When one engine was started the process was done on the second one. I liked the airplane trip. The time of the flight was much less than an hour. The airplane flew not higher than 1,000 meter (3000 ft.) and from the window one could see every little house and the people around the houses.

At that time there was an airplane connection in Hungary from Budapest also to other cities, but all domestic airplane connections in Hungary were cancelled after the Hungarian border was hermetically closed and a group of people hijacked a plane and diverted it to Munich in West Germany. This indicated that Hungarians not only invented Vitamin C and made humanity richer with other important inventions, but Hungarians also invented airplane hijacking.

4. The Airpregnancy System

The Telecommunication Research Institute – Távközlési Kutató Intézet (TKI)] - was officially established in December 1949 by bringing together specialists from various organizations such as the Telephone-factory, Orion, Standard, the Post Experimental Station and from the Technical University of Budapest. The building of TKI's Headquarter and its research laboratory where those specialists were assembled was started in 1950 in the elegant 'Rózsadomb' (Rose hill) district of Budapest. The building was completed at the beginning of 1951[17].

Dr. András Dallos - Managing Director – TKI-2 (1954)

---

[17] Private communication from Dr. Tibor Berceli – Technical University of Budapest – (2008)

The Electron Tube[18] Research and development work carried out in the Tungsram Research Laboratory in Újpest, and the groups working in these fields were transferred to the newly formed Telecommunication Research Institute, the headquarters of which as mentioned was at Rózsadomb. Dr. Ernö Winter was nominated to become the Director General and Dr. András Dallos the Managing Director of the newly formed Telecommunication Research Institute-2 (TKI-2) [the Rózsadomb Laboratory was named TKI-1].

First Lieutenant Károly (Karcsi) Ducza[19]

---

[18] 'Electron tubes' were the name of those devices from which the air was pumped out, that the electrons produced there could be used to operate radios, radars, television systems or fluorescent lights.

[19] Károly Ducza started to work in 1944 at the Tungsram Research Laboratory. Received his diploma in Radio Engineering at the Technical University in Budapest. After that he was drafted to the Hungarian Army's 'Telecommunication Section'..

The entire Telecommunication Research Institute (TKI-1and 2) were under military supervision and Colonel Ferenc Biró was appointed to be the liaison officer for TKI-1 and 2, and reporting to him First Lieutenant Károly (Karcsi) Ducza became the liaison officer for TKI-2. In 1950 plans were developed to provide additional laboratory space for TKI-2 by building a new laboratory building attached to the 1930 built three story 'Tungsram Research Laboratory', and that the two buildings should be connected to each other.

I was working as a chemist conducting research in the field of electron tubes, under the direction of Dr. Ernö Winter, therefore I was also transferred to TKI-2, and in spite of having only one subordinate at that time, I was promoted to become a Department Head with big responsibilities, to design three research laboratories, specify all the necessary equipment and furniture and hire scientists, technicians and workers for these laboratories, and when completed to supervise them.

That was for me an incredibly big responsibility, because I had just started to work in this field. The design of laboratories, specify and procure furniture and equipment and hiring employees was not a subject taught at any Universities including the University of Szeged where I got my diploma. What made this task extremely dangerous, which I knew by that time, was that if something went wrong, - even a minor detail, especially as we became a military research institute - the consequences would be much more serious than just being dismissed from the job. It would have been considered 'sabotage' and even today's reader will understand the consequences of such a crime in communist times.

One of the laboratories I had to plan was a general chemistry laboratory, which was designed with the purpose of studying the materials used in electron tubes and the methods of their cleaning. I was able in a very short time to find and hire Magda Ács who received a diploma in chemistry from the University of Budapest. Magda was a slim, tall woman with dark red hair a few years older than I was. She was a very competent and reliable coworker. She helped me in the design of this laboratory.

The purpose of the second laboratory, which was part of my department, was to study the vacuum technical methods used in the manufacturing of electron tubes.

The purpose of the third laboratory I had to establish was to continue my research on oxide cathodes. The oxide cathode was the heart of the evacuated and sealed electron tube. One had to use materials and processes for the cathodes that they should be able to produce for an extended period of time large amounts of electrons. In those days the best material was a layer of barium, strontium, calcium oxide deposited on a metal, specifically on a nickel tube which could be heated.

In 1950 I was doing research on oxide cathodes only since less than a year, but the research of these "oxide cathodes" for electron tubes used by the military was considered extremely important. And suddenly it became a very important research project for me. I established that this research would require a laboratory, which had to be climatized, which means that the laboratory should be kept at a constant temperature and the incoming outside air had to be filtered, to avoid dust or other pollutants. I came to this conclusion from the bible of this subject at that time, the book written by Hermann and Wagener, but also by studying the “western” literature. I did not see that this would be a problem, because the so called “air-conditioners” used for keeping rooms at a constant temperature all year round in the western countries were not only used for laboratories, but also for private apartments by using a small unit in windows, which one could observe in pictures. These window-mounted air-conditioning systems were blowing air into the rooms at an even temperature, which one could select by means of a thermostat on the units. The air was blown into the rooms through a filter, which guaranteed that the outside dust was removed.

Every language, including Hungarian, is acquiring many foreign words. Everybody agrees that Ferenc Kazinczy was in Hungary the first leading person to insist on converting these foreign words into good Hungarian expressions. Luckily this spirit is still alive and in TKI-2 my colleague Gyurka Gergely also insisted on converting these foreign words or expressions, which invaded the beautiful Hungarian language, and use only the good Hungarian expressions or words instead. One of his ingenious hungarization was when he converted ‘Dialectical Materialism’, at that time a frequently used phrase, to pure Hungarian. We agreed that Gyurka’s conversion of ‘Dialectic Materialism’ to Hungarian (Tájszólásos Anyagelvűség) was an excellent choice, because nobody really knew what the original expression or the Hungarian version meant. When I told Gyurka that I was planning a laboratory which was going to have ’air-conditioning’, he became very upset and told me to use decent Hungarian words. Obviously ‘air’ has a Hungarian word ‘lég’ and therefore the Hungarian expression used was 'lég-kondicionálás;. But in his opinion 'kondicionálás', the Hungarian version of 'conditioning', was not a real Hungarian word and having two meanings in Hungarian it would be confusing to use. One meaning is a 'condition under which an item is sold'. This word in Hungarian is 'feltétel'. Air-conditioning in Hungarian could be understood that some condition is attached to the air. The other meaning of condition is 'the building is in good condition'. This word in Hungarian is 'állapot'. That would be the right word, because the 'air' is 'conditioned'. Therefore the proper expression to be used in Hungarian should be 'lég-állapotoitás'. I pointed out that the Hungarian word 'állapotositás' had two meanings; bringing a building into a 'condition' or bringing a woman in a 'condition' that is, 'pregnancy'. He said that 'leg-állapotositás' was the proper word to use and I only objected, he said, because I had a dirty mind.

The planned Cathode Laboratory was a relatively small room with a floor dimension of 5 x 8 meter. I planned that one of the walls would be the inside corridor of the building. Opposite to that should be the outside wall of the building, which contained a window. One of the other walls of the Cathode Laboratory was planned to be my "General Chemistry Lab" while opposite to that the wall should be the wall of the staircase. My plan was that the entrance to the Cathode Lab should be from my General Chemistry Lab and not from the inside corridor to eliminate to possibility of the variable temperature in the corridor and dust. I prescribed that the temperature in the Cathode Laboratory could vary by 3° C to 4° C. I found from the literature that this wide range would be acceptable and not very stringent. I also believed the window could be covered from the inside to avoid the sun heating the room, and the air conditioning equipment should be mounted in the window, as I observed from western publications. All of that was included in the building plan and in its drawings.

I submitted all of the building plans of my laboratories, including the one of the Cathode Lab., to Karcsi Ducza.

Not even a month later, Éva, Ducza's secretary, came and asked me to see Karcsi. I went with her. Karcsi was in his office sitting in front of a big table on which I recognized the drawing plans of my laboratories.

"Ferenc" – he said – "there are some problems with your Cathode Laboratory. People from the company developing the building plans came to see me and brought these drawings. The size of your laboratory has to be increased, but what is worst, they need an additional room on the first floor underneath your Lab for the air conditioning equipment to be installed."

I went to the drawings.

"What kind of machines are they planning to install there?"

"They say the Laboratory requires more space because of the heat insulation, and they are planning to build a double wall. They are planning to have a half a meter gap between the inner and outer wall and they are going to install in the room below the Laboratory and the equipment needed for the air conditioning."

When I heard his explanation I sat down:

"Why do they need another room, are they planning to install so many machines?"

"They informed me that they need a big compressor, they also need a large steel pipe system, in which the tube will coiled back and forth and they need some other machinery too, so for this they need a room under your Laboratory, the size of which will be half of the size of your Lab."

"I do not understand this. When I made the plans for the air-conditioning, I selected to maintain a wide acceptable temperature range. We looked in several magazines and we considered that for the size of the room and the temperature specification, a small window mounted air-conditioning system would be sufficient."

"That is possible, but that equipment is not available here and the planning office designed this system. We are not experts, therefore we have to accept this, and I cannot do anything about it. As this is included in the plan and in the budget, they are going to build it. Luckily until now there was nothing planned under your Laboratory, therefore we can provide them with that space. We are going to be able to solve the enlargement of your Laboratory because we are able to plan the other laboratories on the floor a little smaller. We are going to be able to solve this problem. I just wanted to inform you so you should know about these changes."

"Thank you. I am very curious what equipment the company is developing and plans to install."

After the meeting with Karcsi, I went with Gyurka Gergely for lunch in the Tungsram dining room.

"You were right to insist that the air conditioning equipment to be installed in the Cathode lab, should use a good Hungarian word, 'legállapotositó' (translated back to English it is 'air-pregnancy system') rather than one borrowed from the English language. In my opinion the one they are going to install for the Cathode Lab will really be an air-pregnancy system.

With this I told him about my discussion with Karcsi Ducza. He was very surprised since he also had seen window mounted air conditioning units and he could not imagine either why they would plan to build a double wall room having an air gap between the walls, as the requested temperature variation was in a wide range.

The new building was completed in 1951. It was connected to the old Tungsram Research building. Somehow the floors did not match, because when the new building was connected to the old and the walls removed to connect them, they found that the corridors of the new TKI-2 building were somewhat higher than the corridor floors in the old building, but this was only a little problem. TKI-2 occupied the entire new building but some of the TKI-2 people also populated the top floor of the old building. Nearly everybody moved to the new building. I moved to an office where two of us, I and Dr. Anna Schneer the head of another Chemistry department, had a desk. Nusi was a very competent and nice person, we liked each other very much. She was about 10 years older than I.

My three laboratories in the new building were completed and had nice laboratory furniture. From my group only my technician, László Navradszky and his machine shop stayed on the top floor of the old building. The Cathode laboratory was also finished and the double wall made it very interesting, because an extremely narrow corridor, into which one could walk, separated the two walls.

Because of the importance of the work on Cathodes I received permission to hire a chemist and also a technician. Mrs. Kitty Ettre was the chemist I hired to work on this project. Kitty received her diploma in chemistry from the Technical University of Budapest. Kitty was a very smart and hardworking, very good looking, medium built girl with red hair. She was a first class chemist, worked a lot and when she got a project she was able to complete it independently with excellent results.

Mrs. Kitty Ettre - 1956

Kitty's first assignment was to study the literature of the oxide cathodes as well as become familiar with the technology used in the production. When the Cathode Laboratory was completed, Kitty and Lajos Egri, the technician we hired to report to Kitty, assembled the laboratory and Kitty started on her first research project, to develop the technology to be able to accurately analyze the materials used in the oxide cathodes.

When we started to use the Cathode Lab. the temperature inside was very pleasant, because the outside air temperature was also very pleasant. I assumed when the outside temperature, because of the season, becomes warmer, the temperature in the cathode lab. would also be warmer, as the air-conditioning system was not in operation yet. Why was the air-conditioning system not yet in operation?

The Cathode Laboratory with its double wall was completed, but what was not completed was the air-conditioning system, which was supposed to be installed in the room under the Cathode Laboratory. When I visited that room the first time I was very surprised. The left side of the room was filled with a very large amount of winding steel tubes. There was a huge compressor and an exhaust system, with a wide pipe to exhaust air through the window. There was also some machinery with a propeller, to blow air from the cooling fins mounted on the winding pipe system into the air ducts leading to the Cathode lab, above the room. There were a great number of instruments and several meters attached at various points to the winding steel pipe. Besides all of this, three men were working in the room. They seemed to be very busy. There was a paper rolled on the floor, which from time to time was studied by one of the three workers.

When I asked: when did they think the equipment will be operational, I did not receive an answer.

A few weeks later Kitty came to my office and announced with a radiant face that the engineer of the air-conditioning system came and said that the work was completed and he would like to turn it on, and asked Kitty to ask me to be present for that occasion. This was very good news and I joined Kitty in the Laboratory. I shook hands with the engineer of the office which designed the air-conditioning system and said:

"The big moment has arrived, please turn on the machinery."

He went to the switch, and looked at me with a smile. He set the thermostat to 22° C (72 F) and pressed the switch. One could hear a faint murmur and one could feel that through the grating of the air ducts, air was coming into the Laboratory. When that happened all four of us, Kitty, Lajos Egri, the engineer and I smiled and applauded. Kitty said that it was a great moment. The engineer opened his arms, indicating the big success. I praised him, that they were able to finish their job close to schedule. During this time the air was coming through the grating.

A few minutes later one could sense a faint smell of ammonia coming from the grating, which smell became stronger and stronger. A few minutes later, when we were not able to get any air, the engineer turned off the machinery and said he was going to go downstairs to find out what happened. The three of us left there were able to open somehow the window partially obstructed by the inside wall and the door to the other Laboratory and run out of the Cathode laboratory.

Not much later Kitty came to my office with the engineer who gave a summary of the situation:

“I reviewed the air handling machinery. The pipes are filled with ammonia gas, which is compressed by the compressor, to force the gas through a small opening into the tube system, where the ammonia gas expands and that causes the cooling of the pipe system and the pipe system cools the air around it. This cold air is then pushed into the duct to cool the Laboratory. Now it seems that the winding pipe system was not properly sealed and ammonia has leaked through this improperly sealed joint and was pushed through the air duct into the Laboratory. Tomorrow we will be able to correct this problem and then everything will be OK.”

That was in 1951.

The end of the story is that in spite of trying to repair it many times the air-conditioning system was not working even in October 1956. As I was not in Budapest after November 1956, I only found out from my colleagues that the air-pregnancy system never worked and sometime after 1957 it was disassembled. Because other Laboratories also required air-conditioning, the necessary number of window mounted air-conditioners were imported and installed.

5. Water-skill examination

Until I moved to Budapest I spent every summer – except 1944 – with my friends on the river Tisza. After I started to work at the Tungsram Research Laboratory, I immediately investigated the water life on the Danube. I was very glad when I found out that Tungsram had on the Danube, not far from the factory, a beautiful water recreation establishment, which included swimming pools and a boathouse, for rowing boats to be rented to employees and to store boats belonging to employees.

Today we cannot even imagine the big, lively life, which existed during the warm seasons on the rivers and on the lakes during the1930s, even during the war except in the years of 1944 – 45, and continued during the 1950s. In those times the banks of the rivers were completely full of sunning or bathing people, men, women, children, and the water was crowded with boats. Today there is water life on the rivers, but it is not even close to what it was in those days. We could say 'The good old times', but the reason that in those days there was a big water life on the rivers was not that those days were better than now, but it was simply due to the fact that in those days in Hungary the families and the great majority of the people were bound to the place where they lived. Practically nobody had an automobile, and the trains were slow and very complicated to use. If for example people wanted to travel from Szeged to Lake Balaton by train, they had to go first to Budapest, where they arrived at the 'West' train station on the Pest side of the city, and from there they had to cross the city to Buda and go to the 'South' station to catch a train going to the Lake Balaton area.

Trips abroad were much more complicated and after 1939, with the beginning of WW 2, it was practically impossible to leave Hungary. After the war, Europe was in ruins and people had no money for trips and when finally they had some money, the communist regime made it impossible to leave the country in any direction. Traveling on airplanes in those times was non-existent. The only recreation during the summer and school vacations, or on weekends was to spend it on the water, on the Danube, on the river Tisza or on the Lake Balaton. The beaches were full, many floating swimming facilities were established and they were also full. The price of rowing boats and kayaks were relatively not expensive, and only few sailboats and motorboats existed on the Danube or on the Tisza.

I was one of those who grew up on the banks of the river Tisza, but not only myself, but also practically all of my friends and acquaintances spent our summers on the river. The 'blonde' Tisza at Szeged was a fairly wide river and during its long trip from the Carpathian Mountains even after it was regulated in 1880 had only a relatively small drop, so if there was not much rain the river was flowing slowly and comfortably. The Tisza got the "blonde" attribute because the river at Szeged contained a large amount of very fine silt, which gave the river a 'blonde' color. A little past the north end of Szeged the river Maros flows into the Tisza. The river Maros comes from an elevation of 1,350 meters from the mountains of Gyergyö in the southern part of Transylvania. The Maros is a totally different river compared to the Tisza. It is a swift river and carries lots of sand type material, having some mineral content. Therefore when it joins Tisza, the mixing of the two rivers is very spectacular because of the two rivers' different content and speed. In this area, where the mixing takes place, one has to be very careful, people who are swimming in that area and also with boats, because of the unpredictable eddy currents. After a half of a kilometer the mixing is completed and the 'blonde' Tisza is flowing slowly, quietly and undisturbed through the city of Szeged.

In Szeged the thriving life on the water lasted until the end of the war. On the Ujszeged (New Szeged), that is to say on the eastern side of the river Tisza, was a large sandy beach, with many cabins for changing clothes. This beach during the weekends was crowded with people, and during the week it was also quite full, mainly with children and their parents. Not far from this beach at the end of the bridge was an Olympic size swimming pool.

Boating Life on the River Tisza at Szeged – 1938

On the west side of the river was the station of the water police. The police had big and very fast motorboats. During summer weekends when the sandy beach of Ujszeged was crowded, there were many accidents in the water.

These police motorboats speeded to rescue – if they could - people from drowning.

On the west side of the river was also the steamboat station, because there was a regular boat service between Szeged and Szolnok, about 100 km (60 miles) upstream. Also on the west bank were the floating boathouses, made of wood. Some of them were private clubs, others, such as the 'Regdon', 'Takács' and 'Szőnyi' – named after their owners - were public boathouses, with cabins, and because they were over the deep water of the river, they had swimming pools made of wooden planks where the river water could flow through and people could stand or swim.

Before the winter set in, these wooden floating boathouses were towed up river into a side branch of the Tisza, where the steamboats were also harbored, to protect them from the ice flow during the spring. After the war, only three of these wooden boathouses were in service.

When I moved to Budapest I liked very much to be living next to the Danube with its big boat traffic. The 2,860 km (1800 mile) long Danube, the name of which originated from the Celts, was since ancient times one of the most important trade route of Europe, connecting Germany to the Black Sea and flowing through six countries. Besides the regular steamboat service, very many freight boats and barges, some of them loaded so that their deck was almost under water, or empty, when the deck was high above the water level, used this waterway.

It was also very good that Tungsram had a magnificent swimming complex on the banks of the Danube. This complex, featuring two very large swimming pools, a large grass covered area where people could sit or lie, and a boathouse, was built before the war, during the time of Lipot Aschner, who was a great supporter of sports. Tungsram had rowing boats that could be used by the employees or if somebody had a boat it could be stored there. The boats were kept in the boathouse on shelves. If somebody wanted to use a boat, it was lifted from its shelf, placed on a cradle which was on a slide and was able to slide it down into the Danube.

When I started my job at the Tungsram Research Laboratory the summer water season was near its end. On an early fall weekend, when the weather was really nice, I visited the Tungsram bathing facility and I found that there were still many people around the pools. I proceeded to the place where they stored the boats and I found the manager of this facility. I wanted to find out that if I bought a rowing boat or a kayak, would it be possible to store it there? The manager of the boat storage place said that he was going to put my name on the list and he was pretty sure I could get a storage place for the next season.

Next year in the early spring I visited Tungsram's beach facility. When I entered I saw that the swimming pools had no water in them but people were on the bottom of the pool and painting the walls. Although it was not the season, music was blaring from the loudspeakers, it seemed the sound system was being tested:

Thank you Comrade Rákosi,
Our thankfulness to you
Burns with clear flames.
When we look at you

Our face is proud
Wherever you go
We bestrew the road with flowers,
We pledge you Comrade Rákosi,
You should lead us
We follow you.[20]

Without any pause, new music started:

Red Csepel your voice should boom
Vaci street answer!
We all going to fight together
We not going to starve.
Red Csepel lead us in the fight,
Bread, jobs![21]

Walking toward the boat storage area and listening to the booming music, I hoped that during the season the music would not be so loud and they would play nicer songs.

I found the manager of the boating facility and asked him if he knew about anyone who was going to sell a boat. He said that he knew somebody who was storing his boat there a kayak equipped with an outboard motor, and wanted to sell it.

Very many times I was kayaking on the river Tisza, but never in my life had I seen a kayak with an outboard motor and I was very much interested to see this one. This motorized kayak was an ordinary canvas covered kayak for two people which had a metal rod fastened to the two sides of the boat in front of the second person's seat. This

[20] Egon Kemély – László Dallos
[21] Eisler - Hidas

metal rod was longer on the left side and on the metal rod which was extending past the side of the kayak a small gasoline engine was mounted. On the front of the motor was a metal disk with a groove onto which a rope could be wound. The person sitting behind the motor could wind this rope around the metal disk and if this was pulled fast, the rope started to turn the disk and the motor started. Above the motor was a small cylindrical tank for the gasoline, and on the end of the motor a pipe was sticking out in which was a shaft on the end of which was a propeller. When the motor was turned on by the rope the propeller had to be out of the water, because of the resistance of the water the motor would not have turned on, but when the motor was running the motor could be lowered down so the propeller was in the water and the kayak would start to move forward. A small handle located on the metal rod could adjust the speed of the engine. In front of the seat of the person who operated the engine were two-foot pedals where the person could put his foot and by applying pressure on the pedal the rudder, connected to these pedals by a metal wire, the kayak could be steered. If the pedal on the right hand side was pushed down the boat turned to right, if the left one was pressed the kayak went to the left.

The owner of the kayak also worked in Tungsram. I visited him and agreed on the price. I told him that the condition was that I had to try the boat. As the weather was not good and the Danube must have been still cold, we agreed that in a couple of weeks when the spring arrived we would go together to the boathouse and I would try the motorized kayak. At the beginning of May on a Saturday afternoon, after work we went to the Tungsram bathing establishment and at the boat storage building he asked the attendant to lift his kayak from the shelf, which was in its storage place and put it onto the cable car and slide it down to the water. The operator started the motor of the cable car and we went down the stairs to the 30 by 10 meter wooden pier floating on the river. The motorized kayak slowly arrived and the owner grabbed the rope attached to the kayak and pulled it off the cradle to the pier. The owner got into the kayak and sat in the second seat, behind the metal rod. I was holding the kayak so that the flowing river water should not take it downstream. He started to explain me how to start the engine. He turned the rope around the disk and pulled it. Nothing happened. He said that this was normal, because the motor had not been used all winter. He repeated this procedure three more times and the engine started, the propeller started to turn. He motioned with his hand that I should get into the kayak. I stepped in and sat down in the front seat. He pushed the kayak away from the pier and moved the propeller into the water. He gave some more gas and the kayak started to move away from the pier as he stepped on the left foot pedal.

The Tungsram bathing facility was located a little below the lower end of the island of Saint Andrew and the river was therefore very wide. He directed the kayak toward the lower tip of the Island, to which he came close in a few minutes. He then turned the boat in a big arc back towards Tungsram's pier. When we got there he slowed the boat and I could reach out from the kayak to get hold of the pier and stop the boat. He stopped the engine and pulled the propeller out of the water.

We got out and he suggested that I should try it. I was reluctant, but he said if I bought the boat, sooner or later I would have to do it anyhow. We changed seats and now I was in the second seat behind the metal bar. I wound the rope around the metal disk, pulled it and because the motor was still warm, the engine started on the first try. He sat in the first seat and pushed the kayak away. The river started to carry the boat downstream. I put the propeller into the water and stepped on the left pedal and the kayak started to move forward and away from the pier. I equalized the two pedals and the kayak started to move straight forward. He turned back and motioned with his hand that I was doing fine. Now I directed the boat towards the lower tip of Saint Andrew Island, and as I got near it, I started to steer the boat back towards the Tungsram facility. It was then I noticed that a fairly well laden barge approaching from upstream. It was still in the distance, but its direction was such that it was going to come between the Tungsram water facility and me. I decided that I was not going to cross the Danube in front of the barge, because if my motor failed we would wind up just in front of the barge. Therefore I slowed the boat and proceeded parallel with the shore going upstream. The barge was between us and the Tungsram side of the river and we could see the waves created by the barge. With my years of experience on the river Tisza I knew that I should turn the boat perpendicular to the waves. The waves rocked the boat a little, but after that, we crossed the Danube to the Pest side in quiet water. We reached close to the shore above the Tungsram pier. I turned the kayak to go with the stream and after we passed the pier I turned back. On the first try I was about a meter away from the pier. I made a new circle and arrived nicely exactly next to the pier. I cut the engine and the owner of the boat reached out to grab the pier. I removed the propeller from the water. We got out of the boat. I shook the owner's hand:

“I am buying your motorized kayak. I am going to bring the money tomorrow to your office, so please prepare the papers needed for the transaction.”

"You handled the boat very well. Congratulations.”

“Thank you. It is a pleasure to sit in a kayak where you do not have to use the paddles and it is still going forward.”

Vera Váradi on the motorized kayak – 1951

Next day I bought the motorized kayak. The now ‘ex-owner’ advised me to become a member of the Motorboat Racing Club of Tungsram, in order to obtain gasoline rationing coupons, which one could get only if one was using the motor boat for racing. On the first weekend after this he came with me to the kayak. I asked them to launch the boat, by lifting it down to the water. The now “ex-owner” gave me some more know-how in connection with the engine.

By the spring of 1950 the Danube was practically the only recreational possibility of Budapest’s over 1.6 million inhabitants. The number of boats, mostly rowing boats, increased incredibly, as people realized that with a boat one could enjoy the pleasures of the summer much more than to be near a swimming pool or sunning themselves on a beach. If one could afford it they bought a boat or just rented one and alone or with several friends or family went "boating", like me, who in a canvas-covered kayak equipped with a tiny gasoline engine braved the actually very dangerous waters of this enormously large river. Many of these people, especially those who used a boat for the first time in their life, and many could not even swim, met with accidents and the police motorboats were often called to save these people, but on many occasions people drowned in the river.

Because of that, the Interior Ministry in its 15.800/1951 B.M. decree ordered that in every boat one person must have a 'Water-skill Certificate'[22]. To obtain a 'Water-skill Certificate' one had to have a certificate that he/she was able to swim 100 meters and was able to demonstrate to operate a boat, that meant to go with the boat in the direction he/she wanted to go. One could get the certificate about the capability to be able to swim 100 meters in any of Budapest's many swimming pools. That one could navigate the boat in the direction wanted to go was done in front of a police committee. The police conducted examinations during the summer in many places. There was a notification at the Tungsram water complex informing when the police would be present for the exams.

I was a good swimmer and operated my motorized kayak for almost a year, so I saw no problem in obtaining a

[22] The mandatory "Water-skill certificate" was abolished in 1970.

'Water-skill Certificate'. I obtained the swimming certificate and signed up for the boat examination for May 17, 1952, afternoon, which was a Saturday and we had to work only until noon. Laci Navradszky, who was my technician in the Laboratory, was very nice and offered to come with me, in case I ran into any mechanical problems. I did not think this could happen, but I told him that it was very nice of him and when we arrived at the Tungsram boating facility we saw that three policemen were standing on the pier and already some of the people were in the process of taking the exam. The exam was very simple, for example the person who had a rowing boat got into the boat. One policeman had a bullhorn and talking into that he told the person in the boat to leave the pier and row against the stream. After that was accomplished the policeman instructed the person to turn left and row in the direction of the lower tip of the Saint Andrew Island. The person was rowing about 50 meters when the policeman instructed the person to turn right and after a short time he said that he/she should return and dock at the pier. After this was also accomplished one of the policeman gave him/her a piece of paper and said that he/she should go up to the boathouse and give the paper to a policeman, who was there, give him also a photograph and the policeman would prepare him the 'Water-skill Certificate'.

When we arrived I got my kayak from the storage rack to the cable car and arranged for it to be sent down to the water. When it arrived Laci and I looked it over. When it was my turn, I told the policeman, that I would like to be examined for kayaking as well as for the motorboat. We agreed that I was going to start with kayaking using only the paddle. I got in the boat and did everything the policeman instructed me to do and returned to the pier. He told me that the result was good.

He also told me that I should now start my motorboat exam. My kayak was at the end of the lower end of the pier facing into the direction of the flow of the river. Laci came there and was holding the kayak until I got in. I wound the rope around the metal disk and pulled it. The engine started immediately. Laci pushed the boat a little away from the pier and I inserted the propeller into the water. I gave some gas and the kayak started to move forward against the stream of the water. I put my left foot on the pedal to steer the boat away from the pier, but in spite of pushing the pedal with my foot down as far as I could, the motor which was on the left side of the kayak started to push the kayak to the right towards the pier. I tried to use the left pedal more, but the kayak moved closer to the pier, finally with the motor in the water the keel which now acted like a ski climbed up on the top of the pier and started with increasing speed to go forward towards the three policemen. They started to escape backwards to avoid being hit by it. I had no idea what happened, in spite of pushing the left pedal continuously. It kept going to the right. The boat, with me still inside, passed the group of policemen, who escaped successfully. Arriving at the end of the pier, the kayak fell back into the water and continued now on the water to make a turn to the right towards the shore. By that time I recovered more or less and cut the engine, pulled the propeller out of the water, but the boat with inertia was gliding on the water until with a large thud it hit an anchored rowing boat. Luckily by that time the kayak lost speed and therefore besides the thud and a mild shock nothing else happened. I pulled out the paddle and started to row back to where I started. In the meantime the police people seemed to recover. I docked and started with Laci to investigate what happened. We discovered that the wire connecting the left pedal to the rudder had broken and therefore I could not steer the boat, and the propeller being on the left side of the boat pushed the boat forcefully to the right and up on the pier. I went to the police and explained to them the situation and told them that we could fix it in a few minutes and I would like to try the exam again. It seemed however they did not recover completely, because they told me to come back in two weeks, when they were going to be back for further exams.

Two weeks later I was back with Laci Navradszky. I already changed the wire on both of the pedals connecting with the rudder. This time I successfully passed the exam and received a 'Water-skill Certificate', which was valid for kayak, motorboat and rowing boat. I am very proud that the Certificate in July 1956 was amended to make it valid also for barges, but as of today I am very sorry, that I did not make the exam to make it valid also for elevators, because I am sure I would have been able to pass the exam.

The Author's 'Water-skill Certificate' - 1952

6. Now you see it, now you don't

In 1950 at the beginning of the summer, around the end of June, suddenly a huge map of the Korean peninsula appeared in many places in Budapest, one was near the main entrance of Tungsram.

At the Conference in Potsdam near Berlin, which ended on August 2, 1945, when the war with Japan was still going on, an agreement was reached between Churchill, Truman and Stalin that the Korean peninsula, which at that time was still occupied by the Japanese, should be partitioned at the 38 parallel. When the Japanese surrendered to the north of the 38 parallel they should capitulate to the Soviet forces, and south of the 38 parallel to the Americans. It was typical of Stalin's cleverness that when this agreement was reached the Soviets had not even declared war against the Japanese. Stalin declared war against them only on August 9, after the Potsdam conference was completed and only after the atomic bomb was dropped on Hiroshima on August 6, 1945.

Immediately after the capitulation of Japan, in August 1945, the Soviet army occupied 'North Korea' the territory north of the 38 parallel and installed Kim Ir Sen's Soviet friendly communist regime and named it the Democratic People's Republic of Korea (DPRK). The American army occupied 'South Korea', the territory south of the 38 parallel, only in September 1945, where Syngman Rhee formed an American friendly autocratic regime, named Republic of Korea (ROK). Most of the American army in 1949 withdrew from ROK and left there a very poorly equipped military, with 40 tanks and 14 military airplanes.

The Soviet military withdrew also in 1949 from North Korea, but the DPRK army was excellently equipped and trained, consisting of about 450,000 soldiers. The DPRK had 200 Soviet made T 34 tanks, which at that time were the best in the world. The Soviet Union provided the DPRK military with about 250 airplanes and the DPRK had also a small navy. That was the situation in June 1950.

The huge map showed the divided Korean peninsula, DPRK north of the 38th parallel and ROK south of that line. The extremely well trained and by the Soviet Union well-equipped DPRK started the attack against the poorly trained and equipped ROK on the morning of June 25, 1950, a rainy Sunday, at 04:00 hours local time.

Every morning the position of the extremely successful offensive of the DPRK forces was indicated on the huge map. The troops of DPRK in three days were able to occupy Seoul, the capital of ROK from where the ROK government ran away.

The advances of the DPRK troops shown on the gigantic maps were incredible. By the end of the first week one quarter of the ROK's territory was occupied. In two weeks half of the ROK's land was 'liberated', and one month from the beginning of the offensive, by August 1, the entire area of ROK was 'liberated', except a small corner in the southeast part of ROK, in the area of Pusan city's vicinity.

Loudspeakers mounted near the maps of the Korean peninsula were blasting communist rallying songs:

The flags were soaked,
reddened by last wounds,
so went the bold squadrons
of the partisans of Amur –
so went the bold squadrons
of the partisans of Amur.

From time to time the loudspeakers also transmitted radio broadcasts, for example that the people greeted the liberating troops everywhere with great enthusiasm, but the government of ROK, the clique of Syngmann Rhee, were not accepting their defeat and in order to maintain their power they were even giving up the sovereignty of their country and requested the help of the imperialist powers.

The USA was absolutely unprepared for this and reacted only several days later. The big mistake of the Soviet Union was that at that time it was boycotting the meetings of the United Nations Security Council, which meant they did not attend its meetings. As the Soviet Union was not present it could not veto the decision that the UN should instruct DPRK to stop its attack of the ROK and return its troops to the north of the 38 parallel. If they did not follow this demand the UN authorized the UN member states under the direction of the United States to retake the territories south of the 38 parallel now occupied by DPRK. As a result of this, 18 UN member states besides the United States sent military personnel to carry out the UN resolution.

When the DPRK started its offensive, very few American soldiers were in the ROK territory, but in Japan, which was not very far, substantial American military, ground, air and naval forces were present, under the leadership of by that time legendary General Douglas MacArthur.

On the gigantic maps displayed at many places in Budapest, during the month of August some adjustments were made, making the 'liberated' territory a little bigger around Pusan. This continued even in September.

Then suddenly, without any explanation, around the middle of September the big maps of the Korean peninsula disappeared from everywhere, including the one at Tungsram.

Only those people who were able and were brave enough to listen to the short wave broadcasts of the BBC (British Broadcasting Corporation), or to the Voice of America, or (after August 1950) to the broadcast of Free Europe, which were aired on several wavelengths, knew the explanation. They were brave enough, because if discovered they could be charged with the crime 'making propaganda against the organization of the state of the People's Democracy'. The Hungarian authorities technically disturbed these broadcasts with radio stations operating on or about the same frequencies that made it almost impossible to be able to understand them. Some of the radio receivers, which one could buy, had extended short wave bands. This resulted in the listeners being able to distinguish the BBC and Voice of America broadcasts from the noise generated by the disturbing stations.

The Hungarian language broadcasts announced that General MacArthur made a successful landing with a large force in and around the port city of Inchon, which was near the 38th parallel on the west coast of Korea, and immediately moved towards the east. At the same time a powerful military force consisting of American and UN nations, assembled in Pusan, started an offensive against the DPRK military surrounding Pusan.

The interesting aspect of the landing at Inchon was that very few DPRK forces were in the vicinity, because it was well known that in the Inchon area the difference between the high and low tides was more than 10 meters, and the time between the tides was so little that it should have made a landing impossible. This was exactly the reason that MacArthur decided to develop the strategy to make the landing for the US and the UN troops exactly at Inchon. This required very detailed planning and was executed with luck.

The successful landing on September 15 practically cut the Korean peninsula in half and the offensive at Puson forced the DPRK forces back to where they came from. In two months the American, ROK and UN troops occupied the entire Korean peninsula, including the entire DPRK, to the Chinese border.

Obviously this defeat could not have been shown on the gigantic maps of Korea. The only thing that could be done with them was to remove them, or rather make them disappear and replace them with another large size placard.

The placard of communist victory which turned suddenly into defeat was replaced by another placard, an ingenious communist system of subjugating people by power and fear:

The Government of the Hungarian People's Republic

Appeal to subscribe Peace-Loan bonds

The Government of the People's Republic decided to issue PEACE-LOAN BONDS and invites our people: to make its savings available to the Country of the people.
Every Forint of the PEACE-LOAN BONDS is a heavy blow to the imperialist adventurers, answer to their shameful war plans.
Everybody should subscribe to the PEACE-LOAN BONDS! We should also serve with this cause of PEACE and progress, the happy, strong, and the future of our independent country.

On behalf of the Council of Ministers of the Hungarian People's Republic:

Mátyás Rákosi – István Dobi Szabad Nép, 1950 September 28

It was clear that the new placards announcing the 'PEACE-LOAN BONDS' instantly replaced in the people's mind the Korean War and all of its details. The Korean War with its great victories and with the defeat of the imperialists became a very distant issue. On the other hand the 'PEACE-LOAN BONDS' which followed a year after the 'PLAN-LOAN' was expected to make a big hole in the people's pocket and occupied everybody's attention.

For the people it was really not understandable that when all the salaries were set by the State, why the Government was insisting that everybody 'voluntarily' should return one, two, three or more percentage from their salaries, when the State could simply provide that much less.

But if one would consider the communist system, the explanation was very simple. It was a part of the system of terror, the system of power and fear. That way, everybody was under fear when individually he/she had to appear before the communist party and Trade Union representative to answer what percentage of their salary they would offer. On the other hand, the system was giving power to these representatives who extricated these percentages under pressure. The system went step by step, because these representatives were under fear when they had to appear in front of the next level of communist party members and show the results that they had been able to achieve, and they were judged accordingly. Now the higher ups had the power and the extractors feared. And this went step by step up in the communist power hierarchy. This system was one of the weapons of the horror system to keep everybody in fear and make him or her respect the power of higher ups.

In the TKI it started with the leaders of the Laboratory and Party and Trade Union representatives who assembled and were told what was the minimum expected to be obtained and that the TKI was in a race with other Laboratories and organizations to outdo the quota they were told to achieve.

The employees of the TKI-2 were assembled and first the Trade Union and the Communist Party functionary described the issues and the expectations.

After this introduction the leaders of the Laboratory had to make a statement. Andris Dallos, Karcsi Ducza, Tibor Sellei who was the Party Secretary of TKI-2 and also Ernö Winter spoke, that they all believed all of the workers of

TKI-2 would enthusiastically participate in the subscription of the 'PEACE-LOAN BONDS'.

After this meeting the Party and the Trade Union functionaries talked individually with every worker and it became evident that all of the workers of TKI-2 would enthusiastically oversubscribe the 'PEACE-LOAN BONDS'.

The Bonds were obviously oversubscribed, but it is interesting to compare the oversubscription of the PLAN-LOAN BONDS issued in 1949 and oversubscribing of the 'PEACE-LOAN BONDS' issued yearly thereafter.

	Issued	Subscribed	Over-Subscription Percentage
1949	500,000	753,715	51 %
1950	750,000	1,045,945	39 %
1951	1,000,000	1,220,141	22 %
1952	1,300,000	1,741,221	34 %
1953	1,000,000	912,572	- 9 %
1954	1,100,000	1,103,000	0 %

Hungarian National Archives M-KS 276.f.66/71.43

The year to year comparison indicates that suddenly in 1953 a resistance against the 'terror' developed, which led to the 1956 Revolution.

7. Slices of the Hungarian Salami

In memory of those martyrs killed physically – mentally by the Rákosi dictatorship

In the history of mankind, Dictators existed already in ancient times. The word: 'Dictator' has a Roman origin. The Dictators do not become absolute rulers by inheritance, like the kings, they obtain it some other way. In history, Dictators obtained their full power with the help of the country's military or without the military, step by step.

The 20th century was the century of Dictators. Europe was the leader in this. The line of the modern European Dictators started in 1922 with Benito Mussolini in Italy. He was followed by Joseph Stalin in about 1924 in Russia, in 1932 Antonio de Oliviera Salazaar in Portugal, Adolf Hitler in 1933 in Germany, Francesco Franco in 1936 in Spain. In 1944/45 two dictators, Mussolini and Hitler, disappeared from the stage, on the other hand as a replica of Stalin, seven new Dictators appeared in the Eastern European countries. One of them was Mátyás Rákosi in Hungary.

Stalin utilized the age-old technique to grab power step by step. Mátyás Rákosi, 'Stalin's best Hungarian disciple' learned from his mentor that the easiest way to become an absolute Dictator was not to eliminate the opponents or problems in one swoop, but to eliminate them in smaller or larger installments, until the adversary or the problem ceased to exist. Rákosi achieved his dictatorial power in Hungary, as Stalin did in Russia, and on his instructions, also step by step.

In 1952 Rákosi was so sure in his dictatorial power, that on February 29, 1952, in his speech[23] at a meeting of the Academy of the Hungarian Workers Party, shamelessly bragging he dared to tell point by point how he – the Communists, were able to acquire the power in Hungary step by step, slice by slice. I assume that for Rákosi, who attended the high school in Szeged, the slicing of the famous Pick salami of Szeged was a daily routine to cut thinner or thicker slices depending on his appetite and need, and he knew that the result would be that the entire salami stick would be consumed, in other words, cease to exist. Based on his experience with the salami, he described the step-by-step method to take over the power by annihilating his opponents by smaller or larger slices and at the end the opponent ceased to exist. Rákosi labeled this method very descriptively as the "Salami Technique".

While Rákosi in Hungary in 1952 believed that his dictatorial position was very strong and arrogantly dared to publicize how he and his cronies were able to take over the power by utilizing the 'salami technique', the very effective and ruthless salami slicing of Generalissimo Stalin on the other hand was not known during his lifetime, thereby he was able to mislead the world. Khrushchev only brought Stalin's horror and the extent of his Salami slicing to the world's attention in February 1956.

Rákosi was only for a short time the brutal Dictator of one of the small countries of the world, population about 10 million. His 'slicing' of the Hungarian salami was however extraordinary. At the peak of Rákosi's regime in four years, between 1949 and 1953, 750,000 Hungarians (7.5% of the

[23] Published in Társadalami Szemle 1952 February-March issue

population) were accused of crimes against the State, out of these 200,000 were jailed, interned or sentenced to forced labor. Besides the 2,000 people sentenced to death, many others died as a result of torture by the ÁVH, ('State Security Authority') or because of the miserable conditions in camps. Many also resorted to killing themselves and their families[24]. Obviously, compared to what was carried out by Hitler or Stalin, his was on a much smaller scale. Therefore Rákosi in the history of the world is going to be mentioned only very briefly or not at all, but coining the phrase 'Salami Tactic', and using it for the first time in the world, made him world famous, or rather infamous. This expression by now is universally used. That Rákosi was the one who used this expression for the first time one can find the reference on the Internet as well as in all of the Lexicons[25]. The only positive result that he achieved was that the world took notice of Hungary's fate[26].

As I was never involved in politics, during my years at the University I never grasped the slicing of the 'Hungarian Salami' by the Communists. When these facts became commonly known, I realized that my luck was that I did not become a Salami Slice and I got away only with a minor thing, that I did not receive permission to have a job at the University of Szeged and after that because of my profession, luckily I was needed. My question was, for how long?

---

[24] Bryan Catledge: The will to Survive - A History of Hungary - Timewell Pres Ltd – London - 2006

[25] The Harper dictionary of modern thought / Edited by Alan Bullock and Oliver Stallybrass, Harper, 1977Time Magazine, April 14, 1952

[26] Time Magazine, April 14, 1952.

In 1945 Rákosi started the slicing of the Hungarian Salami with the agrarian reform, continued with the nationalization of the coalmines, large factories, small enterprises, banks and commerce. It was continued with the churches, a part of which was the jailing of Archbishop Josef Mindszenty.

Rákosi and his Comrades' most important step was the slice-by-slice destruction of all other Hungarian political parties. The winner in the election held in November 1945, the Small Holders Party (FKGP) received a 57% majority, which would have entitled them to form the Government, which would have been the case in a Democracy. But Marshall Voroshilov, the Commanding Officer of the Soviet Army stationed in Hungary did not permit this. He ordered that the parties should form a 'coalition government' in which the Communist Party (which received only 17%) should also participate.

The first result was that the Communist Party demanded that Rákosi should become the Deputy Prime Minister and the Communist Party should receive the Interior Ministry. This was the most important for them, because within the Interior Ministry, the Communist László Rajk became the Interior Minister, who based on the Soviet system established the 'State Security Authority' (Állam Védelmi Osztály – ÁVO, later called ÁVH) This was the most important to them, because through the ÁVO they could arrest people whose slice by slice removal was important for the Communist bosses, accuse them in general with untrue, fabricated stories and thereby eliminate their enemies.[27]

Because the FKGP was the largest party, Rákosi with the help of the ÁVO, slice by slice eliminated their key members, which resulted that the FKGP in 1948 ceased to exist.

The second large party as a result of the 1945 election was the Social Democratic Party, with the same percentage (17%) as the Rákosi led Communist Party. Rákosi's next goal was to eliminate the Social Democratic Party.

The elimination of the Social Democratic Party, in spite that I was never a member of any Party, including the Social Democratic Party, affected me closely. My uncle, Dr. Imre Györki[28] as a member of the Hungarian Social Democratic Party was elected in the years between 1922 and 1939 to the Hungarian Parliament in the second voting district of the city of Debrecen. His popularity in Debrecen was so

---

[27] Rákosi also demanded complete obedience from fellow members of the Hungarian Communist Party. His main rival for power was Rajk, who was now the Interior Minister overseeing also the Secret Police. Rajk became also a slice of Salami and was arrested. At his trial in September 1949 he confessed to being an agent of Miklos Horthy, Leon Trotsky, Josip Tito and Western imperialism and admitted that he had taken part in a murder plot against Mátyás Rákosi and Ernö Gerö. Lászlo Rajk was found guilty and executed.

[28] Peter Sipos: Biography – Dr. Imre Györki (1886 – 1958) Multunk 1999/1 pp 170 - 201

high, that in 1926 he defeated István Bethlen who was at that time the Minister President of Hungary. On March 19, 1944 the German Gestapo arrested Imre Györki and as well arrested Károly Peyer, who since 1931 was the president of the Hungarian Social Democratic Party as well as being the leader of the Social Democrat members of the Parliament. The Gestapo arrested also other Hungarian politicians and they were all deported to the Mauthausen concentration camp in Austria. Peyer and Györki survived the Mauthausen concentration camp and returned to Hungary in May 1945.

Before they arrived back to Budapest, the war was over and the political life started in Hungary. By the time Peyer came back, Árpád Szakasits took over the leadership in the SocDem Party. As the first step the Communists wanted to merge the two parties and thereby obtain the support of those workers who were members of the SocDem Party.
To achieve the fusion of the two parties according to the Salami Tactic Rákosi engineered the expulsion from the SocDem Party first of the 'right side' of the SocDems, Peyer and Györki who did not want to have close ties with the Communists, then the 'centrists', Antal Bán and Anna Kéthly. The 'left side' of the SocDem Party, Árpád Szakasits, György Marosán and Gyula Kállai received – temporally – high positions, for example, Szakasits became the President of the Republic of Hungary and agreed to the fusion, which was completed on June 12, 1948.

I was immersed in Science and did not follow political events. In retrospect I was very naïve and did not grasp the basic principles of Rákosi's and his Comrades' salami tactics. If I now consider how Rákosi sliced up the SocDem Party and what happened to its leaders, then it is clear that not only I was naive, but those who were in the middle of the Hungarian political life and who were affected by the Stalinist system – named by Rákosi as "Salami Technique" - were also very naïve or just could not believe that such a system existed.

Only very few of the Social Democrats realized what could happen to them and left the country: All of the other SocDems, who did not leave the country, the 'right side', the 'centrists' and the 'left side', also those who were promoting the SocDem – Communist fusion and were temporally elevated to high positions (Szakasits, Marosán, Kállai), after the 'fusion' in 1950 were all arrested and as the result of the 'show trials' they were all convicted and jailed.

* * *

After I moved to Budapest in 1949, I visited many times my Uncle, Imre Györki and his wife, Gizella (aunt Guzsi). They lived in Budapest in Falk Miksa Street. I talked with Uncle Imre many times about the situation in Hungary. He clearly saw that in Hungary a one party system and a Communist dictatorship would develop. His daughter a few years before went to Paris to get married. On his advice his son left the country in December 1948 to Austria and from there to the USA.

Imre Györki decided that he was not going to leave the country. From our discussions I came to the conclusion that he believed he was a Hungarian and his ancestors were born and lived in Hungary. From the time when in his youth he entered the politics and for 17 years he had been a member of the Parliament and since 1945 he had promoted the welfare of Hungary. In spite that he clearly saw the development of a Communist dictatorship, he believed that he could do more good for the country at home than those who were going into exile. I think this consideration was based on his own experience, because he was the one, who as a member of the Parliament in the 1922 – 1926 time frame was able to make the arrangement that those politicians who went into exile in 1919, such as Jakab Weltner, the editor of the newspaper 'Népszabadság', were able to return to Hungary.

That I was naïve and did not notice what was happening around me in the world is understandable, but it seems that the Salami Tactic and the Stalinist horrors were covered by a smoke screen. In 1948 not only I, but probably all of the population of Hungary, including the Social Democratic Party's members and leadership, the right wing, the centrists and even the left wing, including Szakasits and his group, could not imagine and could not comprehend what fate was awaiting them. In 1922 – 1926 during the Horthy regime, there was a kind of administration of justice, in the Stalin/Rákosi regime only the administration remained the word 'justice' was removed from the dictionary.

Imre Györki on June 13, 1950 left his home in Budapest, because he had something to do in the City, and somewhere on the street ÁVH henchmen arrested him and took him to the infamous Andrássy út (Ave) 60 Until February 19, 1956 when he was released from jail, nobody knew where he was and did not hear anything about him. His apartment was confiscated and his wife was interned at Tapiógyörgye where she got a room in a house in the village.

What happened to Imre Györki after his arrest, one can more or less reconstruct from the No. 0058/1962 document issued on July 12, 1962 by the 'Hungarian People's Republic's Supreme Court's Military College' and from the research work of Zsuzsanna, B. Kádár[29]. From Andrassy ut 60[30]., Györki was transported to the State Criminal Institute (13 Kozma Street), where his questioning started, and was concluded with his 'confession' which he had to sign.

At the time Györki was arrested, the ÁVH arrested 21 other SocDem leaders. The show trials named József Kálmán, and his 21 associates were held on September 13 at the

[29] I would like to thank Dr. Zsuzsanna B. Kadar for the information I received from her.

[30] In the story I will keep naming this address Andrássy út 60, in spite that after 1950 it was renamed to Stalin Ave, but the infamous Andrássy út 60 was always called Andrassy ut 60, in spite that this Avenue was renamed many times in the history of Budapest:
1883 – 1886 – Sugár út
1886 – 1950 Andrássy út (it was named after Count Andrássy, who was still alive at that time)
1950 – 1956 Stalin út
1956 October – Magyar Ifjuság útja (Avenue of the Hungarian Youth)
1957 – 1990 – Népköztársaság útja (Avenue of the People's Republic)
1990 became Andrássy út again.
Source: Budapest's lexicon of street names, 15 September 1998 edition

Military Tribunal of Budapest and thereafter at the Military Supreme Court on September 20, 1950.[31]

All of the defendants were transported on August 27, 1950 to the Military Prison of Budapest and the Jávor division of the Military Court held the trial. Györki was accused with war crimes, participation in illegal organization and crime of disloyalty, and as a result, like his other accomplices, was sentenced to life imprisonment, loss of position for 10 years and confiscation of all of his property.

Györki[32] (and also the others convicted) received clemency, but with the upholding of their sentence, and was released from jail on February 19, 1956.

In 1955/56 the cases of the 22 convicted were re-examined and they had a hearing (except those who died in jail as a result of mistreatment and conditions in the jail. József Tolnai died in 1951 at age 51 and Ferenc Szeder died at age 71 in 1952). All of the 'convicted' said they made their confession under duress. The following quotations are from the minutes of the July 14, 1962 closed session of the Supreme Court of the People's Republic:

"During the re-examination and during the reopening of the case all accused revoked their previous confession and in connection with all of the criminal accusations they were charged, presented definitive defense.

---

[31] József Kálmán and his 21 Associates show trial is described by Zsuzsanna, B. Kádár: "The History of the Hungarian Socialdemocrat Trials." Multunk1996. 2.

[32] Géza Jeszenszky – "The victim of two dictatorships" – Magyar Hirlap 2008 October 2

"All of the accused without exception declared that after their arrest their interrogators were regularly beating them, and employed physical and psychological pressure. They were threatened with the arrest and physical mistreatment of their relatives. After their arrest their examination was conducted for months, and during the entire time they suffered humiliation as human beings, and systematically pressure tactics were used against them. Because of this illegal treatment they signed the statements prepared during their interrogation the way their interrogator wanted. Before their first trial they had to memorize their confession made during the inquiry and they were accompanied to the trial by their interrogators. In this condition they did not dare to make any changes in the confession made during their interrogation."

Ervin Faludi[33], who was previously a Lieutenant in the ÁVH, during his interrogation in April 1956 confessed that he used physical beating to force Györki to make his confession.

On February 19, 1956 the gravely ill Györki was released. He never told anything to anybody, not even to his family, what happened to him. His body and soul were crushed as

[33] Because of the grave violations of the Socialist legal system, on the order of the Supreme Public Prosecutor ordered the Public Prosecutor to arrest Vladimir Farkas and Ervin Faludi, both previously officers in the AVH, on Friday, October 5, 1956. (MTI Google: http://1956.mti.hu/Pages/NewsArchive.aspx?id=5215dcf7-02cb-4873-94co-5a8b36adc9fe)
On April 13, 1957 Faludi was sentenced to a 4-year jail term by the Supreme Court's Military College, which sentence was reduced later to 2 years in jail.

the result of the horrors he was exposed to and he died in his illness on April 25, 1958.

As a delayed satisfaction, on a closed retrial in August 1962 the Supreme Court absolved Imre Györki from all of the fabricated accusations[34].

Peter Sipos concludes the biography he wrote of Imre Györki:

"We do not know how Imre Györki considered his life and his career. It is possible that it occurred to him: it was a mistake that he entered politics. He was a brilliant lawyer and as such he could have been a successful and popular advocate and live a full life. The historian in view of the facts believes that he did right to enter politics. Without his Socialist belief and consequent strong anti- dictatorship stance, the not very rich Hungarian democratic heritage would be grayer and poorer."

Imre Györki spent his life in the Hungarian country's politics. In 1948 he decided not to leave the country and go into exile as others did, where he would have been able to live a comfortable life secured for him by the European Social Democratic parties, but he wanted to stay in Hungary, because he knew from history that the West never helped Hungary and those Hungarians who fled as emigrants could not change that. Several statues were erected in America to honor Kossuth, the hero of the 1848 Hungarian revolution against Austria, but he received no help for Hungary. Only those who stayed at home helped the fate of Hungary. This was so in 1848 and this was so in

---

[34] Peter Sipos – Multunk 1999/1 pp 170 - 201

1956. Imre Györki believed that he would be able to help his country better by staying at ‘home’.

8. SCH (Secret Case Handling)

At the time when the Újpest section of the Telecommunication Research Institute (TKI-2) was separated from the Tungsram Research Laboratory and at the time when the new building next to the old Tungsram Research Laboratory was opened and we moved in, 'increased vigilance' was initiated.

One could realize 'increased vigilance' when entering or leaving the building. The new TKI building had an entrance behind the old Research building next to the place where the old and new buildings joined. A guard, Comrade Bóka, was employed, who was stationed at the TKI-2 building entrance. The job of Comrade Bóka was when an employee entered the building, to take the employee's Identification Certificate and exchange it for an Identification Pass for the Laboratory. It was the custom in Hungary that everybody who worked received an Employee Identification Certificate from the employer.

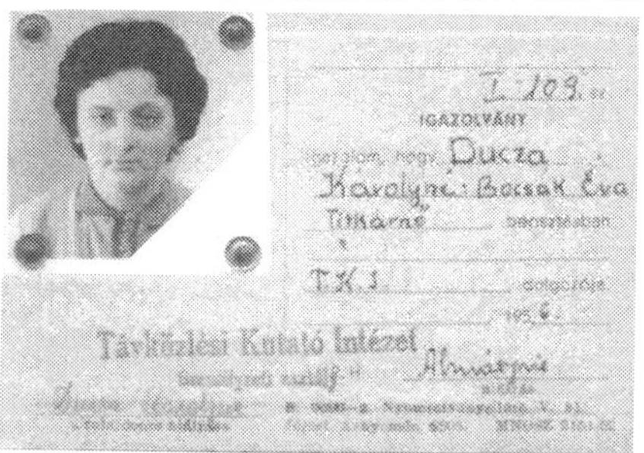

I. 109.

IGAZOLVÁNY

Ducza

Károlyné: Bocsák Éva

Titkárnő

T.K.I.

Távközlési Kutató Intézet

Employee Identification Certificate of Mrs. Károly Ducza (Éva Bocsák)

The example above is only the first page, the second page (not shown) contained data such as birth place, date, mother's name and since when was employed and where, and his/her picture was securely included in the Certificate. This Certificate was stamped quarterly by the personnel department of the employer, to certify that the person was employed. This Employee's Certificate had to be with the person all the times, because when the police made a raid, for example in a movie theatre, everybody had to prove that he or she was working. The police detained those who could not prove employment. In the evening when the employee went home, he or she had to return the Laboratory Identification Pass to Comrade Bóka who exchanged it and gave back the Employee Identification Certificate.

The other important job Comrade Bóka had to do in the morning was to search our briefcases and/or bags when we entered the building and also do the same when we were leaving. Because of this function, which he did very well, we called him the 'best researcher' of the TKI-2 Laboratory. When somebody arrived in the morning for work, Comrade Bóka opened even the brown bag in which the person was bringing his/her lunch. When somebody asked him what he was looking for, he could not tell. Because of this the following joke circulated in the Laboratory:

A worker leaving the factory was pushing every evening a wheelbarrow full of sand. A guard at the door every time searched the sand but could not find anything in it. The guard got himself a narrow steel rod and he stuck the rod several times in the sand, but never found anything. A few years later the employee retired and on the last day the guard searched the sand again, but found nothing. He shook the retiring man's hand and wished him all the best. The worker was already outside when the guard called after him, "Comrade, in the last year you were taking every day a wheelbarrow full of sand. Why did you need that much sand?" The man who just retired without turning shouted back. "I did not need the sand, I poured that out. I needed the wheelbarrows."

The other important new procedure was the introduction of TÜK (in Hungarian – Titkos Ügy Kezelés) [Translated: Secret Case Handling – SCH]. An office was assigned for TÜK on the first floor of the New Research Laboratory, which we called the 'Secret Office'. The Secret Office furnishing consisted of a desk with a chair, a few metal cabinets, a metal filing cabinet, and a table, and where no cabinets covered the wall, metal shelves were mounted. On the upper part of the entrance door of the Secret Office was a smaller door, which could be opened from inside the office. At the lower end of this little door, inside the office was mounted a wooden shelf. A Secret Police (ÁVH) soldier or employee was stationed in the office during the entire day (including the night). We assumed that he was sitting at the desk and when somebody knocked on the door, he went to the door and opened the upper part of the door and received or handed over the objects described below.

In connection with the procedures related to the TÜK, everybody received instructions from the personnel department and had to take an exam set by Karcsi Ducza. It was said that nobody ever failed this exam. The essence of these instructions can be summarized as follows:

<u>The first rule</u> was that for our work or for any other purposes, we had to use sheets which were numbered and issued by the Secret Office. The head of each

group/department received the numbered sheets and had to acknowledge with his/her signature the number of sheets received. The group/department head had to account for each sheet of paper that meant that the sheets could not be thrown out if not needed. Each sheet, if not needed had to be returned to the Secret Office and that number was crossed out from the sheets that the group/department head acknowledged that he or she had received.

The group/department head gave the blank sheets to the people working in the group/department, but all the sheets had to be collected in the evenings and had to be stored in the Secret Office. The procedure for this was the following:

The group/department heads received a greenish-brown approximately 15 cm high metal box, the size of this box was somewhat larger than the standard paper sheet's size. The cover of the box was attached with a hinge to the narrower end of the box and that way the box could be opened and closed. At the middle of the opposite narrow end of the box was a 2 cm wide and 5 cm long metal sheet attached to the top of the box also by a hinge. At the middle of this hinged metal sheet was a slot. The purpose of this was that when the top closed the box, a U shaped strong wire, which was attached to the narrow side of the box, was able to fit through that slot. When the box was closed and the U shaped wire was protruding from the slot one could put a lock through the U shaped strong wire and the box was then securely closed. According to the instructions that we received, we were not supposed to use a lock. We received a Hungarian national, red, white, green colored cord and an aluminum cap resembling the one used on beer bottles and we also received putty.

Every group/department head who received a box, also received a round aluminum seal, which fitted into the metal cup. The group/department head was supposed to engrave, or have engraved, his/her name or initials into the seal.

The procedure for closing and locking the metal security box was by first putting the top down and making sure that the U shaped wire went through the slot of the hinged metal sheet. The national red, white green colored cord was pulled through the U shaped loop and its two ends were guided through the beer bottle shape aluminum piece. We had to put the putty into the cup, making sure that it covered the cord, but level with the top of the cup. Then we pressed our seal into the putty and made sure that our initial or name was clearly visible.

The numbered sheets were collected in the evenings and the group/department head put them into the metal box and took the metal box to the Secret Office. He/she knocked on the door. The person on duty in the Secret Office opened the upper little door of the door. The group/department head in front of the Secret Office official on duty sealed the metal box, gave it to the person on duty and the person on duty noted in a book the name of the group/department head and the time and date when he received the box. He took the box and closed the little door.

Next morning, when the group/department head arrived at work, he went to the Secret Office and knocked. The official on duty opened the upper little door and recognizing the person went to pick up his box, carried it to the little door. Before giving the box back to the person he wrote in the book when the box was picked up. The group/department head checked the seal to make sure it was intact and signed the book that he picked up the box. The official on duty closed the little door. The group/department head in his office opened the box and distributed the sheets to those he received them from the day before.

The procedure with the Laboratory notebooks was the same. The Secret Office issued the notebooks and the pages were numbered. The notebooks had to be collected every evening and put into the Secret box with the numbered sheets and returned to the person who used it the next morning.

<u>The second rule</u> was that the night before the 'socialist holidays' (April 4, May 1, August 20 and November 7) all of the typewriters in TKI-2 had to be transported to the Secret Office and left there for safekeeping. The morning after these holidays the typewriters could be picked up from the Secret office and transported back where they came from and could be started to be used. The time when the typewriters were deposited and picked up had to be noted in a book and when it was picked up the one who picked it up had to verify this by signing the time and the date.

<u>The third rule</u> was that if somebody wanted to take numbered sheets or a notebook out of the Laboratory, that first had to be submitted to the Secret Office and permission received to do so. This obviously needed some time. If somebody was sent on a trip and needed to take some sheets with him, these had to be submitted to the Secret Office and after some days he received them back

in a strong and sealed envelope which was to be opened only after the person arrived at his final destination.

The entire system had one great advantage that work could not be taken home because the numbered sheets or notebook could not be taken easily out of the building and that way one could not work at home.

The result was that one wanted to minimize the usage of the numbered sheets and therefore every office was equipped with a blackboard, and a white chalk was used to write and work. Naturally, in the evenings before leaving, the blackboard had to be wiped clean.

The other result was that if somebody lost the seal or forgot to return the metal box to the Secret Office before leaving, the first time the person received a very serious reprimand and fine. Nobody ever dared to make this mistake twice, because we could imagine the consequences.

We had several theories about the development of the TÜK (SCH) system. It was evident that Hungary adopted the same system that was used in the Soviet Union. The SCH name was most likely the result of a bad translation of the Russian phrase, because it was evident, that it did not describe what the system was supposed to do, namely not the 'cases' had to be handled "secretly" but rather the documents. All of the typewriters had to be deposited in the Secret Office the evening before the holidays. One theory was that the system of having the typewriters removed from the offices, locked and guarded was developed probably around 1918, when only a very few typewriters existed. This prevented them being used when nobody was in the offices, to type leaflets or other propaganda material against the communist system. The system was not changed in Hungary in spite that in the 1950s very many typewriters existed, even in many people's homes, which probably was not the case even in those years in the Soviet Union.

The purpose of the control of the laboratory notebooks that they should not be taken from the premises was to eliminate the possibility that they should get into the hands of the enemy, the damned capitalists or into the hands of their henchmen. This also explained the system that documents carried abroad had to be transported in heavy duty and sealed envelopes, because that way the person traveling abroad could only take the controlled documents and no other paper could leave the country.

It was lucky that in those days no Xerox machines existed.

9. A small excursion, go for a spin

On the first Monday of September 1951 Gyurka Gergely visited me in my office. He sat down and without any introduction said that during the weekend he met at his mothers a lady friend of hers who worked at IBUSZ[35]. The lady brought the news that IBUSZ was planning a collective excursion with about 100 participants to Zakopane, which is a famous winter sport resort on the Polish side of the Tatra Mountains. The lady also said that whoever wanted to participate in this trip should be next Monday in the early morning hours in front of the IBUSZ office located on Vörösmarty Square, where only those people would be present who had pre-knowledge of this trip, because IBUSZ would advertise this trip only later on the same day.

Gyurka said that he would like to participate and would I also be interested? I asked him a few questions, for example how many days would this trip be, would we go by train or by bus and if Zakopane was a winter ski resort. It should not be a problem that I did not ski, because in Szeged the biggest elevation was the embankment of the Tisza River from which if there was any snow one could slide down with a sledge. Gyurka had no answer to all of these questions, and said that he could not ski either and had no intention to learn. He said that none of these questions was important because the main thing was that this would be a trip to a 'foreign country'. That alone would be very interesting. My answer was that he was absolutely right and I was strongly interested. He should count on me and my wife, Vera, to whom I got married a few months

[35] IBUSZ was the Hungarian National travel agency

earlier in July 1951. Vera was a girl also from Szeged, whom I knew from there and after she received her diploma in teaching at the University, was teaching in a school in Budapest.

Gyurka said that his niece, Sára, was willing to go early morning next Monday to obtain priority numbers for us. Sára spoke several languages, she could ride very well and was planning to work at IBUSZ as a guide for foreign tourists coming from the West to Hungary for equestrian tours organized by IBUSZ. She would be their translator and guide.

We were not able to obtain further information about the trip to Zakopane, how were we going to travel, what would be the hotel accommodation, food and so on. IBUSZ was unable to provide any of this information and actually nobody was really interested in these details, the main thing was as Gyurka said was that we are going to a 'foreign country'. The final result was that from our colleagues, Andris Dallos and his wife Zsuzsi, and "uncle" (as we called him) Laci Rotter planned also to go and therefore beside me and Vera there were five participants, including Gyurka and Sára, who was going to stand in line on Vörösmarty Square.

Sára was successful and obtained numbers for us among the first 50. She also received forms which we had to fill out. The completed and endorsed forms had to be submitted by the end of the next three weeks, by October 15th, to IBUSZ when the entire price of the trip had also to be paid.

When we received the forms we saw that these had to be endorsed by the personnel department at our place of work, to show that we were employed there. Meanwhile, we realized that the completed forms had to be endorsed not only by the personnel department at TKI Újpest, but had to be sent to the TKI headquarters personal department and from there they were to be further sent to Közép Gépipari (Middle Machine Industry) Ministry. What 'Középgép' (Middle Machine) had to do with it I did not know, but for some reason the TKI belonged to the Ministry of the Middle Machine Industry.

When we realized this, Gyurka discussed with Andris Dallos, 'Uncle' Rotter and I what we should do. The question was whether it was worth making a high - profile case from this trip, that it should also reach the Ministerial level. This was a complicated problem. Why attract attention - that was the key issue. We discussed all angles of this issue. Each of us said our opinion, which differed only in hues from each other, that such a case, with the waves reaching up to the Ministry, could it be adverse for us. Finally, however, we agreed, that an IBUSZ-tour to visit to a socialist brother country could not be a bad point on our cadre file. Finally we decided to fill out the forms and submit them to the personnel department to start the endorsing procedure. After the personnel department in the Újpest TKI endorsed them, Andris, who anyway had to go to the headquarters of TKI, would take the forms with him and give them to the central personnel department, that they should send them to the Ministry. So we did that way. During the next two weeks we did not receive the approval, so we inquired how it could be speeded up. The information was that it could not be speeded up.

In early October, the secretary of the of Újpest TKI Personnel Department gave us the list of who was planning to take this trip, together with the forms endorsed and signed by the Minister of the Middle Machine Industry which had also the Seal of the Ministry. We all gave the forms to Gyurka Gergely. He said that he would give them to Sára, who would take them to the IBUSZ office and give them to Gyurka's mother's friend that she should arrange to get us into the group of the 100 lucky participants. We also gave him the money to be able to pay the full price of the tour.

Sára submitted the forms and Gyurka relayed the news to us, that not 100 but 120 candidates had been accepted, because the experience was that some people would not receive an exit permit, that is the passport, and there would also be others who for different reasons would not participate. When Sára submitted our forms with the money, she received a brief prospectus. The IBUSZ prospectus stated that the departure date of the Zakopane tour would be on Saturday, December 8.

On November 9, that is four weeks before the advertised departure, we still did not know anything more from IBUSZ. Gyurka asked his niece a few times to make inquiries, but she was not able to find out more information. Gyurka's mother's lady friend, who provided us with the advanced information about this trip, and who worked in the Vörösmarty Square head office of IBUSZ knew also nothing. She said that the travel was included in the plan of IBUSZ, but had not yet been notified by the

ÁVO to authorize the entry or exit for those who had been submitted the application documents.

Sára on Friday, November 16, visited again the IBUSZ office to make inquiries. She was told that on that day they received from the ÁVO the notification that 100 persons from the applicants were going to get the permit to leave and return document. Sára, who was a clever girl, somehow persuaded the IBUSZ officials to let her see the list. She verified that all of our names were on the list, so we were going to get the exit permits. Gyurka informed us about this good news, and now we had three weeks to prepare ourselves for this trip.

We received the official notification from IBUSZ a few days later. In this it was stated that the passport would be a 'Collective passport' and therefore we would not get in our hands an individual one before we departed. The notification also informed us that we were going to leave by train from the Nyugati (West) train station on 15 December, Saturday (and not on December 8, as originally announced) at 10 am. The return date would be Saturday, December 22, also to the West station, but the arrival time was not specified. In the notification it was stated that everybody could bring no more than one suitcase. The letter also wrote that IBUSZ Agents would also be on the train. They were going also to come with us to assist us in everything. They would be able to convert money, the Hungarian Forint to Polish Zloty. We were also notified that there would be no food service on the train, therefore everybody should bring food and water for the trip.

On 15 December morning, we arrived at the West train station by 9 o'clock. We met there and together we proceeded to find the train, which according to the letter we had received from IBUSZ, was supposed to have a wagon marked 'IBUSZ' which would take us to Czechoslovakia en route for Poland. We found the IBUSZ-marked wagon. Only one of the doors was open, in front of which a woman with IBUSZ armband was waiting for us. She was dressed against the cold so that only her eyes could be seen, and her hand which was holding a pencil. The other gloved hand held some papers. She asked our names, and after reviewing her papers put a checkmark against our names and said that we should board the train. We ascended the stairs and entered the wagon. We went to its center and found an empty compartment where we settled down. We put our luggage up on the luggage rack. When we were all settled, Gyurka and I got off and walked in the direction of the train's locomotive. Between our IBUSZ wagon and the locomotive there were three wagons with a sign 'Kosice' which meant that those cars were going to Kosice (Kassa), a city in Czechoslovakia. After our wagon there were four other wagons with a sign: 'Miskolc'.

From this observation we assumed that the train would go to Miskolc, after which it would cross the border to Czechoslovakia and would go to Kosice. From there who knows how we were going to finally reach Zakopane. We returned to our compartment and relayed this information to the others. In the compartment it was pleasantly warm, everyone took off their coat, and settled comfortably . The train, as stated in the letter from IBUSZ, left at exactly at 10 o'clock. It did not go very fast and it also stopped at several places, but finally it arrived at the Miskolc railroad station. The IBUSZ lady who already took off her warm coat and hat, turned out to be a pleasant-looking, middle-aged, brown-haired woman. She came in with a younger man who also had an IBUSZ armband. She introduced herself and said we should call her Zsuzsa. Her IBUSZ companion's name was John. She said that because the train would stop in Miskolc for about 30 minutes we could get out of the train to get fresh air. When we stopped in Miskolc the last four wagons were detached from our train which left only our wagon and the three marked 'Kosice' attached to the locomotive. By the time we started from Miskolc, it was already two o'clock in the afternoon.

The train continued from Miskolc at a snail's pace, but it did not stop at any station. Finally at three thirty it stopped at a small station the name of which was, 'Tornyosnémeti'. Here our accompanying IBUSZ people told us to dress warmly and everyone should get off, but we should leave our belongings where they were. We put on our coats and hats and got out the wagon. We noticed that nobody got out of the three cars marked 'Kosice'. We saw that in the area in front of the small station many border guards, that are ÁVH soldiers, were present. Of these, ten had gone to the wagons marked 'Kosice'. An officer came and was standing in front of us with a megaphone and said that he has a collective passport from which he was going to read our names one by one and whoevers name was called should come forward and he was going to ask a few questions and, if the answers were acceptable, the person could go back to the wagon, from which he or she had disembarked. We saw that in each of the doors of our carriage an armed border guard / ÁVH soldier was now stationed, and we saw that four ÁVH soldiers with bayonets entered our wagon, presumably to see that nobody was hiding there.

After this the ÁVH officer began to read the names. The roster started at the beginning of the alphabet. Whoevers name he called out had to step in front of us. The officer asked a few questions, such as the mother's name, birth date, and so on. Meanwhile, the officer looked at the paper in his hand, and when the response he received agreed with the data on the paper, he motioned that person to return to our wagon. Of course, the people first checked had to wait at the stairs of the wagon and could not enter until the four armed ÁVH had got off. After they came down the stairs from the wagon, and signaled that everything was OK and nobody was hiding there, the first passengers could re-board. The procedure went quite slowly while we were standing and waiting in the cold. Fortunately the day was cloudless, no rain or snow was in sight. It was getting a little dark. By now most of our group was on the train, but because my name started with the letter 'V', my name was not called yet. About fifteen of us were still waiting. Finally Vera and I were called and after we answered the question which apparently satisfied the officer, we were dismissed to get back on the train. When we approached the train, about ten passengers were still standing there outside. When we reached our wagon and the AVH soldier standing there motioned us to get on the train, the officer announced that there are no more names on the list. Still about five or six men and women were standing there. They protested that they were still there. The officer told them that their names were not on the collective passport and therefore they could not continue the trip. He said that they could one by one get on the train with one of the soldiers to fetch their belongings, get off the train and go to the station and they should return to Budapest with the next train.

Meanwhile, it grew dark, but both the station and the train were illuminated with flood lights. When we returned to our compartment I informed my friends that about five or six people had been removed from our train and told to return to Budapest, because their names were not on our collective passport. Zsuzsa, our IBUSZ lady, just looked into our compartment, when the six persons with their luggage went towards the station. We asked her who those people were. She said that she had no idea, because everyone who was on the train was included in the list they received from IBUSZ and she had no idea why they were not on the border guard's collective passport. It was maybe possible that the collective passport read by the officer was of a later date than the list, obtained by the IBUSZ.

She said that she was going to speak to her colleague and would ask who those people were who were returned to Budapest. Meanwhile the train began to move slowly. Shortly after the train started to move, we stopped again, this time at the Czechoslovak border station. As we could see from our window, the Hungarian border guards were traveling on our train's steps, and now they stepped off. The Czech border guards did not come into the IBUSZ car. They bypassed us and went to the three non-IBUSZ cars. They boarded and the train was standing about half an hour. When the Czechoslovak border guards also descended, the train started slowly to move.

By now it was dark outside. In our compartment a lamp was on, but gave not much light. We talked a lot about everything, especially what happened with those unfortunate people who for some or other reason were not included in the collective passport read by the officer and what would have happened if some of us had been told at the Toronynémeti boarder station that we could not continue our trip.

Everyone slowly started to doze, and hours later we arrived at Kosice. Zsuzsa, the IBUSZ lady, came to our compartment and told us that her colleague could not imagine any other reason why those people were not allowed to continue our trip that the six peoples names may have been inadvertently left out of the collective passport received by the officer. She said that if anybody wanted to get out and walk around, we should do so because the train was going to Poprad, but she did not know when we were going to depart. Her colleague was now trying to find out, but considering that new cars were going to be attached to us, and yet there was no locomotive, it was uncertain when the train would actually leave.

That there was no locomotive could be felt, because it started to become cold in our compartment. Again with Gyurka I undertook to get off to see what was happening. As we got on the platform we saw that they were just attaching a few wagons, and it seemed that a locomotive was going to be also attached to our train. We got back quickly, and told them this news. The attachment of the locomotive was noticeable, because the compartment started to get warmer. About a half hour later the train started to move but very slowly trundled along. Occasionally it stopped at a station. Finally we all fell asleep while sitting. We woke up when the train stopped, and Zsuzsa, the IBUSZ lady dressed warmly, opened the door of the compartment saying that we had arrived at Poprad. We should all get off and take our belongings, because we were transferring here to an autobus. We should stay together with others of our group and go together to the front of the station where a bus was waiting for us. This was at night at ten-thirty. So we all dressed, gathered up our belongings, removed our luggage, got off and stopped before our wagon . When everyone was down, the IBUSZ escorts told us to pick up our luggage and go to the front of the station because the bus was there. Everyone should deposit their luggage next to the bus and get on the bus. We all took our luggage and went in front of the station building to the street. Poprad was at the foot of the High Tatras and on the top of the houses there seemed to be a bit of snow. In front of the station stood the bus. We deposited our luggage at the side of the bus, and boarded.

The bus became full, only a few seats were empty. The IBUSZ escorts Zsuzsa and John sat in the front row, and when they had all settled, Zsuzsa picked up the microphone and said it was great that we were all on the bus, and we would leave soon. She told something to the driver, who closed the door. Soon after, we started. The bus was new with very comfortable leather seats. Zsuzsa talking into the microphone said that because it was dark, unfortunately we would not be able to see the beautiful mountains. Looking out the window of the bus we saw that the edge of the road was covered with more and more snow, and in the weakly moon-lit distance we could dimly see the outlines of snow covered mountains.

Our bus went reasonably fast, then around midnight stopped.

Zsuzsa of IBUSZ announced that we have arrived to the Polish border. Here, the driver would unload the luggage from the autobus. Everyone should pick up his or her suitcase, because it must be carried over a bridge, which was over the Bialka River to Poland. On the other side of the bridge, we had to stop, because the Polish border guards would be counting us, and would look at the collective passport. On the other side of the bridge, a Polish bus would wait for us. We should deposit our luggage next to the bus. The driver of that bus would load them on the bus and that bus would take us to the hotel in Zakopane.

Zsuzsa picked up her suitcase and started to walk over the bridge. Fortunately Vera and I had just one suitcase. Vera also had a small bag. Andris and Zsuzsi had also only one suitcase, and Zsuzsi had a small bag. We started to go over the snow-covered and rather sparsely-lit bridge from Czechoslovakia to Poland. The Czechoslovak border guards were on this side of the bridge, but they only looked at us and did not say a word.

The bridge was about 100 meters long. It was snow covered, therefore we had to be very careful to avoid slipping. An uncomfortable and cold, probably north, wind blew. I pulled my hat over my ears. On the other side of the bridge on a snow-covered area was the Polish border guard's post. A few of the border guards with rifles on their shoulders were standing next to the small house. Zsuzsa in the meantime probably received other instructions, because now she said that we should deposit our suitcases and we would be called one by one in alphabetic order to go into the border guard's small house. After one had completed this, one should pick up the suitcase and then go to the autobus stationed at the other end of the snow covered area. Zsuzsa went to the guard's house, while John, the other accompanying

IBUSZ escort, remained and said that those whose name started with A should come closer. When the last one whose name started with A went into the guard's house, he said that now those with the letter B should come closer. This was repeated in the order of the alphabet. The night temperature was well below freezing. As my name started with the letter V, about a half an hour passed until Vera and I could enter the well heated small guard house. In the room we entered, a young Polish solder was sitting behind a desk and Zsuzsa was standing at the side of the desk. She asked us to announce our name. This we did, and the young soldier began to write, but he obviously had difficulty with the Hungarian names. In this case, Zsuzsa tried to help him. I did not mind the slowness, because it had been half an hour that I was freezing outside, but inside it was pleasantly warm. When he finally finished, Zsuzsa told us that when we got out we should pick up our suitcase and take it to the bus.

When we got out of the guard house the young man with the IBUSZ armband told us also to pick up our luggage and get on the bus. We did that. Inside the bus it was pleasantly warm, at least compared to the windy cold outside. When all of us were on the bus the Polish border guards came to the buses with our IBUSZ escorts. Two border guards and Zsuzsa boarded our bus, and Zsuzsa began to read out the names from the collective passport. Whoevers name was read out put up his or her hand and Zsuzsa in front of the border guard made a check mark against the name. The border guard did the same on the list he made in the guard house. When we finished with this, the border guard left the bus and Zsuzsa handed over the collective passport to her colleague.

By the time the bus started, it was already quarter of one in the morning. Half an hour later, we arrived in Zakopane. The bus stopped on a snowy road in front of a multistory large building, on which there was a sign 'Lipowy Dwor', which was immediately translated into Hungarian by Gyurka as 'Linden Tree Yard'. This was our hotel. The driver put the suitcases on the snow next to the bus. Everybody was searching for their luggage. Inside Zsuzsa and the hotel clerk greeted us. Zsuzsa announced that couples would have rooms with two beds, while individuals would be housed in rooms with multiple beds. Thus Vera and I got a key, fortunately to a room on the ground floor, Andris and his wife also on the ground floor got a room adjacent to ours. Uncle Laci Rotter and Gyurka received no key, they were told that their room was number 10 on the first floor, so they went up carrying their luggage. Sára was placed also on the first floor where the women had a common room. As it turned out, ten individuals were housed in a common room. Over the receptionist desk on the wall was a sign in Hungarian: 'Breakfast in the restaurant from 7 to 9 AM'.

Our was room number 6. The furnishing in the room was two beds and a chest with three drawers. I deposited our luggage on the top of that. In addition, there was a clothes rack and washbasin with the taps over it. On one side of it was a metal bar with two small towels on it. I looked at my watch. It showed 1:30 AM. After that I went out to explore where the bathroom was. I found it at the end of the corridor. There were two toilets and two small rooms, shower and sink in both of them.

The next day at breakfast we met our companions. Everyone told their experiences. In Uncle

Laci's and Gyurka's room besides of them they also had eight other companions. Some of the beds were only mattresses placed on the floor. According to Sára in their room all of the ten women had beds. Compared to that, our room with two beds was real luxury. The breakfast indicated that there would be a problem with the food. We got coffee and a slice of bread, each. No milk for the watered coffee, no butter, no jam with the several days' old bread. But the weather and the landscape were beautiful. Opposite the hotel were the snow-covered slopes, and behind the hotel the High-Tatra's peaks appeared, and everywhere bathed in the brilliant sunshine. The clean, white, bright snow was everywhere.

Before we left to explore Zakopane, IBUSZ Zsuzsa came to the restaurant and said that we were going to have great weather for the whole week. She suggested that we should see the village, which was famous as it was founded in 1676, when it had 43 inhabitants. In the small town, since 1929 ski and ski jumping competitions were taking place, and in March 1940 the Russian NKVD and the German Gestapo held a week-long conference in Zakopane's 'Villa Tadeusz' to co-ordinate the extermination of the Polish resistance movement. This was an interesting fact, but under the circumstances it was dangerous information. We looked at each other because we did not know why she said it.

The town center was not far from the hotel. We walked along its nice main street, which was full of small shops. Considering that Christmas was coming, all the shop windows were nicely decorated. Beautifully packaged boxes were nicely arranged. From the signs displayed on the shops we could not find out what they were selling, so we entered one of them to look around and perhaps find something nice to buy as well. In the store a very friendly attendant greeted us from behind the counter. When we looked around, we saw that there were no goods anywhere. Each shelf was empty, and every glass covered cabinet on the counter was decorated with the same type of beautifully wrapped and tastefully displayed boxes seen in the shop window. Given that neither of us spoke polish, Sára nicely said, 'magyarszki'. She nodded, and the she said, pointing to herself, 'polszki'. Now Gyurka asked whether she understood French or German. The woman said that she knew a little bit of German. So we asked what was she selling. She said that she had all kinds of merchandise for tourists but now there was nothing in the store. After a great walk on the nice, a little snowy but sunny streets of Zakopane, we went back to the hotel.

After our experience of the quality of our breakfast, we were not surprised when the lunch was served, which consisted of a small portion of chicken, which I do not think was chicken. It could have been an eagle, because we had seen many of them flying over the city. The dish which was labeled chicken did not resemble any poultry I had eaten.

After lunch we took a walk around the town on one of the walks where there was an excellent view of the mountains. On a snow-covered area, deck chairs had been set up. We sat on them and enjoyed a panoramic view of the mountains and enjoyed the sunshine. Then we returned to the hotel.

László Rotter, Zsuzsa Dallos, Vera Váradi and András Dallos

During the next days we made trips to the Zakopane ski slopes. On a cable car we went up to the lookout tower, saw the Meteorological station situated at a height of 2000 meters, the ski slopes and a lot of skiers, who raced madly down the slopes. At times, two skiers went down from the top of the slope, between them a stretcher on sleds. We saw that where they stopped a body was lying on the snow. The two skiers lifted gently the stretcher now having somebody on it and started probably in the direction of a hospital. One such unfortunate was the roommate of Gyurka and Uncle Laci. He had only a mattress on the floor as his bed, but when that evening he returned from the hospital with a broken leg in plaster to the 'Linden Tree Yard' his roommates voted to go give him a bed, and until we left he did not get up, only when it was absolutely necessary.

Zsuzsa told us that IBUSZ had organized a bus tour of Krakow. We all enrolled. This was on one of the gloomily gray days out of the seven we spent in Zakopane. The trip from Zakopane to Krakow was about 100 miles, which we made in 2 hours by bus.

We learned that Krakow was a very old city and its touristic center was the Wawel Hill. Wawel is a limestone hill on the left bank of the river Vistula. Its height is 228 meters. Wawel is the Polish word meaning 'abyss', because the hill a long time ago was cut in two by an abyss. On the hill once was a fortress, and today it is full of historic buildings, including the Wawel Castle. Wawel was the center of the Poland until the 17th century, when Warsaw became the capital of Poland. The Wawel castle (Zamek wawelski) was the seat of the Polish kings from 1038 until 1596. Stephen Báthory (1533-1586), who was born in Hungary, was crowned king of Poland on May 1, 1576. We also saw the other attractions including the beautiful Wawel Cathedral.

It was sad to see that the buildings in Krakow were greyish in color throughout, probably because of World War II, the German occupation and the many years of neglect. The shops we found were the same as in Zakopane. They had no merchandise and we could not buy anything. The shops here were empty too. By the evening we were back in Zakopane to our usual excellent dinner. The next day was sunny again, and we continued the exploration of Zakopane and its surroundings. IBUSZ on December 21, Friday, at our breakfast drew attention to the following day, December 22, Saturday, when at 8 o'clock in the morning we should be at the exit door with our belongings, because the bus would leave no later than 8:45. We could get our breakfast as early as 7 o'clock.

On the morning of December 22, we were at the exit door at 8 o'clock with our packages. We carried our suitcases to the bus and boarded the bus. Zsuzsa and Janos sat in the front row again, and when Zsuzsa saw that we were all there, Janos counted us and when he was satisfied that we were all there, he announced that there was good news for us. The bus would go straight to Poprad, and we would not have to walk across the bridge which was the Polish-Czechoslovak border.

That announcement was very enthusiastically applauded, some of us shouted"Bravo, bravo". At 8:45, as Zsuzsa promised, the bus really started. The trip to Poprad was made during day time, and the High Tatra Mountains in the beautiful clear sunny weather could be very well seen.

We arrived around noon at Poprad. Zsuzsa told us during the trip that she could change money for us, because the shops in Poprad would be open, and we could buy something. The bus stopped in front of the station. Zsuzsa informed us that the train would leave at 2 o'clock in the afternoon for Kosice, and then we could board the wagon marked IBUSZ. We could leave our luggage in the bus and the bus driver would take it out of the bus and would deposit it next to the bus from where we could pick it up when we returned from the town to board the train. That way we would not have to carry our luggage when we visited the town.

Poprad was a nice little town. The shops were really open. We found a cafe, and entered to eat something. Because of the food which we had not received in Poland we were starving. It was a pleasant surprise that the usual Czech dumplings were available with a good heavy gravy. Then we drank coffee, which was also pretty good. Then we looked round the shops, where goods were found, but mainly technical things, such as compasses, altimeters, clocks and writing materials. These were, at least, something to take 'home from abroad'.

The train left really on time. In Kosice they did the same as when we arrived from Hungary. They removed some of the wagons and added some others. Zsuzsa said that we should feel free to disembark because the train would be leaving only half an hour later. The half hour became an hour because when we should have left it was discovered that two of our companions were not on the train. Our two IBUSZ escorts ran to the stationmaster, who was ready to give the signal to start the train, and somehow made him understand that two passengers were missing and without them we could not re-enter Hungary with our collective passport, which required that we had everybody present. So the train waited. Our traveling companions arrived, about a half an hour later.

It turned out that they still had some Czech money left over and wanted to spend it on something. At the end they purchased a pencil. So an hour after boarding the train we finally departed with wagons marked 'Miskolc – Budapest'. It was reassuring that, at least, we did not have to switch somewhere to another train.

The trip home went smoothly enough. When we arrived at Tornyosnémeti, the Hungarian border, the train stopped. Zsuzsa said that everyone should remain seated

Border guards/ÁVO boarded the train with bayonets fixed and went from compartment to compartment. When they opened the door to our compartment one of them asked us to show our identity cards. The one who had our collective passport in his hand made a check mark against the name of the person whose identity card had been shown. When all of us had been checked, they closed the compartment door and proceeded to the next compartment. They did not ask what we had bought and what was the value of our purchases. They probably knew that neither in Poland nor in Czechoslovakia was anything to buy.

We arrived in Budapest at the Western Railroad station in the evening around 8 o'clock where it was difficult to find a taxi, but finally we arrived back home at 9 o'clock from our trip to a 'Foreign Country'.

10. Capitalism's fatal deficiency

On the road of socialism leading to communism one of the very first and most important tasks was the introduction of the planned economy, in order to achieve the most efficient use of the resources and materials. It was considered that in the defeat of capitalism one of the most important tools was the planned economy which eventually meant a significant difference compared to the planless irresponsible capitalism, the sole purpose of which was clearly the exploitation of the workers.

In capitalism, anyone can initiate anything, the consequence of which is that some of the initiatives are successful, but some of them go awry, with the result of squandering resources and materials. In capitalism they are not making precise plans as to what to produce in the next years but to manufacture what eventually will be needed. A major drawback is the ensuing confusion and rush, and those who realize that this demand can be turned to their own advantage to benefit themselves, start to produce what is necessary. Others, in the meantime, produce what people do not need which is then a total waste and squandering of resources and materials. This squandering has to be eliminated as soon as possible on the road of socialism toward communism.

It was planned therefore to introduce as soon as possible an economy, by drawing up exact plans on the basis of which every need could be satisfied the best possible way and with the greatest possible efficiency. To this end, already in 1947, at the beginning of the very first three-year plan, a National Planning Office was established, and

Zoltán Vass became its President in 1949. The Planning Office according to the example of the Soviet Union started to develop five-year plans. In the planned economy the demands had to start from the bottom, and get up to the leaders. There at the summit the decision was made, where to devote the time and the available economic resources and materials. As a result the three, later five-year plans were decided at the top and imposed on everyone as to the task and function. This meant that all of the government owned companies' management implemented the instructions from the top and had virtually no autonomy.

Perhaps the case of the newsvendors gives probably the simplest possible example to understand the system. The newsvendors could not order many copies of a newspaper or magazine, but somewhere at the top it was decided what newspapers should be printed and in how many copies and accordingly how many copies of that newspaper should be sent to the individual newsstands. Those newspapers which people liked were sold out quickly and after that were not available, those which were not in demand obviously were not sold and every evening they were bound together and shipped to the pulping mills. This was the result of the communist planned economy: 'like it or does not like it, will not get else'.

To improve the system, based on the Soviet model, the 'Innovation program' was introduced. The problem with this program was that if an innovation was introduced inside of the company, and it proved to be successful, the person who introduced it received either no benefit from it, or maybe received a reward. However, if the innovation did not work out, it was clear that the person was a saboteur, pushed the imperialist's cart, perpetrated a crime against the people, which everybody knew had the most terrible consequences. Therefore it did not make any sense to change methods, imposed from above, which already existed. Plans could not have been changed, for example, because the old equipment, which produced some articles, was already in the production plan. If the plant received permission to buy a new machine to produce the same article, then the expected output of the new machine had to be added to the output of the old one, so to stop the outdated, no longer economically operating equipment could not be done.

The planned economy was also introduced in TKI. This of course in a research laboratory was quite absurd, because in the research work the needed equipment or materials in most cases cannot be pre-determined. The introduction of the planned economy resulted in every department of the research laboratory in August every year having to submit a research plan for the following year, the introduction of which research work, and for those projects how many people would be needed, the equipment was what, and how much material would be needed.

The problem was that if a department did not plan something and during the next year needed it, the department was not able to obtain it, because in the planned economy it was only produced, or obtained if in the previous year it had been requested. One can imagine to what this was leading. With wise foresight everyone ordered everything, as one could imagine.

Now, the request for materials for the following year had to be submitted in August, and this was accomplished as follows:

TKI received from the National Planning Office the 'List of Goods and Materials' prepared for that year. This was a massive volume, into which all of the material or substance was listed with its description and a ten-digit 'article number' and its price. The individual departments had to assemble the following year's 'procurement plan'. I sat down with my chemist colleagues and assembled with an educated guess an assumption of the subjects we were going to conduct research on in the next year. As we did not know what new tasks TKI would have during the next year we had to extrapolate from what we were doing at that time and we took that as our basis. The current situation we of course expanded somewhat, and of course some growth was also included in the calculation. All of the departments, including mine, based on guesses, assembled the materials, instruments, equipment list required for the next year. These items had to be copied from the 'List of Goods and Materials' in exact details. For example, how many units will be needed of the so-called 'Beaker-glass' used in the laboratory. These beakers came in many sizes and naturally they had to be detailed in all of their possible sizes (10, 20, 50, 100, 250, 500, 1000 milliliters and so on). Of the extremely thick book: 'List of Goods and Materials' of course only a few pieces were in the lab, we had to fight to get from somebody else who was using it, to fulfill our job.

I requested that each of us, myself as well as my chemists, should compile separately the list of the necessary material, equipment, and so on and when it was ready I summarized the results, which looked like this (the numbers and rates are hypothetical):

Item number	Description	Quantity	Price	Total price
1234567890	Beaker-glass 10ml	30	10.00	300.00
1234567891	Beaker-glass 50ml	15	12.00	180.00

When I reviewed the totals of our request, I saw that the final amount was an astronomical figure which seemed to me unrealistically high. The fact of being unrealistically high, of course, was just my opinion, but in the end I had to fight for it, when everybody submitted their obviously high totals. I started to cross out items or quantities so the total should be something normal, at least normal in my opinion. The final list was at least 40 pages long. I had to compile also the next year's labor force as well as the equipment requirements, and then once we had checked that all the numbers, quantities, and descriptions were correct, I handed the entire package of maybe 50 pages to a secretary to be typed. After typing we checked again and when we found it correct, I gave the dossier to Andris Dallos' secretary.

When Andris, the Managing Director, received from all the Department Heads their requirements, and added them together and saw the final results for the first time, he saw the incredibly large amount of money, and he got nervous. He also showed this to Karcsi Ducza, our military liaison, and they agreed that if they would go up to our Headquarters with these numbers, they would be booted out. They agreed that a quarter of this estimate would probably be feasible, but not even that would be easy to obtain.

Andris convened a meeting with the Department Heads and told them that every one of them had gone mad, and the next day he was convening a meeting where he expected that we all should come with a new proposal in which the requested amount for the next year's budget should be less than one quarter of the outrageous sum they now requested. Of course, for this next round no one reduced the amount to one quarter of the original plan.

When the next time we gathered in his office, Andris took off his glasses. Maybe he did not want to see us sharp, because that way he was more comfortable to yell at us:

"Look, I do not mind what you remove from the budget, only the total amount should be less. Do you think that anybody will inquire that you really need 30 pieces of the 10ml beaker or just 6?"

Our argument was that if 6 were requested, and actually we would need 7, from where the hell would we be able to get the seventh one? These meetings lasted for a week, when Andris resigned himself to the fact that the final amount would be more than a quarter of the original, and we removed as much as we believed would be acceptable. Naturally we had only a vague idea of what we were really going to need for our research during the following year. Eventually we reached a definitive list which the secretary typed in a final form, from the lists which had lots of corrections and crossed out lines. After the list was retyped by the secretary, I as well as my chemists, reviewed it and made sure that everything including the 10 digit part number, the description, the quantity and price was OK, my department's final plan was submitted to Andris, so did every Department head. His secretary was now responsible for assembling the entire Laboratory's final plan, that is to compile all the of the Újpest TKI-2 Laboratory's Department's plans. For example, a 10-ml glass beaker, the part number of which for example was 1234567890, at least five Departments wanted to order some, say, 3, 4, 7, 8 and 11 pieces. The Újpest TKI-2 Lab's final plan looked like this:

Part number	Description	Quantity	Unit Price	Total price
1234567890	Beaker-glass - 10ml	33	10.00	330.00

Given that at the time duplicating machines did not exist, everything had to be typed and retyped. Lightweight thin papers were used, in between them carbon papers to copy the typing to the next thin paper, that sufficient number of copies should be completed. One copy for Újpest TKI-2, one for Headquarters, and so on.

When Andris took the TKI-2 plan to Headquarters, the same story was repeated. The requested amount was too much, some of the quantities had to be reduced, or items had to be eliminated. Andris was now fighting for our numbers. Of course, some items were crossed out, in most cases the quantity was reduced, and now the secretaries of the Central Office were typing the finalized list.

This process was probably at least twice or three times repeated at higher and higher levels, finally the Minister gave his blessing to the final list. This meant that the list with the 10 digit part numbers and descriptions, and so on, which were by now many, many hundreds of pages, could have at least been four or five times retyped by the secretaries of the various offices.

With this our material and so on plan for the following year was completed, on the basis of which the National Planned Economy ordered the domestic production or if that was not available initiated the purchase from abroad of the items which were desperately needed by us for the next year.

We did not have to deal with this anymore, we could be satisfied that now we were sure that the next year we would have enough material to conduct our research work.

During February of the next year, I received a call from an engineer colleague whom I only knew by sight, who was working in one of the electronic laboratories.

“For your chemical laboratory work you most likely are using a liquid platinum paint which when you paint it on a glass surface and heat it up, it will produce a thin and nice platinum layer.”

“Yes, yes, of course I know. Sometimes we use a little of such organic platinum paint.”

“Very good - he said – would you need some?”

“Yes, we could use some, we do not have much and slowly we have to get more.”

“Great, how much would you need?”

I was thinking.

“Oh - I said - if you could give us approximately 5 grams, I would thank you very much for it.”

His tone at the other end of the telephone line drastically changed, I had to take the receiver from my ear because his screams would have raptured my eardrum.

“You are trying to be funny with me, 5 grams? I am not in the mood to joke the minimum I can give you is 100 grams!”

Now I was surprised.

“Well, this is the problem, because yesterday I was delivered 1 kilogram.”

“100 grams is a lot of platinum paint, it is a fortune. I do not understand, you say that yesterday they delivered to you 1 kilogram of platinum paint? Who delivered it and why were you delivered so much?”

Apparently he calmed down, because from his voice I was rather hearing despair, and not the hysterics, as before.

“Last year when I prepared this year’s material and equipment plan I specified that 10.00 grams of platinum paint would be needed. I assume that during the several retyping of the lists somebody left the decimal point out and the 10.00 gram became 1000 grams which is equivalent to 1 kilogram. So now they delivered me 1 kg platinum paint, which, as you say, costs very, very much money. The problem is that I did not order this, but I cannot prove it. The fact is that I have here on my desk 1 kg of the platinum paint, and I would like to share most of it with anyone who can use it, before an investigation will be brought against me."

"I understand. Look, I will take 50 grams, and I am going to ask colleagues whom I think could use it, and going to give them your telephone number so you can discuss with them directly how much they could use? Do I need to sign something that is has been delivered?"

"Yes, I am going to send you 50 grams with my lab technician, please sign it, that you received it. Thank you very much for your help."

A couple of weeks after this incident, I had something to do on the ground floor of the laboratory building. It was a wintry February morning and when I looked through the TKI glass doors, I noticed that a huge flatbed truck was in front of the entrance. On the truck was a huge machine, at first glance I could not figure out what it was. Comrade Bóka who was the guard at the front entrance came to me and when he saw that I was looking at the truck with this huge device on the top of it, he said that the truck brought a huge winch which is used on ocean going ships for hoisting and lowering their anchor. When he saw that I was looking at him with disbelief, he confirmed it:

"Dr. Váradi, the truck driver said what this machine was, when he showed me the receipt to sign it. Imagine that I did not sign it, but I called our purchasing department. Comrade Győri came down at once, and now as you can see, he is discussing the matter with the driver."

I just said to Bóka that the matter was incomprehensible to me, and then hastened back to my laboratory, from the window of which one could see the huge truck, on top of which was a sea-going ships winch which was designed to lift large anchors, and the driver who was vividly talking with Comrade Gyôri, but now Karcsi Ducza also joined them.

The truck with its engine shut off was still standing there when we went out for lunch, but now neither the driver nor Győri, nor Ducza were visible. I went to lunch with Gyurka Gergely to the Tungsram restaurant. On the way we both admired the huge winch. Over lunch, we agreed that this was probably not manufactured on an order of the TKI laboratory, the question was who was the one who had the winch included on this year's material and equipment list.

When we came back from lunch, the situation was unchanged. Eventually around 3 o'clock in the afternoon I saw from the window that the truck with the winch slowly started to back out from the entrance and Gyôri was waving to help the driver extricate himself with such a large vehicle from an area obviously not suitable for such a large vehicle. Eventually the truck was gone.

Later I crossed the corridor to go from my laboratory to my office and saw a few people standing there and Ducza with great vigor was explaining something. He was apparently sweaty and he spoke with agitation which was unusual for him. When I got there, he was just saying:

"From the papers it is clear that this was manufactured by the Shipyard on an order from TKI. The main problem is who ordered it, because it is clear that the consequences will be terrible. We took out our 'Materials and goods' needs' list which we submitted and was approved last year, but the part number of the winch was not on that list. Now the question is, after all the changes were made and the final list was submitted by the TKI Headquarters to the Ministry, was the winch's part number on that list? Well it was a big job, because you can imagine how many pages were the 'Materials and goods' needs' of the entire TKI. Four people had worked on this, but it turned out that the part number of the winch was not included when the list was sent up to the Ministry. Thus, nobody in TKI is responsible for the order of such a useless and expensive machine. Now, we do not know who was the one who accidentally mistyped one of the part numbers. Also we do not know what equipment we will not be going to receive, because its part number was accidentally mistyped to order a winch. But this should be our greatest problem."

With this he wiped his forehead and, went slowly toward his office.

About a month later I got a huge surprise. Our warehouse clerk brought a pretty heavy looking brown box to my office. He put it down on my desk and took out a piece of paper from his pocket and asked me to sign it. The paper was to acknowledge that I had received 10 pieces of 125 mm diameter agate mortar with their corresponding pestles. When I read the paper, I sat down on my chair in the office, and with slightly trembling hands pulled out my pen and signed the paper, gave it to the warehouse clerk and thanked him for the package. The storekeeper said goodbye, walked out of my office, and I just stared at the brown box, which apparently contained 10 pieces of 125 mm agate mortar with their pestles.

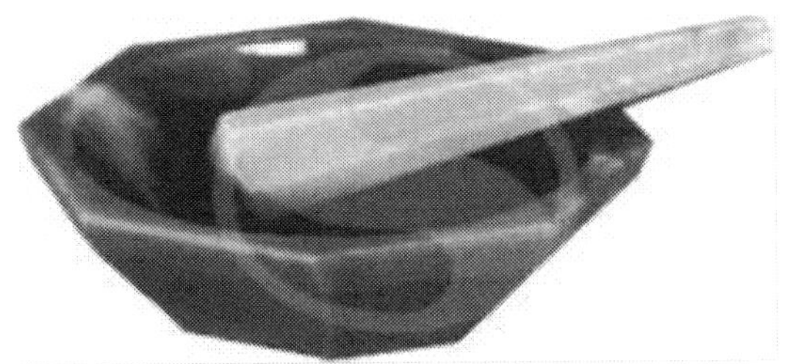

Agate mortar and pestle

The agate is a semiprecious stone belonging to the quartz family. It is used as jewelry, but since it is extremely hard quartz, which can be polished and is acid resistant, therefore it is also used to make mortars and pestles, which are used to pulverize chemical substances. One can imagine how expensive this sort of mortar is.

I opened the box and took out from it the 10 mortars and pestles; each carefully packed in several layers of paper. I unwrapped one, and there was in my hand a beautiful octagonal agate mortar and its pestle. I remembered that in the previous August, when we prepared the procurement plan for this year, I included in the list one agate mortar of this size which I believed may be necessary, though very expensive. I remembered that the price of such an agate mortar and pestle was like my half-year salary. And now here before me I had 10 pieces! My full salary for 5 years! I started to feel sick, what would happen over this?

When I gathered myself a bit, pulled out my department's finalized purchasing plan. I looked the part number and found that I ordered only one piece of this agate mortar and pestle. I put the mortars and pestles into the drawer of my desk and went to Andris' offices. I told the secretary that I would like to see the entire TKI-2's annual procurement plan, because I would like to identify a single item, how many pieces did we order of that?

Magda was very friendly, and immediately took out the awfully thick dossier, which contained the list. I opened the list and as the list was organized by part numbers, it was easy to find the part number for the agate mortar and I was pleased to see that TKI-2 requested only one piece of the agate mortar. I closed the list and returned the dossier to Magda. I thanked her, and now I returned to my office very relieved. Accordingly it was not TKI-2's fault that 10 pieces were delivered.

The question now was how to make nine pieces disappear and keep only one? I was thinking of my colleague who received 1 kg of platinum paint and who tried to get rid of the excess, but I realized that my problem was much simpler. I only had nine pieces of beautiful agate mortars to make disappear without any trace, because if they took an inventory and found 10 pieces of 125-millimeter agate mortars with their pestles, representing a fantastic value, I would not be able to explain that I did not order them and TKI-2 did not order them either, which we could prove, but somewhere somebody accidentally typed the wrong number, or it was shipped by mistake. I could not return them either, because to where should I send them back? Where the shipment came from, they most likely could prove that they were ordered to deliver 10 pieces. If it came to proving that we just ordered one, but someone in the Ministry who retyped the list made a mistake, that would be very bad news for me. For the comrade from the ÁVO, who would deal with this matter, a simpler solution would be if I confessed that I wanted to destroy the People's democracy, rather than to investigate in the

Ministry or anywhere else, who copied the list and made a mistake copying the TKI 'Materials and goods' plan. I thought this over very quickly and before I even got back to my office, I realized that the agate mortars with their pestles had to disappear in seconds, so that only one should be left in my laboratory. I also figured out that these could become great decorative ashtrays and would make anyone happy to display them on their table at home. Now I just had to look for colleagues who would not open their mouth about it and would immediately take them home. My action was so successful that by the end of the day I had difficulty to rescue one agate mortar and its pestle, which I locked up immediately in a glass cabinet in the Cathode Laboratory.

I do not want to leave our dear readers in delusion that these three cases, as we progressed along the rugged road of socialism toward communism, were isolated cases. Absolutely not. For the lower value materials, large quantities were gathered, or as one of my colleague put it: "People were snatching from each other's hand those thick volumes with the part numbers and stupefying quantities of materials materialized in the laboratories, on the other hand unforeseen needs during the year could only be obtained with great difficulty by finding another laboratory in the country and borrowing from them. This practice remained after 1956, because the planned economy continued to rage. This system lasted until about the middle of the 1980s."[36]

How is it that the capitalist system, with its fatally deficient system of planless confusion where many who produce what nobody needs, thereby squandering material and

[36] Dr. János Ádám - personal communication

labor, should have long ago disappeared from the scene, and did not disappear. On the other hand the planned management system leading to communism did?

The answer is perhaps not so difficult: the largest part of humanity is probably stupid, therefore not able to realize what's good for them.

11. Motorboat sport in Hungary

The fuel for my kayak's small engine was a mixture of gasoline and motor oil and the engine consumed only very little. When I bought the motorized kayak, the owner warned me that no matter how little gasoline and motor oil was consumed, gasoline and motor oil should only be purchased with ration tickets. Gasoline and oil could be bought cheaper on the black market, but he recommended me to get gasoline and oil with ration tickets, because if a police officer stopped me and I could not prove that my gasoline and oil rationing was officially granted, then I could have serious problems. He also said that one could get for motorboats oil and gasoline rationing if someone was a member of a motorboat sports club and also took part in boat races. If I obtained such a sports certificate I could officially get gasoline and motor oil with ration tickets.

After I bought the motorized kayak, I immediately visited the President of the Tungsram Motorboat Association, or as it was called 'Vasas Izzo Motorboat Section', and told him that I wanted to be a member of the Association. Once I completed the proper paperwork, I got a membership card and thus became a motorboat sportsman. I reported this to the appropriate government office, and from then on I got regularly the monthly gasoline and motor oil ration tickets.

The Association's President said that as a motorboat sportsman I had to participate yearly in at least three races. Most of the motorboat races took place on the branch of the Danube between Margaret Island and the Pest section of the city. Two buoys were anchored in the middle of the Danube. The distance between them was usually about the half the length of Margaret Island. After the start, one or more circles had to be run on this elliptical course, depending on the category of the motor based on its size. My small kayak with its miniature engine, of course belonged to the smallest category, which had to run usually one but a maximum of two laps. On these races I was always the last, as I did not want to drive my motor too hard. But in a competition somebody always has to be the last. There were also longer distance tournaments around the Margaret Island, around the island of Szentendre, or south of Budapest near the island of Csepel. I did not participate in those, except once when somehow I was persuaded to participate in a competition near Csepel Island. I survived this with great luck. Tungsram's watersports establishment was at the northern end of Budapest, while the island of Csepel was south of the city.

From the Tungsram watersport establishment to reach Csepel Island, I had to go south the full length of Margaret Island, after that through the entire downtown of Budapest and under all the bridges. South of the Margit Bridge in front of the Castle Hill and Gellért Hill was not easy where the Danube was very narrow and deep, but at the Elizabeth Bridge it was the worst phase. The Danube in that area was full of eddies, and if you came up against a ship or a barge, the waves from shore to shore reflected back and were very dangerous. I usually used my motorized kayak near the Szentendre Island, where the Danube was wide and flowing slowly and comfortably, so when I got in this area going towards the Csepel Island with my small and light kayak, I did not feel safe. Eventually I passed the last Danube bridge and arrived at the northern tip of Csepel Island, where the competition was held. I knew that the competition would be in a branch of the Danube. Thus, when finally I saw a branch on the left side of the Danube, with relief I directed my kayak there.

It was a cloudless, pleasant, warm summer day, and on both sides of the narrow branch of the Danube fishermen were sitting waiting for a catch. When they saw me entering the branch with my motorized kayak, everybody waved and tried to tell me that something that was ahead of me. I looked at them curiously, trying to figure out why they were waving. When I got a little further down, one angler put down his rod and with both hands was waving, which looked as if I should stop. When I went a little bit further, I saw not too far from me that there was a weir, and the water of the river was flowing over it. Then I realized why the people were waving and that I was in a very bad place, because if I went further, then inevitably the water would carry me over the weir. I reacted immediately, by pressing the foot pedal and tried to turn the boat around. I almost succeeded, when the engine suddenly stopped. I wrapped the cord around the drum of the motor and pulled it. Nothing. I did this twice, but I felt that the water was sweeping my boat towards the weir, and seeing this, the anglers were excitedly yelling something and pointing at the direction of the weir. At this point I rapidly pulled out the oars of the kayak and started paddling with all my strength, and with the foot pedal moved the rudder to go the shortest way to the shore. Finally the kayak's nose ran up the sand, and I got off the boat. By that time several of the fishermen got there too and started to shout at me, saying how could I be so foolish.

I told them that I did not know there was a weir in this branch of the Danube and asked them to hold the two ends of the kayak. I tried to start the engine, which started on the first pull of the cord. I put the propeller into the water and got successfullyout of this branch of the Danube which was positively not for motorboats.

Finally I found the venue of the race. I registered for the competition to make sure that this would be one of my yearly three mandatory races, and as usual I became the last boat in my category.

I was pretty scared of my return trip, because from the north to go to Csepel was relatively easy, since the water was flowing in that direction. Going backI would have to motor against the stream, and if by chance in the vicinity of the Gellert Hill or under the Elizabeth bridge or under the Chain Bridge my engine stopped, as happened near to the weir, it would not be simple to get to the shore. This could be more complicated if at the same time a steamboat or a barge was coming. Fortunately, the engine did not stop and without trouble I made it back to the Tungsram beach. However, I vowed never again to venture with my motorized kayak south of the Margaret Bridge.

In January of 1952 Comrade Bóka, the Újpest TKI laboratory's guard at the entrance door, called me to say that two Comrades were looking for me. I went downstairs and recognized one of them as Karcsi, the Chairman of Vasas Izzo Motorboat Section. The other was a member of the club, whom I knew by sight. Karcsi said they would like to speak to me, so I asked them to come with me and invited them to an un-used office on the ground floor, and we sat down.

Karcsi started by telling me that I certainly knew that the during the time of Aschner a boat building workshop was established on the grounds of the Tungsram factory, which was responsible for building boats such as kayaks, rowing boats, sculls and canoes used for racing. The boat building workshop was still in existence with excellent professionals who were still there and were building excellent boats. Recently they completed the construction of boats needed for the Helsinki Olympics. Karcsi said that he spoke to the workshop boss, and they were willing to help the Vasas Izzo Motorboat Section so we should have good motor boats which would improve our racing capabilities.

Karcsi went on and said that after such encouragement the Vasas Izzo Motorboat Section should take steps to obtain wood allocation so everyone could build a well-designed, high quality, nice boat, and with such boats we could achieve in the races better results than ever before.

He said that in the workshop one of the experts would design the boat, and then under the direction and supervision of the boat building professionals we would undertake the work. Everyone was going to build his own boat. Karcsi and some of the members of the Motorboat Section had calculated that this could be achieved if at least 10 members were willing to participate and pay for the necessary wood and materials cost.

"I would gladly participate" - I said – "as one of the required ten members, and pay the amount which would be my share. My problem was that even under the direction of the Tungsram boat building professionals I did not believe that I could assemble and put together such a boat."

They both looked at me as if I was somewhat retarded and they had to explain a complicated algebraic equation.

"I can understand your worry very much" - said Karcsi – "because I would not be able toassemble it well either. The cutting to size of the wood has to be done on the machines of the boat building shop which we cannot handle anyway, so this has to be carried out by professionals trained to operate those machines. Of course, they are going to do this after hours, and we have to compensate them for their time. As of the work to assemble the wood pieces already cut, to screw them together and make them watertight, paint them and varnish them, that has also to be done after working hours. The competent professionals have offered their help to do a big part of this, but they would teach us who would use the boats and we would help them to do this work. Of course we were going to compensate them for their time."

Since I am not fast to understand things, I still was not sure that my 'help' would not be detrimental to the safety of the boat. However, I had enough sense not to ask this, rather I continued with another issue which I understood better:

"That sounds very good and interesting" - I said – "my question is that is there any idea what would be the approximate cost of the wood and other materials and the help of the boat building Comrades?"

I saw on their faces that this question began to change their opinion about my mental capabilities. Gábor, the member of the Motorboat Section who came with Karcsi, pulled out of his pocket two papers, smoothed them on the table, and put them before me.

"One of the papers, as you can see, is showing the planned boat's image."

The drawing showed a very elegant boat. The front of the boat was attractively designed. On the edge of the boat and the middle of its deck a narrow stripe ran along, which was a bit darker in color than the rest of the deck. The seats were nicely shaped, each with a small back. From the first moment I really liked the design of the planned boat.

"On the other paper you can see the budget, the compilation of this was done with the help of the boat builder Comrades, so I think it is accurate. We would like to offer two types to our members. One would be for two persons, the other for four. Otherwise, the two types will have similar construction. The only difference is that the one for two persons is for the use of a smaller engine, the one for four people of course will need a bigger one."

"I would be interested in the small two-seater boat, because I could transfer my present motor."

"Then let's look at the budget of that one."

He then went point by point through the expenses. He began with the wood purchase, transportation, cutting, and then explained in detail the necessary construction materials: sandpaper, screws, paints, varnishes, all of which could have been purchased only by allocation, their needed quantity and price. Finally he proceeded with the boat building expenses and the honorarium for our education to learn the painting and varnishing of the boat

When he finished, they both looked at me questioningly.

“You know” - said Karcsi – “these numbers are calculated, so a minimum of 10 boats can be built. If the number of participants is less, then the price will be higher.”

“How many have signed up until now?”

“Eight, who are sure. You would be the ninth.”

I quickly thought the matter over. The cost of the boat building, including the material and ‘honorarium for our education' was acceptable. If I would keep my motor and sell the kayak, the price I would receive for the kayak would be sufficient to pay for the new and very beautiful boat.

“Expect me as the ninth member. I hope that you, or rather we, are going to find a tenth. When are we going to start and how much deposit will be needed, and when the rest have to be paid?”

“I think” - said Karcsi – “we are going to find the tenth member during this week. Béla Lakatos, maybe you know him, he is working in the glass factory, told us repeatedly that he would like to buy a motorboat, but as you know, a new boat and motor cannot be obtained, and there is a high demand for used ones but only very few are offered. Béla said that he is going to assemble this week the money for the boat.

“We will be able to obtain the plywood and the necessary wooden beams approximately in two weeks, because the member of the Tungsram party committee staff dealing with sports matters supported very favorably this matter and said that he would be able to arrange the allocation of the necessary materials immediately. He happened to be one of those who signed up for the project. He has no motor boat, but he will get an engine and he is very enthusiastic to participate in the competitions.

“As regards the boat building Comrades, their work is presently somewhat reduced,because for the Helsinki Olympics the kayaks, canoes, and the regatta boats have all been completed and work is now only needed for possible repairs. So now there will be no overtime, and after work they will be available to direct our work. Two of the boat building professionals and the younger brother of one of them also want to participate in this project and plan to become members of the Motorboat Section because they also want to take part in boat races.

“According to the boat building Comrades, with evening work, 2 or 2 and half months will be needed after the date when the material arrives, to complete the construction of the 10 boats. In their workshop, so as not to disturb their daily work, space is available so that 3 vessels can be built at the same time, so if all goes well, by the end of April or early May all of the boats will be ready.”

“That's great - I said.”

“To begin the work as soon as possible, we are planning to hold a meeting on Friday at 5 pm in the boat building shop. You know where that is?”

“Sure.”

“In this meeting beside of the ten of us, the Comrades who designed the boats and the boat building experts will also participate. The drawings of the two boat types will also be completed showing all the exact details. There we all get together and sign our obligations, the petitions for the allocation of the wood and other materials, and get acquainted with the teachers who will train us.”

“Great. I'm sure I'll be there. Shall I bring some money?”

“No, you do not need it at that time. Gábor by then will have a schedule to indicate how much money you will need and when, who’s boat will be constructed and when, because as I said, with the available space, only three ships can be built at the same time.”

“Thank you for coming to see me, and also to offer me the opportunity. This boat building is a great idea, because our Motorboat Section will become much more competitive.”

I escorted them to the exit door, we shook hands, and they left. I returned to my office, sat down, and started to consider the situation.

When I got back to my office and sat down at my desk, I looked out my office window, which was opposite the Tungsram glass factory. The glass factory was well-known to me, because for different jobs I visited it many times. Also when colleagues came from another research laboratory I was glad to take them over to admire the automated machines, which produced the incandescent lamp’s glass bulb. I always liked to watch these miraculous machines.

The glass was melted in a large circular, at least 8-10 meter diameter, cast cweamic container. Machines, rather robots, were next to the large tank containing the red hot glowing glass, which lowered a part of them into the tank and touched the glass. The end of the machine, which was lowered into the tank, picked up a little of the red hot glass. The machine raised the arm, to the end of which was now a small amount of glass attached, and when it emerged from the glass container, the robot began to rotate the glass, while air was blown into it, slowly starting the glass to inflate., The machine then began to shape the glass and the glass bulb used for the incandescent lamp was formed in less than a minute. A couple of minutes later the glass had cooled and the machine deposited the now ready bulb on a stand. When there was not much molten glass left in the tank, the tank with the remaining molten glass was then pushed to the building's edge where the wall of the building was missing, there they simply pushed the cast stone pot with the residual glass in it, which crashed on a sandy area prepared for this purpose on the wide road between the TKI laboratory and glassworks. When the tank hit the ground, it broke to pieces and the red hot glass and the pieces of the tank's wall sent many glowing sparks up in the air and it looked like a miniature volcano. I liked to watch this.

I was thinking that in many ways I was very slow witted. For example, when I was 17 years old, in the summer holidays I decided to enroll in a typing school, and there in a two-week course I was going to learn to type with 10 fingers. We had a typewriter at home, and I was able to type with 2 fingers, but I considered it too slow. In this course we were about twenty. I was the only male student, the others were all females and the maximum age was about 25. I realized many years afterwards, why I was the favorite of all the students, and why some them were especially nice to me.

Now I had a little more experience of life, I perceived, that the materials such as wood, bolts, paint, varnish, needed to build a boat were only available for allocation, so they were relatively cheap. The conversations revealed that through appropriate connections we were easily going to get the allocations. As far as the 'honorarium' was concerned, that the boat builders Comrades were going to get for working after their hours, who was going to check that? They were going to use the workshop equipment, tools and electricity, so what we were paying them would be all pure profit. So they also had an interest that we should, or rather they should, build the ten boats. That was the reason the price was going to be low.

Now I just wondered why 10 boats had to be built and why I had the good fortune to be included in this great program. Now that I had more experience of life, I started thinking about this quite a bit. My first thought was what my Professor of Chemistry, Dénes Kőszegi, said many times: 'Miracles do not exist, just stupid chemists.' It was characteristic of my simple mindedness that I found the probable solution only a few days later, when I looked in the newspaper at the boats for sale advertisements. Interestingly there were very few boats for sale, and the ones advertised were quite expensive. I became sure that for my kayak, even without the engine, would raise more than this beautiful new boat would cost.

After I had put down the newspaper, I thought it over and found it interesting that from the ten of us who signed up for the boat building, five or six did not have a boat, and had no engine either. Yet they were the ones who were able to obtain the material or could build the boat. But the formal request had to be submitted by the Tungsram's Motorboat Section which required the participation of older members of the Section. So we the 'old-motorboat people' had to be included.

The ten members came together, the application was submitted, we received the material, and the boat building Comrades showed us how to build a boat. I participated at least in five one-hour long training sessions. On my beautiful new boat the boat building Comrade painted the name I selected: 'Pendragon'[37]. Laci Navradszky, my lab technician, helped me to mount my motor on the new boat. I also found at the flea market a beautiful chromium plated searchlight, which we mounted too. Pendragon occupied the birth of the old motorized kayak in the Tungsram beach house and was launched for the first time on April 19th 1953.

It was an incredible difference to be on the deck of Pendragon compared to the poor little kayak! I participated dutifully as before in the motorboat races, but my placement in spite of this beautiful new boat did not improve. As before I managed to be the last to arrive. It happened once that I came in third and also received a prize, a beautiful wooden block with a metal propeller on it and the date 1953. I am very proud of this sport achievement.

---

[37] The name of the boat was inspired by the title of Antal Szerb's book 'The Pendragon legend' (1933)

Pendragon – The author's motor boat. (1953)

The trophy is still the ornament of my desk. It is true that only four boats started in that race, but one boat's motor failed and did not make it, therefore I became the third.

12. The eleventh plague of Egypt

Sándor Varga – nobody knows why, but everybody called him 'Harry' - and László (Laci) Navradszky watched the accumulated water which was not going down in the one meter by half meter size sink. The cause of the blockage was that Comrade Budincsevits two hours ago brought to Harry a great size metal container in which was some kind of treacle, sticky material, to clean it out as fast as possible, for it was needed for a new experiment he wanted to conduct.

Harry was Comrade Budincsevits' mechanic and Laci was mine. Harry and Laci worked in the same workshop, in the 'old' Tungsram research building's top floor, immediately next to the staircase. The restrooms on each floor were on the staircase landings. This building which consisted of a basement and three floors was built in 1930. Since 1950 the top floor of the building belonged to the Telecommunications Research Institute (TKI) which was built adjacent and of which Andris Dallos was the General Manager, while the bottom two floors and a basement of the "old building" was the Industrial Research Institute of Telecommunications (HIKI) the boss of which was Dr. György Szigeti.

On the third floor of the 'old building', which belonged to the TKI were the laboratories of 'Uncle' Laci (Rotter) and also of Andor Budincsevits. Budi, as we called him, was a real jack-of-all-trades. He did not have a University degree, but for 25 years he was working in the research lab, and he was able to solve great technical challenges. So by now he was the head of a Department with a staff of a couple of engineers and technicians.

Harry started to clean the metal container. He was able to scrape out some of the treacle material and throw this in the garbage, but most of it seemed stubbornly insisting to stick to the metal container, and Harry could not do anything with it. Harry and Laci discussed it, and decided to try to fill the metal container with hot water, hoping to lift the goo. This was somewhat successful, the molasses like substance became more pliable and by stirring the hot water and scraping with a spoon some portion of the plastic brown material it could be poured out with the hot water. The metal container was almost completely cleaned from the molasses, the problem now was that the hot water started to accumulate in the sink and, finally did not go down at all. Well, this was the time mentioned above, when Harry looked at Laci and closed the tap and both of them looked at the accumulated hot water. It became clear to them, that the molasses substance did not go down but somehow accumulated in the drain. Laci went to get a plunger, which was a wooden rod at the end of which a rubber bell is attached and was used to open up clogged drains.

Harry took the tool from Laci, put it over the drain opening, and depressed it fast so the pressure, from the bell should push out the blockage. But nothing happened. After a few attempts Laci took over the tool, and he tried to do the process more vigorously. But this had no effect on the water level of the sink either.

After further discussion and consideration, Laci went down to the Tungsram's workshop, where he had good friends, and brought up a "pig" which is an approx. 2 meter long twisted elastic but flexible metal spiral, and told Harry, to stick it down the drain and then it will push down the material that is stuck there. Laci and Harry began to press the bundled wire, of which circa 40 cm went down, but more could not be pushed, even when they wanted to pull out, it was very difficult. When the bundled metal wire finally came out of the drain, a little sticky molasses was attached to its end, which was the material that was removed from Budi's metal dish. They tried the procedure several times but the result was the same, only more of the treacle material did not come up at all. The water which was in the sink, remained there.

Now they thought they would see what would dissolve the material which still remained in Budi's metal container. Acids were tried, alkalis, organic materials of all kinds, in the end it looked like petroleum may dissolve the molasses, because when they poured some of it into the metal container with some of the molasses, the petroleum got a little brown discoloration. The only problem was that the petroleum is lighter than water, so if they would have poured into the sink, which was half filled with water, then the petroleum would have floated to the top of the water. So they came to the conclusion to scoop out the water and collect it in a bucket. That is what they did, but the problem was, that when the bucket was full they had to carry it over to Budi's laboratory and pour it out there, because their workshop had no other drain, only the one which was clogged.

This took quite a long time. Finally, they managed to remove all of the water, dried the sink and poured in the petroleum. The petroleum showed little discolorations but it did not drain. By now the working day was over, and the two mechanics thought to leave the kerosene, to which they added a little more, for the night, thinking that the kerosene will slowly dissolve the molasses in the pipe and by the next morning the problem will be solved.

When next morning Laci and Harry entered their workshop, the smell of the petroleum filled the room, but the petroleum in the sink was the same amount as when they left it the previous night. Both looked at the sink, Laci finally decided to go down and talk with the people in the plumber shop. About an hour later Laci and one of the plumbers came to the workshop. The plumber, a middle-aged mechanic, slightly balding stocky man, dressed in work clothes, brought with him a large toolbox as well. Laci introduced Comrade Pasta, the plumber who came with him, to Harry. Comrade Pista shook hands with Harry, and then took from his pocket a pack of cigarettes and offered them to both of them. With this, all three of them started to smoke in the room filled with the smell of petroleum and Comrade Pista after reviewing the situation, said he was going to remove the smell eliminator part of the drain and they should bring him some bowl into which the petroleum will flow, when he removed the U shaped smell eliminator. Harry brought a bowl which was placed under the U-tube. The role of the U-tube is that when water flows down, some of it remains in the U-tube and the water will prevent the smell from the drains going into the room. Comrade Pista was of the opinion that this U-tube is clogged, and if he will remove and replace the U-tube with a clean one, then the problem will be solved. He removed from the tool box a large monkey-wrench, lay on the ground and with the monkey-wrench began to unscrew the nuts from the two ends of the U-tube. This went without problems, and after the nuts were loose, he grabbed the U-tube and wanted to take it off. This did not happen. The U-tube stubbornly stayed there, in spite that the nuts were not holding it. Comrade Pista called out from under the sink: "Give me the big hammer which is in the toolbox." Harry willingly handed it to him. Comrade Pista attached the wrench to the bottom of the U-tube, and hit it with the big hammer. The U-tube did not move. He continued this for a while, then climbed out from under the sink and got to his feet:

"I think that what you poured down the drain, clogged the tube also before and after the U-tube, and somehow it got solidified and that is the reason we cannot remove the U-tube. I think that we have to cut open the wall, and to knock on the drain pipe to hear how deep it is full, cut the drain pipe on both sides of the U-tube where the sounding will show that it is not clogged and replace it with a new one."

Hearing this, Harry said:

"Give me the hammer and the wrench". - Now he climbed under the sink and started to hit the U-tube very strongly to try to knock it down. Except for the huge noise he produced, nothing else happened. Finally, Harry climbed out.

Comrade Pista took from him the hammer and the wrench. He put the hammer in the toolbox, then climbed with the monkey-wrench under the sink and screwed back the nuts which were supposed to "hold" the U-tube. He tightened the nuts, which in this case was obviously not needed, but he was used to doing it. He climbed out, put the wrench into the toolbox. He closed the box, and then looked at Harry:

“If you want to proceed with the opening of the wall and make the repair of the pipes, it will require that you should bring down an order to our office.” - With this, shaking his head, he left.

Harry and Laci sat on a chair and lit another cigarette. None of them spoke a word. This was the case when Budi in his usual white lab coat came in the workshop.

“I need the metal container which you cleaned.”

Harry practically was unable to speak. He sat on the chair put out his cigarette in the ashtray, and then finally was able to say something.

“Comrade Budincsevits, the metal container is not yet clean, but what came outof it, clogged the drain tube so, that we tried everything but could not achieve that anything should go down the drain. Comrade Pista, the plumber was here now, but could not even take the U-tube off, because it seems that what was in the metal container, solidified in the tube and blocked the entire drain below and above the U- tube. He advised to cut the wall open and to replace the pipe, which is blocked.”

“You know, Harry, these plumbers they love to overcomplicate things to create themselves work. How did you attempt to fix the drain?”

Harry explained in detail what they tried. Budi

sympathetically listened, pondered, and then came to Harry and put his hand on Harry's shoulder.

“You know, things have to be solved the simplest way. This was always my rule, and this was leading always to success. What you did not try was the simplest thing to do. Roll that bottle of nitrogen to the drain. Take the flexible metal tube which is mounted on the nitrogen bottle and push the end of the metal tube as far down the drain as you can. Then you should stuff around the drain some clothing, tightly as well as you can that it should be in and around the pipe strongly and very tightly. Then fill the sink halfway with water. Keep your hand on the tube so it does not pop out, and Laci, you should open the valve of the nitrogen cylinder, that the high-pressure gas should suddenly hit the drain. You will see, within seconds the water will flow down.”

On the way to the door he turned back and said, that if the issue with the sink is resolved, then the metal container should be cleaned quickly, because it is needed for an experiment

They immediately started to implement the process suggested by Budi. Harry inserted the metal tube into the sink’s drain pipe, the way Budi said, he stuffed the hole and let the water fill the sink to its half. The petroleum of course was floating on the top of the water. Laci was standing next to the high pressure nitrogen cylinder, with his hand on its valve and was ready, when Harry, who finished placing the tube and tightening the material around it and thought that everything is ready, then turned to Laci:

"Now, open the valve!"

Laci with a quick twist of his hand opened the tap, a sizzling sound was heard, and they saw that Budi was right. The water began to drain. Laci closed the valve of the nitrogen cylinder, Harry pulled out the metal tube and the water in seconds drained from the sink.

Laci had not yet taken his hand off the valve of the nitrogen cylinder, when coming from the corridor outside the workshop a frenetic roar was heard. They both rushed out into the corridor, and realized that the roar was coming from the stairwell's landing, from the direction of the WC, when one of the toilet doors burst open and the still howling Mátyás (Matyi) Szabó - a technician who worked there on the third floor - rushed out and yelled:

"The toilet exploded! Help, help!"

In the meantime, he was trying to pull up his pants which were soaking wet and some dark matter was dripping from it. Matyi was not yet out of the door, when female screams were heard coming from the direction of the WC two floors below. Matyi was a little calmed down by then, He did not shout for help anymore, just kept loudly cursing, but he was still barely recognizable from the watery smudge. Meanwhile, the woman below kept hysterically shrieking. Laci and Harry staggered from the concentrated odor coming from the direction of the toilet and Matyi.

Within seconds, the entire third floor corridor came alive. People rushed out from the laboratories to the corridor, some of them with less, others with more black masses on their hair, or on their white or gray laboratory coats, on their faces and on their shoulders. They all were screaming. Laci and Harry looked puzzled as to what happened to them. Budi, who was in his office and was not yet in his lab, since he had not received the clean container, hearing the noise came out of his office. Budi in his snow white laboratory coat and Harry and Laci in their clean gray work coat, were in startling contrast in the hallway from the raving, and to differing extents spattered and smelly colleagues.

On the ground floor corridor, Dr. György Szigeti, Director of the Institute was headed towards his office, when people splashed with this amazing concoction and water stormed out to the corridor.

Szigeti first laughed at this sight. He went into his office where the secretary had just typed something. Like all the big bosses, Szigeti of course, had an office with a padded door, which opened from his secretary's office. From his office opened a small wash cabinet where he went in the morning to hang his coat, or when he put his white lab coat on and hung his suit jacket.

When Szigeti entered the office, his secretary said that his wife had called and he should call her back. Szigeti said that he was going to call her immediately and went to his office. From there he entered his wash cabinet, to wash his hands. When he entered, he saw that the entire cabin was filled with the same watery, smelly smudge that he had seen in the hallway, including his clothing which was hanging there. The smile froze on his face and he ran out in the corridor, where the people in their soiled clothing were swearing. He began to shout:

“Sabotage in the laboratory! Our sewage system was blown up!”

Budi, when he came out from his office took stock of things, without a word went back into his office. Harry and Laci went back to their workshop they sat down and lit a cigarette. Laci now assessed the situation:

“Harry, it seems that the high-pressure nitrogen blew out from our drain pipe the blockage and then through all of the smell arrester in the building pushed all the dirt accumulated in the past 20 years, like a geyser into the labs, and in the toilets.”

Harry looked at Laci, put down his cigarette, and as someone who was bitten by a viper, jumped up, went to the sink, pulled out the stuffing, took out a metal tube, pushed the nitrogen cylinder back to the wall, chained it to the wall, screwed out the metal tube, coiled it and put in a drawer. All this in seconds then he sat down and continued to smoke his cigarette.

Pali Havas arrived on his motorcycle at the entrance of the TKI-2 building. He secured his motorcycle and went into the building. Comrade Bóka, the entrance guard, welcomed him. Pali hurried up to the third floor, and went from the new TKI building to the old building where he had a lab and office. Pali was an electrical engineer and worked in Budi’s department. Pali, like Budi, was a jack-of-all-trades, did a lot of everything, he had great imagination and brilliantly solved all the technical problems. When he reached the third floor corridor of the old building, he saw there the dirty people milling around, but he was in a hurry, and entered immediately the lab door, opened the door to the lab, where Budi in his blindingly clean lab coat was discussing something with his lab technician Gizi. Gizi's lab coat was not completely blinding, because black and brown stripes enlivened it. When Pali came in, Budi told him succinctly the story of the last minutes. Pali went to the two mechanics' workshop, where he found Harry and Laci smoking cigarettes.

Harry briefly sketched out the events, including the scene with Matyi Szabó. Pali, who stood listening and was holding his belly from laughing said:

"Well, so they are going to hang you for this…" – Suddenly, panic spread over his face, and he stormed out without a word. He ran over to the TKI-2 new building, to find Tibor Sellei, Party Secretary of the TKI-2. As he ran along the corridor leading to the new building, he just ran into Sellei, who smoked a cigarette in the hallway.

"Tibor" – Pali panting, said – "come with me immediately, because Budi and his people did something incredibly crazy, from which a terrible scandal may develop, if not stopped in time."

"What happened?"
"You will hear it. On the way I am going to try to tell you, but come on, we are going to take Budi with us to see Szigeti, you should only confirm what I say."

Budi was in this office.

"Uncle Bandi, come on, let's go down to Szigeti, to discuss the matter with him."

Budi just nodded and started toward the door with them.

"Uncle Bandi, leave the clean lab coat and come in your jacket!"

Budi without a word did it. Pali in front, the three of them rushed out of the door. Gábor was just there. Pali told him to come with them. Gábor asked why, but Pali said that it is a very important matter, they must see Szigeti, and he will find out there, he should only confirm what he will say.

On the ground floor the four of them went to the Szigeti's secretary's office, and Pali said they would like to speak with Comrade Szigeti.

When the secretary saw the lab's Party Secretary and three engineers with him, she said only that:
"Yes, Comrade Szigeti is in the office."

All four of them entered without knocking, because it was no purpose to knock on the padded door, went to the Director's office, where Szigeti, who had already calmed down a bit, sat behind his desk. When they came in, he looked up with amazement. Szigeti rose, shook their hands, and then motioned that they should sit down at the negotiating table and he sat down too.

Pali began his story:

"We are aware that Budi's people did something terribly stupid" - Sellei looked at Pali curiously – "because of a misunderstanding they blew out the building's drains from which a lot of dirt came out and the people and the equipment became dirty, butno other damage occurred. We discussed the matter and we came to the conclusion that the best is if this thing remains in-house. We should not draw in people from the outside, because who knows what the consequences would lead to, which might be unpleasant for everyone, even could bring the lab into disrepute. I hope that Comrade Szigeti, you do see things the same way."

Szigeti was listening to the story with interest, and was getting his arm raised toward his dirty clothes, to point them out with indignation, but when Pali drew attention to the consequences, he changed his mind, and nodded as a sign of consent.

"Thus, it is recommended - Pali said this already with a deep voice, as if the entire Party was behind him – that we should call Patyolat[38] to send a car, to pick up the people's dirty clothing, and to bring them back clean tomorrow. Whoever does not want their clothes to be given to Patyolat, they should take them themselves to wherever they want them to be cleaned, they should pay and bring the bill, and their money will be refunded. As for the cleaning of the laboratories, the laboratories are fit for a thorough cleaning anyway, and every lab should do it by tomorrow. So the case would be closed down."

Szigeti just looked at them and nodded again, probably in his dreams he would have never thought that such a case could be settled so smoothly, and would not become a major scandal, or would bring an investigation in which the ÁVH would also be involved. Although because of his clothing he was very annoyed, he thought about the matter

---

[38] Patyolat was the Hungarian National dry cleaning company.

and realized that in this particular case his clothing was really a very small problem.

Pali said:

"We are asking, Comrade Szigeti, that you should immediately convene a meeting which everybody in the building should attend and tell them what we discussed. We will be there to support Comrade Szigeti's decision."

Szigeti immediately called his secretary.

"Please call now all employees of the building to come immediately to the library. We will be there waiting for them."

The secretary left to go door to door to round up the people.

When the secretary left Pali said:

"I think the best would be if Comrade Szigeti would announce to the people that a secret experiment conducted at TKI caused the problem, give instructions what to do with their clothing and say that he expects that the cleanliness of the lab will be restored tomorrow morning. Also tell them about the secret experiment which was attempted and that they are prohibited to mention to anyone outside the laboratory, because it would amount to the crime of disclosing secrets. The latter is very important to prevent that people in the factory or outside should begin to inquire about the matter. I hope that Comrade Szigeti also thinks so."

Szigeti, who could not think of anything else, than what would have happened if the factory's party organization or, worse still, if some kind of other authority, in the worst case the ÁVH, would be drawn into the affair. The story which Pali concocted in seconds was a simply ingeniously solution. He certainly would not have admitted this he just mumbled something and finally said:

"What you propose, I agree, let's go to the library. Budi you do not need to come with us" - he added.

The library session was conducted smoothly. Everyone understood what to do and that what happened is a consequence of a secret experiment, and therefore no one should talk about it.

After the meeting in the library, Tibor and Pali went upstairs and entered the Secretariat of Dallos and Ducza. There sat the two secretaries, because the office of Andris was on the right and Karcsi Ducza's on the left.

Pali said to the two secretaries:

"Are the bosses in their offices?"

"Yes" - they replied almost simultaneously.

Pali now turned to Ducza's secretary.

"Éva, please, tell Karcsi to come over to Andris Dallos office, because we want to discuss a very important issue with both of them."

With this Tibor and Pali opened Andris office door again without knocking. Andris was sitting behind his desk, and read some papers, when they came.

"Andris" - said Tibor – "a complicated case happened, which we would like to discuss with you and Karcsi.

Karcsi entered in his military uniform.

Pali began to tell the story about the blockage of drainage and the way it was cleaned. When in the story he came to where Matyi Szabó burst out from the toilet covered with shit and dripping wet and trying to pull up his soaking wet and shitty pants, Ducza from laughter almost fell off his chair and Tibor, who had heard this story at least twice, also laughed. Andris smiled only slightly, since he already imagined the problems which Pali started to explain, saying that this happened in the other building, but unfortunately the case is a TKI problem, because the trouble was caused by TKI staff and that part of the building belongs also to TKI. Of course Ducza stopped laughing, and with quite frightened face listened to Pali's story of how a solution was reached.

Ducza turned to Pali:

"Congratulations that you managed so quickly and skillfully to settle the matter, because really it could have caused awful problems. Thus, the matter was solved very skillfully and is now over."

"The matter is still not completely over - said Pali - because the cleaner's bills have still to be paid."

“This is the only remaining problem?” - Karcsi Ducza asked.

“Yes, we hope.”

“You can tell Szigeti's secretary to collect the bill from Patyolat and the cleaning bills from those who got their clothing cleaned somewhere else, she should give all of them to Eva and I will get the money from somewhere to pay them off. As regards Budi, I suppose he was adviser to Moses in the Egyptian ten plagues, and this would have been the eleventh plague, but was not needed, since for the Egyptians the first ten was enough. Damn it, one cannot have a quiet day.”

13. Refute Heisenberg[39]

To be a Department head in TKI meant great responsibilities. That the Department heads should be able to carry out this very responsible job, they had to participate once a month on Saturday morning in a seminar attended only by a limited number of these leaders. Some of these Department heads participated in a seminar organized in Újpest. I and a few of my colleagues attended the one organized in the Administration Building of the Post Office in Buda. The multi-story building of the Administration Building of the Post Office which was standing on Krisztina ring near Moskva square was recognizable from a distance by its red brick walls and its round gazebo which resembled the look-out tower of a castle.

Our team leader was the Szeged-born Pista Vince whom I knew from my childhood. His parents had a large grocery store - until it was nationalized - in Bridge Street. He may have been about ten years older than I was. Pista became a mathematician and after he completed the university he started his career in Budapest with an insurance company as a statistician. He was a very talented, good-willing, kind man. At that time he worked in the Mathematical Institute of the Hungarian Academy of

[39] Heisenberg (1901-1976) German physicist established the theory of the **uncertainty principle** which resulted in a revolutionary change in the development of quantum mechanics, the impact of modern physics is similar to the relativity theory developed by Albert Einstein.

Science (MTA), where the director was Alfred Rényi.

How Pista became a seminar leader, I do not know, but knowing him I do not think that he would have volunteered for this assignment. Our group consisted of 16 to 20 people. The seminar was held in the Post Office Department's Management building in a conference room overlooking Krisztina Ring. Next to the wall of the conference room stood a lacquered credenza and in the middle of the room was a very nice long lacquered wooden table. At the seminar usually a current event was discussed, and everyone had to comment. Who was taking notes during the discussion I do not know, but we all knew that someone was noting all of our words and forwarding them to the "relevant authority".

At one such seminar, seventeen of us were sitting around the table. Pista Vince was sitting at the head of the table seven people were on each side of the table, and two at the other end. I was sitting in the second chair on the right side of Pista, Uncle Laci Rotter, my colleague was on the other side of the table at the end, next to another colleague.

The seminar started at 10 o'clock in the morning. When we sat down, Pista greeted us:

"It is great that everyone here is so punctual, because the matter that we are going to talk about is close to us, since it is about science. I suppose that all of you are going to actively participate in the discussion. I am sure you all read in the SzabadNép (newspaper) a great article recently published by Comrade Stalin in which he describes how wrong the Heisenberg's Uncertainty Theory is, contradicting the principles of Dialectic Materialism. Who read this article?"

Everybody put their hands up, indicating that naturally they read Stalin's article. I really read it, but I do not know how many of them did not read it, because no one would have admitted that. Pista continued:

"The Dialectical Materialistic philosophy which was initiated by Karl Marx and its development continued by Comrade Lenin and now by Comrade Stalinplays a key role leading to the road to Communism. The advancement of the sciences in the direction set by dialectical materialism is of the utmost importance. Cosmopolitan and reactionary scientists are trying by the interposing science to change the direction of dialectical materialism. This was noticed already by Lenin and in 1906, he pointed out the connection between philosophy and science, that modern physics contradicts dialectic materialism. Comrade Stalin, in spite that he had to defend a huge Empire against the enemy, yet has a very considerable scientific knowledge. Comrade Stalin is a member already since 1939 of the Academy of Sciences of the USSR, and achieved great merits in agriculture and linguistics and now for a long time is considering the relationship of physics and philosophy. Comrade Stalin recently revealed the views according to which modern quantum mechanics, in particular Werner Heisenberg's uncertainty thesis, is incorrect, the cosmopolitan scientists are trying with this to attack the strong foundation of dialectical materialism.

"Such views of Comrade Stalin were detailed in a paper translated from Russian in the newspaper 'SzabadNép'. As you indicated all of you read this very important analysis which deals with the essence of modern physics. Today's seminar lasts two hours, so I give everyone 5 minutes so each of you can express your opinion, we are still going to have time to discuss together Comrade Stalin's article and your opinions in connection with this important paper. Let's start from here to my left side, and continue it from there. Please begin by summarizing your views."

Pista with his hand pointed to Steve our colleague to his left. I met him only at these seminars therefore I did not know him well. In any event, it was very good, that Pista did not start on my side the comments, because it would have given me just 5minutes to prepare myself, because I was the second on Pista's right side. This way it gave for me at least one hour to think over what should be my contribution to the discussion.

The colleague blushed slightly, and slowly began to talk. After the first words, when he started to talk about what constitutes dialectical materialism, I pulled out from my briefcase a sheet of paper and a pencil. I put them down in front of me.

On the paper I started writing the points around which my remarks will be built:

1. From Comrade Stalin's articles it is clearly evident that he is right.
2. I have knowledge in science, but philosophy and philosophical thinking is very far from me.
3. In college, I studied a lot of theoretical physics, relativity and quantum theory, but I was never convinced about the validity of the quantum theory. Why I was not convinced?

I was thinking about this and I wrote it immediately on the paper in front of me, not to forget it, and to use it in my contribution to the debate. This obviously will be said by all of the speakers before me because what else can they say, but the repetition of this may not be harmful to me:

'The foundations of dialectical materialism are known to everyone. This philosophy direction was shaped by Karl Marx in such a manner that he merged Hegel's dialectic with Feuerbach's materialism and that became the basis of 'dialectical materialism', although Marx never called it that way. This was then modified by Lenin, and Stalin declared this as the Marxism-Leninism and declared it the cornerstone and main theoretical basis of the Communist system. Basically the Marxist-Leninist dialectical materialism could be defined that material things - the material - go through a permanency of changes because of the influence of interrelated opposing forces, elements and ideas and tension between ideas. This for example causes the revolution of social classes.'

I never understood the philosophical doctrines, the exercise of the mind in this direction and poetry. These were not tangible to me, such as chemistry or physics, and therefore I could not understand the problem of Heisenberg's uncertainty theory, which I thought to be a science item, what relation it could have to philosophy, and why it is wrong from the perspective of dialectical materialism. Heisenberg's uncertainty theory states that a quantum, which in the world of atoms is a particle, cannot have its movement and position determined with certainty. According to Heisenberg this principle diverted science from the nineteenth century's materialistic direction. When I got so far in my thoughts, I realized immediately that the

Heisenberg theory of uncertainty is really distinctly different from the basis of dialectical materialism, as Heisenberg himself also described.

These ideas I also wrote down in a few words on my paper. When I read through my notes, suddenly it enlightened in my mind what will be my comment.

This was the moment when Pista asked my colleague and good friend Laci Rotter to explain his views.

Laci, as I wrote earlier, was a few years older than I and most of my colleagues, and was a very good and effective engineer. Laci in spite of his Jewish origin worked until 1944 in Berlin at the laboratory of the world famous Dutch company, Philips. In 1944 he returned to Hungary, because his apartment and also the laboratory he worked in were ruined by bombs dropped by British/American airplanes. Uncle Laci took part in the First World War, at a very young age went to the army, and received the highest military honors, which exempted him from the Jewish laws of Hungary. In 1944 he returned to Budapest, went to the Tungsram Research Laboratory, where he immediately was offered a job. When the fighting ceased around Budapest, and life started again he could continue his work. He was given a laboratory, where he was put in charge to solve a variety of engineering problems.

Laci loved everything that was German, in particular the trains. Moreover, he was one of the world's most courteous people, he started his comments accordingly:

"Sorry for the comments, but I'm not a person with philosophical directions, and therefore I would not examine the matter from a philosophical point of view. Not surprising, that Heisenberg's uncertainty theory is philosophically not perfect, and therefore, does not match the views of dialectical materialism. It is not surprising, at least for me, because Werner Heisenberg is a German scientist, who since his birth in 1901, lived in Germany, where he grew up, and he should have known that an uncertainty exists only in systems that are not properly organized.

"Herr Heisenberg must have known the railroad system in Germany as well as in other countries of the world. If Herr Heisenberg would have made a comparison of the railroad systems in these countries, it may have been clear for him, that the cause of the accuracy or uncertainty of the railroad system is not the fault of the railroad, but on the mentality of the people of the country. For example, in Germany, where German precision is born into the People, the railroad system is functioning accurately, and even during the recently ended World War II when the bombing caused major obstacles to the railroad system, it still functioned accurately. If it was posted, that a train will arrive at 9:55 pm and will leave at 10:00 pm then it arrived at 9:55 pm and leave at 10:00 pm. Uncertainty accordingly occurs only in a not precisely operating system. Now, the atoms are precisely operating systems. Heisenberg argues that one reason of the uncertainty is in the measurement. He carried out the measurement with an imaginary gamma-ray microscopy, in which he shot the gamma ray at the photon. If I would have dealt with this problem, I would have tried to determine whether there is a different measurement method, which does not cause uncertainty. Considering this I strongly support Comrade Stalin's views about Heisenberg's uncertainty theory. That's all I would like to say, and I hope that I did not take away time from others who wish to speak and to contribute to this discussion."

Pista with a few words, thanked Uncle Laci for his valuable comments, inquired as to whether anyone has any questions, but nobody had any, therefore he asked the following colleagues, to explain their views.

By listening to Uncle Laci I thought what a great way he solved the problem, he agreed with Stalin, but did not get mixed into the dialectical materialism and in Heisenberg's thesis but he moved the entire issue to a side track. This was my idea also to similarly but more complicatedly get the issue on a side line.

Eventually my turn came. Pista turned to me:

"Ferenc, what is your view about this important topic?"

"Pista and the colleagues before me have given a lot of very interesting and thought-provoking views, so it is difficult to add anything to that. As we know, and some people have said before me, Marxist-Leninist dialectical materialism can be defined that the material things - the material – are progressing through permanent change and go through the interrelated and conflicting forces, elements of tension between ideals and influence. This causes for example the revolution of social classes. As you said in your introductory notes, Comrade Stalin since a long time is occupying himself dealing with the relationship of physics and philosophy, and has recently come to disclose his views of, the modern quantum mechanics, especially Werner Heisenberg's uncertainty thesis is incorrect, and these cosmopolitan scientists are trying to attack the strong foundations of the dialectic materialism."

I looked at the paper in front of me on which my notes were and continued with what I wrote:

"Philosophy and philosophical thinking are very far from me, because I am somehow science-minded. It is interesting that Comrade Stalin considered the quantum theory developed by Heisenberg on a philosophical basis incorrect, because at the University I studied a lot of theoretical physics, relativity and quantum theory, but I was never convinced about the validity of quantum theory, and looking from the science side, also considered it inappropriate. That the validity of quantum theory is not right I was not and I am still not convinced. I am not alone. Interestingly enough, Einstein – to whom I do not want to compare myself - also questioned the validity of quantum theory on the basis of science."

With this I reached into my pocket and pulled out a small piece of paper. I smoothed it and began to read:

"Einstein in a letter to Heinrich Zangger dated 20 May 1912 wrote the following: 'The more success quantum mechanics has, the dumber it looks.' Einstein in a letter to Max Born dated 12 December 1926 writes: 'Quantum mechanics is very impressive. But an inner voice tells me it's not the real thing. The quantum- theory says a lot, but does not bring us closer to the secret of the 'Old'. I am convinced that He (God) is not a dice player. "

I stopped here for a moment and put the paper I was reading on the table, as I looked up I saw that everybody was looking with interest at me. Pista Vince looked at me, curiously, to know where I was heading.

"When I read Comrade Stalin's article, in which he disproved Heisenberg's theory on a philosophical basis, it occurred to me that Einstein was not convinced of the validity of quantum theory, and found evidence about it, examples of which I just read. After I considered this I made the following observations. We humans, we know two worlds. The world of stars, the Sun, Moon, planets, stars, comets, and so on. This is our 'macro-world'. The other world, that we are trying to get to know, is the world of atoms and molecules, which is the 'micro-world'. The macro-world that we see with our eyes, telescopes, and that for which Einstein developed the theory of relativity. The astrophysicists deal with this world. The interesting thing is that the micro-world of atoms within which are protons, neutrons, electrons and the molecules world is closely linked with the macro-world. According to science, in the beginning one atom, the hydrogen atom, was generated and all the other elements, helium, oxygen, gold, and so on.. In the macro-world was created in the glowing Suns by nuclear fusion. In our Sun, which consists primarily of hydrogen in the midst of which a nuclear fusion takes place, where the temperature is 15 million °C and under high pressure, helium and a lot of other elements are produced, which comprise only 0.1% of the volume of our Sun. This means that all the elements, even the molecules which exist in the micro-world, have been produced in the macro-world. Because of this it is clear that a close and inseparable relationship exists between the macro- and the micro-world. The micro-world is the basic element of the macro-world, however the many types of elements and molecules would not exist without macro-world. If you consider this, it must be concluded that in the macro- and the micro-world the same laws of nature should exist. In the nineteenth century, the scientists of that time imagined the atom and its laws according to the macro-world. These ideas were changed by Heisenberg, Bohr and others to the world of quantum physics. Heisenberg said that the quantum theory diverted science from the nineteenth century's materialistic views. This meant that our two world's natural laws according to the quantum theory do not agree with each other."

I pulled in front of me the small paper, on which the Einstein's quotes were written, and continued:

"Einstein wrote in this regard: [40] 'Every of my attempt to use the theoretical foundations of physics to apply to this new science (quantum theory) totally failed. This is similar to when the ground is pulled out under somebody without able to find a solid foundation on which to build anything.' When I considered all of this it occurred to me what one can see from Einstein's remarks, that one cannot imagine the laws of nature should be different in the world of atoms and the world of the stars.

"Maybe it is possible that the theories of Heisenberg, the quantum theory, misled humanity not only in the field of philosophy, but also in the field of science, and if it did not happen, then Einstein would have been able to write a universal theory of the world, where the macro- and micro-world would have been governed by the same laws of physics and the world, as Einstein says: 'He (God) has

---

[40] F. A. Schlipp-A. Einstein: Philosopher - Scientist, On Quantum Theory, 1949

launched it' with uniform laws, and no separate laws for the macro-world and separate laws for our micro-world. If this idea was accepted, then perhaps it is also possible that not only these two worlds would exist, but others could be smaller than the micro-world and perhaps others which are larger than our macro-world and perhaps even others, smaller and larger worlds. It's like Russian Matrjoska dolls, there are smaller and smaller dolls and even smaller and so on. But all are the same. Like I said, I do not understand the philosophy, I cannot follow the philosophical theories, but everyone can see clearly that Stalin's articles are right. However, it is also possible that the quantum theory is trying to derail not only philosophy, but also science? Thank you for listening to me."

There was silence for a moment, then for the first time Pista Vince spoke:

"Ferenc, you've read about it somewhere?"

"No, I have not read anything about it."

"You reached very interesting conclusions which one can think about. Perhaps it would be nice if you wrote about this and publish it."

"Thank you very much you think that what I said was so good. Again, I would like to quote Einstein: 'The quantum mechanics - very impressive but an inner voice tells me it's not the real thing. The quantum theory says a lot, but is not bringing us closer to the secret of the 'Old'. I think that these thoughts are not even much developed to see daylight."

Pista now turned to the group:

“We have one more comment left, and then we can start a discussion.”

Pista pointed to the colleague sitting beside me, whom I only knew by sight.

The colleague who had already prepared Stalin’s paper on the table, andI saw several places that were underscored and annotations were also on the margins of the article. His comments followed Stalin's article, and his opinion, not surprisingly agreed in every respect with Stalin’s.

Very little time was now left for discussion, because of course nobody adhered to the 5-minute speaking time, so rather than debate Pista started to read his notes, summarizing the comments, and then announced the next seminar date.

Once we reached the street, Pista, Uncle Laci and two other colleagues from TKI-1 left together and started towards the Moscow Square tram stop. Pista walked next to me.

“Your comment was very interesting that instead of the dialectical materialism and the philosophy you rather discussed Heisenberg’s uncertainty theory from the point of view of science. Seemed to me that you already had thought about this previously.”

“Like I said, during my time at the University I studied quite a lot of theoretical physics, I even wrote a thesis about ‘Theory of valence angles’, for which I received a prize. At that time I thought about it and also about Einstein's opinion about the quantum theory."

Pista turned to me:

"It was very interesting, that you illuminated the validity of Heisenberg's uncertainty theory from scientific and not from the side of philosophy. I knew Einstein's views of the quantum theory, but you went beyond this, and with Einstein's quotes you extended it to the entire quantum physics."

"It's interesting that what I said, you also consider it this way. What I was thinking and I just said was that Einstein believed that if we accept Heisenberg's quantum theory, then the universal laws for the whole world, macro- and micro-world that he recommended and researched, would be impossible despite the fact that both for the macro- and the micro-world valid universal laws undoubtedly exist. Such as Einstein's famous equation $E = mc^2$, which means that energy can be transformed to mass and mass can transform into energy. Also, the speed of light, which, as we know is 300,000,000 meters per second, is the same in the macro- and micro-world. The question is whether the macro-world that we see, and we can touch, or one of the 'particle' like the Earth, and we might go to another 'particle', such as the Moon or Mars. Perhaps it is the Heisenberg's uncertainty theory which denied the equivalency of the macro- and micro-world, which may be not a valid theory.

"The quantum theory is now universally accepted. But do not forget that the accepted theory of the Hellenistic civilization was that there are four elements, earth, water, air and fire, what Aristotle supplemented by a fifth, the aether. Until the Middle Ages, for more than 500 years in Europe this theory was accepted. This theory was followed by other theories in science and philosophy. It is not impossible that that the quantum theory will also be replaced by a new one and will look very primitive as the Hellenistic is viewed now."

We arrived at the tram station, and parted with the remark, that this was an interesting seminar.

I thought about all this, but I had enough sense not to tell him that every theory, whether philosophical or scientific, is perhaps best described by Hungary's eminent poet Árpád Lőwy in one of his 'poem': [41]

<u>Moral:</u>
All theories are shit which
unsettles a weak mind. **

[41] Árpád Lôwy manuscript poem volume. OSZK Kézirattár Quart. Hung.2660. 33–34., II. fejezet (Élet, halál, szerelem, házasság) 27. Vers.

** I hope that the reader believes that at that time I would have not dared to write the very descriptive lines of Árpád Lőwy at the end of a story containing this subject and I would not have done it especially if it is published in print.

14. Stalin's birthday

On a gray autumn morning in November, 1952, I arrived in my office a few minutes before Tungsram's doors closed at 8 o'clock. A few minutes later Dr. Anna Schneer came and sat down at her usual place at the desk opposite mine.There were three Chemical Departments, Anna, Pista Hangos and I were the three heads of these. Pista's lab was on another floor, Anna's and my laboratories were on the second floor, so the two of us sat in one office. We were on very good terms. Once we had both removed our coats and sat down, Anna started:

"I finally got my transfer to the Technical University as a lecturer."

Anna had already talked about that before, but I did not take it seriously because such a transfer was thought to be impossible, but it seemed Anna had 'superior' help, and somehow it was arranged. She continued:

"You are the first one to whom I speak about this. This morning I am going to Andris, to tell him that in the next days he will receive the official notification. I would like to leave on November 15."

I must have looked at her with surprise.

"Well, that means you leave not even in two weeks!"

"Unfortunately, that's right" – she said – "but on Nov. 17, I have to begin at the University."

This was an unexpected turn of events. The work for the chemical labs was divided such that the chemistry of light emitting materials used in fluorescent lamps and TV picture tubes was Pista's work, I was dealing with the oxide cathodes, the materials for electron tubes, vacuum systems, chemical analysis and with special electron tubes, and Anna's department was dealing with everything else not falling into Pista's department or mine.

"Anna" - I said – "it's impossible that you're leaving us. Partly we are going to miss very much your expertise, also it will be very bad for me, because I will have nobody with whom to discuss various things like we used to do every day."

Anna was at least 10 years older than me. She was a short, good looking, bespectacled, brown-haired woman, and wore her hair clamped at the back. She was always wearing a skirt and I never saw her in pants. Of course, like all of us, she always wore white lab coats. She was an exceptionally good chemist, had a doctorate in chemistry, and joined TKI about 2 years before. She oversaw two laboratories, where about 10 technicians worked. She was a very nice woman and we worked together very well. We used to discuss work-related things and daily affairs. Now that she was leaving, whom were they going to hire?

After lunch, I was reading in my office when Andris Dallos's secretary came in and asked me to be at 2 PM in her boss's office. The secretary just went out, when the door of my office burst open and Pista Hangos with his usual speed stormed in and dropped himself into a chair.

"Amazing" - he said – "that Nusi[42] leaves us. I do not know how they are going to find a replacement so quickly for someone who also has the expertise to know what is needed in that job. Of course, I do not blame Annus, if one can get a university job, then one should take it immediately. At least every morning she does not have to use the terrible trams and travel the fuck out to here. I wish I could leave! Come on, let's go to Andris, because this is the time he asked us to be there".

Andris was sitting behind his desk, which was towards the end of his office opposite to the door, Annus was already sitting in a chair at the long table.

"Hello" - we said almost simultaneously.

"Sit down."

Pista, as it was for him customary, plumped himself down on a chair opposite Annus. The big chair snapped, almost collapsed from the sudden weight. I also sat down opposite to Annus.

Andris presented the facts that both of us already knew:

"This issue came to me very suddenly, but for Annus this is a big opportunity to get a job at the university, and she cannot help that she was just told about it and she has to report there by the end of next week. Obviously as I just learned this, I have not had much time to think about it, but I believe it is the only solution that Annus's laboratories and personnel shall be distributed between the two of you."

[42] Nusi is the Hungarian abbreviation of Annus (Anna)

Pista jumped up as if he had been bitten by a viper.

"You cannot do this, I have so many things to do that I am here in the evening until 10 pm, and even so I am unable to complete the work you gave me. Not to mention that Szigeti or Winter come up almost daily with a new set of ideas, which I should do immedistely. This solution cannot be done!" – He flung himself on the poor chair.

Andris was desperately looking at this outbreak. I just said that Pista was right. Annus did not say a word, she just looked at Andris.

"I know you both have a lot of things to do" - Andris said gently – "but in such a short period of time one cannot find anyone who would be able to continue her work. But if the projects and the people would be somehow distributed between the two of you, the hurdy-gurdy would continue. Annus has only 10 people in her laboratory and many of the projects are routine. I would like to ask you to help me to be able to solve this issue smoothly and that we should not have to involve people who would make a capital case out of it."

This was a very clear definitive request and a very clear indication of what could happen. Pista could not say a word.

"It is my opinion" – Andris continued – "that you should now sit down with Annus, discuss the matter between you about how to distribute the projects, the laboratories and the people. By tomorrow please give me the result so that I shall be able to announce it."

With this he closed the case. All three of us went to the office I shared with Annus and we discussed the matter. The next day the three of us went to Andris and gave our agreement about how we were to divide Annus's domain and the list between the two of us of who was going to do what. When we assembled the list, Pista's main argument was that Annus's laboratories were adjacent to mine and his was on another floor and therefore the best would be if Annus's entire domain would belong to me. Eventually, we agreed that Pista would get a few little things, and I would continue the rest at least until we found someone to take over that segment.

The next work day was Monday, November 10, when I sat down with Annus for her to tell me how far things were advanced in the various projects her group was working on. Nothing seemed very complicated, because Annus's group made nice advances. The last topic was that Annus's group had to develop a getter[43] material, for a miniature electron tube. When we discussed the details of the project I almost fell off my chair.

The miniature electron tube was actually a copy of the one

[43] The operation of the electron tubes (which were the predecessors of the presently used transistors) required an absolute vacuum, without traces of air. Thus, in the production of electron tubes the air must be removed by pumps. The residual gases, which cannot be removed by pump were removed chemically. This was achieved by evaporating in the already sealed electron tube a metal - such as barium - that is able to trap the remaining gases which are still there. The barium is vaporized and like a silver reflecting coating is deposited on the inside of the glass wall of the electron tube. These materials which are absorbing the remaining gases are called 'getters'.

made by the Philips company of the Netherlands, which was used in hearing aid equipment, but was also used in small radio transmitter/receivers. The miniature radio transmitter/receiver was also used in aircraft gun projectiles. It emitted radio waves, and if the radio waves were reflected from the metal casing of the aircraft they were detected by the miniature receiver and the projectile was detonated. The projectile did not have to hit the plane directly. If it was near the airplane and exploded it could damage the plane. That was the reason it was called a "Proximity fuse". TKI offered to develop this miniature tube and have it ready for production, with appropriate documentation, and transferred to the Tungsram factory's electron tube department at the latest by Comrade Stalin's birthday. Everyone knew by heart that his birthday was December 21.

When we had this discussion, it was the 10th of November, and it turned out that Annus's group had not even started to work on this project. The problem was twofold. Neither I, nor anyone else in my group, knew anything about getters, furthermore if it was offered that this miniature electron tube be completed by Stalin's birthday, then whatever happened in the world it had to be completed. If because of someone it was not completed, that person's fate at that time was easy to imagine.

The same would have happened to the person or group not completing their task, as what happened not long ago to our colleague András Karcag. He worked as a chemist at the factory, and it was one of his tasks to determine the amount of nitrocellulose material to be used in a manufacturing process. The nitrocellulose was used for many things, such as being the raw material in nail polish. The problem was that this white powdery substance could not be stored in dry form, because it was flammable. Even if it was heated to over 100°C, it could explode, so it was usually stored moistened with alcohol. Before it was used, one had to accurately determine how much actually the weight of the dry nitrocellulose was. This was done with a very small quantity of the moistened material, weighed, then heated very carefully to about 50-60 °C in a small oven and dried. Then its weight was re-measured and from the difference of weight one could calculate the weight of the dry nitrocellulose powder. This András Karcag did somewhat superficially. In the production area there was no sensitive small weighing machine, only those which could weigh larger quantities, therefore András took a larger dish, filled it with the wet nitrocellulose, and measured its weight. He put this bigger container in a larger furnace, which was located on a table in a larger room. The room had many other tables and a bunch of working women were sitting around them. Their work was to assemble a type of electron tube. That required peace, patience and skill.

András switched on the furnace and left, because he had many other projects to attend to. As the furnace had no temperature controller, the temperature was slowly rising and when the nitrocellulose reached the critical temperature it just simply exploded. Because he used a larger amount of nitrocellulose for this measurement, the explosion ripped off the 40 x 40 cm (16x16 inch) heavy door of the furnace, which like a rocket zipped over the head of the working women, then through the window of the factory building and fell on the road in front of the building. Besides the broken window, the furnace was ruined and probably some of the women had to change panties., No other damage happened. After it was found out who caused this accident, which obviously could be called sabotage, András was called to the office of the Party. We never saw him again.

After I finished the discussion with Annus and it was evident that in the getter project something had to be done immediately, I asked the two chemist ladies in my department to come to my office. One of them was Magda, a slim, red haired, well-shaped woman. She was about 10 years older than me. Magda was a good chemist, and when I told her what had to be done, she carried it out very well, but she never initiated anything. The other chemist was Kitty, the head of my cathode laboratory.

As I was waiting for my chemists and looked out the window, I saw that from the glass factory they were throwing down an empty red hot glass melting container. I liked to see that process, because when the container hit the ground, it broke into pieces and the red-hot pieces of glass splashed and sparked like a firework. I heard that my office door was opening and I sat down at my desk.

When they arrived I told them that Annus was going to leave TKI because she had got a lecturer position at the Technical University, and Kitty was going to get Annus's desk in my office. Magda had a little office next to her laboratory. I told them that I did not see any problem about being responsible for Annus's labs, but there was a project which we had to complete very quickly which in my opinion would be a very serious task.
By that time I had found out that the getter used in the miniature tube was different from any of the getters used in

the electron tubes manufactured at Tungsram. We had no Philips tube to copy in which the getter was evaporated to find out what was the material and how it looked before it was evaporated. When I had the chance to look at the tube I assumed that the getter was a barium- aluminum[44] alloy, which material was stable in air, and the powder of which was probably painted on a metal part of the tube, which when it was heated by radiofrequency the barium evaporated and was deposited as a mirror on the inside of the glass envelop of the tube. I only knew about one such alloy, $BaAl_4$, which according to the scientific literature was stable in air. The question was where and how could we obtain this material in such a short time and if it was not available how could we produce it.

I told Magda, to stop all other work and start to research the literature to find out everything about the $BaAl_4$ alloy. I gave her two days and after that she should bring to me everything she found and save time by not writing a report about it. I asked Kitty to find out where this material could be obtained in Hungary and if it is not available where could we get pure barium metal and pure aluminum powder.

On November 14 Annus assembled her people, I got together mine and Pista Hangos his and we all congratulated her for her good luck that she was able to go to the University and wished her the best.

From Magda's search of the literature she could not find out much, but it looked like the production of this alloy was very complicated. According to the literature the material

[44] The chemical symbol of barium is Ba and of aluminum, Al

was produced in a vacuum system and needed a very complicated mechanism. I asked Magda to continue her research and to bring me everything else she found. Unfortunately our library received only very few magazines from the West and that was the case with other libraries too. It was impossible to get in contact with Western Universities or Research laboratories, because the ÁVH or other organizations watched this very seriously and a connection of this type would have been outright dangerous.

We determined right at the beginning that when we submitted our purchasing plan a year ago for this year for my laboratories we had no idea that we were going to participate in this program and we did not ask for the basic materials metallic barium and pure metallic aluminum. Annuska had no idea either and she did not request them. That meant that inside TKI these materials did not exist. The next step was to find out where one could find these materials in Hungary and how could we get them

Kitty had no luck, she could not find the $BaAl_4$ alloy in Hungary and it turned out to be very difficult to even find metallic barium or even pure aluminum powder. We probably could have ordered it, but to get it would have taken a long time, especially if it was purchased from abroad. It would have taken months. We would have to obtain a number of signatures, as these materials were not in the TKI's 1952 material request. Kitty was a very good looking girl and she knew everybody, so after a few days she informed me, that in one of the research laboratories in Budapest she found half a kilogram (one pound) of metallic barium and about the same amount of pure aluminum powder. She also said that next morning she was not going to come to work, because she was going to pick up the material and transport it to our laboratory.

Magda brought from the library what Mrs. Törzs, our librarian, had been able to find. I read it and came to the same conclusion as Magda, that the preparation of this alloy was a very complicated issue. It required vacuum equipment, which would be impossible to assemble and put in operation before our December 21 deadline. Magda said she was going to the University library to see what she could find there. The project looked absolutely hopeless. I called a few acquaintances who were working in metallography. I called the Research Institute for Aluminum without any result. Finally from the results Magda found and from my inquiries I wound up with the following information.

The metallic barium can be only stored under paraffin oil or in argon atmosphere, because if it is kept in air it will oxidize, if it gets in contact with water it will produce hydrogen which will burn and it may blow up. The aluminum powder itself is stable. The alloy made of barium and aluminum, the chemical symbol of which is $BaAl_4$, contains 55% barium and 45% aluminum. In air at room temperature it is stable, but if it gets in contact with water, it decomposes and is flammable. It could start to burn if ignited by a spark or heated in air,

We did not find anything new about its production, only the way it could be made in a vacuum system. We also discovered that in Milan, Italy, a small company SAES existed which was producing the $BaAl_4$ alloy. Probably that was the company selling the material to Philips whose electron tube we were copying. But naturally we would not be able to buy from them, because that would have broken the increased vigilance related to the copying of the miniature electron tube.

In the meantime Kitty was successful in obtaining the metallic barium in a glass jar in which it was kept under paraffin oil, and also got the pure aluminum powder. This was at least half a kilogram (one pound). She was very proud of this because according to her this was the maximum amount one could find in such a short time in Hungary. She was also proud that she managed to transport the metallic barium under the liquid on public transportation, streetcars and rumbling buses, successfully to TKI in Újpest, because had the paraffin oil spilled out, than the barium would have ignited or in the worst case blow up in the streetcar.

It was already during the middle of the last week of November when Andris' secretary came to my office and said that Andris asked me to go immediately to his office. Andris was seated behind his desk and Tibor Selley, Party Secretary of the Újpest Laboratory of TKI was sitting at the long table perpendicular to Andris's desk. Selley was a mid-sized brown haired about 35 year old engineer, who was appointed to be the Party Secretary of the Laboratory. He was a very decent person and caused no problem to anybody. It was obvious that Andris was in a bad mood. He asked me to sit down and pushed an envelope in the front of me. On the envelope I noticed the address of the SAES Company in Milan which I knew at that time that was the one which manufactured the $BaAl_4$ getters. I had not heard about this letter and did not know who could have written it. I opened the envelope which contained a short English language typewritten letter. It was signed by

Magda and was asking simply for brochures about their $BaAl_4$ getters.

I knew nothing about this, but I did not understand what the problem was? When I read it I put it down I looked at Andris and also Sellei.

"Why did you initiate writing them a letter and asking for data sheets?" – asked Andris who was very upset.

"I did not write this letter and did not ask anybody to write it. As of now I did not know about this letter. But what is the problem?"

Comrade Sellei answered me very calmly:

"As you know, the development of this electron tube is a very secret project, of which one cannot speak outside of this laboratory, Especially one cannot ask about materials used for this tube, especially it is prohibited to call the attention of the capitalists in the Western World to our work."

Considering this I realized that the matter became very serious.

Andris looked at me like I just would have been discharged from a mental hospital: - "Give me that letter'" - I got up and handed the letter over to him. Andris looked at Sellei and murmured:

"Luckily the letter was opened here and did not leave the building. Tibor was nice and brought it to me". – he turned to Sellei, who was used to smoke cigarettes:: "Please give me a match!"

Sellei took a box of matches out of his pocket and pushed it to Andris. Andris took the letter, lit a match and over an ashtray lit the envelope. The letter started to burn and when it burned Andris dropped it into the ashtray. When there were only ashes, Andris picked up the ashtray and dropped the gray ashes of the letter in the wastebasket under his desk.

"Tell your idiot people that they should not do things like this, because next time it may not end so easily." Tibor Sellei just nodded. I got up:

"I guarantee that this will not happen again." – and left the room.

I went immediately to Magda's laboratory where she was working on something. I told her to stop what she was doing and come to my office. When we entered my office, luckily nobody was there. I told her to sit down and I sat down also.

"Did you write a letter to the SAES factory in Milan?"

"Yes, I did. I asked them for the data sheets of their $BaAl_4$ getters." She said very cheerfully.

"Magda, for this the best case would be if they incarcerate both of us, but I can imagine much worse too."

She looked at me very frightened:

“What is wrong that I wrote a letter and asked for data sheets? Companies are sending data sheets of their products to everybody.”

I explained her the other side of the coin. Now she looked at me with total fright:

“I did not think about this. Mrs. Törzs found their address somewhere and as I speak good English I thought I would write them a letter and ask for data sheets. I believed it was a good idea, because we would have known about the qualities and details of the getter.”

“If you write a letter to anybody in this country or abroad you show it to me before you mail it. This is an order! If you write a letter and it is mailed before I see it I will initiate disciplinary action against you. Please go and find Kitty and both of you should come to my office. But you should not say a word about this letter issue either here or at home. Did you understand what I said?”

Very meekly she said “Yes.”. Left the room and in a few minutes she returned with Kitty.

“Sit down.”

I looked at them.

“They called my attention again, and I am repeating it to you, that the work we are doing in this Laboratory is all top secret. Do not talk to anybody about it, including the work related to the $BaAl_4$ getter. Neither inside the Lab. nor outside the Lab. I hope Kitty when you found the barium and the aluminum you did not say what they were needed for".

Kitty looked at me:

"Certainly I did not tell anybody, I know what an idiotic vigilance we have in this joint."

"Kitty this idiotic vigilance is not the end of the world. The end of the world starts when we do not obey these rules. I just wanted to remind both of you that we should not forget that these rules exist. We have to think about them and obey them. I hope I can count on you in this respect? I know I can. I wanted to mention it, because people are forgetful."

They just mumbled something.

November 21 was a Friday. I believed this was the last day I had to make a decision. Until then Magda spent some more time in the library. I went to the Research Institute for the Aluminum Industry and talked there with colleagues and spent there a day in the library. The result of all this was that we did not receive any new information. The only point of reference was that the melting point of barium is 724 °C and of aluminum is 660 °C. These were relatively low compared to iron, which is 1538 °C. This made me think and gave me an idea.

On November 24, Monday morning when I arrived in my office I put on my white lab coat and walked over to the old building of Tungsram's research lab, where on the top floor was my department's mechanic's Laci Navradszky's shop. Laci Navradszky was just getting into his grey lab coat.

"Come" – I told him –" let's go over to my office I would like to discuss something with you."

I did not want to use the numbered sheet of papers, therefore I picked up a chalk and started to draw on the blackboard what I was saying.

"We would need a half a meter long iron tube, the wall of it should be about 4 mm and the inner diameter about 5 cm." – I have no great talent for drawing. But I drew the iron tube and drew the planned experimental set up. Laci asked here and there questions, gave some advice which I incorporated in my scheme. When I finished it I looked at the drawing and summarized it.

"We need this iron tube, its cap, an iron rod and a steel cylinder filled with compressed Argon. Could this be made and assembled very soon?"

"Sure, it will be ready by tomorrow."

"Excellent!"

I then explained him the experiment I was going to do utilizing the iron tube. The essence of the experiment was to throw small pieces of barium and the aluminum powder in the tube, while letting Argon flow into the tube to protect the barium from oxidation. We would heat the bottom of the iron tube, where the Ba / Al mixture was, to 800 °C, so the Ba/Al mixture should melt. We would stir it with the iron rod like cooking jam.

"The question is" – I said – "when the iron tube will be cool what are we going to find inside. I am going to leave this drawing on the board, but when I leave in the evening I have to erase it."

"No problem, I remember the details and everything will be ready by tomorrow" – said Navradszky – "I think we could start the experiment by tomorrow morning."

"Laci, this is excellent, then we are going to start the machine tomorrow morning."

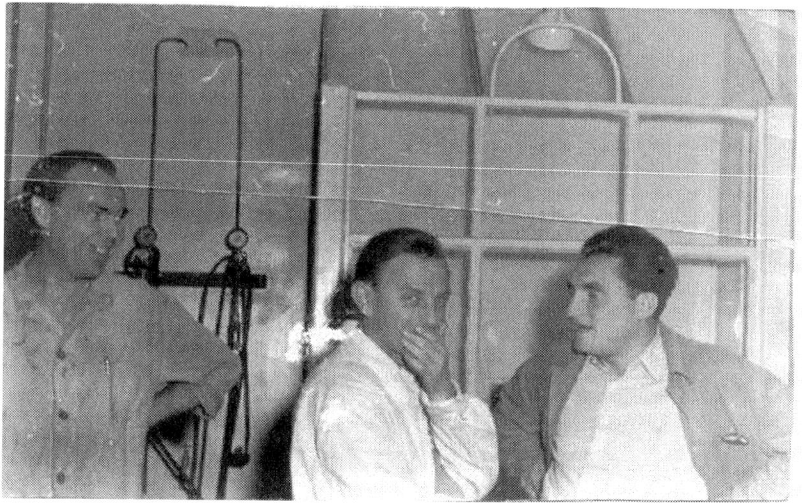

László Navradszky, Péter Ferenc Váradi and János Ádám - 1954

I went into the Lab where Gizike was working on an experimental electron tube.

"Gizike, I heard that the stock room received vacuum desiccators from Czechoslovakia. We would need a large size. Could you please get one?"

Gizike in such matters was extraordinarily clever. What we needed she was able to get. The reason I thought we would need a vacuum desiccator was that if we were going to be successful and produce the $BaAl_4$ alloy, for its storage the best would be to put it into a vacuum desiccator. The vacuum desiccator is a glass container of two parts. It has a bulging lower part in which one can put those materials which would be damaged if you leave them in moist air. They used to put in also material which collects moisture, but that is not important, because one can evacuate the glass system. The lower bulging part has a flat bottom, on which it can stand and the upper part of this glass container has a flat ground rim, on which the upper dome type cover which also has a flat ground rim can be placed. The ground rim is usually coated with Vaseline, to seal it better. The upper cover has also a valve through which the air can be pumped out from the desiccator. After the air is pumped out, the valve can be closed and then the desiccator will have no air in it. The idea is the same as was demonstrated in the famous 'Hemispheres of Magdeburg' by Otto von Guericke on May 8, 1654 in Berlin. He demonstrated the power of atmospheric pressure with a pair of large copper hemispheres with mating rims. When the rims were sealed with grease and the air was pumped out by a pump which was his invention, the sphere contained vacuum and the atmospheric pressure pressed the two hemispheres together so even 15 horses attached to each of the hemispheres were not able to pull them apart. Naturally that meant that the glass walls of the desiccators had to be very thick, that evacuated they should not collapse because of the atmospheric pressure.

About an hour later when I returned to the laboratory I saw that three of the very big glass desiccators were on a table next to each other. I looked at Gizi, who was assembling the experimental electron tube, She just shrugged and said simply:

"They gave me three pieces and Pista from the warehouse brought them up, because they are extremely heavy".

"Let's try them" – I announced. I lifted the glass cover of the desiccator which was the first of the three, to coat the rim with Vaseline. When I lifted the cover somehow I felt that it was not as heavy as I expected. But I knew that the Czech glass was very high quality.

I coated the rim of the cover and also the lower part with Vaseline and placed the cover on the lower part. I went and got a thick rubber tube, attached it to the valve of the vacuum line on the wall and the other end to the valve on the desiccator. I closed the glass valve of the desiccator and opened the vacuum line's valve at the wall. Gizike was still assembling the electron tube. Her workstation was in a corner of the Lab on the same wall where the desiccators were on the table. Next to Gizike's work station was a big metal cabinet.

I told her jokingly:

"Gizike please go to the cabinet next to you. Open the door and stand behind it."

Gizike looked at me with surprise, but got up opened the metal door and stood behind it. I was in my white lab coat and went to the desiccator. I grabbed the valve and from habit I turned away, so that only my right side was in the direction of the vacuum desiccator. I turned to see that Gizike really went behind the metal door I could not see her, because she was standing behind the open door of the cabinet. I slowly started to turn the valve of the desiccator.

As I started to turn it, I felt that the valve started to pull my arm downward. I somehow comprehended it immediately but before I could react I heard a huge bang, and like a machine gun shooting a metal plate, I heard lots of small knocks.

The vacuum desiccator imploded with an enormous bang. Probably the thickness of the glass was not sufficient to withstand the atmospheric pressure and it just collapsed. The result was that a huge number of small and large size glass splinters, like as much shrapnel, flew all over the place. The sound of the machine gun projectiles impact came from the open metal door behind which Gizike was standing. From the vacuum desiccator nothing was left but the valve that I was still hanging on to. My lab coat was covered with small and large glass pieces and glass splinters, but I did not even have a scratch.

"Gizike" – I said – "you may close the cabinet door."

Gizike closed the cabinet door, her face was about as white as her lab coat. In slow motion she went back to her work table and was just staring at me. By that time I put down the glass valve which I was still holding in my hand, I was shaking down the glass splinters and pieces from my lab coat. In the meantime Gizike recovered somewhat and with a little wobbly walk went to the corner of the lab to pick up a broom, but she was still looking at me with big eyes, while I was still removing splinters, smaller and bigger glass pieces from my lab coat.

"Gizike" – I said – "please call the stockroom and ask them to send up somebody to pick up these two desiccators. They should send them back because they are life threatening, when they are used they can blow up."

I already started to take off my lab coat, which was more or less free of glass splinters and pieces of glass. Gizike came to me and for measure of safety she started to brush off glass splinters from the lab coat which was still on me. When I started to leave the laboratory she started to sweep up the glass splinters, and the bigger pieces of glass. She still did not say a word, which was highly unusual for her and which I think never happened before during all the years we worked together.

Next morning around 11 a.m. Laci Navradszky came to the Laboratory where I was and motioned to me that I should go with him. I understood that he had finished the preparations and we could start the experiment. I said that I would be there in a few minutes.

I went over to my other laboratory, where the aluminum powder and the barium pieces were all prepared. There was a beaker in which 45 gram of aluminum powder had been measured in and a flat dish which contained 55 gram of barium pieces under paraffin oil. I picked them up and walked over to Laci's shop, where the iron tube and all the other required parts and pieces were all prepared. The iron tube, which now had a rounded bottom, was fastened to a stand so that its bottom was about a half meter from the floor. On the table next to it I saw all the required parts and the steel cylinder filled with argon was also there. We started the flow of Argon through a rubber tube into the iron tube, that it should replace the air. After a short while I poured the aluminum powder and the barium pieces, which we first dried with a paper, into the iron tube. We assembled the equipment and kept the argon gas flowing.

I waited about 10 minutes then told Laci that he should start the hydrogen/oxygen welding torch and start to heat up the bottom of the tube. Laci ignited the flame and started to heat up uniformly the bottom of the tube for about 15 cm (6 inches). In the meantime I picked up from the table the pironometer, which is an optical thermometer. The tube had to be heated to 750 – 800 oC so that it should be over the melting point of barium. As noted before the melting point of aluminum is 660 oC and barium's is 724 oC. Slowly the bottom of the tube started to become red hot. I picked up the iron rod from the table and inserted it into the center hole of the cap closing the upper end of the tube. I noticed that the rod was now deeper in than before we started heating. Laci was in the meantime still heating the tube with the burner. We must have reached 800 oC and the mark on the rod, which me made when the tube was empty, how far the rod is when it hits the bottom, was almost at the opening of the cap. I slowly started to move the rod in a circle to stir the content of the tube, the way I was helping my mother when she cooked the plum jam. I was stirring very slowly and the mark on the rod reached the opening on the cap. Laci was still heating the bottom of the tube. I slowly pulled up the rod, until it was not in the melting area and fastened it so it could not slide back. I told Laci to turn off the flame and keep checking that the argon gas was flowing, but he should not do anything else, just wait for the tube to cool down.

The interesting part was that the whole experiment went very smoothly, nothing exploded, blew up and no other mishap occurred. I told Laci, when the tube became room temperature he should let me know, I would be in my office. A few minutes later I was in my office, it was noon and Gyurka Gergely came in and, as he did a few times a week, asked me to go to the Tungsram's cafeteria to have lunch. I put on my coat and left. I told him what we were doing during the morning. He stopped, looked at me with horror.

"You are insane! If that barium would have gotten air somehow you could have burned down the entire building."

"Why should it have gotten air? During the entire time it was under argon atmosphere. It seems that the entire production is very simple and nobody tried it, because they were afraid, but I have not had any other choice. Now the only question is, what we have in that tube, can it be used as a getter? I am not sure of that."

He was shaking his head.

"It was crazy what you did."

"You are right, but if I had not tried it then after December 21st you would not have been able to come for me to go to lunch. But on the other hand that is true too, that if it would have exploded, I would not be any more your lunch partner."

Laci came to my office around 3 p.m. and said the tube was at room temperature. We stopped the flow of the argon gas. I asked him to cut the tube where I put a mark.

After he cut it we saw that the lower part of the tube was filled with a hard, metallic, silver gray crystalline material. I asked Laci to try to cut me a little piece of that metallic material. The material which was in the iron tube must have been brittle, because Laci was able by hitting it a little to break off small pieces. I put them in a beaker and asked Laci to find somewhere a desiccator and he should put the iron tube with the material into the desiccator. I went to Kitty's laboratory, gave her a little piece and asked her to analyze it and find out how much barium, aluminum and iron was in that sample. I put the other part of the sample in the only agate mortar which was left over from the ten and I started to pulverize the material using the pestle. When it became pulverized I took the material to Gizike's lab. to put it on a little metal foil and mount it to be able to put it in a glass tube, which we could put on the pump to evacuate. When it was on the pump she should get me and let me know.

Around 4 p.m. Kitty came to my office and said that the material was aluminum and barium and there were no traces of iron in it. That was very pleasant news, now the question was could it be used as a getter. So I walked over to Gizike's lab, where she and Mrs. Fekete were just pumping the air out of the little glass tube in which on a small nickel foil I could see the metallic gray powder

When the vacuum measuring instrument indicated that the pressure inside the small tube was about equivalently to what it should be in an electron tube, I put on the tube the 'bomber', the coil used with the radiofrequency generator, which when it is turned on heats up the metals in vacuum. I turned it on and the nickel plate started to glow and I after a second the top of the little glass tube, over the nickel plate, turned into a silver mirror from the evaporated metal, which obviously was the result of the $BaAl_4$ alloy having the quality of a getter. The production of the $BaAl_4$ was a success.

I asked Mrs. Fekete to seal off the little glass tube. After she did it, I cut the tube open, the metallic mirror turned immediately white, as every getter should do. I took the tube with me and asked Gizike that she should collect Laci and Kitty and the three of them should come to my office.

When all three of them were there I explained them the program in which who has to do what.

Laci's task was to find out how he could get the alloy out of the iron tube and after that how to pulverize it, but not in air. He should also assemble another iron tube for an experiment for the next day, because I would like to make another run.

I asked Kitty to analyze the material which was evaporated onto the glass in the little experimental tube. Also that she should analyze the material which would be pulverized by Laci. Also that she should take some from the pulverized material Laci is going to make and mix it with some liquid having some nitrocellulose, approximately the amount we are using in electron tubes when she prepares a cathode, and give that to Gizike.

I asked Gizike that when she received the powder in the nitrocellulose solution she should paint it on small nickel metal sheets, like she did it yesterday. She should make about 20 pieces and mount them the same way as yesterday in small glass tubes.

On December 12, on a Friday afternoon I went to Andris's office and I put on his desk about a half centimeter (0.2 inch) thick typewritten report and a glass with ground-glass stopper in which was about 50 gram of gray metal powder.

"Andris" – I said – "I am giving you the detailed report about the manufacturing of the $BaAl_4$ getter material, the utilization of the experimental data and also how much residual gases can this getter absorb in an electron tube. You can transfer this to production and we would be glad to help them if they need more information or want to have their material analyzed."

"The only thing we need now is that the rest of the group should also finish their work." – said Andris."

I went to my laboratory and asked Gizike to get everybody in my department to be in this laboratory. I went to my office, where Kitty and Magda were now sitting. I went to my desk, where was one copy of the half centimeter thick report. I sat down and lifted the report.

"Thank you for your help" – I said – "it was a close call, but we survived it with not much difficulty. At least our part of Stalin's birthday present is completed. In a half hour please come to my laboratory, as I would like to thank everybody, that we were able to solve this absolutely hopeless looking job."

I picked up the half centimeter thick report and went over to Laci Navradszky's shop. When I got closer to his shop I heard repeated 'bangs' the source of which was obviously Laci's shop. I entered. Laci was standing in front of a table on which a vise was holding a tube, which was obviously the cause of the explosive bangs. When I saw the set up I immediately realized that Laci was trying to make a little jet engine for his model airplane.

He stopped the noise by disconnecting something.

I shook Laci's hand, lifted the report, showing it to him.

"Laci thank you. Without you we could not have made it."

"Doctor Váradi" – for some reason he never called me Ferenc – "I obviously helped, but I only did what you told me to do."

"Come with me to the lab, because I would like to thank everybody."

Andris on Friday, December 18 invited everybody whose department participated in the development of the electron tube for the 'proximity fuse' which the TKI laboratory offered to complete for Stalin's birthday. He had on his desk a dossier. When all of us had arrived, Andris stood up and lifted the dossier, which must have been at least 20 centimeter (8 inch) thick.

"I would like to thank all of you for completing the work that we offered to do for Comrade Stalin's birthday. Comrade Ács, the President of TKI, called me and asked me to tell you his congratulation, that we fulfilled our offering with success. I asked the Director of the electron tube production to come here, that I should be able to give him in the name of all of us the documentation of the fabrication process of the 'proximity fuse' electron tube and

10 pieces of the tube, which is operational according to the specification."

He just finished speaking when the door opened and three people from the production came in. Andris gave them the file and the tubes and said if they had any problem, those who developed this tube in this short time were offering to help.

The production was started without any problem, including the manufacturing and utilization of the $BaAl_4$ getter material.

* * *

Five and a half years passed. I was working in the Research Laboratory of the Telefunken Company, in Ulm, in what was at that time called West-Germany. By that time several of my scientific papers had been published about the analysis of residual gases in electron tubes.

One day one of the secretaries came to my office and said they had called from the production that a Dr. Paolo Della Porta was visiting there, who wanted to visit me and talk to me. I was very surprised, as I knew that Dr. Della Porta was the founder and owner of the SAES Company in Milan.

Paolo – I mention him only by his first name, because after our meeting in Ulm we became good friends and met several times at various scientific meetings – asked me to go out to lunch to a restaurant he selected. He knew my papers and he was very much interested in them. I obviously also knew his papers. So we mostly discussed that subject. Finally, as he knew I was from Hungary, he said that he was just coming from Budapest where he had met people from the Tungsram electron tube factory. They said that they were familiar with the $BaAl_4$ getter material, which they were manufacturing with a very simple process, but that he was successful to convince them that they should stop making the $BaAl_4$ getter and rather they should buy the $BaAl_4$ getter which he was manufacturing. So now he had got for his company the entire Hungarian market.

Basically I agreed with the people at Tungsram that they would buy the $BaAl_4$ getter from SAES rather than make it themselves. Because the method we developed saved our lives, but was a relatively dangerous process, it was probably better and cheaper to buy from SAES, since they made the alloy in mass production .The Hungarian need was not much and therefore the production was probably also more expensive.

When Paolo told me this, it flashed through my mind that for Stalin's birthday on December 21, 1952 we had to develop within weeks the production of the BaAl4 getter. Magda Ács, the chemist, who worked in my group, wanted brochures from SAES, that maybe we could buy it there and only our luck and good colleagues rescued us that we did not wind up in jail because the failure of the vigilance would have opened holes in the bastions of socialism for Della Porta and through him for the imperialist camp.
Probably the SAES getters were used in 1959 for the TV picture tubes which were mass produced in the Tungsram factory in the city of Vác, which was built for this purpose and which factory provided all of the picture tubes for the Hungarian TV set production. The glass enclosures and the getters were first imported from the West, but because of the high price of the glass enclosures later they started to use the glass enclosures made in the Soviet Union.

From there on the rate of failures was catastrophic. This was investigated by experts from TKI-Újpest (which was renamed in 1967 back to what it was in the 1940s: Tungsram Research Laboratory) who found that the failures were caused by the air which was seeping through next to the metal electrode embedded in the glass. Because of this the factory at Vác had to be closed in 1970.[45]

[45] S. Mészáros - Gy. Gergely - J. Ádám: Yhe history of the domestic TV picture tube - Hiradástechnika, 2009, 64. 9-10 – 7-10

15. “4. Kútvölgyi Avenue”

Gabi Fóti who was the boss of seven technicians working in my Laboratory #1, knocked on my office door and entered. That was on January 27, 1953 on a Tuesday just after her working hours were finished. She came a few steps closer to my desk then stopped.

"Doctor Váradi," – most of the workers in my laboratories addressed me like that, probably they were trying to avoid calling me "Mister" or "Comrade" – "Irén did not come in today and she did not telephone either. It is true that they have no telephone, but if somthing comes up, her husband always calls to inform me, but today he did not call me either."

"This is realy strange, because Irén is a very dependable and serious person. I am surprised."

"Yes I think the same way. For this reason, if you think it would be all right, then I would visit them now and find out if they have any problem."

"That would be very nice of you."

"So, before I go home I am going to visit them."

Next day when I arrived in my office Kitty was already sitting at her desk and was deeply involved in what she was writing.

"Servus,"[46] I said.

She greeted me, but was immediately immersed in her writing. She finally looked up.

"You know, I thought about the paper we are writing about flame photometry with Gyuri Gergely and János Ádám, and I came to the conclusion that some things have to be added to it. That is what I am trying to write now. We would like to send it to the magazine, but in my opinion things have to be added to it. When I finish I am going to show it to János, and after that I would like you to look at it and tell your opinion.

Before I could answer, somebody was knocking on the door, and Gabi Fóti came in. I noticed that she wanted to tell me something, but did not wanted Kitty to hear it.

"Gabi," I said, "I was just going to my lab, could you please join me?" I got up and we left my office.

When I closed the door she turned to me and said, "Irén's husband disappeared."

I realized that I cannot discuss this with her in the corridor, and we cannot discuss it in the laboratory either, so I turned back to my office. My office door just opened and Kitty came out.

"I am going to discuss this matter with János, before I am going to involve you."

---

[46] Hungarian greeting means "Hello"

“Excellent.” I said and Gabi and I entered my office. I motioned Gabi to sit down at Kitty’s desk. She sat down, but she seemed not to know how to start her story. I helped her.

“Yesterday you visited Irén?”

“Yes. Only Irén was at home and was crying all the time, and their small apartment was in shambles. She said that her husband, as usual, went to his job Monday morning to the Kútvölgyi Avenue Hospital, where he is working in the pharmacy department. Irén worked all day Monday here in the laboratory. After work she went to pick up her son from the day care, and they went home. When they got to the door, she realized that the door was a little open, and when she entered she saw that the apartment was in disarray, approximately the way I have seen it. All the things from the closet and the drawers were thrown on the floor. Irén assumed that someone broke into the apartment, but it was strange that the few valuables they had, like the radio and a few other things, were not taken. They had no other valuables. Her husband, who under normal conditions should have been home, was not at home. Irén was very upset. She did not know what she should do. She believed that her husband had to work overtime. She went down and called the Hospital from a pay phone and asked them to connect her to her husband. They told her that her husband did not come to work.

"Irén did not understand it. She returned to her apartment, dressed her five year old son, Tamás, and they went to her parents apartment in Tűzoltó street, not far from where she lived on Üllői Avenue. Irén’s father said that she should leave Tamás with his wife, and the two of them should go to the district police station to report the burglary and to ask if they could tell them anything.

"They went to the police station and told the policeman on duty the story. He wrote down the incident and asked what was taken from the apartment. Irén said that the robbers made a heluva mess in the house, but she could not see immediately that anything was missing. When she goes home now she will look everything over, and she is going to prepare a list of the stuff that is missing. The policeman promised that he is going to ask on the telephone whether there was some information about her husband. He came back after a few minutes and said that they have no information that anything happened to her husband. From the tone of the policeman one could understand that in his opionion, if her husband did not inform her, then some woman issue must have been the cause of his disappearance. Naturally Irén started to cry, and they went back to her parents home. They discussed the matter, and they decided, that Tamás should stay with his grandparents, and Irén should go home, because Gyuri maybe is at home by then. If he did not come home, Irén should go next morning to Kútvölgyi Hospital and ask the personnel department what to do and how can Gyuri be found.

"When Irén arrived home she started to assemble what was around. First the bed, which was disassembled. The mattress was on the floor, and it was cut open, like the burglers were looking there for something. She came to the conclusion that nothing was missing. Only two small framed pictures were mising from the wall. One of them Gyuri received from the "National Committee for Attending

Deportees"[47] (DEGOB) as a recognition that he participated in DEGOB's work helping the Jews returning from deportation. The other was a diploma Gyuri received from the Joint Distribution Committee (JOINT), which was an American organization helping the Hungarian Jews who survived the holocaust, where he worked in 1945 - 1946.

"By night Gyuri still did not come home. Next morning Irén went to the Kútvölgyi Hospital's personnel department. She introduced herself, that she is Mrs. György Fuchs, and she told what she knew. The woman working at the personnel department listened to the story and said she is going to try to find out something. She left the office and Irén stayed.

"The woman came back in a half an hour, sat down at her desk, put down the paper she had her notes on. She turned to Irén and said, "We were able to establish that your husband, György Fuchs, yesterday before he arrived here to the hospital was arrested by two people wearing the military uniform of the ÁVO[48], because they want to ask him questions in connection with some Jewish doctors whose perscription his department was filling for some of the patients in the hospital. We do not know at which office your husband is being asked the questions, but we are sure that they are going to inform you and us too.

"One can imagine what shape Irén was in after she heard this. As of last night she knew nothing, but it can be seen that it was her least problem to call me in the laboratory."

For a short time I could not say anything, but luckily just then Kitty walked in and Gabi, who was sitting at her desk,

---

[47] Deportáltakat Gondozó Bizottság – DEGOB (www.degob.hu)
[48] ÁVO = Hungarian Secret Police

got up. I got up too, and we walked out of my office. In the corridor I told Gabi that I am going to look into the matter and when I find anything I will let her know, but until then she should not tell anyone about this. She should say that Irén has called that she cannot come in. With this Gabi went in the direction of her laboratory, and I went upstairs to find Karcsi Ducza.

On the way up I was thinking that I heard of many such events. My uncle, Imre Györki, disappeared on June 13, 1950 the same way, and we did not known anything about him since that time. Now it happened with one of my subordinates, and I do not have the faintest idea what to do at such a time. As TKI was a military Research Laboratory I assumed the first thing I have to do is to report it to our military liaison officer Karcsi Ducza and inform him about the situation. He will find out what to do about it.

I entered his secretary's office and told her that I have to see Karcsi immediately. When I walked into his office Karcsi looked at me surprised. I greeted him and sat down on a chair at the table next to his desk.

"Karcsi, one of the girls in my lab, Irén, did not come yesterday to work, and she did not call in why she is not coming to work. Gabi Fóti, who as you know is the manager of that lab, offered to visit Irén and find out what was her problem. She went to see her, and this morning when I got in told me the story. I have absolutely no idea what to do about it, but I am sure you will find out and let me know what I should do. Until I find out I asked Gabi not to tell the story to anybody."

I could see that Ducza did not like the whole thing, but he said I should continue. I continued by telling him everything I learned from Gabi. After I finished I looked at him. He looked puzzled, he grabbed his chin with his left hand and started to massage his face with his fingers. He did not say a word, but he pressed a button to ring for his secretary. Éva entered immediately.

"Éva, please order me a car, because I have to go to our central office."

"I am going to order one immediately, and I let you know when it will be here."

"Please arrange it, that it should be here as soon as possible."

Éva left. Ducza turned to me, "I am not surprised that you have no idea what you should do in a case like this, because I do not have either. I do not want to discuss this on the telephone, and I do not know with whom I should discuss this. So I rather go up to Rózsadomb (that where TKI headquarters was). I hope I will know more by the afternoon. Tell Gabi that she should shut up until you talk to her and tell her what she has to say.

Éva came in. "The car will be in 5 minutes at the entrance door."

"Excellent."

He got up, went to the hat stand for his military jacket, "Lucky that today I came in my uniform, who knows with whom I have to speak."

At the door he pressed my arm, “Fuck, I would have had today so many other more pleasant things to do.”

I went to my laboratory, found Gabi and told her, “As we discussed, do not say anything about this. If somebody asks you, tell them that her kid is sick or something similar. I told Ducza and he went to Rózsadomb, because he did not know either what to do. When I find out anything I will let you know immediately.”

After I talked with Gabi I went upstairs to Andris’s office. Andris sat at his desk and was reading some papers. When I walked in he put the papers on his desk. I sat down to the conference table perpendicular to his desk and broadly outlined the entire story.

After I finished he only said “uh."

Ducza’s secretary, around 3 PM, asked me to go to Karcsi’s office. I immediately went with her to his office. Karcsi got up and said, “Ferenc, I have not had lunch yet, come with me to the Tungsram dining room, I am going to get something to eat.” With this he picked up his coat and hat and started towards the door.

“OK, but I would like to pick up my coat also because it looks to me that the weather is cold.”

“OK. You are right, I just arrived and when I got out of the car I felt that the weather was cold and humid.”

When we got out of the building it was cold. The sky was grey and one could feel that sooner or later it will be snowing.

The road from TKI to the Tungsram dining room is very short. Ducza was walking very slowly and started to talk immediately.

“What I am telling you now should stay between us. I have told most of this to Andris, but I am telling you a few details which I did not want to discuss in my office, because who knows? So, I went to Rózsadomb and since that time I either talked with people or was talking on the telephone, and I really had no lunch. The entire matter is very complicated. Irén’s husband, György Fuchs, on Monday was really arrested by the ÁVH before he got to his work place. I assume that he was taken to 60 Andrássy Avenue for interrogation. You may have heard about the trials of the medical doctors in the Soviet Union. Professionally highly regarded Jewish doctors got together to systemetically poison the leaders of that country. Stalin exposed this conspiracy. The waves of this just arrived to our country. It is obvious that the Kútvölgyi Avenue Hospital, where the political leaders of our country are treated, is the most suitable place in Hungary where such accusations could be started. That is how it happened that they arrested György Fuchs to interrogate him, He was in the pharmacy in a very responsible position. I assume that he was not the only one whom they arrested from that hospital.

"From this one could draw the conclusion that the innocence of György Fuchs will not be established in a few days. Naturally, until his innocence is established we cannot employ his wife at TKI because we are working on top secret projects. Somebody from our Personnel department is going to visit Irén and is going to tell her that she is on leave with her full salary until the personnel department is able to find her a suitable job.

"Gabi should tell the other people in the laboratory that Irén is on an extended vacation because of family reasons, and that she is asking everybody not to disturb her while she is away. You are going to get permission to hire immediately somebody to replace Irén. Irén's salary will not be charged to your account."

We just arrived to the entrance of Tungsram's dining room.

After lunch, from my office window I looked over to the glass factory's huge glowing glass melting pots and thought the matter over.

I had already heard about the case of the Soviet Jewish doctors. Around the end of 1952 Stalin said at the meeting of the political committee that every Jew is nationalistic and is the agent of American intelligence, and among the Jewish doctors there are many Jewish nationalists. It was said that Jewish doctors, several of them with excellent professional reputation, joined forces to systematically poison the leaders of the country. I read in a Hungarian newspaper that in January of 1953 an article was published in a prominent place in the Pravda, the title of which was approximately: "Evil Spies and Assassins Disguise Themselves as Professors of Medicine." The article said that these doctors incorrectly used dangerous medicine to kill several communist leaders.

For me it was clear that the influence of the anti-Semitic doctor's trial arrived now to Hungary. Looking at it in this light, it is understandable that such a case would start with those who are connected with the Kútvölgyi Avenue hospital.

Kútvölgyi Avenue hospital was a relatively new and well equipped exclusive medical institution. In 1942 Governor Miklós Horthy and his wife inaugurated it. The Governor and his wife at that time would not have imagined that 10 years later it will be still an "exclusive" institution, but it will serve for the healing of the functionaries of the Hungarian communist party and of high ranking government employees.

A couple of weeks later Karcsi Ducza informed me that they found a job for Irén in the Biological Research Laboratory in Kőbánya a the district of Budapest (the Hungarian accronym of the laboratory was KŐBIKULA), which was across from the Kőbánya Beer Factory on the Maglódi Avenue, close to where Irén's apartment was.

Stalin died on March 3, 1953. The new Soviet government declared that the trials against the doctors were based on trumped-up charges, and the detained were were promptly acquitted.

On the afternoon of a Saturday on an early June day the doorbell was ringing at Irén Fuchs's apartment. Irén could not imagine who that could be, because she did not expect any guest. She was dressing her son because they were planning to go with the grandparents to a nearby pastry shop, where they could sit on the terrace in such a nice day. She said to her son to get his shoes on, and she went to open the hallway door.

At the front door stood Gyuri in the same winter outfit in which he went to work on the morning of January 27. He carried on his arm his winter coat, which he was wearing on that day, and had his briefcase in his hand which he carried when he left home on that date. The only difference was that in his clothing there would have been place for two Gyuris. For a moment they were standing in silence, then they embraced and started to cry on each other's shoulder. That lasted for a few minutes, when Tamás who did not know why his mother did not come back, opened the door to the hallway. When he saw his father, he ran there, jumped on him, and the weakened Gyuri almost fell back.

"Father," he said, "We are going with Granny to a pastry shop."

Gyuri was transferred to a rural hospital, where he had to report on Monday. With this life went on, only four and a half months were erased from the Fuchs family's life.

16. The top-secret, secret project

At the beginning of 1953, on a Monday, Andris's secretary came to my office and relayed Andris's request, that at 3 o'clock that afternoon all of the Department heads should assemble in the big meeting room. The meeting room was a huge room in which all of the employees of the lab could have been accommodated. I asked the secretary what was the subject of the meeting, but she either did not know or did not want to tell me. A few minutes later Pista Hangos came to my office. I was alone there. As he normally did, he slammed himself on a chair, which at this time was the chair at Kitty's desk, which reacted with a snapping noise to this insult.

"For what bullshit is Andris collecting all of the Department heads in that big room? I already asked Gyurka, but he did not know."

"I have no idea either. I asked Andris's secretary who did not knew it or did not want to tell me."

Pista got up, shrugged his shoulders and left.

At 3 o'clock in the afternoon I went to the meeting room, where on the podium was a long table, behind it four chairs and a blackboard. Except Vili Szikora who was not in the Laboratory that afternoon, the rest of the 12 Department heads were assembled. Besides the Department Heads, Henrik Fried was also there. He was the head of one of the electron tube manufacturing departments in Tungsram.

At 3 o'clock Andris Dallos, Ernő Winter, who was the Director General of the Laboratory, the boss of Andris, Karcsi Ducza and Tibor Sellei, who was the Party Secretary, entered. They sat down on the podium at the prepared four chairs.

First 'Old father' Winter[49] started to talk. It was a little hard to understand him because he spoke very softly and had a nasal voice. What he said approximately was that the Laboratory received a great honor as we were going to start a very important research project, which would have great importance for not only our country but for the entire socialist camp. He knew that the staff of the Laboratory would complete this work with success and on time. He asked Comrade Ducza to explain the details.

Karcsi Ducza, who was wearing his military officer's uniform, looked around and found all Department heads were present, except Vili, whom he apparently knew that on that day he was not in the Lab.

"TKI-2, that means our Laboratory, was trusted to carry out an extremely important and confidential program – he started his speech. – The Soviet Union entrusted Hungary and acknowledged the capability of TKI-2 to develop the electron tubes utilized in the operation of the terrestrial radar systems used in the Soviet Union. Because of this, Hungary was able to buy the technical description used for manufacturing the electron tubes used in those radars. Our

[49] In Hungarian the word 'Winter' means the season winter, but could also be somebody's name. Therefore he was called between us "Old father Winter" which does not meant his age as he was only about 53 years old.

Laboratory received the very important task based on the provided drawings and descriptions to develop these electron tubes and to prepare the documentation, the plans and measuring technology and equipment for the production of these tubes, that is to say everything needed for Tungsram to be able to manufacture these extremely important electron tubes used in the radar system.

"I must emphasize that this is an extremely secret project and we are going to do everything that not even the smallest details should leak out.

"We are going to receive tomorrow the Russian language descriptions. These will be delivered by the Comrades of the Secret Case Handling (SCH). The Russian text will be translated on this floor. Three translators will start this job. Typing will be done in another room by one typist who will arrive here with the translators. The two rooms will be equipped with special locks and the translator Comrades will deposit every evening the original Russian and the translated texts in sealed boxes at the SCH.

"The translators may need technical advice. Such requests have to go through my office and I am going to designate the individual who could enter the translators' offices.

"The original Russian and one copy of the translated texts will be transported from here and stored by the SCH. The copies of the translated text and drawings needed for our work will be given to me and I am going to provide it to the people who are going to work on the subject. We are going to organize for these people a Secret Case Handling course, to assure that nothing leaks out from this project.

"Now I am asking Comrade Dallos to appoint those Comrades who are going to work on this project."

In front of Andris was a sheet of paper and in his left hand a pencil. He pushed his glasses with his right hand a little higher, and raised his eye from the paper to the assembled Department heads sitting in front of him.

"I also want to emphasize how important is the secrecy in this extremely interesting work. I would like to emphasize that to realize this program in time, we must work together. The tasks, or in other words the electron tubes to be developed, can be divided into four groups" – he stood up, he carried the paper which he had in his hand, went to the blackboard, picked up a chalk and started to write:

Magnetron
Klystron
TR-tubes
Cathode ray tubes

He wrote these words on the blackboard by leaving space between them.

<u>"Magnetron"</u> – he underlined the word – "this project has two parts. One is the development of the magnetron electron tube. This part will be directed by Comrade Budincsevits. The magnet belonging to this project will be developed at TKI-1 at Rózsadomb." – He also wrote that on the blackboard:

"In the development of the magnetron, Comrade Váradi's department will help, performing the necessary chemical analysis and making the cathodes, as well as cleaning of the materials used in the electron tube.

"Tibor Horváth's group will develop the measuring methods for the magnetron tubes as well as perform the measurement of the completed magnetrons."

Andris wrote the names and also the tasks on the blackboard.

"The second electron tube will be the reflex klystron." – Andris now underlined on the board the word klystron. – "The development of this will be done by the departments of Comrades Rotter and Szikora. Váradi's department like in the case of the magnetron will help in chemical analysis as well as the development and making of the necessary cathodes, and cleaning of the materials used in the tube. The measuring methods of the reflex klystrons and the measurements of the completed klystrons will be done by the group of Pista Ruf."

Andris noted the names under the word klystron.

"The third group of the tubes is the TR, or using its English name: 'transmit and receive tubes', which are diodes filled with gas. Vili Szikora's department is going to make the development. It is evident that Váradi's department has to participate in this to analyze the materials, but also in the filling of the tubes with gas. This work will be done in cooperation with Gyurka Gergely's department. The development of the measuring method and also the measurements of the completed tubes will be done by Pista Ruf's group.

“The forth group is the cathode ray tube which is also called picture tube. This is the tube which displays the microwaves reflected from an object illuminated by the microwaves. For this a so called phosphor material is needed which is similar to the one used in picture tubes for TV, but it has to have a long lasting afterglow. In TV the picture is changing fast, therefore the phosphor has to extinguish fast, on the other hand for the tube used in radars the image has to be on the screen for a longer time, that the position of the airplane from which the microwaves are reflected can be seen for a longer period. The development of such a phosphor is very difficult. It will be also difficult to develop the glass enclosure needed for this tube. The development of the long afterglow phosphor is going to be done by the departments of Pista Hangos and Gyurka Gergely, while the development of the glass enclosure will be directed by uncle Feri Reisz and Ödön Kenczler.”

Andris wrote these names also on the board.

”Besides of those – he pointed to the board – evey person in every department in the Laboratory should consider their primary duty to help, if it is needed.”

Andris sat down, put the paper in front of him on the table.

Karcsi Ducza got up and continued:

”The manufacturing of the developed tubes were trusted in Tugsram to the department of Comrad Fried. – He pointed to Fried, who stood up and bowed. – In order that the production of the developed tubes should start as soon as possible and smoothly, Comrade Fried will follow every step of the development, therefore he will have a free entry to the laboratory and it would be very good if the problems which eventually may come up are discussed also with him.

„We have about one year for the development of the tubes mentioned by Andris. The translation of the Russian specifications and the copying of the drawings with Hungarian text will take at the most one month. But during that time those parts which were completed will be available for those who work on that segment. So the procurement of the necessary materials and equipment can be started already during that time.

"I would just like to mention that I hope everybody realizes that the prestige of our entire Laboratory hinges on the excellent and timely completion of this task.

"Anybody has any question?"

He looked around, but nobody asked anything.

„As there are no questions I just would like to say that those who are working on this project and whom I am going to notify should get together here tomorrow at 3 o'clock in the afternoon to discuss the important aspects of the stricter Secret Case Handling procedure we have to introduce."

While we got up and started to leave the meeting room, Ducza wiped off Andris's writing from the board.

Gyurka Gergely and Gábor Sebestyén joined me when we were in the corridor. We went to Gábor's office to discuss what we learned at the meeting.

Gábor declared that the entire project was nonsense, because there was nothing new in these tubes and the staff at TKI-2 had much better things to do than to spend time to copying them.

He said that the magnetron[50], which was an electron tube placed in a magnetic field, was invented in 1920, and during the second World War the British and the Americans manufactured them in large quantities for their radars. He said that it made no sense to copy now an already developed magnetron. Gábor also said that the development of the magnetron during the war actually won the war against the Germans, because that was the essential part of the high power radars that the Germans did not have. The Germans developed the klystrons, which were able to hold the microwave frequency better, but ithe klystrons power was not sufficient.

He said about the klystron that it was invented by the Varian brothers in America in 1939 and it was an electron tube the development of which was completed during the war. He sketched on the blackboard the reflex klystron and its operation.

As of the TR tubes I said that I knew them. It was actually a special type of tube, which was filled to a certain pressure with Argon gas, but a small amount of water vapor was added, which was not a simple matter. I said that I was working on this issue in connection with another

[50] The magnetron is the heart of today's microwave owens.

project. For me it would be an interesting experiment to produce the necessary gas mixture and also that I would be able to continue my research to develop the analysis of such low amount and low pressure gas mixture.

At the end we decided that we had to do this job in spite of it not being a serious research project. It was primarily only copying, but we had to do it and hopefully there would be time left to work on some more exciting research task.

During the next day there were lots of events in the laboratory. The translators, three men about 30 years old, arrived and occupied one of the rooms equipped with special locks. For the typist lady – who had a scruffy appearance and was about 50 years old – they brought a table and a typewriter. They were not from the Laboratory, everything was brought in from the outside, no typewriter from the Laboratory was used. When everything was in the rooms with the special locks, four persons in military uniform arrived. They carried a big metal box with locks and were escorted by an officer. They all entered one of the rooms, carrying the locked big metal box. They all had a blue patch on their collar identifying them as belonging to the State Protection Authority (Hungarian: Államvédelmi Hatóság or ÁVH). When all that was completed, Ducza came dressed in his military uniform identifying him as being a First Lieutenant and entered the room, where everybody, translators, typist the four military personnel and the officer were present. Finally Ducza, the ÁVH officer and three soldiers came out. It seemed that one of the soldiers stayed in the room as a guard.

For the afternoon meeting, not only the Department heads were invited but all of the employees of the Laboratory, and the meeting room was quite full. When everybody, including Vili Szikora, was there, Karcsi Ducza, Andris, Sellei and an officer in State Protection Authority (ÁVH) uniform came in and sat down at the chairs prepared on the podium. The blackboard was not in the background at this time.

Ducza started by introducing the ÁVH officer. He continued with about the same speech he gave the day before, that the Soviet Union was trusting Hungary and recognized the ability of TKI-2, and so on. He did not go into details about the tube types, but immediately continued his speech by emphasizing the importance of secrecy, because the enemy's' ears and eyes could be everywhere and for this reason we had to be more alert. He described the tightened SCH system and called everybody's attention to the fact that the Laboratory would now have its examination as to how could we increase our alertness. He said that courses would be organized and everybody would be notified when he or she would have to attend one of them.

The ÁVH lieutenant Comrade did not say a word. His presence seemed to be a warning that every failure related to secrecy would have serious consequences, and in the evaluation of a mistake not only the local people would be the judges, but the ÁVH would also participate.

At this point Ducza thanked all for their presence and closed the meeting.

After the meeting, Gyurka, Gábor and I went to Gábor's office. None of us liked the situation, especially as an ÁVH officer was also present. We decided that his appearance turned this work to very serious.

Life went on. The people of the translation office worked very hard. From time to time four ÁVH soldiers led by an ÁVH officer appeared with the big metal box, which sometimes came empty and left full or arrived full and left empty.

We had only rarely to do something for them. Sometimes Ducza asked one of us to see him and told us that we had permission to go to the translator's room. For this he gave us a paper on which the translator with whom we were talking had to write the time when we were leaving the room and sign it. We had to give the paper to Ducza's secretary.

I was also sent in a few times, other colleagues also. In most cases the issue was that the translators got hung up on some words which they could not translate from Russian. They believed that it was some special technical expression and that was the reason they asked for a technical person. In general they were English words which were easy to translate, because we usually knew the expression. At least we were helping the translators.

When the translation of a section of the project was completed, somewhere copies were made of those pages. Every page was numbered and the pages were bound together with the national color, a red-white-green ribbon. From these it seemed that Ducza received as many copies as he needed. He asked the people who were involved in that theme to come to his office – on such an occasion Andris was also present – and gave to each Department head a green colored metal box, the same that we used for our standard SCH system, except that this had a paper glued to it: 'HIGHEST GRADE SECRET CASE HANDLING'. To everybody Ducza gave a box and he put in the pages bound together with the red-white-green ribbon. He also gave everybody a small seal and demonstrated how the box should be sealed, how one should insert the small piece of putty into which we had to push our seal when we closed the box, which was identical to what we had to do for the normal SCH process. Those Department heads who received it had to sign a book and identify what they received.

Ducza called our attention to keeping the box sealed even when it is in our office. If we or any of our people had to read something, we should close and seal the box immediately afterwards and had to deposit the box at the SCH office every evening. If we discovered that the box was opened without our permission we had to report it immediately to him.

After Ducza finished, Andris said that he was going to call a meeting for those who worked on the same subject, in order to discuss who was going to do what and also to determine what we were going to need and what had to be completed and on what date to be able to finish the program in time.

After returning to my office with the metal box I reviewed what I had received. It was evident that my Department had to work on the development of three radar tubes. These projects came on top of the other work we had to do, because it was not discussed that we could stop working on anything we were working on at that time. The problem I saw was that this new work was not planned a year ago and by reviewing the package I realized I would need more people, material and also equipment. Every one of these items presented problems.

To hire people could be easy, but where were we going to find technicians and specialists for the laboratories who had any knowledge about these fields?

Ordering materials and equipment presented also big problems. Because of the 'planned economy', materials and equipment should have been planned the year before, but maybe because of the importance of these projects something could be done about it. After I reviewed the documents I received I made for myself a few notes and on the pages which contained the work to be done by my group I made a mark. I called my two chemistry group leaders, Kitty and Magda. They also participated in the session organized by Ducza admonishing us for secrecy, so they knew what the plans were. When we were together I sketched them the situation.

I told them which work they were going to do. They should sit down and look over the content of the metal box. They should consider how many workers they would need and what material they would require for their part of the project. Magda's office was in another part of the building, so I told her that she had to do the work in my office, the box could not be removed from there. She should get herself a chair and sit at one of the desks.

So when Andris convened the meeting of those who worked on the same project I had everything that my department needed. Not everybody was prepared. Andris got very upset. He said that it was not a good beginning and by next day at 2 o'clock in the afternoon he would reconvene the meeting and by that time everybody should be prepared with what they needed for their part of the project. With little hiccups at the beginning we started the most secret, secret project.

We all agreed that we had to hire people, but we agreed also that one could not find qualified technicians or experienced laboratory assistants, and those already working in the labs would also need more education. Therefore we agreed that inside of the laboratory we were going to start a laboratory assistant and technician education course, the curriculum of which we were going to assemble. Everybody volunteered to teach without compensation. Those technicians and laboratory assistants who successfully completed the course should be put in a higher pay bracket. This way we were going to achieve that the workers in the laboratory should be better educated and they should have a reason to learn. The educational courses were started a few days after we decided to do it and it was very successful.

One of the main problems we had was that when we received the text and drawings which we translated from Russian, they also specified every material and its composition, but we did not receive samples of the electron tubes we had to develop. In connection with copying electron tubes, but also any other technical product, the cardinal rule was that one should not "improve" the copied object. I explained this at one of our meetings and said that one of the compositions of a material specified was strange, and we knew we could use something better but we should not try it. We should use exactly the same material specified. It is possible that the composition of the material was strange, but this could have been for two reasons. Either for those who designed or manufactured the object it was the only material available, or that the equipment for one or other reason worked by using only this strange material. As we were not able to find out why they used exactly that material, the safest was to stay with that material specified because we would not make a mistake. I offered that my department would be able to analyze all of the materials which we were planning to use in the tubes to verify that they were exactly what was specified. This was not easy for my lab. to do because many types of material were specified.

In connection with this I was able get a few very interesting research projects approved. One was analyzing materials by utilizing flame photometry, which project was initiated with Gyurka Gergely's Department. The other was the analysis of residual gases in electron tubes, which project was with the Department of Gábor Sebestyén. For this project I was able to hire a chemist, Éva Rieger, who received her diploma of chemistry from the Lórand Ötvös University of Budapest where she was already working with mass spectroscopy. She started to work in my Department in August, 1953. She was a very competent, hardworking, nice, pretty girl. Both of these projects became very successful and resulted in several scientific publications.

The staff of TKI-2 was able to complete all of the development work successfully and on time and presented the documentation for the tubes to be produced by Tungsram. With luck the incredible secrecy was also kept, we had not had a single incident or problem in keeping the secrecy. When the entire documentation in many volumes was on Andris's desk, to transfer this officially to Comrade Fried and representatives of Tungsram, he called the 12 Department heads to his office to thank them, that the documentation and the sample electron tubes were completed on time.

Karcsi Ducza and 11 of the Department heads assembled in Andris's office. Only one Department head, 'uncle' Laci Rotter, was missing. A few minutes later he arrived too, followed by one of his technicians. Both carried two very voluminous books. The books were visibly a series of books. Each had the same binding. The spine of the hard bound books were red with gold lettering, the covers were dark gray. They deposited the books on Andris's desk next to the volumes of documentation. The technician after he deposited the two books turned around and left the office. Andris looked at Rotter with surprise.

Rotter was a short person and was always talking to everybody always very politely, now he said very quietly and politely:

"Andris, I was just in the library and Mrs. Törzs showed me that finally we received the 28 volumes of the MIT[51] Radiation Laboratory's 1947/48 edition, which is 5 years old, that we ordered a few months ago. I brought four volumes from that series. Please look at them. You will see that Volume # 6 title is: 'Microwave Magnetrons', the title of volume # 7 is 'Klystrons and Microwave Triodes'. The third on is Volume # 14 and its title is 'Microwave Duplexers' and the fourth book is Volume # 22 the title is: 'Cathode

[51] Massachusetts Institute of Technology – a very famous University near Boston, Massachusetts

Ray Tube Displays'. If you would look at them like I did it during the last hours, you will see that what we reproduced during the last year under incredible secrecy from the material translated from Russian, the magnetron, klystron, TR tubes and the cathode ray tube, were published in 1947/48, with their detailed description and drawings, by the American McGraw-Hill, 5 years ago." – Probably to emphasize how long ago these books were printed, he repeated the number of years. – "They appeared in print as the work carried out during the war by the MIT Radiation Laboratory. In these volumes, which anybody can buy, everything is printed that the documentation on your desk contains."

Andris adjusted his glasses, picked up the first volume on his table, which was Volume # 6 of the MIT Radiation Laboratory series about the magnetrons, opened it where Rotter had left a paper marker and in the front of his eyes was in printing the detailed description with pictures of the same magnetron tube, the documentation of which, the result of our "most secret, secret project" was also towering on his desk.

17. Auto, auto, auto

In order that today's reader - who is wishing that all the automobiles, including those in which they are spending a considerable amount of their life and in which they are getting slower to their destination, than if they would walk, should go to hell as they are clearly the devil's invention – should understand the situation when everybody's dream was to have one. I would like to tell a story, which will explain it. In the city of my youth some cars existed and were used as taxis but most of the taxis were fiacres, horse driven carriages; in the entire Hungary in 1949 there were only 13,000 passenger cars[52], of which 538 were taxis, less than one thousand were used by private people and the rest of them were all government vehicles. Well, that was the time I decided, that for me the most important thing should be to learn to drive a car and to obtain a driver's license. In order to show how important that was for me, I just mention, that 46 days before I got my Philosophiae Doctorem diploma, (because in those days diplomas were written very elegantly in Latin), on May 31, 1949 I completed my driver license exam and received the license to drive a vehicle used for persons and operated with liquid fuel. I still have this license which as of today I treasure very proudly.

When I signed up in the town of Szeged for the driver education school at Vár Street, I was offered that for the same price they will teach me not only to drive an automobile but also a motorbike. I said I only want to learn

[52] Statistical yearbook – published by the Central Statistical Office (Központi Statisztikai Hivatal) - 1964

to drive an automobile, because if I receive a license to drive a motorbike I may get the idea to buy a motorbike and not an automobile. In retrospect it may have been a mistake to have the ambition to learn to drive a car and not an airplane, because if I would have done that, this story may not have been written.

But at that time I believed, that in spite of my many handicaps first of all, not to have much money, and even if I would have had lots of money one was not able in those days to buy a car without special permission, and on top of that I was not a communist party member, which would have put me to be the last person to buy a car, I still believed that I was going to have very soon a car. The probability of this was as you can understand from the above handicaps really very, very, very small. On top of that the number of passenger cars in the coming years did not increase, but rather diminished. In 1953 the number of passenger cars in Hungary was only 9437 (compared to the above mentioned 13,000 in 1949) and the ones owned by private people decreased drastically, because the cars became old, there were no spare parts to fix them or the starting communist system declared their owners capitalists and confiscated their automobiles. To buy a new car was impossible. No cars were manufactured in Hungary and none was imported from abroad. If it was imported it was only for a high ranking party functionary. That was the background when disregarding time and money I obtained a driver license as I believed that shortly I was going to buy a car.

When I went to Budapest and got a job, naturally I could not buy a car. Instead of a car, I first bought a motorized kayak, then selling the kayak and keeping the motor as I described, because of the unpredictable bureaucracy's surprising result I was able to change my motorized kayak into a nice real motor boat. A few years later, actually in 1953 this motor boat changed into a car. This did not happen that a fairy came and with her magic wand put four wheels on my motor boat, but it happened because of a little kink at that time in the labyrinth of the bureaucracy.

The story started when a good friend of mine Dr. Béla Lajta who was a dentist in Budapest, and whose wife was from Szeged a distant relative of mine, who for some reason still had his car, which was an ancient Italian made Lancia, said that I should go with him to his mechanics, because his car was just fixed. His car was at the mechanics, because Béla who sometimes was still going back to Szeged, during his last trip on the Szeged - Budapest highway stopped at a railway barrier. The barrier was lowered because a train was coming. His Lancia with his passenger, his wife stopped at the barrier, but a big military truck behind him did not stop and pushed Béla's Lancia with him and his wife into the barrier which obviously broke and the car and the broken barrier were moving towards the railroad track. Luckily the broken barrier and the car stopped by a fraction of an inch from the passing freight train, which just roared by.

The driver of the military truck and his passenger got out, went to the car and to the remains of the barrier and expressed their regret for what happened. After they extricated Béla and his wife Éva from the wreck they determined that Béla's car was totally broken and not operational. They also established that on the bumper of the military truck one could see a few small scratches. As they found out later two of Béla's ribs were broken, but besides of being very frightened nothing happened to Éva. The driver of the military truck and his passenger tried to calm down the hysterical Béla and the far more hysterical Éva. At the end they decided, that they are going to lift the Lancia onto the empty truck. This was possible, because on the truck there was some kind of a lifting mechanism. After lifting the badly damaged Lancia onto the truck, they all got in and Béla asked them to take them and the car to his mechanics and after that to take them home. The driver said that he is going to arrange for the repair to be paid.

The Lancia was taken to Béla's mechanics Béla Méhl. who had in Budapest in the Rózsadomb district in Kapor Street near Marczibányi square a house, a yard and a garage where he had a shop to repair automobiles. Béla Méhl, we will call him Béla M. was at home when they arrived and directed skillfully the driver of the truck where to put the Lancia. When the car which was in a very bad condition was standing on its wheels on the ground, Béla - this was Lajta, from now on Béla L. discussed with Béla M. and the truck driver the repair and payment issues. That was during the summer of 1953.

Two months after the accident when I went with Béla L. to pick up his car as he was told that it was ready. It was a pleasant early fall afternoon. We found Béla M. under a car, which he was repairing. Béla M. crawled out from under the car. His clothing, face and hands were full of oil. He was a squaby, strong, broad shouldered balding man. The house where he was living and had his garage was very nice. The yard was full of cars to be repaired. As I found out later that during evenings several mechanics came to help him as he had so much work. He was only repairing cars belonging to privates, but that was a very good business, because the automobiles owned by privates were very old and they spent more time in Béla M.'s yard than used by the owners. When we arrived, Béla M.'s wife– of which I learned later that her maiden name was countess Márta báthorkeszy Báthorkeszy – came to the yard and was pleased to welcome Béla L. I was introduced to her. In the meantime Béla M. cleaned himself a little bit and he and his wife asked us to sit down at the table in the garden part of the yard. Márta asked what we would like to drink. We asked for raspberry soda.

Béla M. pointed to the Lancia which was not far from there:

"Didn't I tell you that it could be completely repaired so no one can see that it was so badly damaged."

Béla L. got up went to the car and inspected it inside and outside finally came back and agreed that it is very nice. In the meantime Márta arrived with the glasses of raspberry soda and sat also at the table. During the discussion Béla L. told them about me, that I was a Department head in TKI. Béla M. asked me if I have this high position, why I did not get a car for myself.

I told him, that for surely I am not going to get a new car and even if I would get one, one has to wait at least three years. Béla M. just waived with his hand.

"You do not have to buy a new car, but on the junkyard one can buy a car type of which there are many used by the government, because for those one can get parts from the drivers of those government cars very inexpensively. I would then reconstruct the junk and it will become a wonderful car."

I found the idea very amusing.

"You mean I should go to the junkyard and by a junk car?"

"No, you cannot do that, because to buy even a junk will require a permit from a Minister. On the other hand if somebody is working in a military research laboratory in such a high position as you, you certainly will get a permit."

Finally Béla L. and I sat in the Lancia and while Béla M. and his wife were waiving, we rolled out from the yard. Béla L. was very happy with the car. One could not see that the car was so badly damaged because it was nicely painted and was running extremely smoothly.

I got intrigued with Béla M.'s advice. Next day I went to Andris Dallos's office, who was sitting behind his desk and as usual, was studying some papers. I told him that I would like to discuss with him an intersting idea and sat down at his conference table. I told him Béla L.'s story and Béla M.'s interesting advise.

Andris showed no interest:

"I cannot deal with such crap. You would do better if instead of chasing such mirage to think about some useful subject. One cannot get permission to buy a new car, and if one would get permission one has to pay the car in advance and wait five years."

"Look this junk car issue costs nothing. I would be a Guinea pig and would submit a petition to buy a wreck on the junkyard. You and Sellei[53] would recommend it, Ducza would recommend it too. Ducza would take it to Rózsadomb and would ask his military boss, Ferenc Biró to recommend it too and he should give it to Ernő Ács to recommend it and to forward it to the Ministry to get the permission. There are two possibilities. They either say OK or say NO. If they say no, the story is finished. If they give the permit to buy a wreck then I go with Béla M. to the junkyard and buy a wreck. After that you can do it too, Sellei also and anybody from the Laboratory as we found the way to do it. Béla M. would be very glad to reconstruct the wreck for all of us."

"Look, I do not have time to fool around with such hair brain ideas."

With this my audience was terminated. I left somewhat annoyed.

Two days later Andris's secretary was looking for me, to go to his office. When I walked in Andris was playing with a little piece of cord. Ducza and Sellei were sitting at his conference table.

"Sit down" – he said. – "I mentioned your hair brain idea about the junkyard to Tibor and Karcsi. They both said, that they would recommend it and Tibor said if it works out he would also buy a wreck," - Tibor and Karcsi nodded. – "So write a petition, we are going to read it and if it is good, we are going to start the matter."

---

[53] In order to refresh the reader's memory: Tibor Sellei was the party secretary of TKI-2, Károly (Karcsi) Ducza first lieutenant was the military liaison officer of TKI-2 and Ernő Ács was the director of both TKI-1 and 2.

"Excellent" – I said and was surprised that Andris in spite of that two days ago showed no interest in the matter, still did something about it – "OK, I am going to write by tomorrow a petition, all of you should read it and give me advice what to change."

By the next day I wrote a one page petition. It was only one page, because I knew that important people who had to recommend it do not read more than that. I wrote that in TKI-1 I am working on programs which are extremely important for the protection and building the socialism. The experimental work makes it necessary that I can be reached any time of the day to go immediately to my laboratories and it is not always possible by utilizing public transportation. For this reason I would like to solve this problem by getting an automobile which I would obtain by rebuilding myself a useless car wreck. Therefore I am asking a permit to buy on the junkyard a car wreck, which I would rebuild and which after according to the rules passes the examination, I could use on public roads.

The secretary typed it from my handwritten draft. I signed it and took it to Andris to his office. He read it, looked at me above his glasses. You could be a great Hungarian fiction writer. Whoever is going to read this, will see immediately that the future of this country and the socialism will depend entirely that you could buy at the junkyard a car wreck. I believe this petition is good as it is. But I am going to give it to Tibor and Karcsi to find out their opinion.

Two days later Andris came to my office:

"The big stone is flying. All three of us wrote a recommendation and Ducza took it today to Rózsadomb to give it to Comrade Ferenc Bíró that he should also write something and give it to Ács, to recommend it and send it to the Ministry."

The big stone was now really in the air, but nobody knew where it was going to land. When about a week later I inquired from Andris or Sellei, neither of them knew anything, they were rather upset that I asked them, so I stopped asking.

18. Decision at the Highest Level

On November 12, 1953, about two months after I handed over my petition to Andris, I received a letter from the Minister of the Internal Affairs, to inform me, that he as well the Minister of the Middle Machine Industry approves that I should be able to buy a discarded automobile at the Autoker Company's Révész Street junkyard which I could restore and after examination receive a license plate. The letter gave me permission that within two weeks from the date of the letter I could buy a useless wreck at that junkyard.

When I read the letter, I ran to Andris's office, where Ducza was also present.

"Thank you for your actions." – I read them the letter. They both looked at me with big eyes.

"What are you going to do now?"

"It is very simple. Today I am going to discuss the matter with the auto mechanic Béla M., who gave me the idea, and ask him that tomorrow we should go to Autoker's Révész Street junkyard. He should select a wreck which he thinks he could repair well and inexpensively and when it will be completed I will probably be the 501st private person who has an automobile in this city of 1 million inhabitants. On the other hand if you want to get a car sit down immediately copy my fantastically well written petition and start on the path which I opened up for you."

With this I turned and left the two guys, who from surprise were not even able to close their mouth. I went to find Sellei, and told him the news, the unexpected letter from the Minister. He was also very much surprised.

"Tibor" – I said – "now you can follow the beaten path and get yourself also an automobile."

"I am going to see what you are going to be able to get tomorrow at the junkyard. We will talk about it, when you let us know."

I called Béla M. whom I found luckily at home. I told him the good news, and asked whether he is going to be at home in the evening, because I would like to meet him to discuss what to do now? He said yes, but I should try to be there between 6 and 7.

Around 6:30 I arrived in Béla M.'s car repair garage combined with his home in Kapor Street. I pulled out the letter from the Minister.

"Excellent" – he said – "after tomorrow, on Saturday we should go to the junkyard at Révész Street to look what selection they have. I suggest we should meet at 11 AM at the entrance of the yard."

We agreed and started to discuss how much this will cost and approximately when the car could be completed.

"I cannot tell you exactly. It obviously will depend on what will be the brand of the wreck we select, what parts and pieces will be required and how much will be the labor to put it together. If we are lucky we are going to find a wreck the same as many government cars are, because as I told you for those I can find parts inexpensively. I assume that it will take 2 to 3 months to finish the car."

On November 14 on a Saturday we met in front of the entrance of the junkyard. Luckily it was a pleasant November day. We entered the office where a middle aged man with a Stalin type mustache and with rolled up sleeves was sitting behind an old, banged up metal desk. He was smoking and was reading a newspaper. Besides of an inkwell and a pen, a couple of pencils were on top of the desk. These were all placed neatly parallel to each other.

"Good day!" – We greeted him in unison. I took the letter I had received from the Ministry from my pocket – "I received permission to buy at this junkyard a useless passenger car wreck."

"I wish you a good day!" – He said and he put down the newspaper, he picked up the letter. He read it very slowly, took from the drawer of the desk a hard bound book, opened it turned over a few pages, picked up the pen from his desk which was next to the inkwell, dipped it into the ink and started to copy something from the letter into the book. After he finished what he had to copy, he put the pen down, closed the book and gave the letter back to me.

"You can go to the yard and within 2 weeks of the date of your letter, from which there are 8 days left, you may select a wreck and when its price was paid, you can transport it from the yard. I have all of the prices, if you want I can give you the sheet of paper, if you find a wreck you want, you can look its price, how much it would cost. In general the price of the wreck is as much as the metal it is made of is worth. At present there are 87 cars on the yard, but the number of them changes daily."

He took now from his desk a paper the size of a label. He wrote my name on it and how long it is valid and signed it.

"With this label you or representative of yours can come here daily and see what is available."

After he said this, Béla M. and I went out through the other door of the office to a large grass covered area, where according to the attendant in the office 87 wrecks were displayed in military order, one parallel to the other. Luckily there was no rain since at least a week and the ground was dry. We methodically walked row after row between the car wrecks. Béla M. inspected each of them very thoroughly. I walked next to him and tried to determine which would be the best for me. Suddenly I was next to a beautiful ancient Rolls Royce cabriolet, which even as a wreck without tires, laying on the ground on its chassis was still imposing. Its once red leather seats were shredded, but its yellow and black paint on the side of the car was still sparkling. A part of its hood was still there and I was able to see its enormous engine. The car was so old, that the gear shift lever was not in the car near the driver, but it was outside of the car on the right side, because the steering wheel was also on the right side designed for the British traffic, where the cars were driving on the left side of the road. When Béla M. noticed that I did not follow him, but got stuck at the Rolls Royce, came back:

"If somebody would reconstruct this, it would be worth a fortune in the West, but here one could not get a single part for it. The Rolls Royce factory in England would be able to supply every part for this car, but here it would be hopeless. This is a Silver Ghost Tourer made in 1910. It would be interesting to know the history of this car, how it winded up at the Autoker's Révész Street junkyard? But it would be better if you would not admire this car, because we have to look at all the cars." – With this he caught my arm and dragged me away.

We reviewed all of the 87 wrecks. He stopped at some of them, lifted some of the wreck's hood, but he did not spend much time with any of them. When we surveyed all of them, he said:

"Let's go back to the Tatra, which is somewhere near the center, I think that would be the best for you."

He turned around went back and stopped at a gray wreck having two doors, no wheels and as I could see the axis of the car was also missing. On the other hand all of the windows were intact but inside there were no seats. Béla M. lifted the hood where one could see that most of the motor was there.

"In this car even the radiator is missing." – I said.

"It is not missing, because this is an air cooled engine. Tatra is a very old Czech automobile factory. It was the third in Europe after Daimler and Peugeot. It started to manufacture cars in 1897. It started to use the Tatra name in 1919. The car which is here is the Type 57A and was manufactured between 1936 and 1938. This car and its famous variation the streamlined T77 was designed by Hans Ledwinka. The interesting story about the 57A is, that Ledwinka told several details of his plan to the German

Ferdinand Porsche, who stole them and used them in 1938 in the Kdf-Wagen, which was later renamed to VW (Volkswagen = People's Car) Beatle. Because of this his company was sued[54]. So this has an air cooled motor, the difference between the Tatra and the Volkswagen is that the Tatra has double cylinders, which means, that two cylinders are together in one block, while the VW each cylinder has a separate block. But that makes no difference. The essence is, that you should buy this one, because I can get all the parts inexpensively from the drivers of the government cars and it will be easy to make a wonderful car from it."

"But in this wreck very many parts are missing."

"That is true, but the body is in good shape, it is not rusted, deformed or dented. In my opinion we do not have to repaint it. It is true that it is not the most beautiful gray. The repair of the body and repainting would be very expensive. The car's windshield and windows are intact they are very valuable now days. As of motor and other mechanical parts, much is here and the others can be easily replaced. So I recommend you should buy this one. After you bought it I will arrange that it should be transported to my yard."

That was when I noticed that the steering wheel was not on the normal location. It was on the right side of the car and not on the left, so I said:

"The steering wheel of this car is on the right side and not on the left where all other cars have it!"

---

[54] In 1961 Volkswagen Company lost the lawsuit and paid 3,000,000 German Mark compensation.

“That is not a problem. In Czechoslovakia, where this car was made they changed in May 1939 the driving from the left side of the road to the right side. In Hungary the change was made later, in June 1941. I mentioned that this car was made between 1936 and 1938 therefore the steering wheel was on the right side of the car. That is not a disadvantage, you have to get used to it.”

*If you think that is not a problem, well, let’s buy it.”

“The change to drive from the left side to the right side is an interesting story, when we are going to have time I will tell you. Let’s go to the office and buy the wreck, I am sorry the car.”

On the way to the office we went by the Rolls Royce, but my heart now belonged to the little Tatra.

In the office I announced that we found a wreck which I would like to buy. The fellow who was still reading the newspaper and still smoking a cigarette, became friendlier, and asked which one I want to buy. Béla M. took a paper from his pocket on which he wrote the location number of the Tatra.

“It would be the Tatra 57A the location number of which is 48.”

“Ah that one? Well, that is in a ramshackle condition.”

“Does not matter, my colleague liked it, and it is especially good, that it has an air cooled engine, and during the winter there is no problem with it.”

“That is true – said the attendant in his short sleeve shirt - and it is not expensive at all, because it is in such bad condition.”

He opened one of the drawers of his desk, took out a bunch of papers and started to look them over page, by page.

“Here it is.”

He took a few papers which were attached to each other and put the rest of them back into the drawer.

He started to study the pages he selected finally he opened another drawer and took out a form. From next to the inkwell he picked up an ink pencil looking thing and started to fill in the form. He asked me to give him back the letter I received from the Ministry. I put it on his desk. Looking at the letter and the papers on his desk he continued to complete the form. When he finished, he looked up and told me the price of the wreck, which was really not much. It was about equivalent to my one month salary.

“Please sign this form. You want to pay it now or when you are going to pick up the wreck?”

I assumed, that I have to give a deposit when we select a wreck therefore I had money with me. As the price was much less than I expected, I had enough money with me to pay the entire amount.

“I think the best is if I pay it now, that way whoever comes to pick it up does not have the complication to pay for it.”

With this I took from my pocket the money and counted the amount he said and put it on the desk.

"Very good." – He said, counted the money and after completing it, picked up the ink pencil and signed the form in two places. The form had two pages. He separated them and handed one to me.

"Who is going to pick up the wreck should bring this paper and I release the wreck to that person. The person has to sign my copy, that he received the wreck. I would like to congratulate you for this car" – I think this was the first time he used the word 'car' and not wreck – "I hope you are going to have lots of pleasure with it!"

I thanked him for the good wishes and I can assure you that neither he nor I had the idea where this little Tatra will ultimately wind up.

He got up, went around his desk and now with a big smile on his face shook hand with both of us.

When we were outside I told Béla M. that I did not believe I am going to be the owner of a car wreck and now I entrust him that he is going to create from it an excellent automobile. He said that on Monday he is going to organize the transportation of the car to his place and I should visit him a week later because by that time he will know approximately when he could collect all the parts needed and how much it will cost the restoration of the car.

We got into Béla M's car. He realy did not own himself any car, but because he always had a few cars to be repaired, he always had one which he was able to use. The one in which we got in was a gray Opel Kadett.

While he was driving me home he came back to the time when the traffic was swiched from the left to the right side.

„The traffic on the roads had no unified rules. It is said, that the traffic on the left side of the roads developed at the time when people traveled either on horse or on foot and because keeping their sword in their right hand they could defend themself better. It is said, that Napoleon ordered the traffic to be on the right side. When his troops left many of the European countries changed to the left side traffic. In Europe except of England evry country switched to right side traffic in the middle of the 1930s. Hungary changed only in 1941. It was done in two steps. The entire country except its capital, Budapest switched in June, while Budapest made the change in November 1941."

I remembered that, because when I was young I went with my parents from Szeged to Budapest. In Szeged we were already driving on the right side of the road but smoewhere before we arrived to Budapest the police was directing the traffic to drive from the right to the left side of the road.

„I do not think that having the steering whel on the right side of the car would cause you problems in driving. Many cars of this kind are still in service in Hungary."

We arrived to Kohary Street. When I got home I told the news to my mother and wife that we became the proud owners of a Tatra 57A type auto wreck.

Monday morning I went to Andris's office. He must have arrived at the same time, because he was just hanging his jacket into his cabinet.

"Imagine, on Saturday I bought a car wreck."

"What did you buy?"

"I told you, I bought a car wreck. On Saturday taking the purchase permit, Béla M. and I went to the Autóker's Révész Street junkyard where in half hour on recommendation of Béla M. I bought a wreck. The car in its better days was a two door little Tatra, but what I bought had no wheels and no seats and most likely several items are missing from its engine, but all of the windows were intact."

"Don't be silly."

"I am not silly. That is what happened. I paid for the wreck, Béla M. is going to arrange today to be transported to his yard and a week from now he is going to be able to tell me how much it will cost and when he thinks it will be ready."

When I got so far with my story, he was already sitting behind his desk.

"That did go with the speed of lightning. I am also interested in this and beside of me Sellei, Pali Havas and Budi are very interested, that they may try it too, if you are successful in this venture."

A week later, when returning from Béla M. I told the news to my mother and Vera that most likely the car will be ready in 2 to 3 months and it will not cost very much, most likely if I sell the motor boat the amount of money I can get for that would pay for the repair of the car.

That was the week, when life in Hungary came to an absolute stand still, because November 25th was the day when the English – Hungarian soccer game was scheduled to be played in the London Wembley stadium. It was heralded in the British press as the soccer game of the century. The Hungarian team the winner of the 1952 Helsinki Olympics was by then unbeaten since three years. The British team was unbeaten at home since 52 years. It was no miracle, that on November 25 everybody was listening to György Szepesi, who was radio broadcasting and commenting the game. The Hungarian team by the goal of Hidegkúti had the lead in the first 90 seconds and by the end of the game they were winning 6:3, with the goals of 3 by Hidegkúti, 2 by Puskás and 1 by Bozsik.

Hungary : England 6:3 - Wembley Stadium - November 25, 1953

Hungary revolutionized the soccer sport. This was an event for which they issued a commemorative postage stamp and everybody in Hungary momentarily forgot their everyday problems and the oppressive communist system.

At the end of this memorable week the TKI-2 prospective car buyers assembled in Andris' office. Obviously I was the center of attention. Besides of me and Andris, Sellei, Pali Havas, Budincsevics and Ducza were present. Ducza said that he is only interested, as at that time he does not have enough money to spend on this.

I told my story and that Béla M. would be glad to help to select their car, independent that the car is going to be repaired by him or not. The discussion was now centered if they should submit their petition together or should do it individually? I did not know what would be best, but at the end Andris's opinion was what they finally decided to do. He suggested that the best would be to submit the petitions all together and not by piecemeal, because that looks better. The matter was left, those who want to follow the path I established to get a wreck car, each should write a petition and those will be submitted together with a recommendation following my tracks. I proposed they all can get my petition from Andris's secretary and with some changes each of them can easily write one. The matter was left, that within one week each of them should give their petition to Andris and also others who decide to join, because after that it probably will not work.

Andris and Sellei said I should tell Béla M. they would also like to have him help to find the proper car and to assemble it. Pali Havas said he has another mechanics, comrade Bikás who is usually repairing his motorbike and he is planning to use him. Budi said, that he is not going to need a mechanic, because he knows how to assemble automobiles and he will do it personally. This ended the meeting.

About two weeks later this auto society was meeting in Andris's office. Andris had three petitions in his hand which he distributed among us to read it. They all resembled my petition, but there were differences between them and therefore it did not look that they were copied from each other. For example Budi's petition started, that he received the Kossuth prize in 1953. Andris's petition was not among them.
We all agreed that the petitions looked very good, but asked where is his petition? Andris said he thought that we should submit these together and he is going to ask advice from Ács that his petition should maybe be initiated not from here but from the headquarter of TKI. Andris promised he is going to write a letter to recommend these petitions and will proceed on the road I pioneered.

I visited Béla M. weekly to see how his work was progressing. During the first weeks the wreck which I called my car was at the same place in his yard where it was originally deposited. Béla M. said the parts are coming and pointed to several boxes and metal pieces.

On Saturdays we only worked until noon. So Saturday was a good opportunity to visit Béla M. and see during daylight what progress was made on the car. About three weeks later I went there on a Saturday afternoon, it was already December, but it was luckily a dry day and warm compared to the season. I found that my car started to make progress. It was still at the same spot, but it was now much above ground. It was layed on wooden trestles and high enough so one could crawl under it. That what I did. I crawled under the car to see what happened. Béla M. was not in the yard. When I was under the car I saw that the entire engine was missing, the engine's compartment under the hood was almost empty, on the other hand the chassis was repaired so that one could not see from below into the car. The rear axis with the differencial in the center was there and had tires on both ends.

I went into his garage. He was working on a car. He closed the hood, showed his hands full of oil and therefore we did not shake hands. He said that the work is progressing. He pointed out the engine of the Tatra, which was in pieces on the beton floor of the garage and told me, that he is going to close the garage for two weeks around Christmas, so I should only come back at the beginning of January, he believed that by that time I will see great progress.

At the end of the first week of January I visited Béla M. to see what happened since I was there the last time. It was a cold gray winter day. When I got there I saw that my Tatra was in front of his garage door, now standing on its four wheels. The door of the garage was closed, which was not surprising because of the cold day. When I got neerer I smelled smoke. I went into the garage it was filled with smoke. Béla M. was there with another man. There was no car in the garage, which looked empty without an automobile. Béla M. and the other man who obvously helped him were busy to wipe and scrub everything with wet rags. As I walked in Béla M. turned around and I saw that his hand and clothing were black from soot. Obviously he was not in a good mood. While we were speaking he continued without stopping to clean various items, tools, table, cans.

It turned out that he had a fire in the garage because some wires caused a short circuit and that ignited some oil. It was lucky, that my car which was in the garage had already wheels and they could push it out when the fire started. They were able to extinguish the fire before greater damage occured, but the fire of the oil produced lots of smoke and lots of soot. Now Béla M. and his helpers, when they had time were coming to help to clean everything. Naturally all work stopped. He said that it was lucky, they had just completed to mount the wheels and tires on the Tatra and they could push it out very quickly and lots of problems were avoided, because the soot whould have painted the Tatra also black. He said, that because of this accident the car will be restored later than he expected. This was not good news, I did not want to hold them up and left.

The second week of January started much better. On Tuersday, January 12, Andris's secretary came and told me that at 11 AM there will be a meeting in Andris's office and I should also be there. When I entered his office Budi and Ducza was already there. I sat down and Pali Havas and Sellei came in immediately. From this I assumed that it will be an 'automobile club' meeting.

Andris summarized the situation:

"On the weekend Uncle Budi, Pali and Tibor received from the Ministry of the Interior a letter similar to what you received" – he pointed towards me - „they can buy at the junkyard a car. They have two weeks to do it. How are you doing with your car?"

"Excellent news that these petitions went through the system as well. What is left now is the execution of the plans. My car is advancing, but Béla M. not long ago ran into a problem that a fire broke out in his garage and therefore my car will be completed only around the middle of February. I asume that Tibor will be the only one who is going to use Béla M. for the selection of his car and for its reconstruction? Pali is going to work with Bikás and Budi, you said that you are going to do it yourself. Is that still the case?

Budi said, that he already went to the Révész Street junkyard and he already selected a car, but he is still thinking about it and is researching if he could find parts for it.

I turned to Tibor:

"You are still planning to work with Béla M.?"

„Yes."

„Then after work we should go straight to see him so you should discuss the matter with him."

„Today would be OK for me."

We started to get up, when Ducza said:

"In connection with buying the automobiles I would like to mention that I talked yesterday with comrade Bíró and he asked me to tell that the headquarter of TKI finds it very important, that Andris should submit a petitions for the reconstruction of a not useful vehicle, which would be important for the national economy the same way as the other petition were accepted. Andris, please write a petition by tomorrow so I could take it to our HQ to be able to send it with recommendations to the Ministry."

Andris looked at us with unease.

"I have so many other more important things to complete that at the moment I cannot deal with this issue."

"Andris, look" – said Ducza – „comrade Bíró instructed me that to take your petition tomorrow to him. As four petitions were already written if you give them to your secretary to write from them a fifth one she would easily do it by tomorrow morning. We review it and by noon I can give it to Bíró."

Andris seemed not to be very happy and waved us to leave.

Tibor and I agreed that after work we are going together by tram to Béla M.

It seemed that they were able to clean the garage, because the Tatra was in the workshop. I introduced Béla M. and Tibor, I pointed to the Tatra, that it was my car. Tibor inspected it and said that it already looks like an automobile. I just could smile and told them that I am not needed and went home.

Next day Tibor came to my office and told me that Béla M. is a very nice guy and they are going that afternoon to the Révész Street junkyard to look for a car. The weather was cold, but sunny it was a suitable day to review the situation there.

Next day Ducza took Andris's petition to the TKI HQ. By the end of the week Tibor became the proud owner of the wreck of an Austin, Pali of an Adler and Budi of a Fiat Topolino.

Austin is a car type made in England. Interestingly there must have been many of this cars in Hungary, because the parts could also be purchased inexpensively.

The Italian made Fiat 500, which was called by everybody Topolino (small mouse) was manufactured during the years 1936 to 1955. It was a very popular small car in those days. It was a simple 4 cylinder, two seater, which probably had lots of parts in Hungary. Budi's car could have been 15 years old.

Adler was a German car, which was tchnically very advanced compared to other cars of that time. Its gear shift was attached to the steering wheel's shaft. Its Triumph model which was manufactured from 1930 was a front wheel drive car, compared to any other car, which in those days were all rear wheel driven cars. Adler was not manufactured after the war.

Andris's permit to purchase a wreck came about a month and a half after Ducza carried his petition to the TKI HQ. Andris also selected Béla M. as his expert. By that time my car was already operational and I drove Andris to Béla M.

with whom he discussed the matter and during the next day they visited Autoker's Révész Street junkyard and selected a spinach colored Opel Kadett. Opel was a German manufactured car of which relatively many were in use in Hungary, statistics indicated that ten years later, in 1964 they were still 4,575 Opel in circulation in Hungary, which was in that year after the Moskvics, Trabant, Skoda, Wartburg and Warsawa the largest number of automobiles in circulation.

Interestingly nobody else from TKI-2 employees signed up to get a car, not even after all of our cars were in operation. Next to the TKI-2 entrance three cars were parked every working day: Tibor's blue Austin, Andris's spinach colored Opel Kadett and my gray Tatra 57A. Pali when the weather was nice arrived on his big motorcycle – and when the weather was not so nice, arrived in his red Adler. Budi's beautifully painted, chrome and gold plated Topolino was never there. One of the reason was that he lived very close to the Laboratory and he rather walked, he also did not want, that his beautifully painted, chrome and gold plated car should be dusty, furthermore as he assembled the car himself, most of the time it was not working.

19. On My Magic Steed

Béla M. called that the Tatra will be ready by next Saturday (February 20, 1954) and I should go to his garage to take possession of it. Béla L. came in his Lancia to pick me up, so we went together to get the car. On the way he asked me when was the last time I was driving a car? I said it was almost five years ago, in 1949 when I made the examination to get my driver license, but I told him that in my opinion learning to drive a car is similar to learning to use a bicycle or learn swimming, if somebody learns it how to do it even if one has not practiced for years. Instantly developing this theory seems that I had enough self-esteem to start my new adventure.

In Béla M.'s yard my Tatra with its front facing the exit gate seemed to be ready to go. In the sunlight the gray color of the car looked matt. I was prepared for that as the car was not repainted. Luckily the paint well covered the car it just was not bright. Béla M. told me when we bought the car that sooner or later I have to get it repainted.

When we arrived Béla M. was around the Tatra. When he saw us opened the iron gate of his yard and Béla L. drove in. We got out of the Lancia and Béla M. waived to us to go to the Tatra. After greetings he lifted the hood of the car and started to explain what is what.

The cover of the two front wheels was also a part of the hood of the Tatra 57A. This meant that when the cover of the motor, the hood is lifted the wheel covers as part of the hood are lifted together. Béla M. lifted the hood and pulled up a rod attached to the front of the engine compartment and put the end of it in a round sleeve attached to the hood to support it. Standing under the hood with the wheel covers looked like we would step into the open mouth of a hippopotamus. Béla M. pointed out one by one the parts of the engine, which I will have something to do with. He said, that if the weather is cold, for example under -2 °C (about 28 F) the starter probably will not be able to start the car, because the motor oil is too viscous, then I have to crank the engine. He went to the car opened the door and pulled out the crank from under the driver's seat. He went to the front of the car inserted it in a round hole on the front of the engine and showed me how to use it. He also said when the weather is cold it is advisable to push down the little knob on the carburetor once or twice, which would squirt a little gas into the engine. He also said that under -5 °C (23 F) I probably will not be able to start the car, not even by cranking, because the motor oil will be too viscous. He showed me how I can check how much oil was in the engine. There was a little tube on the motor and inside of it was a little metal rod with a handle. He pulled it up and one could see oil on it. He wiped the rod clean and inserted it into the tube and pulled it out. One could see the oil, but only at the end of the rod up until a little engraved mark. He said it is advisable to check this from time to time. If the oil is only half way to the mark, I should add oil. He showed me what I have to unscrew where I should be able to add some oil.

After he explained everything in connection with the engine, he went to the back of the car and showed me the spare tires mounted on the back of the car and also showed the tools to be used if I have to change tires. After this he said, he is going to drive the car. I should sit next to him and he is going to show me how things are operating to drive the car. Béla L. said he is coming with us and sat on the rear seat. I sat next to Béla M. I knew the inside of the car pretty well, because when I visited him before he had shown me the inside, the dashboard and the other parts and pieces to operate the car. When we were in the car, he started the engine. He waited for a minute, until the engine was running smoothly, pressed down the clutch, pushed up the gear shift handle to put it in first gear and the car slowly started to roll towards the open gate of the yard, rolled out to the road, where Béla M. turned the steering wheel to the right and the car turned right. In the meantime he told me what he was doing and what I should be careful when I am driving the car. After we went several blocks, he stopped the car turned the motor off and told me we should change seats as I should drive the car. He told me to start the car and drive it back to his yard. So, not even 5 years after I received my driver license and imagined at that time that in spite of incredible odds I am going to have a car soon, I sat behind the steering wheel of my own car.

As I sat behind the wheel, in spite of the cool February afternoon, a heat wave came over me. I started the engine, depressed the clutch, shifted to first gear and slowly but confidently started to go back to Béla M.'s yard. I stopped on the street in front of his yard. I stopped the motor pulled in the hand break, looked at Béla M. and Béla L., both applauded, and with a modest nod I thanked them for the applause and we got out of the car.

We went into Béla M.'s house where he invited us to sit at the table, Márta came in also, congratulated me for obtaining a car and also for the successful trial run. She sat down too. Béla M. opened a bottle of red wine, picked up four glasses from the dresser, and poured the wine. All of us rose our glasses, clicked them and the three of them wished me good trips. Béla M. took from his pocket the key of the car and the car papers he pushed them to me and wished the best to the owner of the car with the license plate CL 149 - that was me. I thanked Béla M. for his excellent idea how one can buy an automobile in Hungary in 1953, because without his suggestion I would still be the owner of a motorboat which cannot be used during the cold winter months. I did not have any more problems with the motorboat as it miraculously was transformed into this car. At this point I took out the money I received for the motor boat, counted the price he had asked for the regeneration of the car and put it on the table. We emptied our glasses. Márta stood up and said that she has to go back to the kitchen where she was cooking, we shook hands and she wished me again good luck.

Béla M. told me that the tank is full of gas and gave me a few gasoline and motor oil rationing coupons, because the gasoline and motor oil could have been bought only for coupons. He told me, that because I have my auto license these gasoline and motor oil coupons will be sent to me monthly by the proper authority in my case the one which is in the district where I live, the V. district's Council's Finance Department. The gasoline coupons were for 20 liters and the oil for 1 liter each. They were valid for the month the gas stations were selling gas only if one had the coupons. Béla M. said that I should use it every month, but the gasoline on the black market is cheaper, than the gas purchased with the coupons. He said that it is especially cheap at the gas station which is two blocks from the Parliament building, because lots of government cars are in that area and the drivers of the government cars receiving more coupons than they need and leaving lots of coupons at the gas stations the operator of which sells it cheap since he and the driver split the money.

Gasoline and motor oil rationing coupons (1956)

I thanked him for the information and said that because of my motor boat I received coupons also, but I bought gas usually near the shore so I should not have to transport the gasoline on the trams and therefore I did not know about the black market gas prices. The gas station he mentioned on the corner of Marko Street and Bálint Balassi Street, two blocks from the Parliament was very near to my apartment and that is where I am going to buy gas.

Béla M. also mentioned, that the paint on the car is not very good and during the Spring it would be good to repaint it, but he does not know where I would be able to obtain paint. I told him that this was not a problem, because I already discussed this with my colleagues at the Research Institute of the Lacquer Industry and they said that they would be glad to make paint for my car in the color I wanted and I can repaint the car. I repainted it during the spring, but unfortunately the paint used for the car made by the Lacquer Industry Research people lasted only one year, when it started to wear off and I had to repaint the car yearly. So my car had a different color every year. In one year they could not make enough from one color and in that year my car had two colors. The top was white, the lower part, including the hood was gray.

Béla M. was very interested in this, because he said, that several of the cars he is servicing need repainting. But told him, that is not possible, because it is not permitted for them and they do not have enough material for it.

Béla M. also said, that he rebuilt the motor of the car very well, but some of the material he could get is not that good. For example the piston rings he could buy are of bad quality and probably had to be replaced yearly. He suggested that he would buy for me on the junkyard another motor which he would rebuild during the year and a year from now he would exchange the presently used motor with that one. He could do the exchange of the motors in about one hour. He said that this will not be expensive, but would guaranty that my car will always be in good running condition. This was an excellent idea and I told him to do it.

We picked up our coats and Béla M. escorted us to his yard. Béla L. Got into his car and I in mine and started in the direction of the Margaret bridge. It was a pleasure to drive on the empty streets. Today one cannot imagine this, when the streets are bumper to bumper filled with cars, but in those days there was practically no car traffic. At the end of 1954 there were a total of 10,083 passenger cars in the entire Hungary[55]. They were 1872 privately used, 1300 taxis and the difference was government operated cars

---

[55] Statistical Yearbook (Statisztikai Évkönyv) Central Statistical Office (Központi Statisztikai Hivatal) 1965

(about 7,000). 40% of the passenger cars were in Budapest, it means about 4,000 – 5,000 cars. If we divide this with the number of streets in that big city it makes it clear there were at any time only very few passenger cars even on the most important boulevards.

On the empty streets I saw only overcrowded trams and buses and maybe one or two trucks coming from the other direction. Thinking over my story with automobiles that in 1949 I imagined in spite of my many handicaps soon I was going to have a car, and now less than five years later I became one of the maybe less than two thousand people who has his own automobile in this country of ten million inhabitants. It suddenly occurred to me that what can happen to somebody is what the person imagines. This means that one has the possibility to achieve something only if one imagines it beforehand and if something is not imagined it simply will not happen. The world is nothing else but the result of one's imagination?

Tatra 57A – License plate CL 149 and the author - 1954

I parked the car near the sidewalk on the opposite side of the street at the entrance of 16 Koháry Street. I pressed the car's horn three times stopped the engine, got out of the car, closed the door and locked the car. I saw my mother, Vera and Éva standing on our first floor balcony. I waived and they waived back and I went to the door of the apartment building up to our apartment.

I immediately offered if somebody wants to come I would be glad to drive them around the city. There were no takers. As it started to get dark I believed that for one day I had enough excitement. Tomorrow I would take my car on its first trip. I however went down again to try how to drive the Tatra into its garage.

When I bought the car wreck I thought that when it will be completed I shall need a garage for it. One of the reasons to keep the car in the garage is for example snowy or very cold days. It was needed also to keep spare tires, and to store gas cans, tools, etc. I saw that in our neighborhood not a single car was parked on the street, which was not surprising having only few private cars in the city, but I also realized that in this neighborhood – in the Lipót district – when they built the houses, automobiles did not exist yet, so why should have been garages built? I walked all over the neighborhood and did not find a single place which would have been suitable for a garage, except in the Balaton street in the building opposite to our window was maybe a possibility. The main entrance of that building was on 17 St. István Ring. That large building which was not only facing St. István Ring but also Koháry and Balaton Streets and had another entrance from Balaton Street That was a huge double door made of very heavy thick wood, which was always closed. When I entered the building through its St. István Ring entrance, I noticed, that the Balaton Street entrance was similar to the one at the St. István Ring, one and a half floor high vaulted "tunnel" leading from Balaton Street to the building's yard. The only difference was that while from the St. István Ring entrance there was a staircase leading up to the upper floors, there was no staircase from the Balaton street entrance. It was only a connection between Balaton Street and the courtyard of the building.

I believed, that if this door is always closed and is not being used I could have the permission to build a wall at the end of this vaulted tunnel, where the yard is, then this tunnel would be an excellent garage for my car. I found the "caretaker" of the building, and I told him my plan. For this occasion I gave him a nice tip and told him that when I am going to get the right to establish my garage I will not forget him. I found out from him, which office is responsible for the administration of this building and who is dealing with the building. The caretaker seemed very happy about this solution, because of the possible tips also as he said he does not have to clean the area, which he would be very glad to clean if I would ask him.

I visited the office responsible for the building, which was also on the St István Ring in another building. Two ladies were sitting in that office each behind a desk. One of them was a middle aged woman, who in her heyday must have been a good looking lady. Now her brown hair, which she had pulled together in a bun she had some white hair too. The other one was a young woman also with brown hair and with a pretty face. On their desks was a tremendous amount of paper.

I greeted them very friendly and told them, that I am living in 16 Koháry Street, which building belonged also to the same office and I was talking with the caretaker of the 17 St István Ring building, who told me, that I should come to this office and I should look for Zsófika. As it turned out Zsófika was the younger woman.

I told them, I am a department head in TKI and because of my important work I got permission to buy a car, which will be ready very soon. I saw, that this made a big impression on the two ladies, to be the owner of a car in those days it was rarer than a white raven, I assume they believed I am a person in very high position and who knows what kind of connections do I have. I outlined for them my plan that I would like to use the unused Balaton street entrance of the St István Street building as a garage for my car, by putting a wall at the end of that vaulted tunnel, separating it from the yard. Obviously I would pay rent for that area as much as they think would be a fair price. I will take care of the maintenance of the area and would use the caretaker of the building to keep it clean. If they want to use the entrance in the future I would restore it to its present condition and the wall which I would build will be removed at my expense.

Zsófika said, my proposal is very reasonable, because it would yield more income and the entrance is not used at all at the present time, but she has to discuss the matter with the manager of the Building Management Office, I should come back the next day, she is going to arrange the deal.

The next day I went back to the office and Zsófika said they accept my proposal and gave me an agreement to sign. The monthly rent was relatively low so I signed it immediately. Interestingly nobody asked the tenants in the house about their opinion that I am going to wall off one of the entrances to the building. After I signed the agreement I installed the wall to separate my “garage” from the yard of the building, I got the entrance door to the street repaired changed the lock and got new keys and by the time my car was finished its garage was also completed.

I went down to the street, got into my car, turned on the engine of the Tatra and drove to the Balaton Street garage, opened its door and drove in. My mother and Vera were still in our apartment’s Balaton street window and observed from there how I am putting our car into our new ‘garage’.

20. Tatra's maiden voyage

The next day, February 21, Sunday was a cool, gray winter day. We ate lunch early, as I said that after lunch I am going to try out the car. Nobody from my family volunteered to accompany me. My mother said she has laundry to do. My mother in-law's excuse was that she previously invited an acquaintance for coffee and will arrive momentarily.

Vera excused herself saying, that she is pregnant and would not join me. This was legitimate, because we married during the summer of 1951 and were expecting our first child. Vera was also from Szeged, I knew her since our childhood. She attended the University first in Szeged and continued in Budapest. She received a diploma to teach English and German, but in Hungary at that time neither of these languages was thaught in schools. Vera was teaching neither English, nor German, but was teaching math in the Szinyei Merse public school for boys. Magda Szabó[56] was in the same school teaching Hungarian. In 1949 she was awarded the prestigious Baumgarten Prize, which was - for political reasons - withdrawn from her on the very day it was given. She was dismissed from her job and winded up teaching also in the Szinyei Merse public school for boys. Her writings were not published until 1958. Vera and I became good friends with

---

[56] **Magda Szabó** (October 5, 1917 – November 19, 2007) was a Hungarian writer, arguably Hungary's foremost woman novelist. She also wrote dramas, essays, studies, memories and poetry. (http://en.wikipedia.org/wiki/Magda_Szab%C3%B3).

Magda and her husband Tibor Szobotka, also a writer. This friendship and exchange of many letters and mailing for her medicine remained until Magda's death in 2007.

The Szinyei Merse public boy school was raided many times by the police. The reason was that the school was very close to the Zoo and the boys ready for action – for example managed to put their teacher in a closet and nailed its door shut – but also were regularly stealing animals from the Zoo. The purpose of the police raid was to recover the animals for the Zoo.

Vera expected the baby for the end of March and she was sure it will be a girl and she had decided to name her Éva Anna[57]. because her two best friends, one was Anna, whose father bottled the mineral water of Szeged under the name of 'Anna water'. The other was Éva Janikovszky[58] who was from 1953 editor and later Chief Editor of Mora Book Publishing Company in Budapest. Éva later became world famous with her children's books.

---

[57] Éva Anna was born March 30, 1954

[58] **Éva Janikovszky** (April 23, 1926 – July 14, 2003) wrote novels for both children and adults, but she is primarily known for her children's books, translated into 35 languages. (http://en.wikipedia.org/wiki/%C3%89va_Janikovszky)

Éva Janikovszky and Vera Váradi – 1948

As nobody of my family was willing to be my first passenger, after lunch I went alone to take my car for its maiden voyage. My family looked from the window to see what I was doing. I opened the garage door, got in my car, started the engine, depressed the clutch, put into first gear, took my foot off the break, gave careful gas and the car slowly started to move. After I left the garage, stopped the car, pulled in the hand break, got out of the car, closed the big havy doors of the garage and locked it, got back into the car. I started on Balaton Street, turned into Koháry Street and the next corner was St. István Ring where I turned right. My plan was to take Váci boulevard and drive until I arrived at Tungsram, this way at least I was going to learn the road which I have to take daily starting the next morning to reach where I was working. Next to the West Railroad Station I turned onto Váci boulevard and on the empty road at which time a #3 streetcar rattled by, I proceeded slowly and deliberately toward the outskirts of the city. I used the gear shift as neded, it seemed that I was right when I announced that if one learned it one cannot forget bycicling, swimming or driving an automobile. Peoples memory is full of shreds, which at some point get in and just stay there. Like a song from a Hungarian movie hit before the war (Meseauto) just occured to me and as it was fitting the occasion I started to hum:

In a Dreamcar near a sterling silver forest
We fly in the spring of our hearts.
On a gold road's glittering diamond dust
We fly in the car of a fairytale.

Perhaps this is just a dream.
And after the happiness
Already by tomorrow the truth will stare at me
I should not wake up yet.
I beg you, O great God!
Let me continue to dream[59.]

I arrived to the end station of the # 3 streetcar and followed the # 87 tram line on the continuation of the Váci Boulevard.

I arrived to the Tungsram factory, I started to like very much to drive this car, so I did not turn back, but continued, passed Tungsram's water sport facility, which being February was closed and continued now on the highway towards Vác. There was nobody on the road and I wanted to try how fast can I drive this car. According to Béla M. the maximum speed should be not more than 60 km/hour (about 40 ml/hour), because the engines revolution would be too fast and that could be detrimental. So I raised the speed of the car only o 60 km/hour. The motor was

---

[59] Alfréd Márkus, Mihály Eisemann, István Békeffi

humming very uniformly. Next to the empty gray highway some houses started to appear, I arrived at the village of Dunakeszi and slowed to 40 km/Hour. Here the road was between the village and the Danube. When I was out of the village I raised the speed again to 60 km/hour. The car followed very well when I gave more gas. The next village was Göd after that was Szödliget and shortly I arrived at Vác.

There was practically no taffic. In the center of the city several people walked on the streets. I also saw a few smal trucks. When I arrived in the center of the city I turned left in the direction of the Cathedral. I decided that I am not going alloway down to the Danube, but making two left turns and be back on the highway towards Budapest.

As I started to drive on that street going to Budapest, I saw a bus station on the right side where two women were standing. The head of both were covered with kerchiefs. As I neared them one of them raisd her arm and waived indicating that I should stop. I stopped. The two elderly women with their kerchiefs came to the car. I rolled down the window on the right side of the car. One of the two bent down and looked into the car.

"Please, are you going to Budapest?"

I was surprised by the please, but in a second I realized, that she could not have said Mister, because anybody who would be happy to be addressed as Mister would not have an automobile. She could not say comrade because she did not want to offend me or she just could not bring herself to say comrade. Dear would have meant a more intimate relation and that left it with the awkward please.

"Yes, I am going to Pest."

"Would you be so nice and take us to the first tram station in Budapest? We are coming from Rád[60] and we are waiting for the bus since a very long time, but it looks like they either are not operating at this time or on Sunday there is no bus, but we have to go to Pest. Would you be so kind and take us?"

"Sure, with pleasure. Get in the car."

The Tatra was a two door car. I opened the door on the other side and shifted the seat next to me forward so one of the elderly ladies could sit on the back seat. They were my first passengers, but I did not tell them, so they should not be afraid like my family, or be alarmed.

One of the women climbed to the back seat and the other sat next to me. The lady next to me tried to close the car door, but she could not reach far enough, because on a car with two doors the doors are quite large. I set the hand break got out and closed it. I got back in, released the hand break, and pushed the directional signal switch to the left. The car was equipped with a mechanism on both sides of the car, when I switched the direction indicator to the right then on the right side and when I switched to the left then on the left side of the car an about a 20 cm (14 inch) little red colored plastic arm having a lamp inside popped out to indicate which direction I intend to go. There was no traffic, but my passengers should see how meticulously I follow the rules I pushed the switch to the left, as that was the direction to leave the sidewalk and enter the traffic.

---

[60] Rád is a little village near Vác.

I shifted the gears very accurately and in a few seconds it was in the third gear and the car was running very smoothly at a 40 km/hour speed. I told the ladies that my name is Ferenc and they should call me accordingly. I asked their names. The woman next to me was Panni and the other introduced herself as Julia. She repeated what they told me before they got into the car that they are coming from Rád and they waited for the bus more than a half hour, It should have come, but it is possible, that on Sunday there is no service. She said that they are going to her daughter who is married and living on the Buda side of the city.

I offered to drive them to the West Railway station, which is on the Pest side of the city, as I am living in that area. The West Railway station area has very good tram connection to Buda where they were heading.

They were very happy and thanked me several times.

When we got out of Vác to the highway my passengers sort of warmed up. Panni, who was sitting next to me took a handkerchief from her little bag and started to wipe her eyes. When I looked at her I could see that she was quietly crying or was trying to stifle her crying. I did not want to disturb her and said nothing. We arrived at Göd when Julia, who sat on the rear seat leaned forward stroked the shoulders of Panni.

“Panni” – she said – “I trust that everything will be all right and when we will be back in Rád you will also see that I was right.”

In order to divert their attention when Panni was crying, I said that I was a chemist and I am working at the Tungsram's Research Laboratory, which is here on Váci Boulevard before we get to Budapest.

Panni who was continuing to wipe her eyes said nothing, but Julia said that she knew which is Tungsram as they always pass it when they go to Budapest. Then asked:

"Is this your car?"

"Yes, but as I said I am working in the Research Laboratory of Tungsram, which was recently renamed Távközlési Kutató Intézet (Telecommunication Research Institute). I am a reseach chemist, I am neither a part functionairy nor a member of the Party."

"Ferenc are you a city dweller?" – Julia asked, from the tone of her voice one could feel that she closed the previous subject, as it was established that the car they are in is not a government car and the owner is neither a party funcionary or a member of the Party, started to say what was on her mind.

"Yes" – I said – "I always lived in a city. I was born in Szeged and attended schools there, but a few years ago I got a job here at the Tungsram Research Laboaratory."

"You people in the city do not know what life is in the villages." – This was not a question, it was a statement.

"No, I really do not know, I was not outside of a city except when my aunt was deported in 1951 to Tápiógyörgye, which is a village between Cegléd and Nagykáta. Now she was able to transfer to Vecsés and I visited her in both of these places."

"Deported? Why?"

"Her husband, my oncle, in June 1950 disappeared, did not come home, and since that time we do not know where he is. Later we found out that most likely he was taken to Andrássy út 60 and could still be there but it is possible, that he was transferred to some other place. In 1951 she was deported."

Panni hearing this story took out her handkercdhif and started to wipe her eyes. Julia continued:

"Then you cannot imagine what is happening in the villages. Panni and her family and also us we, each of us owned a small land. My husband suddenly died two years ago. That happened when they came to us and told my husband, that he did not fulfill his delivery obligation, if he is not delivering it within 48 hours they are going to come for him. When they left my husband sat down on a chair and asked for a glass of water. By the time I arrived with the water I found him with his face on the table, he just died. When they came back after 48 hours there was nobody to be taken in and ask to fulfill the delivery. They said they will be back after the funeral and left. On the next day I transferred our land to the agricultural co-operative. We have two children, my son who is now 28 years old is a sales person in the Keravill[61] store in Újpest. His wife is also with Keravill in the office on Váci Boulevard. My daughter is also married. Her husband works for the railroad. The are living in Vác. Panni and her husband, like

[61] State owned electric products and appliance stores.

we had, have a small land. Propagandists who were called 'educators of people" visited them and told Panni's husband that he either will join the co-operativ or they will arrange that he should be put on the list of kulaks. The next day other propagandists showed up and in front of their house they were singing:

"This kulak is the type
Who is hindering the Co-ops.

„Subsequently they searched their house and found a pan full of fat. They took her husband away and told him they are going to find out that secretly he had a pig which was not delivered, but sloughtered. She has only one daughter whom we are going to visit, because we think if they would offer their land to the co-op they would let Panni's husband out."

Panni started now to cry more noticeably.

"Do you know what the 'collection plan' is?"

"I only know what I am reading in newspapers or hear on the radio."

With my coleagues we rarely discussed anything about agricultural co-ops, small holders or kulaks. We only discussed it because one could find less and less food in stores and the papers reported that this is the result that the kulaks are sabotaging the delivery, but the government made already steps to solve this problem. When Julia asked me if I know what the collection plan is, it occured to me that I knew about it. They tried to force the independent farmes into an agricultural co-operative. One method to do this was to prescribe how much food stuff they have to deliver, and those who could not do it - even when their family would not have anything to eat – they were severly punished.

”As I said my husbnd died two years ago, our children went to work in the city, as other people fled also, becaause it was impossible to fulfill the delivery obligation. I transferred our land to the co-op and now I am working there. This way they leave me alone and I do not have to work as much as I did while we were independent. On the other hand my salary is not enough to live on. Many people from the village did that, many left and went to the city to work there. If somebody was not doing that they were submitted to land consolidation.”

“What is land consolidation?”

“They said that to produce more the land of the co-op has to be in one piece and not pieces here and there. If somebody's land was near the co-op's they took it away and they received land somewhere else usually the land was useless for growing anything. These people at the end transferred their land to the co-op and moved to the city. There is no purpose to keep animals, because it requires a slaughtering permit and it is required how much they have to deliver to the state. If somebody could not do it the person was arrested and disappeared. For this reason the best is if there are no animals. But then they come and ask why they do not keep animals? Because of this it is no wonder one cannot get food in the cities.”

I noted, that us living in the cities do not even have an acquaintance who is living in villages we only notice that there is less and less food in the stores.

We arrived to the West Railroad station. I stopped my car across from the Railroad station at the beginning of the Váci Blvd. I got out, opened the door on the other side and helped the two ladies to get out of the car. Both women fixed their kerchief, embraced me and I received from each of them a kiss on the cheek and Panni started to cry again. Julia tried to quiet her. They profoundly thanked me for my help, asked God's blessing for me. I pointed out where the # 6 tram's station which is going to Buda is and tried to comfort Panni that things will be better.

I got back into my car and started the engine. The two ladies were waving I waved back and started to drive the few blocks home. Listening to the stories of these two ladies it was not easy to comprehend that in this world I am driving my car practically alone in Budapest. It seemed to me the way I am living here is like a showman in the circus I am driving and balancing this car on a tight rope 20 stories high, but there is no safety net below me, which would catch the car when it is needed. Under poor Panni and Julia there is no safety net either to protect them.

21. Pony Express

Budapest's public transport system before the war compared to other European cities was good. In continental Europe,[62] Budapest was the first city to build an underground line, which was inaugurated on May 2, 1896, and it is still in operation. Because of the war and for other reasons Budapest's public transportation system deteriorated very badly. Another problem was that the number of passengers substantially increased. At the beginning of the 1950s the situation did not change much, if anything it became worse. Tungsram was located in Újpest (4th district of Budapest) on the outer Váci Blvd, but a great majority of my colleagues, including me, lived in the city. The only way to get from the city to the entrance of Tungsram was to take either the # 3 or the # 55 street car lines at their city terminal which was near the West Railroad Station, to the border of Újpest and transfer there to the # 87 tram line which had a station at the main entrance gate of Tungsram. Because of the large passenger traffic, the # 3 and # 55 streetcars had two cars hitched together. The number of passengers was so large that even operating each tram with two cars, when they left the terminus they were not only overcrowded inside, but clusters of people were hanging outside of the cars. People were hanging on steps, standing on the bumpers in between cars and in general wherever they could stand on or hang on to something.

---

[62] The first Underground Railroad (Metropolitan Railroad) was inaugurated in London on January 10, 1863.

Overcrowded streetcars in Budapest[63] – 1948 to ?

At the terminus of the # 3 tram (the # 55 continued into Újpest) one had to transfer to the # 87 line which route was on the outer Váci Blvd next to the Tungsram factory, until its terminus at the Megyeri Inn, which was practically the outer border of Budapest. There the tram driver got out and went to the front of the tram. There was a rope which was connected to the pantograph which could be pulled forward and thereby the tram was able to go back from where it came. He pulled it over. Then he went to the end of the tram, which became now the front. He climbed back to the driving console and when he felt the time was right, he started the tram to go back.

This was the dream, but what was the reality? Before the # 3 (or # 55) arrived at their Újpest station where the passengers who wanted to go to Tungsram transferred to # 87, the # 87, which was a one car and fairly small tram,

---

[63] http://rajnoha.alon.hu/index.php/2011/04/14/mi-jut-eszembe-egy-fenykepr-l?blog=8

departed with a very few passengers aboard. Passengers on # 3 noticed this and jumped off the still moving # 3 and started to run after the now departing # 87. When they caught up with the accelerating # 87 they swung themselves up. The technique of this was that while running they caught the metal railing of the steps, jumped in the air and with the help of their arm muscles swung themselves up onto the stairs. It also happened many times, that those who could not reach # 87 but were close enough caught the rope of the pantograph then pulled it down. As the tram's contact with electricity was lost it slowed down and stopped. That made it possible for more people to transfer to the # 87.

I was an eye witness of this several times. On one occasion our colleague Laci Rotter ran after the accelerating # 87. He was able to catch the rope attached to its pantograph and pulled it down, so the streetcar slowly stopped. The tram driver looked back and started to swear loudly expressing his displeasure although he should have been used to it. Usually there was a policeman in the vicinity, who occasionally started to walk in the direction of the person pulling the rope of the pantograph, but seeing the angry crowd streaming from the # 3 retreated quickly.

The reason for this mad rush was that the working hours started at 8 AM and whoever was late was posted on the factories' – or in our case the Laboratory's – 'Shame-board' in TKI. This 'Shame-board' was posted on the wall in the hall opposite the main entrance. Daily the names of people who were late that day were posted and in a separate column the names of those who were twice or more times late were listed.

To arrive at exactly 8 AM with the ridiculous public transportation in Budapest was very difficult. It happened many times that even if somebody left in time from home, he or she could not make it in time. These ‘Shame-boards’ had to be sent daily to the TKI main personnel department and from there a warning was sent to Ducza and Dallos, that the disciplinary conditions in the Laboratory were unacceptable and they should finally take some action to rectify it. From time to time Andris assembled all the workers of the Laboratory and tried to explain that on the road to socialism one has to get used to start the working day at an exact time and late arrivals must be taken very seriously and a process would be started against those who were notoriously late. There were many of those. The secretary of Andris made a statistic and determined that the majority was less than half hour late.

Finally Andris came to the brilliant idea that he was going to reset the clocks in TKI-1 by a half hour, which meant that when in the entire Hungary, even in the entire Europe, the clocks showed half past eight the clocks in TKI would show exactly eight o’clock. As the statistics made by Andris’s secretary indicated that the majority was late by less than a half hour, those people would now arrive in time, therefore the ‘Shame-board’ would display only very few people. The idea worked out excellently. The number of people being late decreased so much that the TKI HQ’s personnel department sent its congratulations that the disciplinary problem had been successfully solved.

Unfortunately the excellent disciplinary situation did not last long. People got used to the half hour and started to come late. A few months later there were about as many names on the 'Shame-board' as before the clocks were reset. Andris was requested to go to the TKI HQ personnel department where he was confronted with the shameful data of TKI-1's 'Shame-board'. They told him that this could not be tolerated. Andris became very angry.

When he returned to the Laboratory in Újpest he requested that everybody should show up at a meeting. When everybody was there, Andris entered and looked at us, like Moses must have looked when he arrived from the mountain with the stone tablets and saw people dancing around the golden calf. His voice was thundering like Moses's, he said that he tried to solve the 'Shame-board' issue by shifting the time, but it looked like this did not help the workers of the Laboratory, so from the next day on the TKI -1 would return to European time and whoever was not arriving in time would get proper disciplinary action.

The public transportation improved a little on the Váci Blvd by adding a new autobus line, the # 50, the terminus of which was on a small square on the west side of the West Railroad Station. The bus went on the Váci Blvd to Tungsram and also a little bit past it. The bus used on route # 50 was probably the smallest and worst autobus of the Budapest public transportation system. In all respects it was a blessing. It was a bit more expensive but improved the commuting for those working on Váci Blvd. This naturally applied only to those who were able to find a place on it.

During the morning obviously everybody was going out from the center of the city, the buses returning were empty. Those people who were athletic waited for the returning empty bus arriving at the entrance of the small square where the bus had to slow down and jumped on the moving vehicle. The autobus slowly arrived at its station, where a huge crowd was waiting for it. The crowd had no mercy for anyone, stormed the bus and transformed the inside of the bus into an overcrowded sardine can. Outside the bus the same system was used as on streetcars. Clusters of people were hanging outside on steps, standing on the bumpers, in general where ever they could stand or hang on to something.

Naturally the buses were not designed for such a load and the bottom of the chassis practically touched the pavement. If the pavement had a bump one could see sparks flying. As the bus left, a long row was standing in front where the bus had just left and behind the first row a big crowd remained. One could not tell that the waiting crowd became smaller.

On the morning of a rainy winter day when such an over-filled bus just left, Andris was amongst those who almost were able to hang onto something, but he could not do it and was left in the first row. He noticed that in the void left by the departing bus a gum overshoe remained. He was always a decent person, so he immediately picked it up and lifted it over his head and started to wave it, assuming that somebody from the throng fighting his way onto the now still slowly moving bus must have lost it. He waved it so whoever lost it could see that a gum overshoe – which in those days was a big value - was left there. A man jumped off from the steps of the bus and started to run back towards Andris, who was still waving the overshoe above his head. It seemed that after the first step he realized that he had gum overshoes on both of his feet and the one waved by Andris was not his. With lightning speed he turned around and started to run after the bus. He managed to reach the bus and jump back onto the stairs. All this happened in seconds. Andris was standing there alone in front of the crowd where the bus was before. As a film in slow motion he lowered his arm, because he realized that on one of his feet the gum overshoe was missing. What he was holding in his hand and waving was actually his own. He started to put it on in front of the crowd and the crowd broke into uncontrolled laughter.

These were the conditions of public transportation in Budapest when on February 22, 1954, on a cold, cloudy Monday morning, when the thermometer in my window showed 0 oC (32 F) it happened for the first time that I did not have to hurry at 7 AM to the streetcars or buses to fight the daily battle, instead at half past seven I casually walked from our apartment to my car parked on the other side of the street. When I arrived, three of my colleagues, Gyurka, Lajos and Pista, were waiting for me and started to applaud with their hands in their gloves. I bowed and with an elegant motion of my hand waved towards the door of my car.

Before we got into the car I went to the motor, opened the hood supported with the rod used for this purpose and, as I was advised by Béla M. because the temperature was 0oC, I tapped quickly three times on the little button on the carburetor, removed the holding rod and closed the hood. My three colleagues looked at this operation with big eyes. When this was finished I opened the doors of the car and all three of them got in. Gyurka and Lajos in the rear seat and Pista in the front seat, as he had long legs. I got in too, started the car and amid the fellows' applause started in the direction of St István Ring, from which I turned onto

Váci Blvd, like I did the day before. The street was empty with very little traffic. We passed a # 50 autobus and several # 3 trams, finally also a # 87 tram, from all of these the usual clusters of people were hanging outside. 15 minutes later I drove through the gate of Tungsram and stopped at the parking area in front of the TKI main entrance. 10 minutes before 8 AM four of us entered the TKI building, smiled on the 'Shame-board' and each of us went to our office.

With this we inaugurated the Pony Express between my apartment and the TKI – 2 in Újpest. The arrangement was simple. From then on, every workday morning – except when the thermometer was below -5 °C, because I could not start my car – my three passengers were waiting for me at 7:30 at the automobile. From then on I could not become ill and not show up at the car, because they would have pulled me out of my bed. The timetable was that we left at 7:30 from Koháry Street, and after I had parked my car at the TKI-2 parking area next to the entrance, we walked through TKI's enrtance door 5 – 10 minutes before 8 AM. Even a half year later we still looked at the 'Shame-board' with a grin where our names did not appear anymore.

22. Hunting stories

According to Darwin's theory, mankind and the apes have a common ancestry.

Maybe a million year ago a species of the monkey family made themselves different from the others by standing on their two hind legs and thereby losing their ability to jump from tree to tree and from vine to vine and grab food that way. The one which got on its two hind legs, let us be scientific and call it an 'anthropoid ape'had, if we think it over, a very poor chance to survive. The 'anthropoid ape'which gave up its mobility in the tree life was, on the ground, not fast enough to catch its prey or run away from a predator which wanted it for a meal, was not strong enough to wrestle with, or big like an elephant to sweep away the enemies. We know today that in spite of these handicaps this 'anthropoid ape'not only managed to survive hundreds of thousands of years, but became the pinnacle of the living world, and was even able to exterminate many of its contemporaries. It achieved this, because by standing on its two feet, somehow the brain volume of this 'anthropoid ape'enlarged, and with this enlarged brain it invented tools and contraptions, and was able to use them with the front limbs which were free and were not needed for transportation, with - we call now arms and hands - which could be used not only for defense but also for hunting. For many hundreds of thousands of years hunting was important for survival. As the result of its achievements the 'anthropoid ape'was promoted by scientists and named 'humanoid'.

Humanoids became omnivorous, which means they could survive on vegetable as well as on animal food. According to local conditions, humans, as humanoids became, could be vegetarians or carnivores. At any rate, the majority of humanity over time got used to eating meat and for the acquisition of meat, to hunting and fishing. This situation changed about 10,000 years ago, when agriculture and keeping livestock was developed and hunting lost its significance.

The many hundred thousand years of hunting was embedded in some deeper part of the brain and in spite that in many places there was no need for hunting anymore, the tradition of the acquisition of prey by hunting survived. During the times of the Egyptians, hunting was changed into a sport practiced by kings, dignitaries and rich people to show their courage, cleverness and strength.

In Europe, as well as for example in China, except for domesticated animals the other large animals were slowly exterminated. Only, birds, rabbits, deer foxes and maybe some left over boars could be hunted. The foxhunting with dogs and hunters on horseback was started already in the 16th century and became the sport of the nobility.

Those human beings that obtained food by agriculture or keeping livestock were able to get their food easily and they did not concern themselves with hunting, but when it was needed the passion for hunting which was hiding in the instincts and in the deep levels of the brain broke out.
One of these cases was when elegant fur coats became the fashion. An army of Russian hunters invaded Siberia and after that also Alaska, and killed animals en masse, the fur of which was needed for the fashionable fur coats.

After the Russian hunters in Alaska, with the help of the Indians – who still lived from hunting – succeeded in converting probably the last otter also to fur coats, the only business that remained for the Russian hunters was to sell ice and ship it to San Francisco for cooling beer. As animals with useful fur practically did not exist in Alaska anymore and selling ice was not producing much money, the Czar sold Alaska, which was not useful anymore for anything, in 1867 to the USA for $7,200,000, which at that time was big money.

The other new occasion when not only professional hunters used their ancient instincts, emerged also in Russia (by that time Soviet) as the result of the introduction of the socialist-communist planned economy. Probably as a result of the centralized organization, products which were indispensable for daily life, such as food, clothing, and household goods, were from time to time available, sometimes disappeared, and then popped up here and there. Everybody needed food and to obtain it required cleverness and ingenuity, which was when even in common people the hunter spirit which was dormant in their brain, surfaced.

People, like their forefathers in the Stone Age, started early morning to follow their instinct to trace down what they needed at that time. They got tips from acquaintances or when they saw people lined up in front of a store went there and asked around what could be purchased and joined the end of the line.

Hunters in ancient times used mallets, spears or arrows as the tools to secure a prey. Later on dogs, horses and firearms were given a very big role. On the road leading to communism, the collapsible bag was the most important hunting tool. It was important that this should be always available, because if one succeeded in finding something it had to be carried away. In the stores no packing material was given to carry away the merchandise.

With my colleagues during our lunch hour we frequently visited all the stores across from Tungsram's main entrance. We organized lemon hunts, pea hunts, fruit hunts and so on. Sometimes we were successful, sometimes we were not.

One of my colleagues who was in Moscow for one week on an official business trip said that Hungary was the disciple of the leading Soviet Union but we were very far away to catch up. In Moscow he saw enormous lines standing waiting to get into a store, and passers-by joined the end of the line. When my colleague went to the end of the queues which stretched to the end of the block, he heard that those who were standing there really did not know what was sold in the store. The people standing in the line speculated, some of them believed it was toilet paper, others guessed that it was sardines. The opinion was that it did not really matter what they were selling. If they did not need what the shop was selling, one could barter it with somebody for something that the person needed.

"You see" – I said to a few people whom I knew quite well - "when are we going to catch up with the leading Soviet Union? We are standing in line here also, but at least we know for what. Lots of water has to flow down the Danube until we are going to be able to approach our leading example".

This was a lucky day, because after lunch I looked into one of the stores, where there were only very few customers, but I saw they were selling lemons. I walked in, took out my collapsible bag and I became the proud owner of four lemons. I bought only four lemons, because they sold only four to one person. When I got back to the Laboratory with my prey my colleagues asked where did I buy the lemons and they immediately ran out to buy some.

As parents worked during the day, the older kids going home from school were also involved in food hunts.

The hunt for household appliances or for the so called luxury goods required serious preparedness. We had an old record player on which we played the 78 rpm (revolution per minute) phonograph records. The 78 rpm records had been available since the 1930s and people had several of them in their collection. The playing time of those records was about 10 minutes. The early versions of the phonographs were operated by a spring, which had to be wound up, and the sound came from a sound box which was equipped with a needle riding in the grooves of the record. Later on the records were rotated by an electric motor and the sound came from the radio which was connected to the sound box and amplified it and its quality was also much better.

All of this changed when the Hungarian born Dr. Peter Goldmark in the Columbia Broadcasting System's Research Laboratory in the American city of Stamford Connecticut invented and developed the 33 1/3 speed, which was named '33' or LP (long playing) records. The quality of the sound was much better and one record was able to play about a half hour of music. This was a great advantage over the 78, because one could listen to a longer piece of music without changing records. Therefore everybody wanted to get that one, the LP.

At the beginning of the 1950s, these LP records were available also in Hungary, because the Czech Supraphone Company manufactured them and small quantities were also available in Hungary. The problem was that the machines able to play them were not available, or rather the Supraphone Company shipped a very small quantity to Hungary and from time to time there were a few Supraphones available in some of the Keraville stores[64]. On these Supraphone machines one could play the old 78 and also the new 33 records.

To obtain such a record player was also a hunt, with the difference that for food and clothing the hunt was for survival, like for our forefathers. The phonograph hunt was rather in the category of the newly developed sport of hunting, where one could prove the person's patience, ingenuity and cleverness. Friends and acquaintances could admire the Supraphone phonograph, like on the walls of a sport hunter the antlers or the stuffed trophies.

When I started the Supraphone hunt, I visited first several Keraville stores, where I either talked with the sales people or with the managers of the stores. They all said that they had in their store a few pieces, but they were immediately sold and they did not know when they were going to get new ones, but they have some Suprahone 33 phonograph records, I could buy those.

---

[64] As mentioned before: Government owned electrical and household goods chain store.

I told them that I would love to buy the 33 records but I did not have anything to play them on. They were very sorry about that. I told them that I would like to give them my address and my telephone number and that they should call me when they got a shipment. I would come immediately to buy one.

They wrote down my name and telephone number with great enthusiasm and assured me that they were going to call me.

As within a month I did not receive any telephone call from the stores I visited, I went to one of them, where I talked with the manager. He recognized me immediately and told me that he was going to call me, but the people who were in the store when the next Supraphone phonograph shipment arrived, which was only 2 pieces, bought it immediately and there was no purpose to call me. I realized that in a shipment they did not get sufficient quantity, so I had to develop a hunting plan to be able to get such a rare trophy.

If the store was getting only 2 Supraphone record players why should the store manager take the trouble to call me? Obviously he was giving it to somebody with whom he had some connection. I could not offer him money, because he did not know me and he would be afraid that they wanted to test him and if he accepted the bribe, he would be jailed or dismissed because somebody wanted to get his job, or his superiors wanted to show him as an example to other corrupt store managers. Maybe he would even file a complaint against me to protect himself.

I thought over whom did I know who had some connection with the Keraville stores. Suddenly it appeared to me, that the wife of one of my colleagues, Pali Rózsa, whom I knew from Szeged, worked at Keraville. Pali was an engineer in the Laboratory and worked on telephone switching technology. When I thought this over I went to his Laboratory and asked if his wife was still working at Keraville.

"Yes" – he said – "she just got annoyed very much, because she got a promotion and became the manager of the Keraville store located on 'Római part'[65]. That is a small store where there are two employees besides her. The annoying thing is that it is far away from our apartment and she has to travel on HÉV[66] daily at least three quarters of an hour".

"How long has she worked there?"

"About a month. It was very unpleasant at the beginning of February, when she started. She had to be there for store opening in ice or snow and they are open until 6 in the evening, so she gets home only late evening."

I told Pali that I was chasing a Supraphone two speed record player, but stores only got very few and they were sold out immediately. I asked him to ask his wife if I could get one if the Római Part store got a shipment.

---

[65] "Római part" is named, because there was a Roman city Aquincum, the ruins of which are still there. It is on the shore of the Danube in a northern suburb of Buda

[66] A local train.

"I am going to ask her. Kati bought one three months ago in the store where she worked where a few Supraphones arrived. We are using it a lot. It is an excellent machine and the 33 disk cannot be compared with the 78 types."

Next day Pali came to my office where I was alone.

"I asked Kati. She said that Keraville occasionally receives a few of the Supraphone record players, which they distribute to some of the stores. They do not know when the next shipment will arrive but she promised that if one is coming she is going to call me to tell you".

On the afternoon on Thursday March 18 Pali came to my office where I was discussing with somebody an issue related to one of my Laboratories.

"I do not want to disturb you but I would like to talk to you."

I asked him to sit down. I finished the discussion in a few minutes. After the person left, Pali told me:

"Kati just called and asked me to tell you that if you can go to the Római Part store and be there at closing at 6 PM she will have something for you."

After that he wrote a number in his palm – I assumed that was the price of the 'something'. I looked at it, I nodded. He rubbed his hand and the number disappeared.

At exactly 6 PM I was in front of the entrance of the store. It seemed that the employees had left because only Kati came out alone, carrying quite a large box wrapped in brown paper and bound with a string. She carried it holding it by the string. She put the box on the pavement and motioned that I should put it in the trunk. In the meantime she closed the store. I put the box in the trunk and by that time she got to the car.. I arrived at the door of the car, I opened it for her, embraced her and offered to take her home.

"I deserve that. It would be good if you would do it every day".

I started the car and when we were a few blocks away I stopped at the curb, took a bunch of banknotes from my pocket and gave it to her.

"Thank you".

She did not even count it, just put it in her handbag.

"We received two Suprahones. One was purchased by one of the employees and this is the other one."

On the road we discussed how inconvenient it was for her to come to this place which was far from where she was living. We also discussed, that they had absolutely no idea what was going to arrive in the store and on which day. It was the same with refrigerators, electric irons and also with anything else. They received a few of them and they were sold immediately, the same way as the Supraphone.

After I deposited her at their house I started to go home with a big surprise: the trophy.

On the way home I remembered the poem written by Vörörmarty[67] and I thought if he lived then, based on the conditions and experiences, he would slightly rewrite his poem entitled 'Beautiful Ilonka':

> The hunter sits still for a long time,
> He is waiting from dusk for a sign of luck:
> Eagerly waiting for the day to be over,
> And luck appeared as expected:
> Ah, but not a stag, but
> A Supraphone gramophone.[68]

At home the Supraphone record player was a great success. I told Vera to put in the Sunday's newspaper an ad that we were selling our old phonograph for 78 records. According to my family that made no sense, because who would buy a gramophone for 78 records? My opinion was that as one could not buy any kind of record player, many people would call. Nobody believed this in my family, nevertheless Vera put in an advertisement.

The next day there was a meeting in Andris Dallos's office. After the meeting I told to the people who were still there, that I had been able to buy a Supraphone record player, obviously I did not say how. Miki Simek, who helped Andris in various issues related to the Laboratory, asked me what happened to my old record player. I said that we wanted to sell it.

---

[67] Hungarian poet and writer 1800 - 1855

[68] The original text is: 'but a butterfly, with a girl pursuing, flutters by'.

"Excellent" – said Simek – "I have a friend who wants to buy since several months a record player, but he could not find one. He tried everywhere. What do you want for it?"

I said that I was not thinking about that.

"How much you paid for the Supraphone?"

I told him.

"If you would get 10% less would that be OK?"

"Sure."

"Then it is bought. Tomorrow, Saturday, after work we will come to you, he will pay and take it. When people call about the ad, you tell them that it was sold."

I said it was OK and shook hands.

"Where is your friend living?"

He told me.

"When he comes he could put the phonograph in my car and we can take it to his place."

"OK, then he is going to pay also the 10%".

When I went home I said that Simek's friend already bought the old phonograph and they were coming for it. We agreed that if somebody called to buy it, we should tell them it was already sold.

On Sunday morning the first telephone call came around 7 AM. When I heard the ringing I could not imagine who would call us that early. I picked up the phone and from the other end of the line immediately came the question, how much was I selling the phonograph for? I told the person that it was already sold.

"I told my wife to call sooner, but she said that it was not decent. The problem is that I always listen to her. I do not know how much you sold it for, but I would have given 50% more." – He hung up.

The calls came continuously. I put a paper and a pencil next to the telephone and asked everybody that if they picked up a call they should draw a line. By 10 o'clock in the morning there were 40 lines on the paper, and the telephone was ringing also after that time, but nobody picked up the phone, because some of the callers got really upset that we had already sold the phonograph and some of them used really bad words.

I felt that I deserved to cash in on the glory of my forecast.

"You see, I was right."

23. Red striped pants

Mrs. Fekete, with flaming red cheeks, trembling hands and with great speed, using a small brush, tried to collect from the floor of the Laboratory millions of smaller and larger fragments, glass splinters, mercury drops and so on. When she collected some amount, with her trembling other hand holding a little shovel she tried to brush it on the shovel and pour the debris from the shovel into a bucket. She did this work with great speed, while there was deadly silence in the Laboratory. Gizike was sitting in front of her work table with her head turned towards Mrs. Fekete to observe what was happening.

Sanyi Hegedüs, who was the technician of Gábor Sebestyén, was standing petrified in front of the experimental set up – a stand assembled from metal sheets – from the bottom of which Mrs. Fekete was removing the debris. On top of the table made of metal sheets sticking out was a short glass tube on the top of which was a small electron tube. In the metal stand was a pump, the operation of which could be heard, but inside the metal box there was nothing. Namely the entire systm was made of glass which lay now in pieces in the bucket where Mrs.Fekete poured it from the shovel. That the enitre metal box was empty one could not see form the front because it was all covered with the metal sheets.

Next to the metal sheet covered table stood an instrument console as high as a person. – full of instruments – and on the console was also a printer at eye level. Sanyi, the color of his face was pale, looked at Mrs. Fekete's activity with fear. I was about a few meters from this and when I saw that Mrs. Fekete had practically completed cleaning up the debris, I turned to Sanyi:

„I can see that the printer has enough paper."

Sanyi bent down and looked at it.

„Yes, there is enough paper."

„You know how the spectrum used to look? We used to get two peaks from the residual oxygen, two peaks from the residual nitrogen and one peak because of the carbon dioxyde. I assume you also remember what was the ratio of the peaks relative to each other?"

Sanyi nodded.

"Then we are going to do the following. When I ask you to start the mass spectrometer[69], simultaneously the printer is going to start. When this happens please look at me When I wink with my right eye, please turn the black knob on the right side of the machine, so the printer's pen should go as far as far the first peak usualy goes, when it reaches that level, turn the knob back to its original position. If I wink again do the same with the second peak and so on. When all of the five peaks are printed, stop the mass spectrometer, take out the paper and give it to Dr. Dallos."

Sanyi nodded again.

"Now lets make a trial run. Start the spectrometer."

---

[69] The mass spectrometer is a chemical analytical instrument for determining the exact mass of the material. In vacuum it is used to measure the type and quantity of the various residual gases.

He started it, he turned the knob and soon the spectrum was printed on the machine.

"Excellent – I said – let's try it again."

The result was as good as the first time.

"Once again."

The printer produced again a beautiful spectrum.

By that time Mrs. Fekete had finished the clean up, poured out the bucket, but her cheeks were still flaming red. Gizike was still sitting at her table looking petrified.

'Now everybody should settle down. Gizike do not stare anymore here, Mrs. Fekete please go back to your working area, Sanyi, please calm down, if you do everything as we practiced we are not going to have any problems."

A few minutes later the door of the Laboratory opened, Karcsi Ducza entered first and kept the door open for the the three Chinese generals who in their elegant uniform, lots of gold on their caps and on their shoulder straps, with lots of awards on their chest and a broad red stripe on their pants, filed in. After them came a civilian, I assumed the interpreter and the group was completed by Andris. When they were all in the Lab., Andris got to the front of the group and directed them to the metal table on the side of which was the equipment rack in front of which Sanyi was standing and I was on the side in an elegant white lab coat.

The Chinese delegation was visiting us in order that we showed to them the research results of TKI-2. One of this was the “radiofrequency mass spectrometer” which was developed here.

During the development of the magnetron and the klystron electron tubes it became evident that the air could not be perfectly removed from the tubes, and the gases which remained in the electron tube would strongly influence its operation and life, therefore it was very important to conduct further research work to identify those residual gases and their quantity.

No Instrument existed until then for the analysis of the residual gases. One of the tasks of my vacuum laboratory became to solve that problem. When I suggested this task, I started to study the literature published in the various magazines and found out that the mass spectrometer was the most suitable instrument for this purpose. By studying the literature it also became evident that from the systems used at that time none of them was suitable for this purpose. However, a special type of this instrument which was recently proposed seemed to be able to do this job. Its theory was known, but nobody worked out its practical application. I believed that we would have the opportunity to develop this so called ‘radiofrequency mass spectrometer’ and utilize it for the analysis of residual gases.

The radiofrequency mass spectrometer or as we called it ‘RF’ consisted of two parts. One part was the detection tube mounted on the vacuum system which was able to separate the various molecules in a suitable electric field, the other part was the electronics, which made the proper measurements. My group was working on the development of the sensing tube, but there was a need for an expert to design and make the necessary electronics. I discussed the matter with Andris and he called Gábor Sebestyén who was the head of one of the electronics deparments. I explained what we needed and he said that he and one of his technicians, Sanyi Hegedűs, could work with me. He expressed great interest to work on this project to develop this new instrument.

Gábor designed the electronics and Sanyi built it. Using it, my group after much experiment was able to build a tube which had the necessary sensitivity to perform the task. This was a worldwide outstanding achievement. That was the reason that my vacuum laboratory was included in the Chinese Generals' program.

Andris first introduced me. The interpreter translated Andris' speach to Chinese. The Generals nodded. I bowed. I looked at Sanyi, who looked that he somewhat recovered in the meantime, at any rate he looked calmer.

Andris described what they were going to see.

"The air has to be evecuated from the electron tubes, in which the residual gas pressure must be less than ten parts per million of the atmospheric pressure. It is also important that the components of the tube should not give off gases. In good quality electron tubes and especially in radar tubes it is important that after they are completed this situation should be stable. For this reason one has to analyse the residual gases in electron tubes and also in radar tubes".

He stopped here and the interpreter translated this to Chinese. When the interpreter finished Andris continued:

"Dr. Varadi" – he pointed to me – "and Dr. Sebestyén" –“he pointed to Gábor, who in the meantime came to my laboratory and was standing next to me – developed an instrument, called Radiofrequency Mass Spectrometer which is able to analyse this small quantity of gas, even in an electron tube.”

He stopped again and the interpreter again translated. The Chinese Generals nodded understandingly, stared at me, Gábor and the instrument. From time to time they also looked at Andris, who continued:

"We are now going to demonstrate the operation of the instrument which is going to analyse the residual gases in the little electron tube you can see above the platform of the equipment.”

He now pointed to the glass tube coming from the top of the equipment and to the small electron tube on top of the glass tube.

The intrpreter translated.

I nodded towards Sanyi, who as we discussed before, turned on the equipment. On the large instrument rack a disk started to rotate, the needle of the printer started to move, I winked and Sanyi produced the peak beautifully, then the second, third, fourth and fifth. He stopped the machine, ripped off the paper with the beutiful peaks from the printer and gave it to Andris.

Andris took it to the Generals.

"In this tube there is a small quantity of oxygen, nitrogen and carbon dioxyde."

It got translated. The Chinese Generals took the paper observed it with great understanding, they talked something between themselves, which did not get translated. Then the one who had the most gold on his hat, shoulder strap and clothing turned to the interpreter and said that the experiment was very interesting and they realise the importance of this equipment and research and they are wishing great success. They saluted and started to leave towards the door. Again Ducza in the lead, after him the broad red striped pants, then Andris and after him the interpreter, who when they left closed the door behind him.

After they left I thanked Sanyi for his excllent performance. I asked Gizike to go to the glass technicians and talk with uncle Neszlényi to come up immediately. Gábor, who arrived at my lab only later, had no idea what happened, but there was no need to get into lengthy discussion, because so many other things had to be arranged very fast.

I asked Mrs. Fekete to go to Comrade Dallos's office and tell his secretary that as soon as the Chinese delegation has left he should come to my laboratory.

Andris arrived in about of a half hour and looked at me with question in his eyes.

"Andris please come here and look at the vacuum system of the mass spectrometer."

"That is the reason you asked me to come here? I have seen the vaccum system of your mass spectrometer."

But he stepped to the metal stand, bent down and looked into the stand. By that time we even stopped the vacuum pump, so not only was the stand empty, but the vacuum pump was not thumping. Everything was quiet.

"What happened to the equipment. The entire thing is empty."

"Well that's the point. The entire thing broke. We had an accident which happened about 5 minutes before you arrived with the delegation. As you see there are two vacuum systems back to back. The one which is now empty was the vacuum system for the mass spectroscope, the other, that you see there is for making experimental tubes. Sanyi Hegedűs put his measuring instrument on the top of the vacuum stand for the mass spectrometer to test before the guests arrived, so that everything worked in good order. At the same time Mrs. Fekete was working on the other vacuum system and that oven, which you see there and can be moved on a rail back and forth, had moved the oven. She had not seen that Sanyi had put a measuring instrument there and simply the oven pushed down Sanyi's equipment, which fell between the two vacuum systems and unfortunateely landed in the vacuum system of the mass spectrometer, which as you know was made of glass. The equipment broke the glass and as it was all evacuated and as one of the evacuated tubess broke, the pressure blew up the entire vacuum system in a second."

"Then how on earth could you have demonstrated the operation of the mass spectrometer for the Chinese Generals?"

„You see Andris, this is an excellent question. The explanation has two parts. The first was our problem: Mrs. Fekete in two minutes cleaned up the ruins. In the next two minutes I discussed with Sanyi what we should do. In the next minute you came in with the people with the red stripes"

I turned to Sanyi."Please demostrate to Comrade Dallos the operation of the mass spectrometer."

I nodded with my head, Sanyi started the machinery, I winked, the peak appeared, we repeated it. Sanyi stopped the printer and with an elegant gesture he took the paper out and handed it to Andris.

"The second part was that you did not know anything and therefore without any hesitation explained to the Chinese how the machine works."

Andris's mouth was left open. When he recovered he said:

"Fu..sorry" - and looked at the ladies in the room – „gosh this was a close thing."

He adjusted his glasses and left through the door of the laboratory through which Mr. Neszlényi was coming in.

"Uncle Neszlényi please come in and look at what happened to this vacuum system!"

He looked into the empty stand.

"What happened, how did the entire thing disappear?"

"It is a long story, the question is by what time could you rebuild it?"

Neszlényi adjusted his glasses and started to scratch his head.

"At presant we are very busy, because..."

Gizike was standing close to us.

"Uncle Neszlényi" – she said – "in this matter we are all at fault. But before we get into trouble because of this, we have to get it repaired. I am going to assemble by tomorrow a new mass spectrometer tube and uncle Neszlényi you are so clever, that you are going to repair this like nothing had happened by tomorrow evening."

"Gizike" – said Neszlényi - "I do not know why but you always can convince me and get me to do something. I am going to measure what has to be done. Doctor Varadi, you and I are going to make a schematic of the system which was here and by tomorrow evening I am going to try to build it. This is not a promise I said only, I am going to try."

Next day, late afternoon, I happened to meet Ducza in the corridor.

"Andris told me what happened. And how resourcefully you solved the problem. The entire mass spectrometer equipment broke and you could still demonstrate it to the Chinese Generals. I do not want even to imagine what would have happened to you and to your entire group if it would not have succeded."

We just went by my laboratory's door.

"Come in and look at it with your own eye the mass spectrometer machine that you say was broken."

We arrived to the equipment. Ducza bent down. When he straightened out he looked at me with surprise.

"This is not broken. It looks like everything is operating."

"It seems Andris must have eaten some poisonous mushrooms and had nightmares in his dream."

24. Coca Cola, the embodiment of capitalism

On October 14, 1956, when my colleague Gábor Sebestyén and I, at Budapest's Ferihegy airport the first time in our life boarded an airplane going abroad, we had no idea that we were going to spend in Berlin October 23, 1956 the day of the Hungarian revolution, which will be written in the world's history. On top of that I was not only going to spend the planned 12 days, but was going to be stuck in Berlin until mid - November.

The story started, with the research work on which Gábor and I and also several of our coworkers, Éva Rieger, Gizike Szremcsevics and Sanyi Hegedűs worked, progresed very well. We developed the Radiofrequency Massspectrrometer, which we nicknamed RF and published articles in many Hungarian as well as western scientific magazines about its design and its application for the analysis of residual gases in electron tubes. That was the reason, that on June 1956 we were invited by the East German, or as it was called at that time DDR Chemical Society to give a presentation about the RF at their annual conference to be held Octobr 16 – 19, 1956 in Leipzig. This was a great recognition that the reseach work carried out at TKI was valued so well that abroad, especially in East Germany the two researchers were invited to give a paper about that subject.

Both of us, Gábor and I were very much impressed that we got such a recognition for our work. We knew that we were the first worldwide to utilize the RF for the analysis of residual gases, but that the Chemical Society of the DDR would invite us as speakers for their annual meeting, we did not expect.

We took our invitation to Andris –as he spoke German – he read it immediately. He asked his secretary to ask Ducza to come over. When Ducza arrived he translated it for him. They both came to the conclusion, that it is for TKI an excellent political as well as scientific acknowledgement. We received recognition from another socialist country's scientific society and also from one in which the scientific life was very highly regarded in the entire peace camp.

Andris said that we should translate the letter and with a cover letter give it to him. He, Ducza and Sellei will recommend it. He is going to take it to our HQ at Rózsadomb and will personally ask Biró to approve it and to give it to Ács to forward it to the Minsistry for approval and stress its urgency that to get into the printed program we must answer by the beginning of July that we are accepting the invitation.

Next day morning Andris asked me and Gábor to come to his office. He motioned for us to sit down to his conference table. When we were sitting he told us, that comrade Bíró as well as Ács were very happy that we were invited by the Chemical Society of the DDR to give a presentation about our work of the RF. They support our request to go to Leipzig for the meeting and to give our presentation about our research results. They sent the request to the Ministry for approval and it is assumed that in a week we are going to get the answer.

The next day when in the morning I arrived to my office, Kitty was already there sitting at her desk, greeted me and said:

"Not only you are going to East Germany, we are going too! Remember a few months ago I told you that Laci (Kitty's hursband) applied for a chemistry position in the Buna Rubber factory near Leipzig. He was notified yesterday thet he received a job offer for a position to start on the first of September. Therefore we are going to East Germany at the end of August, becasuse this is a two year long assignement. Unfortunately I have to leave TKI. I hope that we are going to finish by that time our flame photometry work and the papers describing them and I hope that when we come back two years from now, I could continue my work at TKI."

By that time I was also sitting at my desk.

"Yes, you told me that Laci submitted his application for the job at Buna. It is excellent that they accepted it, because this means lots of money for you. I am very sorry you are leaving and I hope that when you comeback we will be able to continue our work at TKI. I do not know yet if we are going to the Leipzig chemical conference, because we have not received the notification for the approval of our trip."

I was very sorry that Kitty was leaving, she was an outstanding research chemist and we published in Hungarian as well as abroad in scientific magazines several very successful joint work.

The next week passed without us hearing of approval. I met Ducza in the corridor, but he did not hear anything about it. About 10 days after Andris took our letter and the invitations to the HQ at Rózsadomb a secretary of our personnel department left a message for me and for Gábor that during the next day we should go to the personnel department at our HQ because the approval for our trip arrived and we have to complete a bunch of papers. The people at our personnel department at the HQ are going to tell us what we have to do and when.

I found Gábor and went together to Andris to tell him the news. Andris already knew about it and told us that we should take the trip seriously and write the presentation in Hungarian as well as in German, because we have to send it for approval, which probably will take several weeks. He said we should write immediately to the Germans and to send them the abstract which they were asking to be published in the program. He asked us to write the abstract also in Hungarian and in German and give it to him, because he has to get that also approved.

The next day I drove up with Gábor to our HQ on Rózsadomb and reported to the personnel department. The boss of the department received us immediately, he appreciated that a fellow worker of TKI was ivited to give a paper at a scientific conference in the DDR. When we sat down at the conference table in his office, he immediaely offered us cigarettes, which we did not accept because neither of us smoked. He asked his secretary to bring us coffee. The secretary returned in a few minutes with steaming coffee served in nice china cups. The chief personnel comrade gave us a number of forms and told us to complete them. He explained, that most of these papers are neded for the passport and the others to obtain the necessary visa, because he assumed that when we have to change planes in Prague we are probably going to need a Czech visa and also a visa for the DDR, furthermore the approval of the National BanK so we should be able to buy Czech as well as DDR currency.

It took us about an hour in his office with his help to complete all of the forms, he took the papers and assured us that from now on they are going to make all of the arrangements including, airline tickets, hotel reservations in Leipzig as well as in Berlin. Our trip preparation went according to schedule. Everything progressed except we did not have our passports and nobody knew if we were going to get them and if we do, when will that happen.

After a few days we received approval for the 10 line abstract of the paper we sent to the secretariat of the DDR chemical conference accompanied with our thank you note. We wrote the text of our speech and as both of us knew German we translated it. Father Lőrinc Hantos who was teaching me German for eight years in the Piarist highschool in Szeged ought to be proud of me. We submitted to Andris the Hungarian as well as the German text including the slides which we planned to use and Andris sent all that to the HQ on Rózsadomb. Mid August the airline tickets were ordered for Octobr 14 for the flights Budapest – Prague where we had to change planes to fly to Berlin. At the end of August we went to the National Bank, where we received Czech and German money.

At the end of August Gizike went around in the building and told everybody who was a good friend of Kitty's, that it was her last day in the laboratory because two days later she was leaving for East Germany and we were organizing a small farewell party. Many peole showed up. Gizike baked for this occasion a cake and we all wished Kitty a good trip and nice time. I told her separately good bye and said, that when she is back for vacation she should let me know so we could meet and I expect her back two years from then in my department. Kitty gave me her address abroad and promised she was going to write me her telephone number when she gets one and with Gábor when we are going to Leipzig we should for sure visit them. I promised.

In the meantime Gyurka Gergely and János Ádám came also to my office to say good bye. They worked with Kitty and me on many subjects and published scientific papers and some of it was just in the process to be published, we discussed how are we going to be able to send them to Kitty for her review.

A few days later Gábor told me that his wife, Terka, would be able to get illegaly some US Dollars and Terka will sew them into his winter coat's lining. I enthusiastically agreed that it will be excellent. He said they could get me also some. I said that 100 dollars would be excellent for me. The reason I asked only 100 dollars was becasue we had at home about 200 – 400 dollars, which at that time was quite a bit of money, especially if they would have found it would have resulted in large punishment probably years in prison. Besides of these dollars we also had some Napoleon gold coins which would have also resulted if found in punishment and prison. Naturally all these were well hidden, because when it was declared that foreign currency, dollars and also the Napoleon gold coins had to be surrendered we obviously did not want to surrender them we had to hide them somewhere, where even if they search the apartment they could not find them. Vera had a standup piano, I believed that the inside of that would be a very good hiding place. I opened the rear plate of the piano to find a safe place. The inside of a pianino is a very interesting place, I suggest if the reader has not seen one yet it is recommended to see it. If has a great number of tunnel type structures, empty cracks like cavities in it. I assume that these are to improve the sound of the piano. I pushed with a rod into one of the cavities the bank notes and also the gold coins wrapped in paper so one could not see them, but also that one could get them out with a rod if needed. So I really did not need Gábor's wife to buy me dollars, but I could not say that I have a supply of them in the piano, which I can take with me, so the simplest was to ask to buy me only 100 dollars.

Mid September Andris asked us to his office and gave us an envelope and said that the Hungarian and German text as well as the slides are in the envelope. They were approved. He said, that what is in this envelope are only copies, we should put them away but we cannot take it with us. The papers which we can take with us abroad will be presented to us officially by the Secret Case Handling (SCH) in a sealed envelop.

It was already October and we still knew nothing about our passports in spite of that we made several inquiries at the personnel department. We would have to leave in a couple days and we still did not have passports. On October 8, Monday, the secretary of the personnel department called us to go to the HQ at Rózsadomb because our passports had arrived. I found Gábor, we got into my car and drove up to the TKI HQ at Rózsadomb.

The head of the TKI personnel department received us in his office which we saw during our first visit. Now he did not offer us cigarette or coffee, but asked the secretary to send in a man whom we never had seen before and when he arrived and we all sat down he took our two passports from his drawer and also took two forms and put it in front of us to sign. I quickly read the paper but it contained only that I received #008453 official service passport of the Hungarian Peoples Republic, dated October 3, 1956. I signed it and he gave me my passport. Same thing with Gábor. I had also to sign it on page #5, under my picture. When I turned the pages I saw that they wrote in three languages, Hungarian, Russian and French that I am a Department head., medium built, my face is oval, my eyes are blue and my hair is blond.

I flipped through the passport and noticed there were no Czechsklovak or DDR visa in it. The unknown man spoke and said, that it is stamped in the passport which country it is valid for and therefore one can travel with this passport to Czechslovakia, to the DDR and to Poland and for the countries no visa is needed. He also said, that we are going to get the text of our talk and the slides in a sealed envelop from the TK-2 SCH office.

The boss of the personnel department stood up, shook our hands and wished us success for our talk. The other man stood up also, shook our hand, but said nothing.

On the way back to TKI-2, I told Gábor that now it looks like we are going to Leipzig. We agreed that after the work hours we should go to a coffee house and think over the details.

When we arrived in the laboratory we went to the SCH office to pick up the text of our talk as the man said we were going to get it from there. The SCH emplyee looked into some papers and told us, that it will be delivered on October 13 and that is when we are going to get it. We told him, that October 13 is a Saturday when the working hours are only until noon and our airline ticket is for the next day and as it is forbidden to take any other paper with us we need that sealed envelop. He assured us, that we are going to get that envelope in time.

Next stop was Andris and Ducza, we told them the news that we received our passports which we showed very proudly because in those days a passport was as rare as a white raven. On the other hand I told them we did not receive our presentation the comrade on duty in the SCH office told us we are going to rceive it Saturday monning. I mentioned that if for some reason we would not get it, it woul be a bad joke. Ducza said he is going to look into this.

I visited my laboratories and told the news that we are now really going to Leipzig and present our work. Everybody was very glad and I got lots of congratulations. Eveybody admired my passport as in my entire department nobody ever got one or even saw one.

After work Gábor and I went to the city. I stoped on Pozsonyi Ave in front of a coffee house and we went in to discuss the details of our trip. It seems that everythig is now OK except the text of our paper and the slides which we hoped we are going to get. What is left is to pack and Terka should sew into Gábor's coat the dollars. Our plan for the trip was simple. We are going to fly to Berlin, from there by train to Leipzig and after the conference to Erfurt where we have to visit an electron tube factrory and its laboratories and going to meet Kitty and Laci. After that we are going by train back to Berlin where we shall spend a week and on October 27 we are going to fly back to Budapest. We agreed that I am going to read our paper in German and on the eventual questions one of us is going to answer depending whether the question was related to the Mass spectrometer of to its electronics. We agreed that we are going together to the airport in case there would be a problem with the departure of one of us, the other should know about it. This sort of thing happened and we had heard about such cases.

On Saturday, the day before our planned departure they called us to go to the SCH room, where besides of the usual soldier a lieutenant of the ÁVH was also present.The lieutenant handed over a large sealed envelope and said that in the envelope we will find two copies of the Hungarian and German text of our paper and also the slides. He repeated what the taciturn guy in civilian clothing told us at the TKI HQ, that we can only break the seal after our arrival in the DDR. He also said that they know, we have to give the text of our talk and the slides to the conference organizers so we do not have to bring those back. He also advised us, that we cannot take any other paper or picture with us and he wished us a good trip. We agreed with Gábor that as I am going by car, I should take the envelope home and bring it tomorrow to the airport. He also admonished me, that under no circumstances shall I break the red wax seal.

At home I told Vera and my mother that everything is ready for our trip the next day and I started my task to conjure the dollars from the guts of the piano. That turned out to be not an easy task. I remembered approximately in which crevice I had put the banknotes and I started to explore it with a small rod. I did it very slowly and carefully so the dollars and the Napoleons should not fall into another crevice in which they could disappear forever. I successfully fished out 15 banknotes which was about 100 dollars. I said that I am going to mix them with the East German banknotes and that is the way I will take them. Everybody had its own opinion if this method is good or bad, but I stayed with this solution. I mixed the dollars with the East German Marks and put the mixture into my wallet. If they should look at them I could say that I received all of that from the bank and I never saw an East German Mark and since I got it from the National Bank I assumed they are all the same currency. They should select which is the good one and which is not. So we left the matter that way.

I went to the gas station, filled up my car and left it in the Balaton Street garage so that for the 12 days we are going to be abroad the car should not stay on the street.

The next day Gábor arrived in a taxi to pick me up. Before I went downstairs with my small luggage I said good bye to everybody and my two and a half year old daughter Éva inquired why we are going by taxi and why not the airplane is coming to pick me up. We arrived to the Ferihegy airport, where I was the last time about six years ago, when I went to Szeged and there was still passenger air transport within Hungary. We made it through the passport check and both of us, Gábor with the dollars sewn in his topcoat and I with the dollars in my wallet boarded the airplane. We landed in

Prague without any problem and transferred to another airplane and continued our trip to Berlin. In Berlin we took a taxi to go to the railroad station and went by train to Leipzig. On the Berlin train station when we boarded the train there was passport control and after the train left DDR soldiers we assumed were the equivalent of the Hungarian ÁVH went through the entire train and checked very thoroughly everybody's passport or identity card.

The Leipzig railroad station had only one railway track, because all the others were removed after the war. Our train and all of the other trains arrived and left from this one track on the minute they were scheduled.

The Conference opening was on October 16, but on the 15th, Monday evening was a reception and we were invited to attend. That was when we met for the first time our colleagues who worked at the physical-chemistry department of the Humboldt University in Berlin and who were very interested in the RF mass spectrometer.

The Conference opened on October 16 by a Minister. During his speech there were more people in the corridors than is the auditorium. After the Minister a Beethoven String Quartet was played, the Conference's meeting room was full and the corridors were empty.

Our presentation was scheduled for the next day[70.] I gave the lecture in German and my teacher – whom I mentioned before – Lőrinc Hantos would have been very proud of me. Apparently, the public understood my Hungarian accented German because after the lecture we

[70] P.F. Váradi - L.G. Sebestyén: Quantitative Gasanalyse mit Hilfe des Radiofrequenz Massenspectrometer.

received several questions, which were answered either by Gábor or by me, depending on what part of the RF mass spectrometer the question was related to. After the talk during the intermission the colleagues from the Humboldt University came to us and invited us to visit them when we are back in Berlin. We promised it.

On the last morning of this very interesting conference were the closing ceremonies. Several people gave lengthy talks. When finally ended we went back to our hotel picked up our luggage, went to the railroad station and purchased tickets. During the afternoon we arrived in Erfurt. On the station was a "Zimmernachweis" which means room accommodation service. The woman in the Zimmernachweis made room reservation for us and explained on which tram we should get there. We showed the paper at the reception desk of the Hotel which we had received from the woman at Zimmernachweis and they asked for our passports. After we settled down, we called Kitty and Laci who came immediately to our hotel where we discussed everything that happened since they left Budapest in August. By the end of the evening we consumed all of the alcoholic beverages in the bar of the hotel, said goodbye to each other because we planned to visit the next morning the laboratory of a factory making electron tubes and after that we were going to Berlin.

The trip to Berlin was very interesting. At the last stop in the DDR before Berlin the story going to Leipzig repeated itself. The military in the same uniform that we saw going to Leipzig got on the train and inspected everybody's passport and identification papers very carefully.

The hotel room in Berlin was reserved for us by the Budapest IBUSZ agency. We inquired at the station how to get there and we started our visit in Berlin. The day was October 20, 1956.

We went by taxi to our hotel, the Hotel Coburger Hof. As it turned out the location of our hotel was excellent. It was close to the Friedrich Street rail station, where not only the trains stopped, but was the station for the underground trains the U-Bahn, as well as the trains running on elevated tracks, the S-Bahn. The hotel was in the middle of the city close to the famous Unter den Linden Blvd and the Brandenburg gate.

We had a very nice room equipped with old furniture. When the desk clerk noticed our Hungarian passports he became very friendly. He knew a few Hungarian words he said that during the war he was stationed for a few months in Hungary. He did not mention in what regiment he was and what was he doing in Hungary. He gave us lots of interesting information. For example that in West Berlin which was the name for the English, American and French sectors having a Hungarian passport one can buy everything at half price and one could get a bigger discount at the movies.

According to our plans the next day, October 21, Sunday we would tour the city, on Monday October 22 morning we were planning to go to the Hungarian embassy in Berlin, to call TKI and try to talk with Andris and Karcsi Ducza, to report to them how the Conference was, tell them about our success and what we are going to do in Berlin. After we arrived in the hotel we were able to call our family in Budapest. This was not very simple. We gave to the hotel's telephone operator our home number in Budapest she was able in a couple of hours to arrange a connection. Terka as well as my family was very happy to hear from us. We told them about our successes and were informed, that since we left, nothing happened in Budapest.

In those days Berlin was divided in four sectors. The Russian sector, where our hotel was located belonged to the DDR but the Russian occupation was very visible. Beside this was also a British, an American and a French sector. One could go from one zone into the other smoothly without any problem. In Berlin a very extensive underground and elevated train net existed. The trains were going in and out of the various sectors. One could easily determine which station was in the Russian (DDR) or in the British, American or French sector. The DDR sectors were dimly lit and one could not buy there anything, while in the other sectors the stations were well lit and full of vendors, newsstands, food and other merchandise. If somebody wanted to go on the streets from one sector to the other there was no problem to do it. At the border of the zones one could see guard stations with the proper soldiers, but nobody cared who is going to which direction.

As we planned, on October 21th Sunday we went sightseeing in the city. This actually consisted, that we stopped at various U-Bahn and S-Bahn stations and looked around. Obviously for lunch we ate the Pick salami we brought from Hungary with some bread, but decided, during the afternoon we are going to go to Kurfürstendamm in West Berlin to the famous Kempinsky Hotel's terrace to taste Coca Cola which in Hungary was labeled as the embodiment of capitalism.

That is exactly what we did. We found the Kempinsky Hotel sat on its terrace and each of us ordered Coca Cola. The waiter brought on a plate two bottles, the shape of which we knew from pictures. He also brought two glasses in each of them a slice of lemon. Put it on the table, removed the cap of the bottles with a little metal tool and poured its content into our glasses. The lemon slices floated to the top of the brown colored liquid. When the waiter left, we lifted our glasses, clinked and solemnly tasted the symbol of the damned capitalism, Coca Cola. After we tasted it we immediately decided that the Communist propaganda is absolutely right, because it is possible, that Coca Cola is the symbol of imperialism, but for sure it is certainly one of the worst tasting drinks ever invented. As we spent compared to our wealth a great amount of money on this drink, we had very bravely to drink the whole thing and decided that this brown colored wishy-washy liquid is very far to be as good as the Hungarian raspberry-soda drink. Most likely they advertise it to be drunk ice-cold, because the cold numbs the taste buds and if one would drink Coca Cola not cold it probably would taste even worse.

After this disappointment we went back to our hotel, but before that we went into a building's entrance to remove the dollars hidden in the lining of Gábor's topcoat. I was holding the coat until Gábor removed the thread Terka sewed in the lining, reached in to remove the dollars. I saw immediately that there was a problem, because Gábor instead of pulling his hand out of the coat started to move it around in the lining. He moved his hand up and down but he could not find the dollars. We decided that we are not going to find it there and we should go back to the hotel and systematically inspect the coat.

Gábor did not dare to get into his coat, but put it carefully on his arm, so the dollars should not fall out at some point. That would have been very unpleasant if it would have happened when we were walking in the DDR sector.

Before we got on the U-Bahn we bought a few bananas that we had not seen since our childhood, thinking that after our salami and bread dinner it will taste very good. After that we went to our hotel very fast. Arriving in our room we locked the door and started to methodically search the lining of Gábor's topcoat. We could not find the dollars. We decided we should open the sewing of the coat at some other points, because from the area which was opened we put our entire arm into the coat, but we did not find the bank notes. With our pocket knife we started to cut the thread holding the fabric and the inner lining together to get to the inner wadding. We did that inch by inch but no result. Finally we found the dollars under his coat's left shoulder pads. By that time the topcoat was demolished.

After we found the money, exactly the amount Terka had sewn into the coat the only problem was how we can reconstruct the coat into a useful form. It was evident that we were going to need needle and thread and some knowledge of sewing. Gábor volunteered to go down to the desk and ask for a needle and thread. Our problem was that we both remembered the German word for needle, but neither of us remembered the word for thread. In spite of this, Gábor triumphantly returned in a quarter hour with the needle and a small spool of black thread. I made a remark, that a gray thread would have been better, because it would have matched the lining. He did not even answer my remark. I volunteered to start the sewing. I threaded the thread and listening to Gábor's critical remarks started to reassemble the coat. Finally we reassembled the coat into a decent shape and after he tried it, he was satisfied with the result.

25. October 23, 1956

Our plan was that on October 22, Monday we are going to report to the Hungarian Embassy which was located 72 – 74 Unter den Linden Blvd in East Berlin, which some time ago was the Messel Palace and was not very far from our Hotel. From the Embassy we planned to call Andris or Ducza depending of whom we could reach and to report about the Conference in Leipzig also about our successful paper as the result of which we received an invitation to visit the Humboldt University to give a presentation about the RF, because their research people would like to work on this subject. At the Embassy a nice, young, blonde girl – Editke – greeted us sitting at a desk near the entrance. We introduced ourselves. She said she is happy to meet us, because they already heard about us that we are very famous scientists, as the DDR Chemical Society does not invite everybody to present a lecture at the Conference in Leipzig. She was going to inform Béla that we are there.

After she put the receiver down she told us to go to a small reception area until Béla is going to come out. Béla, about a 30 year old brown haired fellow with glasses showed up in minutes. He told us to be seated and offered cigarettes. We sat down and told him we are not smoking, he lit a cigarette. He knew about us too. We told him about our program since we arrived in East Germany and what our plans are in Berlin. He praisd us that we are making such a good name in science for Hungary. We told him, that we would like to call TKI. He called Editke, she got very fast a line, we thanked Béla. Said good bye and told him we are planning to come visit him periodically to inform him of what we do. He said that he will be very glad if we would visit him and if we need anything we should let him know. He was aware that we are stayig in the Coburger Hotel.

Béla left and Gábor picked up the telephone which was in front of us. Karcsi Ducza must have been in Andris's office, because he participated also in the conversation. Gábor informed them of what we had accomplished. Andris was very happy that the conference and our paper went so well and that we also going to visit Humboldt University in East Berlin, which was not in our plan. After Gábor, I talked with them too. I asked them how are things there. They said that everything is going on as usual. There was no problem in my department and they are waiting that in a few days we are going to report about everything in person. I said we are going to call again before we go home. As an interesting item *I would like to mention that this happened during the morning of October 22nd.*

The day before we went to West Berlin, because it was Sunday many of the stores were closed. This day was now Monday, a normal week day and everything was open and it struck us the incredible difference we saw between the communist DDR's East Berlin and the west sector's Berlin. We could observe that in a square, where one side of the square belonging to East Berlin was dark, dirty ruins without any stores, while the other side of the square which was a part of West Berlin had restaurants with neon signs, shops and department stores. We heard about this only from the BBC or the Voice of America broadcasts and believed it was empty propaganda, but now we were seeing it with our own eyes.

On this occasion we purchased in West Berlin a bunch of bananas and also two grapefruits. We remembered grapefruit from the times before the war, and we have not seen one since more than 15 years. We believed that after our bread and salami dinner, fruits, such as banana and grapefruit will be an excellent addition. In West Berlin one could buy everything for East German Marks which was worth only 50% of the West German Mark, like it would be West German Marks, so everything was half price for us.

Our salami dinner in the Hotel room was very good, we had only a problem with the grapefruit. We did not know that a grapefruit which looks like a big orange cannot be peeled like an orange. We considered that it was a big orange and we tried to peel the deceptively similar orange colored, skin like an orange, with our fingers. The end was that we were sprayed all over with grapefruit juice, but we also had to clean the bed and some of the chairs with a wet towel to remove the orange-red juice of the grapefruit.

The following day, October 23, we went to Humboldt University to discuss the RF masspectrometer with the colleagues. The University was only a few blocks from our Hotel. I talked with Margaret, who was a lecturer in the physical-chemical department to visit them at 10:00 AM. She proposed that after our arrival we should get a tour of their department after that we should have lunch with them in the University's restaurant. After lunch she would invite those people who are interested in the mass spectrometry and planning to work on the project. After that she would have a question/answer session. Our visit was very successful. They asked many questions and they told us they are very sorry that in a few days we are going back to Budapest, because they would like to take advantage of our advice. They invited us if we have some time left to come back again. During the afternoon we went over to the West Berlin side where as Easterners we could see for half price the performance of Berthold Brecht's Three penny opera (Drei Groschen Oper).

The next day, on October 24, Gábor went to our Embassy to call TKI to tell them that we are planning according to schedule to fly back to Budapest on October 27, Saturday. I went to West Berlin to buy a few things. When we met late afternoon in our Hotel room Gábor said that he was at the Embassy, but he was not able to get a telephone connection with TKI in spite that he was waiting there during the entire afternoon. I told him I was not surprised, because in West Berlin on every newsstand posters were hung and with huge letters it was headlined: Blutige Aufstand in Ungarn. (Bloody revolution in Hungary)[71]. I also checked on the way back the News stand in East Berlin, but there was nothing posted about a revolution.

"I am not surprised," - I told Gábor – "because if something happened on the afternoon of October 23 or during the evening it could not have been in the newspapers today, those are printed during the night, but those one page news hanging in West Berlin at the newsstands can be printed very fast. So it is possible, that something happened at home but the papers got the news when the paper was already being printed."

Gábor was so surprised that he practically left his mouth open. That was for us a highly unexpected turn of events. We agreed that we should try to reach our families by

---

[71] The day to day description of the October 23, 1956, Hungarian Revolution is narrated by Béla Lipták in his excellent book: A Testament of Revolution – Texas A&M University Press, 2007

telephone. We called the telephone operator of the Hotel to call Budapest. That evening we could not get any connection.

Next day October 25 morning we went to see the newsstand at the train station next to our Hotel to find out what the DDR papers are writing. At those newsstands only DDR papers were sold, those wrote nothing about Hungary. We got on U-Bahn and went to West Berlin to look at the West Berlin papers. We purchased three papers, der Tagesspiegel, Telegraf and Berliner Morgenpost. The events in Hungary were all over their front page.

Telegraf

Blutiger Aufstand in Ungarn

Sowjetpanzer greifen ein

Standrecht verhängt – Nagy neuer Regierungschef

Gomulka fest im Sattel

Ueberall Gefechtslärm

Ungarn völlig abgeriegelt

Rentendebatte hat begonnen

October 25, 1956: Front page headline of the West Berlin newspaper: 'Telegraph'

[72] On the first page of Telegraf with large bold letters was what I had seen the day before on the posters displayed at newsstands: 'Bloody revolution in Hungary - Soviet tanks engaged – Imre Nagy is the new prime minister'.

ERLINER
MORGENPOST

ippe droht wieder – Wie wir uns schützen können

ngarn kämpft um seine Freiheit

October 25, 1956: Front page headline of the West Berlin newspaper: 'Morgenpost'

In the Berliner Morgenpost: huge letters on the front page: 'Hungary is fighting for its freedom'.

Der Tagfesspigel's headline was: The Soviet army was deployed against the people of Hungary - Budapest is surrounded

[72] Special thanks to Mr. Alexander Fiebeg, Statsbibliothek zu Berlin, Germany, for researching the files to find the relevant Front pages of three Berlin Newspapers. Also thanks to Bildarchiv, Berlin for the permission to use them.

These ruled out any doubt that in Hungary totally unexpectedly a revolution was started. We decided the best we can do is to go to the Embassy and find out what is the situation.

On the way we discussed what can we say. We cannot go and tell what we were reading in the West Berlin papers. The best is if we go as nothing happened and ask to reconfirm with the airlines our tickets for October 27. This was a very natural request. When we entered the Embassy the nice, young, blond girl – Editke, whom we knew from our previous visits, was apparently totally confused. When we asked her to get in touch with the airline to reconfirm our tickets, she did not know what to say. Finally she said that she is going to find Béla and we should discuss it with him, because she is very busy at that moment. She left and soon came back with Béla. We told him the same story and also mentioned we would like to talk with TKI to find out if they want us to do something else. He asked us to sit down – as he did at our first meeting – and offered us cigarettes – he excused himself that he forgot that we are not smoking. He took a cigarette and took some time to light. He said that he is going to call the airlines and asked Editke to switch the phone line to the telephone on the table in front of us. He asked on which day and on which flight are we leaving. Gábor took out his notes and gave him the date, the flight number the time of departure and also the date of our connecting flight from Prague to Budapest. He wrote all of that on a piece of paper, from time to time he took a puff from his cigarette, carefully dropped the ashes into the ashtray.

When he completed to write down everything the phone was ringing and Editke said that the airline is on the line.

Béla told on the phone our name and the other information. After that he was listening for a long time what the airline employee was telling him. Béla from time to time said only Ja – Ja – Ja. Finally he said thank you, and took another sip from his cigarette.

“Your ticket is OK from here to Prague, the problem is that the flight from Prague to Budapest was cancelled. It is cancelled today and also tomorrow and the airline guy could not say when will be a flight from Prague to Budapest.”

We both looked at him. Gábor wanted to ask him something, but Béla continued:

“Our understanding is that there is some problem in Budapest and the Ferihegy airport is not operating. It looks like that is the reason the Prague – Budapest flights are cancelled. Comrade Ambassador was trying to call the Ministry but for some reason the telephone connection is not working either, so he could not get any information.”

Obviously we did not start to discuss what we had seen in the West Berlin Newspapers, but being a practical person I asked a question about our stay, which seems to be extended.

“I f we cannot leave on Saturday as scheduled then we are not going to have any money for the Hotel and for our expenses. How are we going to solve this problem?”

A few more puffs from his cigarette, of which he got now to the end and squashed it in the ashtray.

“This is a good question. Wait here I am going to ask how we could solve this problem.”

He left us and disappeared through one of the doors. In about ten minutes he returned.

“Today is Thursday. Please come back tomorrow morning, by that time we are going to know better when the flights will be resumed and if they are not leaving, how we can solve the financial problems.”

We said good bye, shook hands. Leaving we waved to Editke. When we got further from the Embassy building we could talk more freely. It seems that the reports in the West Berlin papers are true, because Budapest is not accessible.

For that night we were invited to the Michael Opperts, Laci Rotter’s friend in West Berlin.

Laci Rotter worked until 1944 at the Dutch Philips Company’s Berlin laboratory as an engineer. Before we left Budapest he told us to visit his best friend from those days, Michael Oppert.

The Oppert’s he and his wife lived in the West Berlin district of Zehlendorf. We were able to reach Zehlendorf which is one of West Berlin’s very nice suburbs very easily, because the U-Bahn goes from the Unter den Linden station directly to Zehlendorf. The Opperts were very friendly to us and obviously the first subject was to discuss their friend Laci Rotter. We told them, that Uncle Laci is a very good friend of ours. We are seeing him daily and he has a very good position and highly regarded, because he is an excellent research engineer.

Naturally we talked about the Hungarian situation and about the fights which recently broke out. They knew about it much more than we did. Besides of the West Berlin newspapers, they were able to listen freely to any radio stations, including the BBC. We learned a lot, including that the soviet troops had to leave Budapest and the Russians seem not to know what to do. It also became clear that this will not be finished very soon and that we were probably going to be stuck in Berlin for some time.
After dinner our host offered us a glass of cognac, which we accepted with delight. Mrs. Oppert did not drink, so the three of us toasted to the liberation of Hungary from the Soviet rule. Michael summarized what he knew. The Russians have serious problems with the Poles. At the moment they are trying to solve that. After Stalin's death the stability of the Soviet regime is not as strong as it was during Stalin, and now suddenly came the Hungarian revolution, they did not expect that the entire population and also the military will be united and the local communist oppressor organization should fall apart. The big question is, how the World especially the USA will react – according to Oppert – as the American elections are only less than two weeks away and as neither party was prepared for the events in Budapest, they probably are not going to do anything.

We had an excellent dinner which felt especially good after the many salami sandwiches and when we left we agreed that we are going to let them know when we find out when we are going to be able to go back to Budapest.

On the way back to the Hotel we discussed what we learned. We had no idea what is going to happen now and that detached from everything what are we going to do here in Berlin? We agreed, the situation is not going to change very soon, unexpectedly and for the long duration we are stuck in Berlin, while our family is in Budapest and God knows what the situation is there. Obviously we did not discuss this when we got back to our Hotel room, because who knows ....?

Next day as we agreed, we went back to the Hungarian Embassy where Editke called Béla immediately, who again asked us to sit down, lit a cigarette and told us that the situation had not changed. He knows nothing new. The Prague – Budapest flights are cancelled and looks like there will be no flights during the weekend. Accordingly we should stay in Berlin and we should call or come to the Embassy daily. It would be better if we would come, because that way we could get money daily to pay our Hotel and all other expenses. With this he took an envelope from his pocket and counted some money on the table which will be sufficient for us for the weekend. Monday we should come in again. On the way out we said hello to Editke and went back to our Hotel.

From the Hotel I called Margaret at Humboldt University and told her, that for the time being we cannot go back to Budapest, because the Prague – Budapest flights for the next days are cancelled, so we stay in Berlin. From her voice I noticed that she knew more about the situation, but did not want to talk about it on the telephone. I said that on Monday we could visit them at the University, because the last time we met they told us they would like to see us again.

She became very enthusiastic and we immediately agreed we are going to be there Monday, October 29 at 2 PM. I did not want to tie us up for the morning, because we had to go first to the Embassy.

I informed Gábor about my discussion with Margaret and after that we went over to West Berlin to buy some newspapers. We bought the Tagesspiegel the headline of which declared: There are still heavy fighting in Budapest. The subtitle was: Hungarian military units sided with the revolutionaries – The most part of Budapest is in the hands of the Revolutionaries.

Evening, when we returned to the Hotel we tried to call our family, but we got no connection, finally the telephone operator called and said that her workday ended and she could not get a connection. She said that she called the telephone company and she was told that all day they were not able to get any connection to Budapest and they were also unable to get a connection to any other city in Hungary.

26 He who dares wins

We were trying to call Budapest over the weekend, on Saturday as well as on Sunday, but got no connection. On October 29, Monday we went again to the Embassy. Editke looked very depressed and said that she tried to call her family over the weekend but could not get a connection. Without asking anything she picked up the phone and called Béla. Béla arrived shortly and as usual asked us to sit down, took his cigarette, lit it. It seems he remembered that we are not smoking and he did not offer us cigarettes. He was not in a good mood either, he said immediately, that he has no new information, they could not talk to Budapest and openly told us, that the only information he has is from the West Berlin radio stations that there are probably serious fighting in Budapest presumably with the Russians. He told us to wait for a few minutes he is going to bring us some money. He left and came back shortly and gave each of us an envelope.

“The money in the envelope should be enough for more than two days. Get receipts for your expenses and come back two days from now account for the money and you will get money again, but we are hoping the situation is going to change and you can go home.”

Handshake, waving to Editke we left the Embassy and went back to the Hotel. We decided that for lunch we are going to West Berlin and look at the newspapers. On the first page of the newspapers reports were about the situation in Budapest. The change they reported was that the Russians are moving out of Budapest and its vicinity and also they are leaving from the military bases located in several parts of Hungary. According to the newspapers the troops are being transported by train towards the Soviet Union. The problems of the Russians with the Poles did not get finished yet. According to the newspapers in Prague there are no problems and the traffic between Berlin and Prague is uninterrupted.

Early afternoon as it was agreed we went to the Humboldt University where we briefly explained that because of the Hungarian situation we have to stay in Berlin for the time being. They asked us if we would know how long we are going to be in Berlin we should let them know as they would like to start their own research project in connection with the RF and as long as we are in Berlin they would like us to help them. We said that we are going to find out and be in touch.

During the evening we tried again to call Budapest but no luck. Gábor decided he is going to attempt to go home, because at the train station we learned that the train traffic to Prague is really uninterrupted. So Gábor on Tuesday, October 30 took the early afternoon train to Prague. I went with him to the railroad station and told him I am going to wait until I will be able to get telephone connection and talk with my family or when according to the Embassy the trip to Budapest will be feasible. I said that I am planning to go to the Humbodt University and start there with the colleagues a research project which I planned to start at TKI.

Gabor's trip to Prague was according to schedule. From his friends in Prague he knew that the Hotel Axa is near the railroad station and he walked there. In view of the Hungarian and Polish problems the Hotel had very few guests, so he had no problem to get a room. In the Hotel he learned, that the Hungarian border was closed by the Czechs so the „revolution should not spill over", therefore there is no traffic between Czechoslovaky and Hungary. So Gábor got stuck in Prague. His problem was that he had very little money. He converted his DDR Marks, but that was not much. He also converted the dollars left over after our excursions to West Berlin. The Hungarian Embassy did not know him so he could not receive support from them, so his days were numbered.

Every day he tried to call his wife, Terka. Finally on November 1 he succeded. Terka told him with great enthusiasm, that the Russians are leaving, and this is the end of the
communism.

Gábor was lucky, because on November 3 he found out that from Bratislava[73] some freighters may sail down the Danube to Budapest and he may be able to get to Budapest. He got on a train which arrived at 3 AM in Bratislava and he really found a freighter which was going to Budapest carrying cement bags. He found the captain, who was a Slovakian, but spoke Hungarian and told him what his situation was. The captain told him, that there are a few Hungarians already on the boat and he would be glad to take him, but there is no place to sleep and the trip could last more than 10 hours. Gábor told him, it is not a problem, he can catch up with sleep after he arrived in Budapest. The boat really left in the morning and by November 4 noon got as far as Visegrad[74], where the bed

[73] A large city on the Danube, capital of Slovakia.
[74] A Hungarian city on the Danube with an ancient castle on the top of a small hill.

of the Danube narrows. Here from the shore Hungarians started to shoot at the ship. Gábor assumed and the captain agreed that they are shooting at the boat with rifles and not with guns. They heard some of the bullets strike the steel side of the boat with a ping. The captain realized the situation: the problem was that the boat was flying a Czechoslovak flag. He gave one of the crew a Hungarian flag and also a white sheet and ordered him to remove the Czech flag and hoist the Hungarian and somehow he also should attach the white sheet. The fellow like a rabbit ran to the end of the boat to the flag pool, while the sporadic shooting was going on. With one motion he pulled down the Czech flag and replaced it with the Hungarian and somehow attached the white sheet to it. A few minutes later the shooting stopped.

The ship berthed on the Buda side of the river. Gábor thanked the captain for the trip and started to walk home. That was on November 4th. Gábor since he talked with Terka a few days before and until he left the ship on the Buda side of the Danube knew nothing about the situation in Hungary. The last he knew was that the Russian troops departed from Budapest. He was surprised when he arrived in the vicinty of their apartment at Széna Square to see a Russian tank start to shoot at the house in which his apartment was. But somehow he managed to get home.

Terka was a pediatrician and she worked at the Tőzoltó Street children's Clinique. Even in the confusion of the Revolution she still had to go to attend her patients. It is the reason that on November 19th she learned from a worker of the railroad whose son she was treating, that in spite of the railroad strike a train is going to leave to

Szombathely[75]. The railroad worker, who came to pick up his child, said they should come that evening to the train station. Terka ran home, packed a little bag and she and Gábor went to the South station, found the train and went with the train employee, his now heatlhy son, another woman physician from the Hospital, her boyfriend and her mother to Szombathely. They slept in the train employees house and the next morning took a local train and arrived at the border where everybody had to get out. The Hungarian border guards asked if they have money. The five of them gave the Hungarian border guards all of the money they had. The border guards informed them, that a certain part of the border will not have Russian troops and so after 10 PM they could go over the border to Austria. The border was a small creek. They waded through it in knee deep water, while they heard shooting in the distance. They winded up in a village near the border and spent the night in a Hospital. There were many wounded Hungarians for whom the crossing of the border was not as easy as for them. Next day they went by train south to Graz, where a transitional camp was established for the Hungarian refugees. From there they went by train to Linz, a town on the Danube, west of Vienna where they winded up at a British refugee Committee. Gábor and Terka spoke English and German so they helped with translation. As a favor next day the British put them on an airplane going to London. Gábor and Terka three days after leaving Budapest winded up in London.

---

[75] A city on Hungary's Austrian border, very close (about 15 miles) to Austria.

27. Heads or tails

After Gábor left the conserve yhr money I was getting, I discussed with the Hotel management how much I shall pay being now alone in the room stuck in Berlin against my will. The Hotel was quite empty so we quickly agreed on a daily room rate. I developed my daily schedule. It was easy. On every second day I had to visit the Hungarian Embassy to find out if I would be able to go back to Budapest, if not to receive money for my stay in Berlin. I went every day to the Humboldt University where with my colleagues I started a massspectrometer program and usually daily I visited West-Berlin for uptodates from the newspapers about the Hungarian situation, of which naturally there was nothing mentioned in the East-Berlin news services, radio or newspapers. I also had to go to West-Berlin to buy what I needed, because on the East side there was pactically nothing available. Another reason was to go to movies, because by showing an „eastern identification paper the price of the ticckets were almost nothing. They showed magnificent films, Carousel, which was the movie adaptation of Ferenc Molnár's Liliom. Anastasia in which I saw for the first time Ingrid Bergman and Yul Brynner, Carmen Jones with Harry Belafonte, which was the modern adaptation of Bizet's Carmen. In front of one of the movies towered a three story high image of Elvis Presley with legs spread wide, guitar in hand plucking the strings advertising his movie: Love me tender. Whenever I went to a movie I found there were many people contrary to the movies in Budapest where the movies Lenin in October, Lenin in 1918, Lenin here, Lenin there were played to empty auditoriums. I told many times to my friends, that the movies in Budapest would be full if they would add to each the title under the quilt, for example Lenin in October under the quilt, etc.

Evenings I tried to call my family. Finally on November 1 I got a connection. Vera came to the telephone. As we did not know when the call will be interrupted and when I will be able to call again she quickly told me, what had happened, but one cannot judge the situation of what is going to happen during the next days. The communist system ended. On October 23 there were large demonstrations and Stalin's huge statue was pulled from its pedestal. Her information was that there were fights between the Russians the ÁVH and the demonstrators, unfortunately many people died. The building where we lived was also hit by bullets. She said many of our friends left for Austria, because the border is practically open. I suggested she should find somebody who can drive an automobile and she and Éva should come in my car to Vienna and I will go there from Berlin, but if she cannot find anybody to drive my car she should join some of our friends who are going to Austria. This she did not want to do, she said that rather I should go back to Budapest and we could drive to Vienna together. Finally she agreed that she is going to look for somebody who can drive a car. I told her, that I am going to try to call daily.

I was very surprised, that our friends and acquaintances just simply went to Austria. But after a short consideration I realized that this was quite feasible. The Hungarian – Austrian border was part of what Churchill named the iron curtain which prohibited people from the Baltic to the Adriatic Sea to leave the Russian zone of occupation. Namely mine fields between barbed wire fences, military watch towers, border guards and dogs, one could not escape from Hungary to Austria. Austria and Vienna were after the war divided into four sectors, the same way as Germany. Austria's eastern strip adjacent to Hungary, called Burgenland was the Russian sector. If somebody was lucky to cross the barbed wire, minefield, watchtower fortified iron curtain, that person would have to cross the Russian sector to get to freedom. The Russian sector in some areas was wider and at other narrower, but the Russian patrols were everywhere. The mined border and the Russian sector made it almost impossible for an illegal border crossing.

Two years after Stalin's death in May 1955 the Soviet Union signed a peace treaty with Austria and withdrew its troops from the Russian sector. Simultaneously the Americans, British and French did it too. Austria became an independent neutral country.

In 1955 and during the beginning of 1956 the communist regime's power in Hungary became somewhat unstable. There were times when Rákosi was demoted, but other times he got back to power again, and alternating sometimes Ernő Gerő, sometimes András Hegedűs, other times Imre Nagy became the leader. Imre Nagy regarded Austria to be a model for Hungary and started discussions with Austria. The result of these discussions was that the Hungarian government at the beginning of 1956 removed the barbed wire fences and the mine field from the border of the two countries. Only the border guards remained and whoever was able to get through was in security after they crossed the Austrian border. It was very likely, that as a result of the October 23 Revolution the border guards fled and therefore whoever managed to get to the border was able to walk over to Austria unharmed.

I could not sleep all night. I remembered my discussion with Professor Bruckner on December 1948, when I confessed to him that I would like to go to the West. At that time I missed the opportunity, because the „iron curtain closed the border before I finished my studies at the University. Now suddenly a new opportunity was offered. Shall I take this opportunity? I considered the arguments for and against. After my University studies I was able to join Tungsram's Research Institute, where I had very interesting work. In the country, as during the Nazi times, in the brutal communist dictatorship the evil people surfaced again and also those who by climbing on the bandwagon of the communist ideology tried to get on account of others a better position. Many people for no reaon winded up in jail, many were deported or driven to poverty, but luckily in my surrounding I had only very decent people, so nobody was harmed. This was not everywhere and lately there were signs that the good situation in TKI will also change. Some of the newly hired „cadre who could not obtain success professionaly one could feel that they are trying to achive progress by ruining others. When I thought this over it became clear to me, that TKI in the present communist dictatorship was a unique oases in which the management was still valuing results and surrounded these people with a bulwark, but this will change sooner or later[76]. Maybe this is a good opportunity for me and my family to go to the West. But I am in Berlin and my family is in Budapest and by the time I go back the situation is going to change back to what it was before and again become impossible to leave the country.

[76] This situation took place after 1956 in TKI.

To meet Vera and Éva in Vienna they had to find somebody who can drive a car or an acquaintance who is planning to go to Austria. If I am going from Berlin through Germany to Vienna I am going to need an Austrian visa. On the other hand if I get an Austrian visa and it is stamped into my official passport and I go back to Budapest and if the regime will become communist again, then according to the rules I have to return my passport and if they see an Austrian visa in it I will be jailed immediately because of it. I had to think a lot what to do now? On one side of the coin was that in spite of the risk I should choose the free West, on the coin's other side were the many unforeseen hazards leaving my country. Heads or tails?

I did not have to flip a coin that fate should decide what I should do, because I already made the decision. I was very sure that Vera will find somebody who will be glad to take the opportunity to drive them to Vienna and get out of Hungary elegantly by car. When on November 2 the day after I talked on the telephone with Vera, I went to the Austrian delegation, they stamped immediately and free of charge a visa in my passport valid to go from Germany to Austria. I should have thought of what Julius Caesar said when he crossed the Rubicon river: "Alea jacta est" (the dice is thrown), but instead I said my favorite saying: "Now the monkey jumps in the water".

Days passed and I was not able to talk with Vera. I visited in the meantime the Opperts, they as usual provided an excellent dinner. Mr. Oppert's opinion was that because the Russians still have problems in Poland, and because of the world's public opinion, they are going to make an agreement with the Hungarian revolutionaries. In his opinion the problem is that England, France and Israel attacked Egypt and the world's public opinion is also preoccupied with that issue. Michael Oppert's opinion was very encouraging because they were able to listen not only to the German stations but also to the BBC and the Voice of America.

Finally on November 5, Monday, I was able to get a telephone connection to Budapest. Vera said she was not able to find anybody who would drive them to Vienna, she asked me to go back to Budapest and we should go together to Vienna. This was an incredible surprise for me. It also did not sound that she made any effort to find somebody, because she could not mention a name with whom she was talking about this. I told her, for me to go back for the time being is not possible, because the Czechs closed the entire Hungarian border and all traffic is prohibited from Czechoslovakia to Hungary.

This changed everything for me. The time when I would be able to go back to Budapest would be only when the Czechs opened the border, but then the situation in Hungary probably would change back to what it was before the revolution. Also the Hungarian – Austrian border could be closed by that time.

I felt stupid that I got the Austrian visa, but I could not even imagine that Vera would not find somebody who would drive the car, or find friends to go with to Austria, when she said before that many of our friends were leaving for Austria. For me, with the Austrian visa in my passport meant that if I go back to Hungary and cannot get out and ultimately I have to return my passport to the authorities, the jail would be the best among many other possibilities which I knew the system that existed before the revolution could give me.

When I was thinking over what to do one of the possibilities was that I proceed as I planned to go to Vienna and tell Vera that she should organize through friends for her and Éva to go through the still open border to Vienna and we will meet there. The other possibility was that I will go back to Budapest and try somehow to get out of Hungary, before I have to return my passport.

From my discussion with Vera I realized that she is either not willing or not capable to organize their trip to Vienna, which left me with the only possibility to go back to Budapest and somehow get out before the communist system returned to Hungary and I have to return my passport.

I came to the conclusion, that the most complicated, but the most secure method would be to go to Budapest and from there with my wife and daughter in my car to return to Berlin. The Austrian visa may present a little complication, but as I have my passport in my hand which is a rare privilege I could return to Berlin. I only need to get for Vera and Éva an exit permit. I even figured out the reason I had to come back to Berlin and that was the research work I started at Humboldt University. If I could get from the colleagues at the Humboldt University a letter or if they would agree that if they are asked they would state the work we started here should be finished and for this they need me to come back to Berlin. Obviously I can say that I cannot leave my family in Budapest in this unsecure times and I want them to return with me to Berlin.

If this scheme would not work we can try the Austrian border and if that is closed we could try the Yugoslavian one, because my understanding was that Hungarian refugees were going through that route too.

When I considered the situation I gave myself an optimistic 50% chance that it will work, which I realized was much better than a 0% chance.

My first step should be to talk to colleagues at Humboldt University. It was agreed that on the next day I was going to Humboldt to discuss the planned experiments. When I arrived in Margaret's office she just lit her cigarette. They put a desk and a chair for me in her office to use for my work when I am in the Institute. I greeted her, and after the obligatory handshake I sat down to my desk and sketched to her my situation. As everybody was listening to the Western broadcasts and saw the Western newspapers I did not have to make explanations. I started to discuss my main problem, that after the traffic will begin to Hungary I have to go back to pick up my family. I told her the problems related to my coming back with my family to Berlin, that I would need some kind of paper that I need to finish here the work I started.

Without hesitation she said, that this would be feasible, but it is unlikely that I should be able to receive a paper with official stamps. She explained why this is unlikely. Margaret and her colleagues cannot write such a paper. It has to be sent to various offices for approval. This would take a long time and most likely it would not be successful to get an approval. On the other hand she would give me her and her colleague's office and home telephone numbers and if they want confirmation she and the others could be called any time of the day to give verbal assurance that I have to come back to Berlin because of my work. I realized that to obtain a written confirmation that they ask me to return to Berlin is almost impossible, because the DDR authority would be suspicious that if I am planning to come back to Berlin with my family, that means I may not want to go back to Hungary. On the other hand Margaret's proposal was very good and even that would be somewhat risky for them. I thanked her very much and said I will be back late afternoon to discuss some of the planned experiments and could I get those telephone numbers by then. She promised and I went back to my Hotel.

I thought over my possibilities in case I would be able to come back to Berlin where I could find a job. I remembered Dr. Walter Dahlke who was working in the West German Telefunken Company's research laboratory and had a very good reputation for his scientific work on electron tube cathodes. I also worked in that field and had several publications in western scientific magazines. Besides of that I also worked on the analysis of residual gases in electron tubes which was a new area of research and that was the reason I was invited by the East German Chemical Society to give a paper. I assumed that maybe Dr. Dahlke would be interested that I should continue my work in his laboratory. To explore this possibility I had to find Dr. Dahlke at the Telefunken Company's electron tube research laboratory.

In my East Berlin Hotel obviously there was no telephone book and I had more sense than to ask at the desk about a West Berlin company, because who knows what and to whom the employees of the Hotel had to report. So next day I went to the Kempinsky Hotel, which I also visited previously, and where by visiting them before considered myself to be a guest, and went to its telephone room I looked up the addresses of the Telefunken Company. Telefunken was a large company founded in 1903 and it was the manufacturer of radio transmitters and receivers and their components. I found the company in the telephone book very easily, but the problem was Telefunken had in West Berlin many sites. I selected which looked the most likely one: Telefunken Röhrenwerk - Telefunken Electrontube factory. I wrote down its address: Berlin – Tiergrten/Moabit district, 71 Sickingen Street.

From the Kempinski Hotel on Kurfürstendamm, where at this time I did not drink Coca Cola I went to Telefunken's Sickingen Street factory. I entered Telefunken's big four story factory building and enquired from the doorman about Dr. Dahlke. He could not tell me anything so I said that I would like to visit the personnel Department. I assumed they could tell me in this big factory complex where I could find Dr. Dahlke. The young girl with big blond hair and glasses picked up a booklet which looked like a small telephone book she leafedthrough it and finally said, that Dr. Dahlke is located in Telefunken's Research Laboratory in Ulm. I must have looked at her somewhat perplexed, because she added that the city of Ulm is located south east of Stuttgart. When I realized that Dr. Dahlke is not working in Berlin, but he was in the Telefunken Research Laboratory in Ulm I decided the best would be to talk with the local head of the Personnel department and to explain why I am looking for Dr. Dahlke. I told the blond girl that I am coming from Hungary because I was invited to give a presentation at the DDR Chemical Society's yearly meeting in Leipzig and that I am working on similar subjects as Dr. Dahlke and that is the reason I would have loved to meet him. But as he is in Ulm I would like to talk with the head of this personnel department. The girl when she heard I am Hungarian became very friendly. She got on the phone and called her boss. After she put the receiver down told me that I should go to the door behind her, her boss is waiting for me in his office.

The head of the Personnel department was about a 50 year old bald bespectacled man. He was sitting behind a fairly large desk in a large armed chair and smoking. When I entered he stood up extended his arm over the desk, shook my hand and motioned for me to sit down in front of his desk. I introduced myself, naturally mentioning doctor before my name, as I knew that in Germany who does not have a doctorate is considered to be in a lower caste. The title Professor is the absolute top. I told him what I told the blonde girl but added that my intention is to stay in the West and my question to Dr. Dahlke would have been if I could get a job in his laboratory.

"Herr Doctor Váradi – he started – my responsibility extends only to the electron tube factory and the research department in Berlin. As Dr. Dahlke is in the factory and research laboratory in Ulm I am not competent for that. But because your knowledge and qualification could be important to Telefunken I am going to call the President of the Electron Tube factory to ask his recommendation."

He picked up the telephone and started to talk I assumed to the secretary of the President. When he stopped the discussion, he motioned with his hand, which looked like I should wait. Soon he started to talk again. When he finished he turned to me:

"The President asked if you have now time to go to his office he would like to talk to you. My secretary will escort you. Thank you for your visit and I hope we are going to meet again."

He got up, came to the other side of his desk and escorted me out from his office. He told his secretary to take me to the President's office. Turned to me, shook hands and I followed the blond girl very surprised at this turn of events.

The office of the President of Telefunken Electron Tube Factory was on the top floor of the building. We went up by elevator. The secretary from the Personnel department knocked on the door and we entered into the very elegant room of the President's secretary. Beautiful oil paintings were on the wall on the shining polished floor Persian rugs. Next to the walls were vitrines in which old and new electron tubes were displayed. The blond girl, who came with me, greeted the also blond but short haired, very elegantly dressed middle aged secretary of the president sitting behind a large polished brown desk, with something that sounded like "schuss". The President's secretary repeated this greeting. My escort introduced me, that I was Herr Doctor Varadi. The short haired blond lady smiled at me, got up came to me and we shook hands – I already learned that every German shakes hand at every meeting or when leaving -, she said.

"Herr Doctor Varadi, please follow me."

She started to go towards a big double door to her left, knocked and entered. I found it interesting, that compared to what was customary in Hungary here the door of the big bosses were not padded. The President's office was a huge corner room with big windows. The short haired lady introduced me:

"Herr Doctor Varadi, Herr Director."

The President was sitting in a huge leather chair behind a huge desk located in the space before the windows. There were a few documents on the desk and in the corner towards me was a vase with flowers. The room's wall had brown wood lining. On the walls the paintings were of marine theme, sailing ships, lighthouses, on the floor Persian rugs. He got up came to me and we shook hands. The President was a tall, lean, balding man with light blue eyes and I noticed how straight his posture was. With his arm he pointed towards the sitting arrangement, four big leather arm chairs in the middle of them was a low brown lacquered table. On the table was a metal tray with a bottle, which looked it was of lead crystal full of water. There were a few ashtrays on the table and a box full of cigarettes.

He motioned for me to sit down and offered me cigarettes. I declined. He sat down opposite me, took a cigarette and lit it. I again noticed how straight his posture was even when he was sitting.

"Herr Doctor Váradi" – it was interesting, that he pronounced my name with a perfect Hungarian pronunciation – "our personnel director informed me, that you are working in Hungary as a research chemist and you are here, because you were invited by the DDR Chemical Society; yearly convention to present a paper about your work. And that you would like possibly to work in Dr. Dahlke's research department because your present work was in that area."

"Herr Director" – I said – "this is exactly right. Presently I am working in the Telecommunication Research Institute in Budapest, which was before Tungsram's Research Laboratory and I am the head of its chemical department for electron tube research and several of my papers related to this field were published in Hungary as well as in the West. One of my latest work is related to the analysis of residual gases in electron tubes, which is a new area even globally and I was invited to the conference in Leipzig to report about this subject. I was never a member of the communist party and I am very glad, that Hungary was liberated from communism a few days ago, but the way I see the situation the Russians are going to bring back the previous communist system and I would like to take advantage of the present situation and with my family, wife and daughter leave Hungary and continue my work in the West, for example under the direction of Dr. Dahlke."

During the continuation of our discussion the President turned to the Hungarian situation. He said that by now at least a hundred thousand Hungarians fled through the border to Austria and more and more are coming daily.

I explained, that for the time being I cannot go back to Hungary, because the Czech closed the border. But as soon as I get back I am planning to come back to Berlin immediately. I left Hungary a week before the revolution started with a passport. I have this passport and because of that I believe I can come back. It was obvious that he wanted to do something for me and said that he is going to call Dahlke. He picked up the telephone which was on the table, pushed a button and said:

“Mrs. Maetzel, please look my calendar and tell me when am I going to have tomorrow a free half hour?”

It seemed that the secretary told him, he thanked her and hung up the telephone.

“Could you come to see me tomorrow at 10 AM?”

“With pleasure.”

He stood up, escorted me to the door of his office, shook hands and said good bye.

I said good bye to the secretary, but she said she is going to escort me to the elevator.

“We see you tomorrow! – she said – we shook hands as is the national custom in Germany.”

On the way to the Hotel I bought a bunch of bananas. I still had salami and salami and banana was my usual dinner.

During the evening I was thinking about the issues. After all it would make lots of sense if I would really come back to Berlin, God knows what conditions are going to wait for me at home. My discussion with the President was very encouraging. It was very perceptible that everybody is trying to support the Hungarian refugees. But I would like to go through Berlin sooner or later to America. On the other hand to work with Dr. Dahlke was also very tempting, because I read many of his interesting work.

The next day, November 8 at 10 AM I entered the President secretary's office. She greeted me with a smile and told me, that the president is waiting for me I should go to see him in his office. I knocked on the door and entered. He came to me, shook hands and motioned that I should sit down. He sat down too. Now it was not the cigarette the first item, but in a friendly tone he told me, that he talked with Dr. Dahlke, who read my papers and would be very glad if I would work with him.

He told me, when I will return to Berlin I can start to work here in the Research Laboratory.

I was very happy to hear that and told him, I am going back to Budapest as soon as I can and I hope that soon I am going to visit him again, because I would be glad to continue my work here.

"Good luck and see you again! – Handshakes and with this my problems in Berlin became closer to be solved. The only little problem was left, how can I get back?."

The West Berlin papers reported of Russian intervention and were not very optimistic. On the next day, November 9, Friday, I visited the Hungarian Embassy. I talked with Béla, but he was not able to tell me anything new. We left, that I am going to visit him again on Monday.

I spent the following week going every day to the Humboldt University where we started experiments. On every second day I went to the Embassy where the mood gradually declined, I was able to get two times a telephone connection with Vera. The situation in Budapest deteriorated a lot. Russian tanks appeared in the city. She also said that Gábor Sebestyén called and said that he arrived in Budapest and they are planning to go over to Austria. Vera did not say that she wanted to join them. It looked like she expected I should go back independent of the consequences.

The change started the next Monday, November 19. At the Embassy Editke looked very low spirited and called Béla immediately. Béla showed up and did not light a cigarette. He gave me the envelope he had in his hand and told me, that the Embassy ran out of money, at best the next time he could give me something, but they will not have any money. According to him the Czech border is still closed. He inquired but there is still no air connection between Prague and Budapest. His opinion was that my ticket from Berlin to Prague is not valid anymore, and that maybe the only possibility would be to go to Hungary by train to Komarno. There is a bridge on the Danube and to cross the bridge to the Hungarian town, Komárom. But he did not know whether one could go through that bridge or not.

I was able to talk with Vera that evening. She said that the Russian troops occupied everything. Imre Nagy, the Prime Minister asked asylum at the Yugoslavian Embassy. There is a great uncertainty about what is going to happen. This news made it urgent if I want to come back to Berlin that I should get home, before the old regime is reestablished. I told Vera that I am going to leave as soon as possible and try to get to Budapest therefore she should not worry if she will not hear from me in the next days.

Next day November 20 I went to the railroad station and inquired about the train schedule Berlin - Prague and from there to Komarno. I wrote down the schedule and the connections. I also went to the Humboldt University. I told Margaret my plan that I am going to try the next day to go back to Budapest and I hope we meet soon. We discussed what experiment they are going to do in the next weeks when after that hopefully I will be successful to come back and will continue my work. We said goodbye, she embraced me and wished me good luck and hoped to see me soon.

Early morning on November 21 I was on the railroad station to catch the train going to Prague. The road between Berlin and Prague was very interesting. The train stopped first in Dresden, which was a total ruin. Some people got off the train but nobody got on. I was left alone in my compartment. After Dresden the train followed the river Elbe to Czechoslovakia. The picturesque Bad Schandau on the banks of the river Elbe was the border town of DDR. The DDR border guards came on board checked papers and stamped my passport, the train went through the Czech border and stopped at the station of Dêĉin where the Czech border guards came and thoroughly examined everything, checked the baggage, under the seats and finally they also stamped my passport.

In Prague I had to transfer to the train going to Bratislava. I had plenty of time for speculation. In my thoughts it was clear that I can very well justify the need I have to return to Berlin. Namely I have my passport in my hand the colleagues in Berlin can verify that my knowledge is needed for the experiments we started. Furthermore I have a car which makes it easy that the three of us could go from Hungary in any direction. We can also take with us many important items.

During the long train ride I thought over what tasks are waiting for me in Budapest. On the slow advancing train from Prague to Bratislava I wrote the items on a piece of paper. I considered two cases. The first was that in spite of the Russian intervention the situation has not yet stabilized in Budapest. Naturally the second possibility was what should be my plans if the old system was restored. Both cases I thought through and noted on a piece of paper what I should do. I rewrote some of the points I changed the order of things to be done but finally when we arrived in Bratislava I believed I had ready a battle plan for each of these possibilities, naturally with lots of question marks and other possibilities in case a road is not feasible. Naturally I took care that if these papers would get in somebody's hand one could not tell what this is about.

This train went very slowly, stopped at many places, but finally arrived in Bratislava. How I am going to get to Komarno? There was a train listed, but only very late evening. I boarded that train with the idea that when I arrive in Komarno I will find out if the bridge over the Danube is open? If it is open I go over to Hungary immediately, if not at least I am going to find out when the border will reopen again.

The local train between Bratislava and Komarno also advanced very slowly. I reviewed my papers several times. I made corrections, crossed things out, because I considered, that whichever is the case I will have only a maximum of one week available to me to start my trip back to Berlin or leave Hungary by another route. The time was passing. By that time I was on a train more than twelve hours. At the end I could not think of anything anymore, half asleep, listening to the clattering of the train's wheels I started to hum a tune from my home town:

> 'Under the bridge of Szeged, my little angel.
> Girls baked fish, my little angel.'

The train arrived in Komarno late at night and stopped not far from the bridge over the Danube. On my enquiry I was told that the bridge was open for passenger traffic. So I started immediately. The Czech border guard stamped the date into my passport that I left the country on November 22. On the other side of the bridge besides of the Hungarian border guards were also Russian soldiers with sub-machine guns. They also examined my passport.

I asked the Hungarian border guard where the railroad station was and are the trains going to Budapest. He pointed out where the train station was and said that in his opinion trains may be going to Budapest. Getting this information I started toward the train station.

28. Steeplechase begins

It was a big surprise for my family, when on November 22 around 11 o'clock in the morning I entered our apartment. Nobody was able to speak except Éva, who immediately inquired what is in my luggage.

My mother's first sentence was that I should immediately eat something. Vera recounted the last day's events. The János Kádár-government appeared the first time on November 4, it became known only later that his speech was broadcasted from the Uzsgorod (Ungvár)77 radio station. On the same day Russian tanks started to attack. There was fighting on the streets, which lasted a few days. Kádár was now in Budapest and started to take control of matters. Imre Nagy and his associates fled to the Yugoslavian Embassy and the Kádár-government guaranteed in writing that if they leave the Embassy they are not going to be harmed. There are still strikes and the Kádár regime is not yet stabilized. But it is assumed that is only a matter of time.

From the narrative I came to the conclusion that the Russians want to reestablish the system which existed before the revolution or a variation of it and therefore it is very advisable to leave. I decided that out of the two plans I worked out on the train, I should proceed with the one which I planned for the case when the situation was not consolidated yet. The one week time during which, according to my plan, we have to leave is maybe realistic,

[77] Ungvár (Uzsgorod) is a city in Ukraine (in those days it was a part of the Soviet Union, now it is in Ukraine) inside of the Carpathian mountains, close to Hungary.

but I have to use every minute, because one cannot tell when Kádár with the help of the Russians will be able to consolidate his position and reestablish the old system. Vera talked on the telephone with some of my colleagues, they told her, that since November 4, when the fighting began they did not go to TKI of Újpest. Gyurka Gergely who lives on the Rózsadomb district of Budapest, a few days ago walked up to TKI HQ which is also on Rózsadomb and met a few colleagues who also lived not far away from there. He said that he saw a few people also in the Personnel department, but they also lived nearby. One could not rely on public transportation.

The first thing was that I showered, ate something and according to my program started with the first step, went down to the garage to start my car. It was a nice sunny day, not cold. I opened the door of the garage to take my car to the street. Sat in the car and tried to start it, but the battery must have been discharged because the starter clicked but did nothing else. I got out, opened the hood, took out the crank and tried to start the car. Nothing. The engine did not start.

That was not a reassuring beginning. I closed the hood, closed the door of the garage and went home. On the way I was thinking what can I do? If I could reach Béla M. maybe he could come here with a new battery. This problem was not in my program and this unfortunately could cause a sizable delay in my plans.

I thought over whom I could reach to help me. The first was obviously Béla M.. I called him on the telephone. Probably they were not at home, or their telephone did not work, because it was ringing but they did not pick it up. The next was Béla L.. They were at home. He was very glad that I called him and that I was back in Budapest. They were living quite far away on the other end of Buda. I hoped he would know how I could reach Béla M. He did not know. I told him, that we are going to talk about my trip in detail some other time. The third was my colleague Pali Havas who lived only a few blocks from me. Pali was the one who purchased from the junkyard the Adler automobile and he was a top expert in cars, motorbikes, machinery etc. Pali was at home and picked up the phone. He also greeted me with joy. I summarized for him my problem. He said that this was not a serious problem. I should go to my garage and he will be there in five minutes.

By the time I opened my garage door Pali was there with his red Adler. I asked him what does he know about TKI when was he there the last time. He said, he was there two days ago, very few people were there, but let's concentrate first on my car. He lifted the hood to look into the engine compartment, sat in the car and tried to start it, no result. He went to his car and drove it into my garage so that his car and my car almost touched. Went to the trunk of his car, opened it and took out two thick cables. He opened his car's engine compartment. His motor was running. He attached the clamps of the two cables to the two terminals of his battery and asked me to get in my car and try to start the motor, when he is going to indicate it by lifting his arm. By the time I was in my car and put the key into the ignition, I assumed that he already attached the clamps of his cable to my car' battery terminals because he stood next to my car, and I could not see him in front of the car when the hood was lifted. When he lifted his arm I turned the ignition key and the starter began to slowly crank the engine. The motor did not catch on. He motioned with his arm that I should continue. This went on for about a minute, when the motor started. Pali came to my car, where the window was down and said I should give full gas. I did. The motor coughed a few times but started to speed up. He motioned I should keep it full speed and when the motor started to run smoothly he motioned I should slowly take my foot off the gas pedal. I did it and when my foot was completely off the gas pedal the motor was still running very smoothly. I got out.

Pali took the cables off my battery, then from his. He closed the hood of the Adler and told me to close the hood of my car. I did it. Pali backed out from my garage and came to me:

"Do you have enough gas?"

"Yes, before I left, I filled the tank."

"Then now leave and turn to Váci Blvd, where you can drive fast and drive until the Hungaria Ring. There turn around and come back to Koháry Street and stop opposite to your house. I am going to drive behind you, in case your motor stops to help. When you are back I will come back too, but do not stop the motor until I am able to look at it."

When I got back, Pali arrived back too. He lifted the hood of my car. The motor was running very smoothly. He said I should stop the motor. I did. He said that I should start the car but with the crank and not with the starter. I did it. The motor came alive after the first turn of the crank. He said that I should drive the car as much as I can at high speed, but it would be good to change the battery. That was naturally a problem.

He asked me when I arrived. I said about two hours ago, but I am planning to go back to Berlin. He looked at me with big eyes. I presented the situation and told him that in my opinion every minute counts. I also told him I will call him in the evening. I got into my car and started toward the direction of Saint István Ring. Pali turned left to Balaton Street to go home. By that time it was about 2 PM.

In my plan the next step was to revalidate my passport, which was in my hands, for another exit from Hungary and to obtain for Vera and Éva a passport. I believed that for this I needed a recommendation from the Personnel department at TKI headquarter at Rózsadomb. When I reached Saint István Ring I turned left in the direction of the Margaret Bridge and on the empty Ring I went as fast as I could. When I crossed the bridge and was on the Buda side of the city I thought that Béla M.'s shop was on my way to Rózsadomb and I should go there first, he is maybe at home, he may not pick up his phone, because his telephone line was damaged during the fighting and his phone is not working. I arrived at his house. The yard's gate was open. I drove in. There were two cars on the grass, but I did not see Béla M. I did not stop the engine. I got out and went to his garage. I heard a noise that somebody was working inside, so I entered. Béla M. crawled out from under a car, showed his hands, which were oily, so he could not shake hands. I told him, that I tried to call him. He said his telephone line during the fighting went kaput and there is nobody now who would deal with repairs.

I told him briefly what happened to me and that I am planning to go back to Berlin, but I got this problem with the battery, which is very bad, because I have now a big need for my car. He said the battery is not a problem. He wiped his hands with a rag, went to the sink, washed them, and came to me and we shook hands.

We went to the yard, where my car's engine was still running. He opened the hood and supported it with the rod, he looked at the battery. I stopped the engine. He told me to go with him to the garage. There he gave me a few tools and said that I should carry the tools he is going to pick up a battery. He took the battery to my car and put it down on the grass in front of the car. Like a surgeon he took a tool from my hand, loosened screws holding the battery, and then the screws holding the cable. He gave the tools back lifted the battery out and put it on the grass. Picked up the new battery and put it in the place of the old one. He picked some tools from me, fastened the battery, put the cables on the terminals of the battery tightened all of the screws. He went back to the garage with the tools, but motioned that I should wait. He came out with an oil can and some rags. He poured from the oil can a little oil on the rag and wiped it on the terminals and screws of the battery. He put the oil can on the grass and checked the level of the oil in the motor, he nodded approvingly and said that everything is OK, but I should take at least one liter of oil with me. I should check the oil level daily and if it is down I should add to it. He took a small tool from his pocket and started to check the pressure in the tires. It seems he found all of them OK, because after the fourth tire he put the small tool back into his pocket.

I asked how much I owe him. Looked at me, shook my hand and said:

"I do not say au revoir, I only wish you good luck. Servus" – he embraced me.

I did not know what to say. I wanted to thank him for helping me to get this car because he discovered the way to get it and for keeping this junk in such a good shape, but finally I embraced him and said only:

"I hope I am going to get with this car to Berlin. Servus." – and for the first time I realized that I was closing a chapter of my life.

Leaving Béla M. I drove up to TKI's Rózsadomb HQ. At the entrance was a guard, but he just waved me in. I went directly to the Personnel department. A secretary was there whom I knew. We exchanged greetings then she waved me to go to her boss's office. When I walked in the boss was sitting behind his desk smoking. He obviously was happy to see me, maybe that I returned from Berlin, or maybe he had finally something to do. After we greeted each other and shook hands, he indicated, that I should sit down in front of his desk.

I told him, that I arrived today back from Berlin and told him my story also that I have to go back, because I worked for almost a month on some experiments with colleagues from Humboldt University and they asked me to continue it but I want to take my wife and my daughter with me because I am afraid to leave them here under these uncertain conditions. He nodded appreciatively. I said that in about three weeks, in the middle of December we would finish the experiments and plan to come back, by that time the situation here will normalize and I can continue my work in Újpest. He liked it very much. I asked him if he would think that it would be possible and would he support this.

"Very logical, what you said and I will support you in everything. I am going to give you a paper in which I certify that you are doing an important job and ask everybody's support. I suggest you should go to KGM (Ministry for Middle Machine Industry) and ask there a paper that they are requesting to extend your passport and recommending to issue the passports for your wife and daughter."

"Who shall I look for in the Ministry?"

"I have no idea who is there. Wait a minute, I am going to call there the Personnel chief, a good friend of mine and going to ask for his recommendation."

He called his secretary:

"Call the Personnel Department at KGM and if you find somebody switch the phone to me. Also please bring in a Hungarian – Russian language certification card, and fill it out for Doctor Váradi, I am going to sign it."

After this he lit a cigarette.

The secretary came in a few minutes later the paper in her hand.

"Nobody is picking up the phone at the KGM Personnel Department. I assume they did not go to work. I talked to the telephone operator who said there are only a few people at work in the Ministry. Here is the card for Doctor Váradi."

She put a half page document in front of him, which he signed immediately and gave to me.

The paper in Hungarian and in Russian had the following text:

CERTIFICATE

We confirm that Ferenc P. Váradi is the emplyee of the Telecommunication Research Institute. We are asking the Hungarian and Russian authorities, that for him – in view of his important work – a free transit should be allowed.

Budapest November 19, 1956

Telecommunitaion Research Institute
Revolutionary Workers' Council

Signature
Stamp.

"With this you can move around in the city and if you find somebody in the Ministry this will help to extend your passport and for your wife and daughter to get a passport. If there would be any problem they can call me, I am giving you my private number."

On a piece of paper which was on his desk he wrote his telephone number and gave it to me.

I stood up he did too, came around his desk and escorted me to the door. I opened it, we shook hands. He wished me success for the experiments in Berlin. When I was half way out the door I turned around like I would have forgotten the most important thing, I asked:

"As I arrived today and was not in the Laboratory in Újpest, I would like to find out how I am going to get my salary for the time I was in Berlin and the time I am going to spend there?"

"Since October 23 nobody received their salary, because we could not receive money and send it to Újpest. I hope that by next week everybody will receive the missed salary. In case if by that time you are on your way to Berlin, leave an authorization with somebody to pick up your salary."

I was already at his secretary's desk, so I turned back and said to both of them:

"Thank you, see you soon."

When I left TKI and sat in my car it was half past three. I thought that as he suggested I should go now to the Middle Machine Ministry (KGM).

As there was practically no traffic in 20 minutes I reached the entrance of KGM. A guard in civilian clothing was at the door. I told him that I am looking for the deputy Minister responsible for the TKI issues. The guard looked at me perplexed so I repeated my question and added that I am coming for a very urgent matter and showed him the Certificate the TKI personnel chief gave me.

The Certificate must have had a big effect on him, because he said he is going to look into the matter and went into his little cubicle to call somebody. He took a sheet of paper and studied whom to call. He did not have much luck, because whoever he called did not pick up the phone. When he called the fourth number somebody on the other end picked it up. He talked briefly, hung up and came out:

"There are only very few people in this building, therefore the best would be to go on the elevator to the top floor. When you get out of the elevator there is a com.... (he did not say the end of the word) desk, that you will see and the guard on that floor can tell you to whom you can speak."

"Where is the elevator?"

He showed me in which direction I should go.

As I stepped out of the elevator on the top floor I immediately noticed the desk with a beefy guy in civilian clothing sitting behind it. It looked like he knew I was coming. We greeted each other I showed him also my certificate. He read it with interest. I told him that the Head of TKI's Personnel Deapartment sent me to immediately talk with the deputy minister who is responsible for TKI related issues.

He said that he does not know who is responsible for TKI. Apparently he had no idea what TKI was. He added that he was sent here only today and he does not know anyone. He said, that there is practically nobody on this floor except someone is working in one of the offices, maybe I should go there and ask. He showed me which door I should enter.

The room I entered was a fairly large office with a secretarial desk in the middle. The lights were on and there was a paper in the typewriter, but no secretary. Judging from the furniture this must have been the entry room to a high ranking official. I knocked on the door which led from this room, but got no answer. I assumed that it was a padded door and one cannot hear the knocking, so I entered.

The room I entered was a very elegantly furnished very large room. In the right hand corner was a sitting area. Opposite the door a huge window and in front of the window a very large desk behind which was sitting an about 50 year old, balding, tall gentleman. Obviously he was smoking.

He looked at me curiously. I greeted him politely, apologized to bother him, I handed him my Certificate, and told him, that I am not sure if I am at the right place, because I could not get any directions from the guards. I told him, that the Head of the Personnel Department at TKI, with whom I talked this afternoon advised me to come immediately here because of my work I need some papers from KGM.

He motioned I should sit down. I sat down and tried to briefly summarize the reason I am visiting KGM. That I was in the DDR on their Chemical Society's yearly conference in Leipzig, because I was invited to give a talk, but as I could not come back to Hungary I worked almost a month at Humboldt University's physical chemical department where I helped to start some experiments. I came back today but I would have to go back for about three weeks to finish the work. In order to go back I would need to get my passport – which I showed to him – to be validated for another exit and my wife and daughter would need a passport, because I would not want to leave them here under these uncertain conditions.

He looked at me understandingly and asked if I have an invitation letter from the Humboldt University? I said I did not get one, because when I found out from the Embassy that the Czech border was open the time until my departure was very short and also because of the uncertainty of the Hungarian situation they were not able to arrange a letter of invitation.

He nodded understandingly.

"Then how could I do anything if there is no letter for which I could give permission to extend the passport?"

"You are perfectly right, for that reason my colleagues at the Humboldt University proposed, that they could be called on the telephone and they will verify that my presence is needed because of the experiments we started. They want to publish the results in a scientific magazine as the continuation of the paper I presented at the conference in Leipzig as soon as possible."

I now took out from my pocket a folded sheet of paper which I received from Margaret. On the Humboldt University's letter head were the names and telephone numbers of my colleagues assembled by Margaret. I had this paper with me, because I thought I might need it at TKI. I opened the folded paper and put it on his desk.

“There are the names of my colleagues you may call any of them to verify that what I said to you is the truth.”

He looked at the paper and it seemed that Humboldt University’s letterhead had an effect on him.

“I am going to try to call them.”

This was an obviously good decision for him not to take any risk, because it was very unlikely he could get a telephone line in a short time and then he could say it is getting too late that he is going to try it tomorrow. I should come back tomorrow morning. He must have been very sure of that, because he most likely speaks no German and what would he do if the call goes through and somebody picks up the phone in Berlin?

He looked at the paper form Humboldt University and dialed the number. It looked like he was able to get a direct line and he knew by heart the area code of the DDR. I was surprised.

After he finished dialing he waited and looked at me. It sounded like, whomever he called and I assumed that it must have been Margaret, because her name was the first on the list, answered the phone, because he started to speak with somebody in German.

I was surprised that he spoke a very decent German, I did not expect that. I understood whatever he said it was obvious they were discussing my case. He said that I am sitting in his office and according to me I have to go back to Berlin. After this he was listening for a long time I assumed to what Margaret was saying. At the end he thanked for the information and said that he is going to do everything about my travel. He very cordially said goodbye and hung up the phone.

First he started to take from the cigarette-box a cigarette, but he changed his mind and picked up the box to offer me a cigarette.

"I am older than you are I propose that we should talk to each other not so formal[78]. My name is Mihály. Would you like a cigarette?"

"I am Ferenc. Thank you. I am not smoking."

He picked up a cigarette took the lighter form the table and lit it. He inhaled the smoke than exhaled it.
"I think we both got surprises. My first surprise was that I got a connection to Berlin immediately and the lady whose number is on this paper picked up the phone immediately. After this you were surprised, which I have seen from your face that I speak German, which you did not assume about me. I worked for three years at our Embassy in Berlin and I learn easily languages, I speak a very decent German. My further surprise was that the lady whose name you gave me is a lecturer on the Humboldt University, which title makes the person in Germany equivalent at least to a small God, a full Professor which is higher, is a full God. If somebody is a lecturer at the Humboldt University that is a big position.

---

[78] In Hungarian as in French vous and tu or German sie and du there is a distinction to be formal or friendlier. He proposed to use the less formal style of talking.

“What was interesting for me is the story you told me that you have to go back to the world famous Humboldt University, because you are needed for the experiments. I called them as I considered your story totally unlikely because you were too young for that. My big surprise was that it seems in science you are really considered an important person, the people at Humboldt University were very glad that while you were stuck in Berlin they could have worked with you on a research project and they want you back to finish the project.”

I interrupted him at this point.

“They depict scientists as old people, but people considered to be scientists are like football players. A football player at the age of 35 is considered old. Scientists at age 35 are also over their peak. Einstein who died at age 76 made all of his work which made him famous in the years between the age 25 and 35. But forgive me, do not misunderstand me, I do not want to compare myself to Einstein or to other really great scientists. There are many excellent scientists in Hungary and I do not deserve this title, I may have had luck to be working on a subject considered new and for this reason my colleagues working in similar field found it interesting.”

He pushed a button on the table and in seconds his secretary about 60 years old with graying hair came in.

„Éva, - he said – I know that it is very hard to find anything here as nobody is around in this building, but we need two forms in which we are requesting the issuing of passports. Could you please find them and fill them out. Here is comrade Váradi's service passport. The other is for his wife and daughter. He looked at me."

"My wife's name is Vera and my daughter's is Éva Anna."

"I would ask you to complete them, stamp them and I am going to sign them."

29. Race against time

I got home by half past five. I parked the car in the garage. When I closed the garage door, I realized I arrived only this morning from Berlin and successfully completed a part of my plan developed on the train. I briefly told the day's events to my family, ate something and was in bed by 7 PM, because suddenly I felt very tired and wanted to be at the passport office by the time they opened at 8 AM next morning.

The next day, November 23, I got acquainted with the 'chaotic situation' in Budapest. In the morning the news spread that Imre Nagy and his associates left the Yugoslavian Embassy after being reassured of their security. Allegedly they were transported by a Russian bus, but nobody knew to where. Furthermore, the other news was that in remembrance of the October 23 Revolution, between 2 and 3 PM, all traffic would stop in Budapest.

As I planned in the morning, I went to the National Police Passport Department, which was located on Andrássy Ave. Surprisingly it looked like this part of the government bureaucracy was functioning. Two policemen in police uniforms stood at the entrance. I told them that I needed to extend my passport and also I needed a new passport. I showed them the Certificate I received from TKI. They looked at it and sent me to the second floor, even telling me the room number. It seemed that office was also functioning. It was strange, however, that they let me in so easily and that they had so few clients. Two women were sitting at two desks. One of them was dealing with a client who was sitting in front of her desk. The other was a woman about 30 years old and pleasant looking with brown hair. When I walked in, she motioned that I should go to see her. She told me to sit down. After I sat down I gave her the papers I received from KGM, in which they asked for an extension of my passport. Namely to validate it for another exit, and to issue a passport for my wife and my daughter. I gave her the Hungarian – Russian paper from TKI and also my service passport. The woman studied all these very thoroughly.

After she read all of that, I told her that this is very urgent, because I have to be in Berlin by the beginning of next week. She nodded understandingly, took some papers from her desk which she pushed over to me.

“One of the papers is for the extension of your passport, or rather to authorize another exit. The second should be completed by your wife, but due to the urgency you could complete it. However, I need two pictures.”

I told her I have the pictures.

“I suggest you should go to this empty desk and complete the papers, and when you finish, give them back to me with the pictures."

In about 10 minutes I filled out all the papers. In the meantime no new clients came in. When I finished the paper work I went back to the brown haired lady and gave her also the two pictures. The woman studied everything very carefully again. When she finished all of that, she turned to me and kindly smiled at me and asked:

“Both you and your wife are from Szeged?”

“Yes.”

“I was born there too, but about four years ago my husband was transferred to Budapest, so we are living here now. In view of the urgency KGM requested for you, come in tomorrow, Saturday, and both will be ready. Our working day on Saturday is only until 12 noon, so I would ask you to come in between 10 and 11. You have to leave your passport here, because we have to stamp the new exit permit in that document. I am going to give you a receipt that I received it. Because you submitted your identification papers when you received the passport I am going to give you a temporary one which will be valid until you receive your passport.”

She took some more papers from her desk, put my service passport in front of her and started to fill out a form. When she finished, she said she had to get it signed and stamped, got up and left through one of the doors at the rear. About five minutes later she came back and gave me a folded document.

“Please bring this back tomorrow.”

When I got to Andrássy Avenue and was walking towards my parked car, I started to really wonder that to obtain a passport before October 23, as I had experienced, was a long and complicated affair. Now it will be so quickly arranged. I thought one reason could be the paper I received from TKI, and another the request from KGM that the passports be issued immediately. But it was possible that at the National Police Passport division there is an internal directive to accelerate the issuing of passports, which I just cannot understand because I am only one day in Budapest.

With this, I completed by 10 AM everything which I planned to accomplish during the entire day. Now the only question remained am I really going to get the passports by tomorrow morning?

I had time left to solve another problem. That was the acquisition of the proper amount of gasoline. During my trip between Bratislava and Komarno, I made calculations. As I knew that the Komárom – Komarno Bridge is open, I planned that I am going from Budapest to Komárom and from there over the bridge to Komarno, and from there to Bratislava. This distance is about 250 km (155 miles), but the roads are not the best. If I am leaving with the car's tank full, that will be sufficient for this leg of our trip. From Bratislava to Prague is about 350 km (about 217 miles). From Prague to the DDR border is about 130 – 150 km (80 to 93 miles). If I would take 2 cans, 20 liter (5.283 gal) each, it could be enough, but not sure. Therefore I probably have to buy gas in Czechoslovakia and will need Czech currency. As we are going to be three people in the car, and I would like to take as much luggage with us as possible, I should take only one 20 liter can as I anyhow have to buy gas in Czechoslovakia.

My problem was that because of the "strict vigilance" there were no up-to-date Hungarian or Czech maps available, only those that were printed during 1945 to 1948 before the communist "strict vigilance" was introduced. I had one of those, and the question is, are the roads shown on the map still in existence or did they build new roads since.

I went home and told about my successful morning, but left immediately, because I considered it important to be back at home with my car before 2 PM, when the one hour traffic stoppage is planned. As Russian tanks were on every corner in Budapest, a demonstration on the street would have resulted in a blood bath. On the other hand, it was a brilliant idea that all the traffic should stop in the city, because with this the Hungarian population can demonstrate that the Revolution is still alive. The opposition led by Gyula Obersovszky initiated this.

In order to get home by 2 PM and put my car in the garage, I immediately put two 20 liter cans into the trunk of my car. I wanted to take one with me, and use the other to fill up my gas tank before we left.

When I saw Béla M., because of my battery problem, he mentioned that buying gasoline would be a problem as the supply is much depleted. The gas stations are not selling gas on coupons, only for cash and for a premium price. Therefore I wanted to start buying gasoline as soon as I could. The question was where I am going to find some.

My first stop was the gas station near the Parliament building. I knew the people there, as I was a good customer. I had bought many times from them on the black market, which was cheaper than what they sold for the coupons. Luckily Uncle Sanyi with his big mustache was there. He knew me very well. I bought from him lots of "black" gas. He was very happy to see me, we shook hands. He said that he had not seen me for some time. I told him that I was in the DDR since October 14, because they invited me to give a scientific paper, and I got stuck in

Berlin because the Czechs closed the Hungarian border. I just arrived back yesterday, and now I have a big need of gasoline.

He started to scratch his head. I suspected that he is mulling over the fact I am a very good customer buying lots of "black" gas, and if things will consolidate, I will be again a very good customer. I believed that he had gasoline but wanted to sell it at a premium price. He was afraid to offer it at premium price since he might lose me as a future customer. In order to prevent him from saying he has no gasoline, I found the following solution:

"I assume, it is very hard to find now gasoline. The coupons are worth nothing, but I would be glad to pay some premium if you could find me some. I need some in my car and also would like to fill up two 20 liter cans to make sure I have some reserve."

He looked at me:

"You know what? I cannot pump gas into your car from the pumps, because they will see it. But you should leave here the two 20 liter cans and come back around 4 PM. I am going to see how much I can find for you."

I went to the trunk of my car and opened it. I took out the 2 cans and put them next to the pumps. I shook hands with Uncle Sanyi, said good bye and drove away. By 1 PM I was at home. I put my car in the garage that it should not be on the street when the traffic stoppage starts and went to our apartment, where they waited for me with lunch. At 2 PM the traffic stopped in the entire city. In the mid-town where we lived the silence was an absolutely incredible experience. At 3 PM the traffic started again and the city noise was back.

At 4 PM I went back to the gas station and my two 20 liter cans were in the same place as I left them. From this I assumed Uncle Sanyi did not touch the cans since I left them there. I became very sad and started to go towards his office. Uncle Sanyi came from his office towards me and said I should put the cans in my car and come back in a half an hour. He said nothing else. He went back to his office. I picked up the handle of the can, lifted and felt that it is full. I put both of them in the trunk. I did not understood what was happening, but it dawned on me that in a half hour I could go to his office, and nobody will remember that I put two cans in my car.

To pass the time I thought to visit Pali Havas, they lived in Miksa Falk Street two blocks from the gas station. I parked in front of the entrance of their apartment building. I saw that Pail's red Adler was parked nearby, so I believed that I would find them at home. He and his wife Lenke were at home. Lenke offered me coffee, but I said I only can stay for a few minutes, because I have to look after many other things. Since I met Pali in connection with my battery problems, I briefly told him about my plans. I just told them what happened since, especially at the passport office.

Pali said they are also planning to leave in a few days[79], but as he does not have a passport they are planning to go by train to the border and on foot from there. The reasons

[79] The Havass left about 10 days later by train to the border and on foot they managed to arrive in Austria. They went from there to the Netherlands, because Pali received a job offer from the Dutch Philips Company's research laboratory in Eindhoven.

they wanted to emigrate were about the same as mine: insecurity of their life. Lenke, in connection with her work, was many times in Western Europe. She told us many times that the communist system is hopeless because in the West, in the past 10 years, they experienced a huge boom. The system which is called 'socialism' prevented any development, there is a shortage of everything, one cannot buy anything and what is available is inferior in quality.

Half an hour later I went back to the gas station. I stopped in front of the office and went in. Uncle Sanyi was sitting behind his desk. I told him I would like to buy a liter of motor oil, as Béla M. told me I needed it for the trip, because the motor was using some oil. He got up went to a shelf picked up a can of oil and put it in front of me.

"How much I owe you?"

He told me the price of the oil and also the price of the 40 liter gasoline. I calculated in my head that the price of the gasoline was 50% more than the gas on coupons, which was 40% higher than the price on the black market, which I usually purchased. I gave him the requested amount.

"Uncle Sanyi it is possible that in a few days I need some more gas."

"No problem, but let me know a few hours before. The purchasing of the oil was a good idea. Keep the can of oil visible when you leave."

"You can be sure of that. That was the reason I bought the oil."

"You have a sharp mind."

I left his office and went towards my car. I was holding the can of oil in front of me. If somebody is watching the gas station, at least they can see why I was there. Because, who knows? I spent the rest of the afternoon calling colleagues and friends, telling them I came back. I told nobody on the phone about our plans, because they may have restarted the telephone eavesdropping.

The next day exactly at 10 AM as the brown haired woman who was born is Szeged told me, I entered the door of the National Police Passport Department. Instead of the two policemen guarding it, there was only policeman. I told him the reason I came, and he gave me the same number of the room where I was the day before. I went to the second floor and entered the office. The desks I knew from the day before were there, but nobody was sitting behind them. There were no other people, except on the chairs next to the wall four people were sitting. They were older than I was, between 40 to 60 years old. One out of the four looked familiar to me. I quickly remembered he was Alberto, a magician performing in circus and well known in Hungary.

When I entered I greeted them, they greeted me back, and I sat down on one of the chairs.

"Are you all here for your passports?"

"Yes," Alberto answered. "I am here since an hour, but it seems the employees of the passport office are not here. Nobody came to this room, and even when I went out to find a rest room I have not seen a single person on the entire floor."

"That is interesting, because I was told yesterday by a woman sitting behind that desk," I pointed to one of the desks, "that I should be here by 10 AM. By that time my passport will be ready."

On this news, the others got involved in the discussion, and it became clear that all of them had to come today for their passport.

The only woman in the group, about a 50 year old well-dressed lady with gray hair said:

"I was told to be here by 9 AM. I was the first to arrive, but even at that time there was nobody here. The office was empty. It seems to me that today nobody came to this floor. It is interesting that the policeman down at the door let me in without any problem. He asked me where I was going. I told him the floor and the room number, and he said I should go up."

We discussed this issue, and all of us told where we wanted to travel. It turned out that Alberto, who really was as I thought a magician in the circus, was supposed to go to Italy, where he has a contract. He must be there by next week. I also told them that I have to be back in Berlin.

With such discussions we passed the time. But we were told when we got our appointment that the office is open only until 12 noon. Therefore, at around half past 11, we started to become impatient and started to discuss what to do. I said first I am going to the rest room. Let's decide what to do when I return. As all of them were there before I got good directions, I had a chance to explore the entire floor. My colleagues were right, I did not find anybody on the entire floor. I looked into some of the offices. Curiously, none of the doors were locked, but I did not find anybody either.

When I returned, I said that I could not find anybody either and lets discuss what to do now. We came to the conclusion that the passports could be ready and they may be in the desks or in the tall cabinet with two doors behind the desks. On the top of the desks was nothing in which passports could be, so we started to pull out the drawers. Each of the three desks had on each side three drawers. We were able to open all the drawers. We searched them. It was full with all kind of material but no passports.

We could open the tall metal cabinet. It was full with all kinds of papers and files which were filled with papers. We examined everything, but we found no passports. The question arose what to do now, ultimately we cannot search the entire floor. If somebody walks in and notices what we are doing, we could have serious problems.

I thought the matter over.

"Yesterday the woman dealing with my case told me that until I get back my passport I should have an ID card. When she completed the form she had to get it signed by her superior. She left through this door" – I pointed to the door – "a few minutes later she came back with the signed and sealed ID card, but she did not have the passport with her. I believe she must have left it with her superior. I suggest we should go through this door, maybe we are going to find the passports there."

I started to go to the door and pressed the door handle. I entered into a spacious office. There was a large lacquered desk and behind it a gray metal closet with a double door, the same as was in the previous room. Besides these, next to the wall, was a worn large table. On the desk was a holder for pencils and another one for pens. There was also a framed picture of a man standing in front of a house and next to him two 6 – 10 year old girls. There was a telephone and a calendar on the desk. On the wall to the left of the desk was a place where a picture must have been hanging before, but there were no pictures on the wall.

On the worn table were three boxes, judging of their size they must have contained documents. All five of us were in the room and we got divided. Alberto and another of our group went immediately to the worn table and opened the boxes one after the other. The woman started to open the drawers of the desk.

I went to the metal closet and pushed the door handle. The closet was not locked. Its content was very organized. At eye level was a stand with several seals hanging. On the middle of the shelf was a box, and I saw that many passports were stacked in it. I picked up the box, took it from the shelf and put it down on the lacquered desk. My partners were still occupied with the great table and the drawers. The only lady with us, who was standing next to me still occupied with the drawers, saw the passports I just found.

"Wow, maybe we found the passports!"

Everybody stopped the search and came to the desk. I sat at the desk in front of me was the box which contained about 30 passports. I found mine very fast and next to it Vera's.

"I assume your passport must be also here. Please tell me your name and I am going to look for them."

Alberto said, "You could have made a career as a magician, because if you were able to conjure from this closet the passports, then pulling out a rabbit from a cylinder would have been a child's play for you."

Everybody agreed and started to laugh, their anxiety evaporated. They gave me their names one after the other and I found their passports. They all opened it immediately and checked if it was OK. That was also the first thing I did.

Everything was OK. I found in my passport an almost one page size new stamp with the title: "Permit for Repeated Travel". Its text was only in Hungarian and French. There were two octagonal places for the exit and entry stamps. It had the stamp of the National Police Passport Department and signed by the Head of the Passport Department (who according to the name was a woman). We probably were in her office. The interesting point was that in the place "Date of the Permit" was stamped November 24, 1956, Saturday – that was the day we were now there.

Vera's brand new passport #014526 was also OK. Her picture was glued into the passport and stamped with the National Police Passport Department, twice on the top as well as on the bottom corner of the picture. Éva Anna – girl - was also included. Everything was properly stamped and signed by the lady who was the Head of the National Police Passport Department, and obviously who was not there.

I put the passports in my pocket and put the box back into the closet to the place where I found it. I took the stand with the many stamps and put it on the desk. I sat down and started to inspect the stamps. I found one with the text 'This passport - during the period of validity - without special approval authorizes multiple border crossings.' Interestingly this stamp was only in Hungarian.

I liked this very much. I took my two passports from my pocket and carefully inserted the stamp on the first empty page of each passport. The woman and a man also asked that I should stamp their passports. The others did not want it. I received their passports and carefully stamped them.

I continued to review the stamps and found three which I felt were useful: one was the signature of the Department head. The other was: 'Head of the Passport Department'. This was in Hungarian and French. The third was the round stamp of the "National Police Passport Department".

I applied these stamps in all of the passports I stamped, that the multiple border crossing was now absolutely official. The two owners whose passport I extended to multiple comings and goings looked at it and thanked me.

I noticed a few curiosities, but did not mention them to the others. One was mentioned above, that in my service passport the date of the permit was today's date, yet we found nobody in the office or even on the entire floor. It is possible that the Department Head stamped it yesterday but made it valid from today. It is also possible that before the first person in our group arrived at 9 AM people were doing their daily job. The woman who was the Department Head prepared the passports promised for today, and for some reason between 8 and 9 AM everybody left.

It was also interesting that the person who signed my passport on October 3 was a man, and his title: 'Head of the Passport Department', appeared in Hungarian and in Russian. While now the head was a woman and had the same title listed in Hungarian and French, and no Russian translation.

It was also remarkable that in my passport dated October 3, my description was in Hungarian, Russian and French with all three was filled out. While in Vera's passport dated November 24, 1956, contained the same pages, but the Russian page was not completed. As a matter of fact, a line was drawn across it.

There was another interesting difference. In both of our passports, on page 6, the passport text stated: 'States that the passport is valid'. Under this was a stamp in both passports stating in Hungarian that the validity of the passport is Czechoslovakia, Poland and the DDR. In my passport the validity of the countries were written in Hungarian and it was repeated in French and Russian. In Vera's passport, while the stamp was the same, it repeated the names of the countries only in French, and one could see that the Russian text was cut off from the stamp.

Where it should have been one could see some spots where there may have been some text before.

I came to the conclusion that the employees I was dealing with the day before were obviously the people participating in the Revolution. As of this morning Kádár's people did not take control of the Passport department. Those who were delegated by the Revolution strangely were not in the office today, at least not since 9 AM when our first person arrived. One can assume that by Monday the Passport Department will be manned by other people. Maybe that was the reason that they completed my passport case in one day. The officials knew the "old guard" will retake the office, and with this they wanted to help those who wanted to flee the country.

We put everything back into the closet and discussed whether we should leave a paper on the desk as a receipt that we took our passports. Based on my thoughts of what might be happening, I suggested not to leave any trail. God knows who will be in this office tomorrow or after tomorrow. I do not know what the others were thinking, but unanimously we decided that we are not going to leave any traces that we were here. We went down the stairs together. When we passed the policeman we greeted him and he greeted us back. At the street we said good bye and shook hands.

I realized that if the "old guard" will be back here, then they also will be back at the border and significant changes could be expected. I realized that I entered a new phase: the race against time.

30. Pitfalls

I went home with the passports. Everybody was tremendously surprised. It was really a miracle that in one day both passports were issued: my passport which needed another exit from the country and a new passport for Vera and Éva. I told my theory that it was probably the last day before the “old communist team” will take the office back, and those who were there gave everybody a passport. That was the reason Vera did not even have to appear to sign her papers requesting a passport.

The next day was Sunday. We visited and met several of my colleagues and friends. One of the topics of our discussion was that Kádár breached his promise to Yugoslavia, and that Imre Nagy and his associates will not be prosecuted if they leave the Yugoslavian Embassy. On the other hand, even with the Russians, Kádár does not yet have enough power to reinstall the old communist system. Several of our acquaintances agreed that Kádár, with the help of the Russians, will bring back the so called "socialist system” with all of its horrors, and that with such an outlook the best is to leave the country. The problem was that my friends, like myself, had a fairly good job in Hungary. With insufficient knowledge of those languages, to secure a reasonable existence would be highly uncertain. It is also not easy to leave family and friends, but if we put it on a scale, considering the communist system which we already knew very well, one would select the uncertainty of our future in the West.

I reviewed my list of what to do so we should be able to leave. I have a service passport in which apparently I do not need a visa to the countries we are traveling. For Vera's passport I have to get Czechoslovak and DDR visas very fast, and we need Czech currency. I have some left over DDR currency. If I cannot get more, what I have will be enough. I hoped that on Monday, November 26, I can get the visas and maybe change money, and on Tuesday or latest Wednesday we could leave. This would be better than what I planned on the train. Because of the fast changing situation, we need to speed things up.

I believed that I should go first to the DDR Embassy to obtain a visa for Vera and Éva. With that visa, I could get the Czech transit visa fast. So on Monday, November 26th, early morning I went to the DDR Embassy, which was at that time on Voroshilov Ave (now Stefánia Ave) which is close to the Városliget (City Park). I took with me the two passports. I also carried the program of the Leipzig conference in which I was listed as an invited speaker. I told the official at the Consulate that I have to go back to Humboldt University, as I started experiments with my colleagues there, and I have to go back the next day, Tuesday to Berlin. He asked me if I am going by train, because he did not know if there are any flights from Budapest. I said that I am driving in my own car. Obviously the program of the Leipzig conference, the fact that I am driving my own car and that I spoke a decent German made a very good impression on him. He said that I do not need a visa in my service passport. I should complete for Vera and Éva a visa request form, and they will give the visa forthwith. I completed the paper and gave it to the official at the visa section. He read it, said it is OK. I asked if I can wait for it.

He said it will take 1 or 2 hours. I asked him to make it as soon as possible, because I also have to get a Czech transit visa. He promised that I will get it by 11 AM.

By half past 10 I received back the passports, and the visa was stamped in Vera's passport. I immediately went to the Czechoslovak Embassy and asked for a transit visa to be stamped in Vera's passport. They looked at the DDR visa and asked me to complete some papers, which I did. By that time it was close to noon. They informed me to come back at 4 PM. I did not like this, because with this the entire day will be gone, and I wanted to go also to the National Bank to exchange money. I was not able to convince the official to complete the passport with the visa sooner, so I could not do anything else but wait until 4 PM to receive Vera's passport with the Czechoslovak visa.

It became too late to go to the National Bank. Late afternoon I met with a friend to whom, when I returned from Berlin, I told my plan to go back there. He had also very good connection to the people at Humboldt University and started to do the same as I was doing. He also had a service passport in his hands. He only needed the same as I did, a new exit permit in his passport and a passport for his wife and child. He was also told that their passport will be completed by Saturday, but for some reason he was not able to go in Saturday before noon. He went in on November 26, Monday morning. At the door were two policemen, and he was also told to go to the same room where he had to submit the passport request. When he came on Monday, at each of the two desks was a woman, but not the same we met the week before when we submitted our request. My friend received his passport with the exit permit, but he was told that his wife's passport was not yet completed. He should return for it a week from Monday.

This was a surprise, but for me not an unexpected turn of events. This only proved my theory that over the weekend the personnel in the passport office will be changed. But this also meant increased uncertainty of the situation we are going to meet at the border when we are leaving. That evening János Kádár gave a long speech about the Imre Nagy situation. Our conclusion after the speech was that events are accelerating and the power is getting back into Kádár's hands. That made it clearer that very little time is left to carry out my plans to go back to Berlin.

Next day on November 27 when I was trying to change money at the National Bank, I was told that I need a request from TKI asking that the National Bank should convert some money into foreign currency. I immediately drove up to Rózsadomb where I found the Head of the Personnel Department in his office. I described what I accomplished until then and that I need from TKI a request to convert my Hungarian currency to Czech and DDR money. He immediately asked his secretary to write the letter.

During the time his secretary was writing the letter he lit a cigarette and asked me when I am planning to return. I told him the experiments will last a maximum of three weeks, and then I come back immediately. But from time to time I am going to call him, and when the laboratory in Újpest will function again, I am going to call Dallos or Ducza regularly to give them a report about the progress of my work.

He mentioned that he heard the Czechs are now requiring that even if somebody has a service passport valid for Czechoslovakia and in transit, they must have a Czech visa. This was shocking news.

I told him that when I got the DDR visa for my wife, I asked the DDR consulate if a visa is needed in my passport and they said no. For this reason I did not ask the Czech consulate. They gave the transit visa for my wife immediately, but I did not ask one for myself. He said the Czechs are probably requesting this because the border on their side towards Hungary was closed until now, and this may be the result of the border closing. I asked if this could be verified.

"I am going to try to call the Czech Embassy."

At that moment his secretary entered his office with a piece of paper which probably was the one needed for my money exchange. She put it on his desk. Before he signed it he asked his secretary to call the Czech Embassy and ask them if a visa is now needed in a Hungarian service passport which is valid for Czechoslovakia, when the person is only in transit to DDR. The secretary left and he signed the letter and gave it to me.

The secretary came back in a minute and told us she talked with somebody at the Czech Embassy, who informed him that it is a new rule, that a visa even in this case is required. The person also told her that today they are not issuing visas because those people who would doing it are on a meeting at the Embassy, but on the next day, November 28, the visa service will be operating during business hours.

I thanked them for the information, which was extremely bad news, but I did not tell them. I said good bye and left.

"Good bye, see you soon!" I hoped very much that this will not happen.

I had no problems at the National Bank. I presented my passport and the letter from TKI to one of the cashiers and told him how much I want of each of the currencies. The cashier left and came back with two envelopes and said that he is not able to give all that I asked in Czech money, because the Bank does not have enough.

This was also not good news. It is true that coming from Berlin I changed money at the railroad station because I needed it for the train tickets, and I had some left over. But according to my calculation, the amount that I received will not be sufficient to cover our two day expenses, hotels, food and gasoline. That meant that I have to change money somewhere in Czechoslovakia. As I could do nothing about it I thanked him and said it is OK. He checked the exchange rates and with a small calculator on his table, he calculated how much Hungarian Forint I have to give him.

At home the ladies were busily packing. The number of luggage and other packages was beyond what I could imagine. I did not believe that all of that could be put into my car, in which, besides of the packages, the three of us will also need space. It is true that Éva will need only a very little space. I expressed my opinion, and as a result, I received long lectures from my and Vera's mothers why all this will be needed.

Now it was obvious that next day, November 28, we are not going to be able to leave because of the Czech transit visa.

Very early next morning I went to the Czech Embassy, where they confirmed that I need a transit visa even for my service passport valid for Czechoslovakia. I was told, it will take a few hours to issue the visa. I should come back at 12 noon. I told them that I rather wait there. I did not want to risk that they should leave or hold a meeting, like they did the day before, and close the Embassy. So I sat down in the waiting room from which they could see that I am not leaving until I get back my passport with the Czech visa stamped in it. At least I had 2 hours to consider the situation. Finally at half past 11, I was called to receive my passport. Interestingly I had to pay some money for the visa.

Now it looked certain that during the next day, November 29, we could leave. The very worrisome question was, how far are we going to be able to get? Only to the border or further? I drove home and put the car in the garage for the night, not to get an unpleasant surprise if I left it on the street and something might happen. I had to start to assemble my papers, such as my high school and University diplomas and publications, but I very carefully avoided taking with me anything related to TKI and my work there. If on the border they would search what we are taking with us and would find something about TKI, they certainly would regard me as a spy, who is taking incredible state secrets which could be used by the Western Imperialists to ruin the entire communist world.

The other important thing was to find and remove from the piano the hidden dollars and the Napoleon gold pieces. I started this exploratory work early in the afternoon. I knew where the bank notes were from my previous exploration and also knew the location of the Napoleon coins wrapped in paper, but the work needed patience and skill. A bad move and the banknotes or the Napoleon coins could fall into a crevice from which it would be impossible to extricate. As I mentioned, the inside of a stand up piano, for a layman like me, is a wonderland. At the end, with various tools and with ingeniously bent wires I was able to find $225 dollars and the small French gold coins. The dollars were of various denominations from 1 to 10, and there were a few Canadian dollars, too. At the end we decided that nobody knew for sure how many dollars were in the piano, but this amount, plus the one I removed when I went to Berlin in early October, was about what we were hiding. We were sure that we had only 10 Napoleons when we put them in the piano, and I found all ten of them.

We had to make the dollars and Napoleons disappear in a big hurry, so they should not be around in case somebody might visit us. As I mentioned before, to have these items was heavily punished. The decision was that the dollars and the Napoleons will be sewn into the very heavy lining of my winter coat, which was made of heavy gray cloth filled with wadding and inside covered with brown fur. As the weather was quite mild I did not need this coat. In the car it will be placed under the luggage and packages. It could not be put into a luggage as the weight of this coat is 5 kg (over 11 lb.). I know this because after 56 years I still have this coat and can hardly lift it. From curiosity I weighed it.

The rest of the day was spent on packing and calling friends. Naturally in the telephone we did not mention that we are leaving tomorrow. From time to time either my or Vera's mother started to cry, and Éva did not understood why they are crying.

I went down to the garage to once more check the car and to fill the gas tank from one of the 20 liter cans. I learned already how to do that. I mounted the can with gasoline on a shelf over the car's gas tank, the cap of which I removed. I had a rubber hose, one end of which I inserted into the can down to its bottom. I took the other end of the rubber tube in my mouth and drew on it. That required lots of skill to compress the rubber tube before the gasoline gets to your mouth – I did that always very well because I learned it from my father when I was a child. I inserted the tube into the tank of my car and loosened my fingers on the rubber tube so the gasoline started to flow from the 20 liter can into the tank of the car. Now I only had to make sure to squeeze the rubber tube when the tank of the car is full. After I squeezed the rubber tube, I lifted from the tank the 20 liter can, loosened my grip on the tube and the gasoline which was in the tube flowed back into the tank. When I closed and lifted the can I felt that half of it must have gone into the car's tank. I took the second full 20 liter can and put it in front of the rear seat of the car, closed the garage door and went up to our apartment.

At home I started to study the old map. I thought that if we would leave early morning we could be in Bratislava late afternoon. We would be there overnight, and the next day we would continue our trip to Prague. Naturally the first and most essential component will be to get over the Hungarian border and to be in Czechoslovakia.

Studying the old map I made plans, to go from Budapest to Budaörs – Tatabánya and reach the Danube at Almásfüzítő. After that Komárom and to drive immediately across the bridge to Czechoslovakia on the same bridge I walked over to Hungary on November 22, one week ago.

If we could leave at 9 AM then we would be able to reach Komarno in Czechoslovakia by noon, if and this should be written in capital letters, IF we cross the Hungarian border smoothly. From Komarno I did not know what roads exist. I estimated the distance between Komarno and Bratislava could be 100 to 110 km (62 to 70 miles). On the old map, it was indicated that the road from Komarno goes to Velky Meder to Dunajská Streda to Somorin to Bratislava. I was hoping that we are going to eat the salami sandwiches which were prepared for lunch between Komarno and Velky Meder.

During the evening we visited our neighbors Dr. Surányi, who was a medical doctor. They were good friends of ours. Their daughter Borika, who was a little older than Éva, played many times together. We visited the Surányis to say good bye and ask them to look after our mothers if they need something. At the Surányis we found a big disorder. When we told them our plans, they said, that in a few days they are also planning to go through the border to Austria. The reason of the disorder in their apartment was that they were trying to assemble what to take with them. We wished good luck to each other and expressed hope that we are going to meet somewhere[80]. When we went back to our apartment and told our mothers about the Surányis plans they started to cry again.

[80] Dr. Surányi and family went to Canada and several years later we met in the USA.

Next day at 8 AM I took the car from the garage and parked it in front of our building's door. We started to carry down the enormous amount of packages, luggage etc. The trunk and the rack on the car roof became very full fast. After that we started to fill the back seat leaving a little room for Éva. There were several luggage which we were not able to squeeze into the car. The ladies insisted that we need all that stuff. I tried to explain this amount of luggage could give us difficulties at the borders. Finally I put them also on the roof and tightly tied everything with strong straps which I had bought not long ago. This was not an easy task.

Ready to go with insane amounts of 'essentials'

Finally we succeeded to pack up everything, and we left a little after 9 AM, after lots of kisses and weeping by the two mothers. They instructed us many times to take good care of ourselves. Our future, under the circumstances especially at the Hungarian border, was not dependent on taking care of ourselves.

31. Trip to no return

On a sunny, pleasant fall day around half past 11, we arrived at the building of the Hungarian border guard at the bridge over the Danube at Komárom. Ours was the only vehicle. None was before or behind us. As a matter of fact, there were no pedestrians in either direction. I saw no vehicle coming from the other end of the bridge either. Two Hungarian and one Russian soldier were standing in front of the building. On the belts of the Hungarian soldiers was a holster with a revolver. On the shoulder of the Russian soldier was the well-known sub-machine gun. The soldiers were standing on the left side of the car, because the car's driver used to sit on that side. They looked surprised at Vera before whom there was no steering wheel, and they smiled friendly at Éva, who looked at them from the rear seat. When they comprehended that this is a car where the steering wheel is on the right side, they slowly came to my side. I had already lowered the window, and with the two passports in my hand waited for them. They saluted (the Russian soldier was not saluting and we exchanged friendly greetings. I told them that we are going to Berlin, and we are only in transit through Czechoslovakia. One of the soldiers leafed through the passports and said he is going to check them in the building. He and the Russian soldier started to go towards the guard's building. The other soldier remained with us. I did not like that they took our passports with them.

Éva announced that she would have to go to the bathroom. The soldier said that the bathroom is in the building and there is no problem to go there, Vera should go with Éva. While we discussed this, Vera got out of the car, and because this was a car with only two doors, opened the door a little wider that Éva should also be able to get out from the rear seat. When this happened the Hungarian and the Russian soldiers just came out from the guard's building.

The Hungarian soldier gave me the passports and said that everything is OK. The Russian did not say a word. I took the passports and opened them to see if they had stamped them. On the other side of the car Éva got out too, and after her, like an avalanche, what was piled up on the rear seat next to her started to pour out from the car to the ground at the feet of Vera, Éva and the soldier. Among the dropped out items were smaller packages, such as in a nice brown paper bag the sandwiches we planned to have for lunch, water luckily in a plastic bottle, and clothing. At the end of the avalanche with a loud clang, came an aluminum espresso machine which probably one of the ladies put in at the end as an essential equipment for us.

At this noise the two soldiers rushed also over to the other side, and everybody started to help Vera to put everything back into the car. When that was completed, the soldier who stayed with us while the others went to check on our passports told Vera that they should go with him. He is going to show them where the rest room was.

I did not dare to get out of the car, because I was afraid that if I open my door the avalanche from the rear seat will start on my side too. The Hungarian and the Russian soldiers now came over to my side.

"Horrible, I told them, women believe that everything is essential. We are going only for three weeks to the Berlin University, and look at how much luggage we are taking."

"That is true my wife is also traveling with an incredible amount of luggage when we are going anywhere."

The Russian soldier was only nodding. I did not know whether he spoke Hungarian and understood what we were talking, or just wanted to participate in our discussion.

In the meantime Vera and Éva and the soldier returned. Vera and Éva got back in the car. As I did not stop the engine because I was afraid if I stop it may not start again, I pressed the clutch, released the hand break, and shifted to first gear. The car started to move slowly in the direction of the bridge while everybody was waving to everybody. I rolled up my window, and the car rolled up on the bridge. I remarked:

"It is amazing that with so many packages they let us through so easily."

I had to watch the road, but Vera and Éva looked from the bridge at the flowing water and remarked that the Danube is really a big river.

On the Czechoslovak side I stopped at the entrance of the guard building. The two Czech border guards leisurely walked over to my side when they realized that the steering wheel was on the right side of the car. By that time I rolled down the window. When they got closer they saluted and said something I assumed was Slovakian. I handed over to them the two passports, opened at the page where the Czechoslovakian transit visa was. One of them took the passport and went into the building, while the other stayed with us. In a few minutes the border guard came from the building, circled the car to me and handed over the passports. Both of the border guards saluted again, I asked them:

“Bratislava?”

One of the soldiers spoke in Hungarian:

“Here at the bridge take a left turn and drive on the road next to the Danube and follow the road in the directions to Velky Meder. Have a good trip.”

“Thank you.” – I waved to him, rolled up the window and started to go.

According to the instruction after the bridge I took a left turn and drove on a city street and stayed close to the river. Finally I saw a sign, Velky Meder, and an arrow showing to continue straight. When we got out of the city we found a suitable place and stopped to eat our sandwiches. It was about one o’clock when we continued our trip. It seemed that everything was proceeding according to our plan. Before we left I looked at the old map again and matched with the paper on which I noted the village’s name we have to go through. After Velky Meder we have to find the direction to Dunajská Streda. I hoped that we were going to arrive in Bratislava by 4 PM.

The road was flat. Sometimes it went upward a little, and the traffic was sparse. Very rarely a truck came, and once in a while a horse carriage was ahead of me. I had to slow down and carefully pass it. So the road was fairly uneventful. In the meantime my passengers fell asleep, and I was thinking over the events of the past week.

A week ago on the slow moving train from Bratislava to Komarno I finalized my plan how I was going to accomplish to be able return to Berlin with my family. I was able to carry out this plan as scheduled, and now, a week later, we were crossing the Hungarian border without any problem. We are with valid papers driving towards Berlin, where as I found out one can be transported to the West and leave behind Hungary, which is now for sure heading back into the communist system.

Suddenly the feeling of uncertainty took hold of me. How do I dared to undertake to start such an uncertain future with a wife and a very small child in a dilapidated car, which in case it has some problem I would not be able to get it fixed, having only a few pieces of clothing and with a few small items, with $225 and ten Napoleon gold coins in my pocket, which was believed in Budapest to be worth a fortune, but who knows their real value.

I weighed on one aide of the balance that we had to leave our mothers and that was the hardest part of our decision, the well-equipped and furnished apartment, and a good job which provided a decent living and a very interesting work, in which I luckily enjoyed some success, good colleagues and friends. As of my colleagues, the Tungsram Research laboratory and the TKI-2 were an oasis in the desert. The managers of the laboratory, Dallos, Szigeti, Winter ,and also the colleagues besides being very talented, were also outstanding in human quality. In my department everybody was a very good colleague. It was a pleasure to work with them. All this weighed down the scale's pan. On the other side the scale was full of uncertainty. I am getting into an absolutely foreign country and foreign conditions. I know German and English, but it will take some time until I will progress in speaking and writing to be acceptable in my work and social contacts. It is true that I was offered a job in Germany in an excellent research laboratory, but that was only a verbal offer. What will happen if for some reason Telefunken does not keep its promise? In that case my money would be sufficient only for one week. Furthermore I finally would like to wind up in America. At least I had there a few relatives, but I do not know anybody else. I shall have to develop a new livelihood which will not be a simple matter.

According to the scale I should have remained in Budapest. Then why did I venture on this trip? Why did I decide already in Berlin that we have to leave Hungary? The same question was probably asked by many of my friends, acquaintances and according to the news, two hundred thousand or more Hungarians.

In my thoughts I returned to Szeged, where in 1948 December I tried to talk Professor Bruckner to let me complete my University studies sooner, because I wanted to go with my friends and relatives to the West. It was not possible for me to finish my studies sooner, and six months later when I received my degree, one could not leave Hungary. Now eight years later an opportunity opened up again for me to leave.

In 1949 DISZ (Kommunista Diák Ifjusági Szövetség = Communist Student Union) arranged that I should not be able to get a job at the University of Szeged. That was not a good omen. Luckily their arm did not reach to Tungsram. As there was a need for special technical people, such as me, with luck I was able to achieve a relatively decent standard of living. That I was able to work in scientific research is a very unstable situation. The question is for how long they would need me.

I saw examples of how uncertain is the position of people like me. That was not only valid on my level but also at the highest communist leadership, for example László Rajk, Gábor Péter, György Marosán[81] and also in the case of others. One can find examples on all existential levels, and on the top of that if somebody, like me, is not even a member of the communist party, he really becomes a free prey. I developed myself a good position, I worked hard and had good results, and one of the results was the invitation to the conference in Leipzig. But if somebody is producing or not producing results, in the communist system it makes no difference. If anytime a good cadre desires my job, my days will be numbered, because they can easily find a hundred and one reasons to eliminate me.

The communist regime in Hungary basically copied the dictatorial system developed in the Soviet Union. Censuring our mail, the writers, theatre, and radio became our daily life. Phone conversations were tapped, the freedom of people hampered, and everything was constrained. The informer system worked effectively, and the people were even exposed to have their garbage inspected to find something on the basis of which the person could be jailed.

---

[81] Rajk was executed, Péter and Marosány were jailed.

I remembered that after the war I decided that I will never live in any place where the laws are to persecute people and not to protect them, and now I have a chance to fulfill what I decided. But I have also an added reason, that I should not force my daughter to grow up and live in such a place.

When I got so far I felt that the balance is strongly tipping in the direction to leave Hungary, because even if it is true that I am facing lots of uncertainties, these are in their great majority financial problems which I can rely on myself to solve. While if I stay, my and my family's entire existence will be questionable, and that is out of my hands, nothing I can do to avoid it.

I became very proud of what a clever fellow I am to be able to arrange our escape in this relatively safe and convenient way, and to arrange this in one week. It was clear to me that at the beginning of October this would not have been possible. When I got so far in my thoughts, suddenly it dawned on me that my cleverness was only a very small part cleverness. It was rather my luck that I arrived in Budapest before the iron curtain was lowered again, and I should thank my smooth departure to those who started the Revolution of October 23, directed against the communist system and against those who served it. The Revolution of 1956 was similar to the one in 1848[82], it was also a fight for freedom demanding the withdrawal of the occupying Russian troops and for the elimination of the Russian oppression. In spite that in 1956 the Hungarians had no serious weaponry in their hands, it was successful. The country declared its independence, neutrality and

---

[82] The Revolution of 1848 was against the Austrian Empire's oppression of Hungary.

declared its withdrawal from the Warsaw pact. As I could see, the Russian text was eliminated or ignored in the passports.

The similarity of the 1848 and the 1956 Revolution for freedom was also that both of them were broken by Russian forces coming from the east, and we are reminded by the Hungarian martyrs of both of these Freedom Fights.

My passengers started to awake slowly. Éva was asking for water. So I stopped, which was good for me also, I could stretch my legs. After this short stop slowly, but according to schedule we arrived in Bratislava. When we arrived in the center of the city we saw the old Danube river the third time in one day, first time in Budapest, the second time in Komárom and the third time now in Bratislava. We saw now the Castle of Bratislava and accidentally came across a hotel. I stopped in front of it. They had a room, so we stayed there. From the hotel there was a magnificent view of the Castle and the Danube. According to plans, we arrived in a hotel in Bratislava before sunset, which on November 29, 1956 was at 15:03.

32. Brandenburg Gate

On November 30, Friday, we left very early in the morning. The Bratislava – Prague distance was 350 – 360 km (217 - 223 miles), and with the maximum speed of my car and stopping for various reasons, I estimated it will take 7 – 8 hours. Since I already transferred with my rubber hose the entire content of the 20 liter can into the car's tank; it will be necessary to convert money and buy gas in Prague.

We arrived well after sunset in Prague. In spite that the headlights of my car had a "shining" chromium coating, they proved to be very dim. The greater traffic and driving in darkness required quite a bit of concentration.

After a night in Prague, we had to leave also very early, but first I had to change money and then try to find gasoline. That was quite difficult, because automobiles from abroad needed a card to get gasoline. Naturally, I did not have such a card. Finally at one of the gas stations I received some gasoline, and with that I estimated there was sufficient amount to get us over the border to DDR and maybe even to Dresden. On the map which was printed before the "vigilance", the main road to the border crossing to DDR was going in the direction to the city of Teplice, which according to my map was about 90 km (55 miles) from Prague. The border from there was only 15 km (about 9.5 miles), and the first large German city, Dresden, was only about 60 km (37 miles) beyond the border. So according to my map the distance from Prague to Dresden was about 170 km (106 miles). I had about that much gasoline in the tank. Because of the bank and the gasoline purchase, we left Prague around noon, but I believed that by 6 PM we probably will be in Dresden.

On the road from Prague to Teplice I could go only very slowly, because of trucks and horse driven carriages. Around Teplice the road started to climb as we continued towards Dubi. Dubi was about 20 km (12.5 miles) from where the "customs" sign was displayed on my map. The mountainous regions started. We were climbing on a winding road towards the border. We could see snow on the mountains. Past Dubi there was no traffic and the winding road continued to rise and the snow line started to get closer to the road. It started to get dark. I believed that by the time it will be dark we will be past the border.

Suddenly a barbed wire fence closed the road in front of us. I saw that the road continued past the barbed wire fence, and two or three parallel barbed wire fences were in the distance. On the barbed wire fence in front of the car was a sign, but I was not able to understand what was written on it. It was probably in the Czech language, but a sign indicated this is the border and it is forbidden to go further.

I got back to the car and using a flashlight looked again at my map which clearly showed that this was the place to cross the border. It seemed they had closed it since the map was printed. Interestingly the road was closed much before the border. We could not see the building of the border guards, and here must have been a building when the border crossing was used. I could not identify from the map where the nearest border crossing was. I told Vera that we have to go back to the last village to find out in which direction we should continue. Silently I was cursing the 'vigilance' of the communist system not to print up to date maps so it should not get into the hands of the enemy.

I could not do anything else, but turn the car around and start to drive back to where we came from. The gasoline in the tank would have been enough for another 60 – 70 km (40 – 45 miles), but now that we were going back, the first village, Dubi, was about 10 km (6 miles). I did not see a single gas station on the road, and God knows how far the next border crossing is from there. As I observed that the road was downhill until Dubi, I turned off the engine to save gas, and we were rolling down without the motor. This was not without risk, because we were dependent only on our brakes to get down safely.

It was pitch dark when we arrived in Dubi. The village looked totally deserted. I started the engine and slowly drove across the village. We did not see anybody.

I was prepared to go back to Teplice, when suddenly on the road past Dubi I saw a truck parked on the side of the road. I stopped behind the truck and went to its cab. Two men were sitting in it, smoking.

I greeted them and asked them in Hungarian which direction we should go to find a border crossing to the DDR. I pointed to myself and said "Hungarian", and asked this in Hungarian, as I knew that in Czechoslovakia to talk German because of the memories of the war is not a good introduction. The driver of the truck motioned that he did not understand it, but got immediately out of the cab and saw my car. He had a flashlight, and when he shined it on my car he saw the Hungarian license plate and the packages on the roof of the car. He got nearer the car and saw Vera and Éva. He became friendlier and started to speak in broken German. After this I sketched my problems. After repeating the story a few times he comprehended that I was trying to cross the border but after Dubi the road is closed and one cannot cross to the DDR, and I don't know where I could find the next border crossing.

He nodded that he understood and motioned for me to follow him. We went back to the truck's cab. He got in, started the engine and turned on the headlights. He was looking for something in the compartment of the door. Finally he pulled out something and got out of the cab. He had a blank piece of paper, a pencil and a small book in his hand. He put the paper on the book, and in the light of his headlight started to draw. He pointed towards Teplice and drew a line, which must have meant the road. He put an X on the beginning of the line and pointed to the ground, from which I understood, that is the point where we are now. Not far from the X he put on the line another X and drew a line to the left. He also put 2 km between the two X. I understood that 2 km from here there is a road going to the left. He showed that the road was meandering and ended in another road. He drew an arrow that I should continue towards the left. At some point he made another X and wrote "Dêĉin." From Dêĉin he drew another line again to the left and made a sign which I recognized. It was the border crossing, and he wrote "Hŕensko" and looked at me with great satisfaction. I realized that when I came from Berlin to Prague the train stopped at Dêĉin, because that was the first station in Czechoslovakia. I smiled at him and asked for the pencil. I got it and wrote 'kilometer?'

He took off his fur hat, scratched his head, went back to the cab and started to discuss with the other guy. Finally he came back and wrote ‘40’ from the first X to Dêĉin and ‘10’ from Dêĉin to the border.

I assumed that in Czechoslovakia the rule was also the constant high ‘vigilance’ and he had no map either, because he would not have drawn the lines on a piece of paper if he would have had a map.

It became clear to me that Dresden, from the border marked on my map, was the same distance as the border crossing marked by him from here. The gasoline I had would have been probably sufficient to Dresden, but with this detour it certainly will not be enough. I did not see a gas station anywhere and even if my gas supply would be sufficient until the border, who knows where I am going to find the first gas station in the DDR.

My only possibility was to try to get some gas from these truck people. But the first problem was, how can I explain it to them and furthermore do they have gas to give or sell to me? How can I make them understand my problem?

I pointed to the truck's gas tank, and then to my car. I took the paper where he scratched my route, turned it over and wrote:

“Petrol, benzin=max. 50 km?”

I saw that he understood my problem. He nodded and went back to the cab and briefly discussed something with his partner. After that he came to me and motioned that I should go with him. He opened the gate on the rear of the truck. I saw several gas cans on the truck. I pointed to one of them, which was a 20 liter can. He reached behind the can and pulled out a rubber hose. He picked up one end of the rubber tube. He picked up the other end and motioned to my car, which meant I should bring it closer. I nodded that I understood, got into my car, started the motor and maneuvered the car so that its gas tank opening was near the gas can of the truck. It is true that my car this way blocked most part of the road, but there was no traffic anyway. He opened the gas can on the truck. I opened my gas tank. He motioned to go there and hold the rubber tube in the gas can. I did it, and he went to my car. He took the tube in his mouth and sucked the tube and very cleverly pinched it before the gas got to his mouth. He put the tube into my gas tank, released the grip on the tube and the gasoline started to flow into the tank of my car. I pushed the rubber tube deeper into his can until I felt it hit the bottom. Finally the entire content of his gas can was transferred into the tank of my car. I pulled the rubber tube from his can, lifted it so that all the gas in the tube should go into the tank. He pulled it from my gas tank, wound up the rubber tube around his hand up to his elbow. I indicated with my finger that I would like to pay and gave him the paper he used to draw the map and pencil. He indicated that I should not pay anything. He took the paper and pencil and wrote a zero on it, and he even crossed it out. I shook my head and also indicated with my hand that it is not acceptable. He indicated with his hand that he does not want anything. At which point I reached into my pocket and took out all of the Czech money I had and put it on the truck next to the gas can and thanked him in Hungarian. We shook hands he motioned which direction I should go. I got into the car, started the engine and started to leave on the road the truck driver pointed out to me and told the entire story to Vera and Éva.

I was only able to go slowly because of the very dim headlights. We reached the point where, according to the truck driver, we had to take a left turn. From here the road was a little better, but we were still driving in the mountains. Luckily there was no traffic. In about an hour we drove through a little village. It had a sign, 'Jilové'. The village was deserted. The road made a great bend. We drove on a bridge over the Elbe River and arrived in Dêĉin, which was written by the truck driver on his penciled map. From here we had to follow the Elbe River to get to the border of the DDR. After a half hour we arrived to Hŕensko at the Czech border. Here was a real border with a building and in front of it two Czech border guards. I stopped. The two border guards looked again with amazement at the steering wheel not on the left side. They came over to me. I gave them the two passports. One of them leafed through them, and in a big circle went around the car to the building. The other stayed with us. Soon, maybe less than 5 minutes later, he came back and gave me the passports. The two soldiers saluted. I waived to them, rolled up the window and started the car.

Not far away was 'Bad Schandau/Schmilka', the DDR border station. Two soldiers were there. I gave them the passports, but at least I could talk to them and greeted them in German:

"Guten Abend!" (Good Evening)

They were surprised and became very friendly. Again, one of them went to the building to stamp the passports. While he was away I talked with the other border guard. I told him that we are with a child, and since it is becoming very late, where could we find close a hotel?

He pushed up his cap and started to scratch his forehead.

“That is a problem, because the next small city is Bad Schandau on the river Elbe. It is a summer resort with many hotels, but this time of the year the hotels are closed.”

In the meantime, the other soldier came back with the passports and gave them back to me. The soldier with whom I was talking briefly explained to the other that we are looking for a hotel, which would be good to find, because we have in the car a small child. The soldier who brought back my passport said that he is going to call the biggest hotel in Bad Schandau. Maybe that one is open. He left.

He came back in a few minutes and said:

“I called them, but they are closed. However they promised that they are going to open one room and will heat it, so you can stay there for the night, and they could make some dinner in their kitchen.”

“I thank you for your help very, very much. How far is Bad Schandau, and how can I find the hotel?”

"Go on the road near the Elbe. Bad Schandau is about 8 km (5 miles) from here, but before you get there you have to go through the village Schmilka. When you reach Bad Schandau, don’t go into the city, but stay next to the river. Somewhere near the center of the town on the riverbank is the Park Hotel. That is where you should go.”

I thanked them again and started the car.

The interesting part of our border crossings were that nobody was interested in the large amount of luggage we were transporting, including several strapped to the roof. On top of that, on the Hungarian border they even helped us to put back into the car the big avalanche which fell out of the car.

In the very elegant Park Hotel they were already waiting for us. At the entrance was a counter arranged in a semicircle. Behind the counter were a man and a woman. We only took with us one small luggage. When we entered they greeted us and asked for our passports. The man said that our room is on the first floor and gave me the key to the room. The woman said they are going to prepare for us a small dinner, because the kitchen is not fully open. Vera discussed with the woman what we should get for dinner. The man reassured me that I can leave everything on the top of the car, nothing will disappear.

We received a beautiful, well heated room with a view on the Elbe River, and we received immediately our dinner. They brought it up to our room, because everything, including the dining room in the hotel, was closed. After our dinner I went downstairs. Behind the counter I found two men. They took papers from a box and studied them. One of them was the fellow who received us. I thanked them for receiving us on such a short notice with such a beautiful well heated room, and the dinner was also excellent. Even my daughter, who is very picky about food, also found everything very good. I inquired how one can get from Bad Schandau to Berlin. They did not have a map either, so they drew it on a paper like the Czech truck driver did.

They said that first we have to go from Bad Schandau to Dresden, which is about 25 km (16 miles). We have to go through the city, and from there the road is very good to Berlin. The distance from Dresden to Berlin is about 200 km (about 125 miles). Considering that the maximum speed I can drive my car is 60 km/hour, I assumed we needed about 5 – 6 hours for that trip from Bad Schandau to Berlin, considering some stops on the way. They were able also to tell me where I could find a gas station to buy gasoline. They also informed me that at the outskirts of Berlin authorities are conducting identity checks. They are going to check our passports, because without passport or special permit one cannot enter Berlin.

Next day on December 2, Sunday, we left quite early to be able to arrive in Berlin when it is still daylight. The people in the hotel were very nice. They even packed for the three of us sandwiches with cheese, and also gave us a bottle of mineral water.

We had to cross to the other side of the River Elbe where the road was going through a forest. The forest was not very dense, and we saw that parallel to us are the train tracks and past that the river. When the forest ended the road was directly on the bank of the Elbe River. Finally we left the river and drove through Pirnán, and after several suburbs arrived in Dresden.

Dresden was destroyed more than any other German city during the bombing raids conducted by the English and American bombers on February 13 to 15, 1945. One could see in Budapest the destructions caused by war, but when we arrived to the city of Dresden, an unbelievable shocking sight greeted us, because there was not a single building standing. Dresden's old city area is about 15 square kilometers, and it was demolished to the ground, including many museums and famous monuments. The streets and avenues of the city still existed, and we were driving on deserted streets toward the center of the city. It was a gruesome sight to see the ruins to the right and to the left of us. In many places one could see through the ruins as far as the third, fourth or fifth blocks, because there was no building standing in between to obscure the view.

We arrived to what was pre-war the most famous church of Dresden, or rather to what remained of it. "Frauenkirche" was built 1726 – 1743 and its 96 meter (315 feet) dome was considered an engineering marvel. It did not collapse from bombardment, but in the fire storm it's holding cracked and the dome, weighting 12 thousand ton, collapsed and fell down. Driving by, we could only see the enormous amount of blackened shambles.

On Vera's advice we went on through the ruined streets to find the 'Zwinger', because she read somewhere that the famous picture gallery, or at least a part of it, was reopened on June 3, 1956. This was because during the war they were able to hide a part of the pictures in secured places. The commander of the Nazi military forces, before fleeing from the advancing Soviet forces, gave an order to blow up a part of the picture gallery, but only a very few pieces were left to perish. After the Soviet troops occupied the area, a large number of pictures were collected and transported to the Soviet Union where they were stored in museums. In 1955, the Soviet Union returned to Dresden

831,240 paintings which were restored in the Soviet Union. The population of Dresden decided in a referendum that the ruins should not be removed in order to replace them with buildings in the Socialist Realist style, which was customary in those days in the DDR. In order to restore the beauty of the city, they should rebuild from the ruins the middle and east part of the huge building complex that was named the Zwinger and housed the Museum of Fine Arts. That made it possible that this part of the Zwinger, with the returned paintings, was able to be reopened on June 3, 1956.

It was easy to find the Zwinger. Through the ruins it was easily to see the restored large building. We stopped in front of the entrance. Vera went in to look at the restored paintings. Because Éva was sleeping I stayed outside with her in the car, which I liked very much, since I was never much of a museum visitor.

The road between Dresden and Berlin, being a Sunday, had very sparse traffic, so we were able to reach the outskirts of Berlin in the afternoon by about 3 PM. As it was described in the previous Chapter, East Germany, or as it was named at that time, Deutsche Demokratishe Republik (DDR), was occupied by the Russians and was totally surrounding Berlin, which was divided into four sectors for the occupying powers, American, British, French and Russian. At the borders of the city of Berlin the DDR security forces controlled who is entering Berlin, because whoever crossed this line could go to Berlin. There in 1956 one could go from one sector to the other without any problem. From the Western sectors one could get by air across the Russian occupied DDR area and wind up in the

[83] The Splendors of Dresden. Newsweek, New York, 1979

west. Compared to the previous border crossings, here we encountered the most serious control. In spite of the spars traffic at least ten cars and trucks were in line waiting to be checked out.

Finally it was our turn. Four soldiers had sub-machine guns and only one had a revolver, who probably was the officer. This one was somewhat surprised that I am on the right side of the car. He circled around the car, came to my window and asked for the passports. He looked into the car, where Éva happened to be in a good mood and smiled at the officer, who smiled back. He went through both passports page by page. At the pictures he stopped, looked into the car to compare the faces with the pictures. Finally he returned the passport, saluted and wished us good trip. For some reason he had also no interest in our luggage.

In Berlin more or less I could find my way since in October/November I had lived here for almost a month. I easily found the Coburger Hof Hotel in the Friedrichstrasse, which I had left about a week ago to go to Budapest. The staff greeted me as an old guest. I introduced to them Vera and Éva, and I told them I need now a room in which they can install a bed for a child. They said that would be no problem, and they would charge me my old rate. I told them we are planning to stay only two nights, because we are going to be here for about a month and we are going to look for an apartment. I said I would pay two days immediately. I asked for help to carry up most of the luggage, but we would leave the big ones in the trunk of the car. I left the car in front of the hotel.

All this happened in daylight before sunset. We were very lucky, because our entire trip was in a sunny and mild weather.

After we settled in our room, Vera started to unpack a few needed things. I removed from my winter coat the dollars and the Napoleon gold pieces and simply put them into my pocket. During our trip we agreed, that the first thing I am going to do is to call Michael Oppert and visit them, and that I am going to rent in West Berlin a hotel room for us to where I am going to transfer our luggage one by one without attracting attention. When all of our stuff will be there, Vera and Éva are also going to move there.

Éva Anna Váradi and Tatra 57A– December 1956

It was also clear that I have to avoid getting in contact with the Hungarian Embassy, and I should not get in touch with colleagues from the Humboldt University. I have to avoid the Embassy, because they would notify the DDR police or the State Security Agency. In spite that without the help of the Humboldt University colleagues I would not be here now, I could not get in touch even to thank them. They obviously would not report that I am here, but if the authorities found out that I am here and they knew about it and not reported it that would get them into a very unpleasant situation. On the other hand, I have to call the Opperts urgently.

So I called the Opperts and told them I came back and I would like, if possible, to visit them immediately. They said they are waiting for me. I went down to the hotel's reception. I found at the desk one of the employees whom I knew well. He already had in front of him my hotel bill for two days. I paid, went to my car and drove to the Opperts in Zehlendorf.

They were very pleased to see me. I told them that I came with my wife and daughter, and we are not going back to Hungary. I briefly told them that we would like to go to America, but if that will not be possible, we are going to stay here because I have a job offer from Telefunken. I asked them to recommend me a hotel somewhere in their neighborhood where I would rent a room and would leave my luggage which is in the car. I would transport our belongings to this hotel piece by piece, and at the end my wife and daughter would come over from our present Hotel from East Berlin.

They said this is a good plan and immediately recommended a Hotel which they knew quite well not very far from them. They were very interested in my car, as I told them that it is a jalopy which was assembled from a wreck. They came with me and admired it, but this was not so unusual in Berlin, because many people living in East Germany had also only a jalopy.

Michael got into my car, his wife went home. Michael directed which way I should go, and soon we stopped in front of a three story hotel.

We got out. Michael greeted the man at the reception desk – it seemed they knew each other – and told him that we need a room for two adults and a child. The man at the reception said that would be no problem, took a key from a board where next and below to each other several keys were hanging on small hooks. Every key was attached to a big metal plate on which the room number was engraved.

He said we should go up to the room with him to see if it is acceptable. He opened a very nicely furnished room. I said that for the child we also need a bed. He said that it is no problem, he will arrange it. I asked him how much the price was per day. He told me. Obviously it was more than I was paying in East Berlin. I told him that it is Ok, and I am renting the room from today. I am going to leave a luggage here, and we bring the rest, and my wife and daughter will come tomorrow.

We went downstairs. At the desk he gave me a paper to fill out. I completed it and told him that I would pay him an advance in dollars. He said it is not needed for Mr. Oppert's guests.

I went to the car, took the luggage from the trunk and brought it in the Hotel. He saw that it was large and heavy. Immediately he got a trolley, he put it on, and we went in the elevator and I left the luggage in the room. When we came back he hung the key back on the board.

When we were back in the car it was about half past six. I said I am going back to the hotel in East Berlin to my family. He said they would like to invite us to dinner for tomorrow. I thanked him very much. He got out of the car and said that it is running very well. I was heading back to Hotel Coburger Hof. The road went through the Brandenburg Gate, which was the border between the British and Russian zone. A few blocks before I got to the Brandenburg Gate a policeman on a motorbike cut in front of me and motioned I should stop. I could not understand what he wanted, because with my car I could certainly not speed. The policeman got off the motorbike and propped it up and came to me. I felt lucky that the trunk of the car was empty as I had left the big luggage in the hotel. I lowered the window. I calmed down when I saw he was a West Berlin policeman and not an East Berlin one and not some official from the East side.

"Sir, the rear light of your car is not on".

The car had only one back light on the left side of the car.

"Thank you, I am going to check it."

I got out and went to the rear of it. In the meantime my motor was running because I did not dare to shut it off. I was afraid it may not restart. I saw the light was really not on. It happened once in a while, and I knew how to fix it.

During the evening it was cold, and I had a coat on and thick gloves on my hands. I hit the lamp with my gloved palm, and the light turned on immediately.

"Sorry" – I said – "it looks like it was a bad contact."

The policeman watched this operation in awe. For a short time he said nothing, because he was not prepared for this sort of repair.

"You should please check it next time"

"Naturally I am going to check it."

He started to go towards his motorbike, but he immediately remembered, that in his surprise he did not say good bye and turned back:

"Good evening!"

"Good evening!" – I greeted him back with relief.-

I went through the Brandenburg Gate without any problem and returned to our hotel. I left my car on the deserted street in front of the hotel.

Next morning I started to take our luggage one by one to the West Berlin hotel. Naturally, every time I went through different check points both going and coming. When all of our belongings were in the West Berlin Hotel, I went back for Vera and Éva to permanently leave the Russian zone in an otherwise empty car and without any luggage. We could be leaving the communist East on side street crossings, but I decided that one should do this in style and leave through its most famous crossing, the Brandenburg Gate.

Brandenburg Gate[84] (Caution - You will leave after 70 meters West Berlin)

[84] http://www.mhoefert.de/brandenburger_tor.htm

33. A Day of Change

At the end of the war Germany was divided into four zones: American, English French and Russian. In l949 the unification of the American, English and French zones established the German Federal Republic (GFR). From the Russian zone the German Democratic Republic (DDR) was established. At the beginning it was easy to cross the border between East and West Germany at several points. Therefore between l950 and l953, about 875 thousand East German citizens fled to West Germany[85] to escape from the dictatorship built on the Soviet example. In 1952-53, the DDR closed down the border between East and West Germany, following the example of the Hungarian-Austrian border.

After 1953 the only way to the Western free world for East German refugees was through Berlin. Berlin, inside the borders of the DDR like an island in the sea, was located fairly far from the nearest point of the GFR's border, about 180 kilometers (112 miles) away. The four zones, established in Berlin at the end of the war, in 1956 were still unchanged. As I have seen on my way to Berlin, the East German border-guards performed their job very strictly on the border which surrounded the whole of Berlin, but there wasn't any barbed-wire fence yet and no watch-towers, either. If somebody succeeded to get through this border into Berlin in 1956, he was able to move around between the four zones without any difficulty. The actual division of the two halves of Berlin was only accomplished

---

[85] Dale, Gareth: Popular Protest in East Germany, 1945 – 1989, 2005

by drastic means: with a wall built on the streets of Berlin, and with the closing down of some stops of the U and S-Bahns (trains). The East German authorities did this in l961[86]. However in l956 the Berlin Wall was not built yet.

So the East Germans who wanted to flee to the West, simply walked over to the American, English or French zone and presented themselves to the authorities there, announcing that they wish to leave the GDR and settle either in West Germany or somewhere else. The Americans, the French and the English established refugee administration offices with the assignment to take care of the applicants, check their identity and their intentions about living in the West, and if no objection was found against them, to transport them by airplane out of Berlin, first to Frankfurt in West Germany.

Because we wished to go to the United States, on the advice of Michael Oppert, we turned to the USA office dealing with refugees. Michael found out for us, that the American Refugee Center was at Berlin-Lichterfelde-West, at Manteuffelstrasse 31, and he explained to me how I could get there from our hotel.

The morning after our moving to the hotel in West Berlin, on the 4th of December, I left Vera and Éva (who saw tropical fruits for the first time in her life) at the breakfast table, promising to be back in the afternoon. I got into my

[86] Between 1949 and 1961 – 2.6 million East Germans were fleeing to the West. This situation changed in 1961, because on Russian incentives the DDR surrounded West Berlin – the American, British and French sector – with a fortified wall. This wall, was destroyed by the people of Berlin after the fall of communist rule in 1989.

car and drove to find the American office dealing with refugees.

I parked the car in front of the building and entered. After the entrance door, I had to get through a second door into an office, where two secretaries were sitting at their desks. One of the secretaries had beautiful blond hair, long black eyelashes, and her face was meticulously made up. I estimated her to be about forty years old. The other lady had brown hair, gathered into a small coil at the back or her head, she was also a pleasant looking lady, probably older than the other, and her face was less made up. I went to the brown haired lady and told her in German my reason to be there. She gave me a form and told me to fill it out. She gave me a ball-point pen to write with. I took a good look at the ball-point pen, because although it existed already in Hungary, I was still using fountain pens. I knew that the ball-point pen was invented by two Hungarians, László Biró and György Biró. After a lot of unsuccessful experiments, they started to manufacture them in Argentina, although they were not perfect yet. Finally they were perfected in America and France, and manufacturing started in great quantities. The French ball point pen, which was manufactured by Marcel Bich based on the patent of the Biró brothers and was distributed with the name Bic, was already quite cheap. I got one of these to fill out the questionnaire. I found it interesting that on the side of the plastic pen the name "Biró" was also visible.

I sat down in the ante-room and filled out the printed form. The form was very simple: my name, my date of birth, my marital status, name of my family members and their dates of birth, the address from where I came, how I arrived to Berlin, my address in Berlin and where I would like to go.

After I filled it out, I returned it to the secretary, who looked it over and told me to sit down .She stood up and went out through the door behind her desk. She came back after a minute and said that the person who will handle my case will be here soon. I sat down.

Indeed, in not more the 5 minutes a tall, balding, about 40 years old gentleman appeared. He was dressed in dark gray pants with black belt, black shoes, white shirt and blue and black striped necktie. He greeted me in broken German and asked me to go with him. I followed him. We went through a corridor from which rooms opened on both sides. He entered one of the rooms and waved me in. In his office there was a fairly big varnished desk with a great amount of papers neatly arranged on it. There was a framed picture on his desk, but I couldn't see who or what was on the picture, because from my side only the back of it was visible. In front of him there was a fairly big writing pad with lined pages. Besides this there was a metal tray with a bunch of pencils and ball-point pens on it. On the wall was a picture of an autumn landscape. It seems the owner of the office was a smoker, because on the table there was also an ash-tray, a box of matches and a pack of cigarettes with "Lucky Strike" written on it. He sat down behind his desk and motioned me to one of the two chairs in front of his desk. After we both were seated, he said, again in pretty bad German, that I should call him Karcsi and take off my coat and hang it on the coat rack. I did this and sat back on my chair.

This was the moment when I told him that we may as well speak English. He broke into a broad grin and said that sounds splendid because his German is not the best. I told him that my English is just as bad as my German, so for me it makes no difference which language I speak, but I offered the English because I thought that it is better for him. He thanked me.

He started to read my questionnaire. When he finished with the reading, he looked at me with interest:

“The three of you, you, your wife and your daughter came from Hungary?”

“Yes.”

“When did you arrive to Berlin?”

“The day before yesterday.”

“How was it possible to leave Budapest now, by air, by train... but I see that you write here that you came by car?”

“Yes, we came by car.”

“By car?" he asked, "What kind of a car?”

“My car.”

He looked at me uncomprehending and asked it again:

“Whose car did you come with?”

“With my car. I came here with it, too. It is standing in front of the building, and I will show it to you gladly. It is an old car, but it brought us successfully to Berlin.”

He looked at me more-or-less as if I had said that I arrived with a space-ship from Mars.

“Interesting," he said, "I would like to have a look at it.”

Saying this, he stood up and took his jacket from the rack. I stood up, too. We left his office back to the room where the secretaries worked. He stepped to the window from where he could see my car.

“Interesting," he repeated, "This is a 56A Tatra.”

“Yes. I see that you are very familiar with old cars. I think this car was manufactured 20 years ago, in 1935/36. As you see, the steering wheel is on the right side, because at that time in a great part of Europe, including Hungary, the traffic was on the left side.”

“I am a great admirer of antique cars. May I have a look at it?”

“Of course.”

We went out to the street. It was pretty cold, so I was sorry that I didn’t bring my coat with me, but I couldn’t guess that my car will arouse such a great interest. I opened the car door, and he got in and sat on the driver’s seat.

“This car really might be 20 years old, but it is in very good condition.”

“I bought it at a junk-yard, because that was what I got a permit for, but I have a very good car mechanic, who reconstructed it. Whenever I had a problem, he repaired it."

He got out, shut the car door carefully, and he looked at me with obviously greater interest than when I first sat down to his desk. We returned to his office. He offered me a cigarette, I told him I don't smoke. He lighted a cigarette and asked me if I would like something to drink, Coca Cola or water or coffee? He said he will have a coffee. I said I would like that too, without milk, but with sugar. He lifted his phone, and I assume he talked to his secretary, saying in English that he would like two coffees, one plain and one with sugar.

After this, he pulled the lined white notebook in front of him, took a ball-point pen and asked me to tell him in detail, who I am, what I do, how we came to Berlin, and what are my plans for the future. He said emphatically, that I should tell him everything in detail, he has plenty of time. He asked how come I speak relatively good English?

The blond secretary came in, smiling, bringing the coffees on a metal tray and putting it on the desk between the two of us. That's when I noticed that the lady had long nails with fire-red nail polish on them. Karcsi thanked the coffee and raised his cup. The cup looked as it was made of paper. He tasted the coffee, but it seems it was too hot, because he did not drink but put the cup back on the tray. The secretary turned around and left.

So I started with my English. I told him that in schools in Hungary until 1945 I learned for eight years German and for four years French, but my parents hired for me a private teacher who taught me English at home. At the

University I translated for my professor and his assistants, who didn't speak English, a lot from English scientific magazines, and I still read a lot of English scientific papers in connection with my profession, and other books too, so my vocabulary is large, only my pronunciation and my grammar is bad.

After this, I started to tell my story. I said that I wanted to move to America right after I finished my studies at the University for several reasons. Many of my near relatives and friends went there before the borders were shut down, all of them escaping the beginning of the communist dictatorship. I was not a member of the communist party, partly because I had nothing to do with politics, and partly because I had seen already the horrors of dictatorship during and before the war, and I did not want to live in such a system. I saw the advantages of capitalism, of which Berlin is the fantastic example. Unfortunately, I never imagined that by the time I finished my studies and I could leave, it was too late, because when in 1949 I received my diploma, the borders were already closed down.

I continued my story with the University. My professor wanted me to stay in his institute as a faculty member, but I could not stay there, because the Communist Students League of the University opposed my appointment, as I was not a member of the communist party. On the other hand, they let me get a job in the Tungsram electric bulb factory's research laboratory, because the communist state needed me as a chemist. The part of this research laboratory where I was working was transformed into Telecommunication Research Laboratory and placed under military supervision. I explained briefly the field I was working in. Finally I talked about the East German Chemical Society's convention in Leipzig to which I was invited as a speaker, and about my fortunate situation afterward, in consequence of which I was able to come back to Berlin with my wife and daughter.

He was very attentive during my story-telling. Sometimes he asked a question, and he wrote notes constantly on the lined white paper. When he finished a page, he wrote the page number on the right top corner, he tore out the page from the perforated note-pad and put it on the desktop. Sometimes he stopped me, looked through the finished pages, asked another question, and wrote my answer on the page on which his question was based. For example, he asked a question about my membership in the communist party. I said that as I mentioned already, I never was a member. So he returned to the first page, probably to where I said that I could not stay at the University, because I was not a party-member. I suppose he added here that I was "never" a member. Meanwhile he was smoking all the time and drinking his coffee. At such times I stopped talking too, and drank my coffee from the paper-like cup.

When I got to the end of my story, he looked at the questionnaire I completed. He read out loud the name of the hotel and the street where we are staying now, and asked why I choose this hotel. I told him that when we arrived, first we went to the Hotel Coburger Hof in East Berlin, because I was staying there when I could not go back to Budapest. I have an acquaintance in West Berlin who lives in Zehlendorf, and I asked him to recommend a hotel. He recommended this one, because he is familiar with it and is near their apartment. He wrote this down.

He asked me if I would tell him my acquaintance's name and address, and how have I got to know him. I said of course, no problem, and I gave him the information he asked for. He wrote that down.

Finally he looked at his wristwatch, and I, too, looked at mine. I saw that it showed exactly half past twelve. He tore out the page where he wrote the hotel's address, put a number on it and positioned it neatly on those sheets which were already arranged on his desk. Then something must have occurred to him, because he started to look through his notes. It seems he had found it.

"You said that you would like to go to America, but you have a job offer from Telefunken here in their Berlin laboratory. We will do everything in order for you to get to America, but I recommend that you should not stay in Berlin. We, I mean my department, can easily arrange that you, with your family, be able to go from Berlin to West Germany. It would be dangerous for you and your family to stay in Berlin, because from here they could easily take you back to Hungary even if you don't live in the Russian zone. As it is already dinner time and you obviously want to go back to your family, I recommend that you come back tomorrow morning, let's say at 9 o'clock. By then I'll look through my notes, and we can discuss the plans."

"You suggest that I should ask the Director of Telefunken, who offered me the job, if I could still get an offer if I do not want to stay in Berlin?"

"I think it would be wise of you if you would ask."

We stood up. I put on my coat. He opened the door and escorted me to the secretary's room, where only the woman with the brown hair was there, and we shook hands at the exit door.

“Tomorrow when you return, I would love to drive your car. It would be a great fun to drive a 20 year old car which is in such a good shape. Goodbye.”

“Goodbye.”

When I got into my car I saw that he was looking from behind the door as I was starting the car.

After lunch I called the Director of Telefunken. His secretary, whose voice I already recognized, picked up the phone. I told her who I was and that I managed to come back to Berlin with my wife and my daughter, and I would like to meet the Director.

She was very glad to welcome me back and said that she is going to check the Director’s schedule. Half a minute later she was back and said that this afternoon at 3 PM he could meet me. I said this is great and I will be there.

When I came to this hotel with Michael Oppert, I had noticed a bank a few block away. I thought that I am going to change my dollars to German marks. Having some time, I went to the bank. After changing the dollars, and as I had some of the Napoleon gold pieces also in my pocket (the rest of them were with Vera), I showed one of them to the cashier and asked how much it is worth. I thought that it must be a very big value if in Hungary one could have been jailed for having one.

The cashier looked at the coin. He took from his drawer a sheet of paper, looked at it and said:

“Sir, the value of this coin is $27, which I could also change for you into German marks.”

That the value of the Napoleon is only $27 shocked me. That the communist system, for a value of $27, should jail people? This Napoleon, reminding me of an insane system, is worth more to me as memento than to sell it. I thanked him, got my Napoleon back, and put it back in my pocket.

I went back to the hotel to give some money to Vera, because she planned to go with Éva to look some shops and store windows.

Exactly at 3 PM I entered the room of the Director’s secretary. We greeted each other like old friends. She got up, approached me and, according to German habit, shook hands.

“Herr Doktor Váradi, the Herr Director, and I also, are very glad that you were able to return with your wife and daughter. I assume it was not a simple matter.”

“It was really not easy, but the Revolution and the anti-Russian sentiment helped, but besides of that I had a great deal of luck.”

"Please follow me.” We entered the office of the Director.

"Herr Doktor Váradi, I am very glad to see you again.” He circled his desk, came to me and shook hands.

""Herr Director, you can imagine how happy I am to see you again."

Before the secretary left, he asked her to bring two espressos. He motioned me to go to the brown leather chairs where we were sitting almost four weeks ago for the first time. The same way as four weeks ago, he picked up a cigarette and lit it. He asked about the Hungarian situation and how I managed to leave.

I said that I came from Budapest in my own car, and my wife and daughter is also with me. I told him that by the time I was able to be back in Budapest, the Russian troops already occupied the country, but the resistance was still active and the Russians could not yet completely reinstate the old communist system. More or less because of this I was able to leave the country.

"I would like to thank you again that you offered me a job in the Berlin research laboratory. This morning I went to the USA office dealing with refugees to obtain the papers needed. They recommended that because we can be easily picked up and transport back to Hungary, I should not stay with my family in Berlin. I think that there is some truth in this."

"I heard about this sort of cases. They are right."

"Would it be possible if instead of Telefunken's Berlin Research Laboratory, I can get a job in Dr. Dahlke's department in Telefunken's Research laboratory in Ulm?"
"I do not see any problem, but I have to discuss it with Dr. Dahlke and with the personnel department in Ulm. The problem could be that because of the destruction caused

by the war there are very few apartments available in Ulm for Telefunken. Therefore the question is, if we employ you there, could Telefunken provide you with an apartment. I am going to find out by tomorrow afternoon, but consider it that there will be a great probability that we can solve this problem. This would require however, that the Americans would transport you by air to Frankfurt. I suggest that you leave as soon as possible. The Hungarian authorities have bigger problems than dealing with you, but who knows? The Americans can get you the needed papers to stay in Germany."

"By 9 AM I have to go back to the American office, and I am going to tell them."

"If possible please come back tomorrow at 3 PM. By that time I will be able to tell you whether they can accommodate you in Ulm."

I promised that I will be back.

By the time I was back to our hotel it was past 5 PM. Vera and Éva told me with amazement what they have seen in West Berlin, wonderful shops, the abundance of merchandise and food, the lights, many cars and the well-dressed people. They have not seen anything like that in Budapest or in East Berlin.

We ate dinner, and Vera put Éva to bed, when the telephone in the room started ringing. The desk called and said that a gentleman would like to speak with me. It was Karcsi. He said that he would like to talk with me, and I should go down. I said I will go down.

When I got downstairs he motioned that we should sit down in the armchairs in the lobby. To get to the chairs we had to pass the entrance door of the hotel and I noticed that in front of the hotel was a large black limousine with a man at the steering wheel. I asked Karcsi if he arrived in that car. He answered very matter of fact that, yes.

When we sat down he said:

"We got information that you and your family are in danger in this hotel, because it is possible that they want to take you back to Hungary. The best would be if you would collect your stuff immediately, and I will take you and your family in the car to a safe and well guarded hotel, and you would move your car there."

The story sounded bizarre as nobody beside of the Opperts and Karcsi, not even the Director of Telefunken, knew that we are in this hotel. I have been in many places today, and in West Berlin are many more autos than in Budapest or East Berlin, but I did not notice that somebody was following me. Furthermore, we just left Budapest only a few days ago, and I was able to judge that the communists are not able so fast to mobilize the machinery of state security, which does not even function well yet. My common sense made me think that there must be another reason why Karcsi wants us to move into another, according to him "well-guarded," hotel. I simply did not believe this story from him. Furthermore, Éva was sleeping and it was evening, and I am not going to pack up and move the family.

"Thank you very much that you are so worried about us, but I think that we arrived only yesterday. Nobody wants to abduct us tonight. Let's stay with our plan, I will be tomorrow morning at 9 AM in your office."

"Then please promise, that you are not going to go anywhere tonight."

"I cannot promise you this, because I have to go to the grocery store across the street. The ladies asked me to buy some oranges."

"OK, than go shopping now, and I am going to wait in the car until you return. I can see from the car the shop, so I can take care of you."

"OK, that is very nice of you," I said, getting used to the English language.

"But tomorrow morning after we met in my office, we are going to come here and transfer you to another hotel. Do not be afraid that it will be expensive, because we are going to pay for it."

Considering our financial situation, this was an offer I could not reject. I agreed immediately. I simply said:

"OK."

We left the hotel together, and Charlie sat in the big American car, which I established was a Chevrolet. I did not wanted to look at Charlie's colleague, but I saw he was of Charlie's age, similarly dressed and also smoked. I went to the other side of the street to the grocery store to buy the oranges. I went back to the hotel and saw that Charlie's car was still there. He was sitting in the driver's seat, his partner was still smoking on the side next to him. When I entered into the hotel I motioned to them. They waited until I was inside, and then Charlie started the engine.

I handed over the oranges to Vera, but I did not mention my discussion with Charlie, that they want to kidnap us. I rather said nothing. In my opinion Charlie saw too many spy movies, and Vera would have been frightened. On the other hand, I told her that next day we are moving to another hotel, which was recommended by the Americans, but the best is that the Americans are paying it. Vera said that this is also a good hotel, but I told her that there is no reason to argue, especially for the hotel. She agreed to this. I called the Opperts and told them that the Americans insist that we should move into another hotel which they select, where they would pay everything, and I do not know why this hotel is not good for them.

“Oh," Michael said and started to laugh, "I know what the problem is. We here in Zehlendorf are in the American sector. The hotel where you are at present, which is a couple of blocks from here, is however in the British sector. I assume that the Americans want to move you into a hotel in the American sector. There are no borders between the Western sectors, but officials can only operate in their own zone."

Michael was able to assess the situation pretty well, and his explanation was more understandable than Charlie’s.

34. Becoming "Eligible" Refugees

I arrived next morning exactly at 9 AM at Charlie's office. The secretaries were sitting behind their desks. In addition, two men were also in the office. One of them was sitting at the table where I had sat the day before, and it seemed that he was just completing the same form I had. The other man was sitting on one of the four chairs next to the wall. The secretary with whom I was talking a day ago told me she will tell Charlie that I have arrived, and until he comes I should sit down. I sat down.

In a few minutes Charlie came, and after greetings, he said we should go to his office.
He said that he has some questions in connection with yesterday's discussion, and after that we should go, I with my car and he with his, to my hotel to transport our belongings to the hotel they selected. His questions were interesting and showed that Charlie is a good observer and a professional. He asked me to show our passports, because from his notes, which were before him on the desk, he noticed that in the passport issued after the Revolution there were no Russian translations and that the page in Russian was not filled and was crossed out.

I told him that is correct and gave him the two passports. He looked at them page by page and made some notes on his white lined paper.

"Very interesting that after the Russian occupation, which started on November 4, they were not able to restore the old system even until November 24, when your wife's passport was issued. Now I can understand how you were able to get a passport."

After we talked about his questions, he proposed that we should go to my hotel to move our belongings. I did not mention to him Michael Oppert's opinion as to why our move was necessary. The big black car which I saw yesterday was now behind my car. The same man, who was yesterday smoking a cigarette while waiting for Charlie, was at the wheel. Charlie said I should follow them and got in the black car. The black car left, and I followed.

We stopped in front of the entrance of my hotel. Charlie and the man dressed almost in the same attire came with me into the lobby. I told the clerk behind the desk that we are going to leave. Charlie, who stood next to me, told him that he should prepare the bill, and he is going to pay. I was very surprised about this generosity.

All three of us went up to our room. I introduced Charlie to Vera and Éva. Charlie shook hands with both of them. He said he is glad to meet Vera and Éva, and introduced our companion, whom he simply called Bob, who shook hands with everybody.

I told Charlie that he could continue to speak in his mother tongue, because Vera speaks good English, and it does not hurt Éva to start learning it. Charlie and Bob grinned. Charlie said, now in English, that we are going to carry down everything. The ladies should carry nothing.

At the reception he paid the bill, for which I thanked him very much. We packed everything in the two cars. Charlie suggested that Vera and Éva should sit in my car. Charlie and Bob sat in the Chevrolet. The black car went ahead again. About half way between the hotel we came from and Charlie's office, the black car stopped in front of a building which had a sign 'Hotel'. It was a little bigger than ours. We entered. It seems they knew Charlie. They did not ask for passports or any other identification. The concierge at the desk gave Charlie a key and told him which floor the room is and the room number. Charlie told him in English that an additional bed will be needed for the child. The concierge nodded and wrote something on a paper and said OK. The room was bigger than in our previous hotel, but the furnishing was about the same. The three of us, Charlie, Bob and me carried our packages and deposited them in the room.

Charlie said that we can eat in the hotel and charge it to the room, for which he is going to pay. He gave me ten 10 Mark bank notes and a paper and asked me to sign it that I received the money. I said that we have some money.

He suggested that we should not spend our money, on the other hand I should write down what we have spent and when we spent it, and I should give him the paper when we spent all and he will give me more money.

Charlie told me I should be in his office next morning at 9 AM. This afternoon he is busy, but tomorrow for sure he wants to try my car.

I was happy with this arrangement, because at 3 PM I had to be at Telefunken.

I was exactly at 3 PM in the Director Secretary's office. The secretary got up from her desk, opened the door to the Director's office and announced me. After greetings and a handshake, we sat down in the armchairs, he lit his cigarette.

"The job in Ulm is OK. They can provide you with an apartment. I suggest that when you are transported to Frankfurt, call the personnel department in Ulm and discuss which day you could go to Ulm to meet Dr. Dahlke and also Dr. Brück, the director of the research laboratory there. You can go there by train and back the same day, and obviously we are going to reimburse you for your expenses. By that time you will know when you are going to get the needed identification papers, and when you could start your work. Dr. Váradi, I am very glad that you are going to be working at Telefunken."

I thanked him for personally having dealt with our problem. He said this is the minimum he can do to help those who fled the communist oppression.

When I returned to the hotel I called Michael Oppert to tell him the address of the new hotel and also the news that I was offered the job in Telefunken's Research Laboratory in Ulm. Michael invited us for dinner, where we could discuss the matters.
I kept my telephone conversation short, because based on my experiences in Budapest, I assumed they may have an eavesdropping system in this hotel. I did not want that our discussion should go to some other area.

At 9 AM the next day, December 6, I was in Charlie's office. I told him that based on his recommendation I talked with the Director at Telefunken, and in case I stay in Germany, I am going to have a job at Telefunken's Research Laboratory in Ulm. I thanked him for his advice that it is safer not to stay in Berlin. The Director at Telefunken saw it the same way.

He picked up a paper from his desk and gave it to me. It was the certificate from the "American Refugee Center" in Berlin, written in English and in German, that I was registered under "Control number 1390" as a refugee and a separate stamp was on it: 'ELIGIBLE'. As of now, I still do not know what this meant.

He said he started the process for our flight from Berlin to Frankfurt and also for our application for admission to the United States. As we are going to fly on a passenger plane, I will not be able to take my car, but as soon as they have a suitable airplane they are going to send it after me.

"At the present it looks like on December 8 there will be an airplane on which the three of you can fly from Berlin to Frankfurt. I suggest you should park your car tomorrow here in one of the side streets, and I am going to take you in my car to your hotel. On Saturday morning I am going to pick you up and will take you and your family to the airport. A colleague is going to wait for you in Frankfurt and will take you to your accommodation in the city. In Frankfurt you are going to be able to receive your German residence permit, and also you are going to be able to start your visa application at the American Consulate."
"This sounds very good. However to start my car in the morning could be a problem when the temperature is low."

"As I told you, I am a great admirer of antique cars and know quite well these problems. If you show me how one can start the car, I can surely start it as soon as we get space on one of the air freighters."
He had other questions in connection with my story. He asked me why they invited me to the annual meeting of the

DDR Chemical Society, and where my colleague with whom I was giving the lecture is now. I told him about my scientific work and about the many scientific papers published in Hungary as well as in the West. I also told him that my colleague arrived back to Hungary sooner than I did and escaped immediately. At the present time he and his wife are already in London.

He told me that now he understood why Telefunken offered me a job so fast, because they knew my scientific work from publications. During our discussions he said that because of the Revolution they – I assumed that he meant his organization – were not able to obtain "material" from Budapest. I interpreted this to mean that if somebody is applying in their office as a refugee, they try to trace down his past from Budapest, but because of the revolution, it seems the usual channels were not functioning. When I asked a question about this he changed the subject, and I assumed that he made an error saying it.

When we finished our discussion, he suggested I should go back to the hotel and spend the afternoon with my family on a sightseeing tour of the city, but I should be back the next day at 9 AM.

As we are going to stay only a few days in Berlin, I also thought the best is to do a sightseeing tour of the city. By that time I knew Berlin quite well, but for Vera and Éva, who just arrived from Budapest to the Western world, everything was very interesting, especially the enormous difference between the communist East and the capitalist West. This was especially visible in Berlin, where they were seen one next to the other. That evening we went to the Oppert's for dinner, where we discussed the situation.

We also talked about that the Americans are going to fly us on Saturday to Frankfurt, and they are going to bring my car after me as soon as they have a suitable airplane.

The next day, on December 7, I went again to Charlie's office. I did not even remove my top coat, when Charlie showed up in a short winter coat and told me to go to my car. He said I should teach him how to start the car and also to let him drive it.

We went to my car. I sat in the car and showed him that when the motor is warm the car starts immediately. I demonstrated this. I stopped the motor and took from under the driver's seat the crank. I stepped in front of the car and motioned him to come there and showed him how one can lift the very large hood. I supported the hood with a steel rod, which was attached to the front of the motor. I told him in detail how one can start the car when the temperature is at freezing or below freezing. He listened very attentively to this.

"Now I know how to start your car when they are going to transport it. If you let me, I would like to try it. I will be back in a minute, please wait."

He went back to the office and in a minute he was back with Bob, his colleague. We greeted each other. Handshakes were not an obligatory routine with the Americans.

"Bob would like to join us in this antique car."

"Excellent." I said.

Bob got in the back seat, Charlie to the driver's seat, and I next to him. When we all were seated, doors closed, Charlie stopped the motor and turned it on again with the starter.

"This car has three speeds."

On the gear shifter I showed him where the one, two and three positions are, and how he can put the car in reverse. He said he did know this system. He depressed the clutch, and expertly put it in the first gear. He released the clutch slowly and the car started smoothly. There was only little traffic in that area, so he drove the car through various streets. It was obvious that he enjoyed it very much, and after a 10 minute ride we arrived back to the small street next to his office. He parked the car at the sidewalk and stopped the engine.

"This is a magnificent car and is very well maintained."

"The gas tank is about half full."

'Very good. Let's go back to my office, because I have a few more questions, and we also have to talk about tomorrow's trip. Do you have anything in the car that you do not want to leave here?"

"No, I have nothing."

"OK. I am going to lock the door and keep the key of the car, and after our discussion I am going to take you back to your hotel."

He closed the car door and put the car key into his pocket.

We discussed the next day's program. They will pick us up at 10 AM and drive us with our luggage to the airport. In Frankfurt they will wait for us, and we are going to get an apartment in the city. The colleagues of Charlie are going to take care of everything. They are going to put in motion to get us the German identification papers and the American visa application. We had discussed all this the day before. The only new information was that in Frankfurt we are going to get an apartment and not stay in a hotel. He also said he is going to drive my car from the street to a parking garage, so that it should be in a safe place until they can find space on one of the freight planes.

He could not tell me how long it will take to obtain the German identification papers and the American visa. He said that his colleagues in Frankfurt have more experience in these matters, and they can better answer my questions. He could not give a date when my car will be transported. He said the transport planes are usually full, but they eventually will find space.

After we discussed everything, he offered to take me back to the hotel. The big black Chevrolet was already in front of the exit from the building. Bob was there, too. Charlie sat in the driver's seat and said I should sit next to him. Bob got into the back seat. We passed by the Tatra, and I waved to my good, faithful automobile and said good bye, see you soon.

The next day, on December 8th, Saturday, exactly at 10 AM, they called me from the hotel's desk in the lobby that somebody wants to talk to me. Charlie was on the telephone and told me they would like to come up to help us transport our luggage down to the cars. I said OK, and soon four people, Charlie, Bob and two others whom I have not seen before, but dressed in similar attire as Charlie and Bob, came to our room and picked up our packages. I only had to carry some small items. Vera had only to direct Éva. We went downstairs where two of the big black cars were waiting for us. They put our packages in the trunks of the two cars. Charlie said I should go in the car he is driving. The seating arrangement was the same as last time. Charlie was driving, I sat next to him and Bob was in the rear seat. In the other car a fellow dressed like Charlie was driving, Vera sat next to him. Another guy and Éva were sitting in the rear seats. When I got in the car I took out a paper on which our expenses were written. I gave it to Charlie, and also gave him the money that we did not spend.

"This is the accounting for the money, and the money to be returned."

Charlie reviewed the paper and counted the money.

"Thank you, it is OK. I would like to ask you to put a date on the accounting and sign it."
I did it and gave it back to him.

"The colleagues in Frankfurt are going to give you money with the same system."

He put the paper and the money in the pocket of his coat. We started towards the Tempelhof airport.

I am a person who comprehends things very slowly, because I just then realized that the presence of two Americans, and the way we are sitting, is not unintentional.

Charlie must have a very dangerous occupation. Many refugees are coming with whom he and his colleagues have to deal. One can assume that the great majority of them are bona fide refugees, but it is also possible that one of them is sent over by unknown employers to kidnap an American, British or French official. This would not be very difficult to do in Berlin. Such a "refugee," if he is alone with one person in a car, can simply bash the head of that official, then drive to the border of the sector, where normally there is no control, and the official disappears in the Russian sector. That is the reason there are always two Americans in the car, and the refugee never sits in the rear seat from where he could easily bash the head of the driver. One of them is driving the car, while the other from the rear seat keeps an eye on the 'refugee'. Looked at from this angle, my case could have been suspicious for them. I am driving from Budapest to Berlin by car, the wife and daughter are only to arouse confidence. Charlie's slip that because of the Revolution they have difficulties to gather 'material' from Budapest was probably in connection with my case. When I got so far in my thoughts, I turned to Charlie:

"Your job is am extremely dangerous, life threatening job."

He took his eyes off the road for a second and looked at me.

"Yes, it is. If a person is not cautious, he will not live until his retirement age. With you I was lucky because we still could not receive any concrete information from Hungary, but in connection with the Telefunken job offer I could easily establish that you are considered a very good professional who was not involved in any complicated political or spy business. It also helped that you told me the name and address of your acquaintance in Berlin. That was the reason we could clear you here so fast and arrange the trip to Frankfurt. But we always have to follow the rules. We have to be prepared that not everybody is a “refugee” who tells us that he or she was."

With this, with a wide grin, he opened his jacket, and a big revolver was visible.

"Bob is equipped similarly.”

“You and Bob are well equipped, but you do not know what I have.” I opened my coat under which obviously was no fire arm.

He looked at me a little afraid, his hand was moving towards his gun, but saw that I have nothing under my coat.

“You know that during our short acquaintance I learned you have a good sense of humor, but I suggest that you should not make jokes like this. If I would not know as much as I learned about you in the past few days, we would have to change direction and not drive to the airport, but to the emergency section of one of the local hospitals. Bob, what do you think?”

“Dr. Váradi, Charlie is right, this would be a good line in a movie, but here in Berlin it is a question of life or death, and it is not a joke.”

“You are so right. I apologize.”

We arrived to the Tempelhof airport which was in the American zone.

Tempelhof was a crucial airport when, a few years before, Stalin on June 20, 1948 decided to take over the entire Berlin and force the three western powers to abandon their sectors. At that time the Soviets closed all the access from the West to Berlin on land and water. That meant the two and a half million people living in West Berlin could not be supplied with food or anything else. The Western powers were facing the choice of either forcefully opening the roads to Berlin or abandoning their presence in Berlin and withdrawing their personnel. Stalin knew that to open a road to Berlin by force, because of the Soviet superior land forces, was not an option. He must have believed the Western powers will have to abandon West Berlin.

Stalin miscalculated. The American President Harry Truman was not willing to give up even one inch more territory than Roosevelt agreed to in February 1945 in Yalta. While Stalin had superior ground forces in the area, the Americans and British had superior air power in Europe. The bad luck for Stalin was that the American sector included the Tempelhof airport[87]. They could easily keep the agreed air corridors open and organized a program to supply the two and half million 'West Berliners' by air, landing the airplanes at Tempelhof. In order to be able to land airplanes almost every minute, the Americans built two more air strips in a great hurry. The Berlin "air bridge" supplied food, gasoline, and everything else for the population. The three Western powers kept their sector

[87] The Tempelhof airport's operation was discontinued on October 30, 2008.

and the “air bridge” operating until September 1949, when the Soviets gave up and opened the land route to Berlin.

We arrived at one of the gates of the fence surrounding the airport, which was guarded by two American soldiers with sub-machine guns. One of them came to our car.

Charlie showed him a card and waived back towards the second car. The soldier nodded, saluted, waived towards the guard house inside the fence where somebody probably pushed a button and the door opened. When both of the cars were inside, the door closed. There were lots of airplanes on the field, some near the airport buildings, and some far away on the tarmac. A big four engine airplane was at the end of a runway ready to leave. Its engines got louder and louder, finally the machine suddenly started to roll, accelerate and was running with increasing speed on the runway until it took off. One could see big letters BEA on it. I knew that it was the name of one of the British airlines.

Our cars did not go towards the airport, but turned on the inner road towards a group of airplanes. They were all identical machines. Charlie turned to me and said:

“These are the famous C-47 two engine airplanes, a large amount of which were built by the Douglas airplane factory during the war and since. They were the ones which carried that large amount of material during the Berlin air bridge.”

I knew these machines as DC-3, and their plan was also given to the Russians. They built it, too, but it was named Li-2. They were used in Hungary after the war for passenger traffic inside of Hungary. I flew on them between Budapest and the town I where I was born, Szeged.

Charlie steered the car to the side of one of the C-47.

“This is the plane you are going to fly to Frankfurt.”

We got out of the car, the second car stopped behind us. Everybody got out. Charlie got four soldiers who were next to the airplane to come and transport all of our belongings to the plane and load them into the hold. Vera had flown already on an airplane also from Budapest to Szeged, but for Éva the airplane was a new experience. I had a hard time to answer all of her questions. After all of our packages were loaded on the plane, Charlie said we should board it. He came with us to the stairs, which were lowered from the plane. We shook hands with Bob and also with Charlie. I thanked him for all his care for us, and I entrusted him with the care of my car.

We boarded the plane using the lowered stairs. Three men in military uniform waited for us. We shook hands. Éva was a big success. All three of them tried to talk with her but she spoke no English. They said we should sit down. This must have been an airplane used for military purposes, because there were no seats, only a long bench on each side at the wall of the plane. The plane had no windows. The ‘light’ came from the lights on the ceiling of the cabin. At that time I did not know, I only learned later from war movies, that this type of seating arrangement was used for transporting paratroopers.

On the two benches eight people were sitting, six men and two women. We exchanged greetings. It seemed we were the last ones, because one of the men closed the door, and all three of them went forward and sat down. The two pilots sat next to each other in the front, and the third, who must have been the radio operator, was sitting behind them. The engines were not started yet so we could talk to each other. We introduced ourselves. All eight of them were East German ‘refugees’. When the engines were started it became very noisy, there was not much soundproofing. We did not take our coats off, as there was no heating.

The machine finally reached the runway. The noise became louder when they revved the motors up for takeoff. The plane took off, and we were on our way to Frankfurt.

35. Cage with open door

The airplane came to a halt and the engines stopped. We assumed this from the reduction of the noise, as there were no windows on the plane. Shortly after this a pilot came back to us and enthusiastically informed us in English that we had arrived. He opened the door of the plane, lowered the stairs and motioned for us to disembark. Our travel companions waived to us that we should leave first. So I went down first, and then Vera started Éva going down. I helped her on the last steps, from there she jumped to the ground. Vera went down followed by our eight travel companions. We arrived at the American airport in Frankfurt on December 8 on a gray, wet and unfriendly cold day.

Not far from the airplane was a small bus. An American soldier motioned for us to go to that bus. I asked him what will happen to our luggage, and he pointed to the rear of the airplane where a few soldiers were removing the luggage from the plane and putting them on a trolley. The soldier standing at the plane said that the luggage will be also put on the small bus. I saw from the distance that one of the packages was ours, so I was very relieved and started towards the bus.

On the bus was a civilian American who was our guide. That he was American one could tell, because he spoke German with a heavy accent. He welcomed us in a very friendly manner to the "free world" and told us that during our stay in Frankfurt we will get our ID cards, which will document that we were accepted as refugees in the German Federal Republic (GFR). He also said that we are going to stay in a very nice place. We are not going to have any limitations, everybody can go when and where they want to. While we are waiting for the card from GFR, we will get a temporary card, and all of our needs will be provided by the United States of America.

After about a half hour ride we arrived in front of a big house with a large garden in front of it. We all got out, and the driver put all of our belongings on the sidewalk. As we had lots of luggage our traveling companions, the driver and the American guide helped to carry them into the building. Inside a woman with a white apron greeted us in German, but without an accent, and told us that everybody is going to be in a separate room, and she is going to escort us there. We received a very nice room with a bathroom. The woman also said that in a half hour she is going to serve us lunch in the dining room.

After lunch I went out to the street to explore the neighborhood. Wherever I went I saw only houses very similar to ours, a big garden and in the garden a nice building. I did not see a single person on the streets.

Returning, I told Vera that I do not know where we are, but we are surely not in the city. Besides the residential villas with big gardens, I have not seen anything else, like stores, and not even a single person. I was told we are going to stay in the city of Frankfurt, but it does not look like we are there. I said that I am going to inquire when we are going to be transferred to the city.

As I stepped out from our room and met our housekeeper, who was not wearing her white apron anymore, I asked her if we are in Frankfurt.

"No, this is not Frankfurt, this is Bad Homburg."

"If we are now in Bad Homburg, then where is Frankfurt?"

"Frankfurt is not far away. It is about 10 – 15 km (6 – 10 miles) to our south."

That proved that I was right. They did not bring us to Frankfurt, but to another little town near Frankfurt.

"Do you know what our program will be? Are we going to stay here, or are we going to go to Frankfurt?"

"I know that you, who came today, will stay here until you get the German Refugee Passport."

"How long does it take until someone receives a Refugee Passport?"

"It varies, but because it is soon Christmas and New Year, and people go on vacation, it could take at least a month."

"When do you expect that somebody from the Americans will come here who is dealing with our issues?"

"Today is Saturday. I am sure Monday somebody will come."

"That means that today or tomorrow nobody will come dispite that eleven of us arrived today?"

"It could be that somebody may come to talk with the newcomers, but I do not know that."

"How could I get in touch with somebody?"

"You can call them on telephone. There is always somebody on duty."

"Could you please tell me their telephone number?"

"Naturally." She was standing next to the table where there was a pencil and paper. She immediately jotted down the telephone number and gave it to me. "If you want to call them you could use that telephone." She pointed to the telephone next to us on the wall.

I was annoyed by this. The pleasant-mannered fellow on the bus told us we can go wherever and whenever we want, but as I have seen from here, one cannot go anywhere. At least not very easily. It seemed to me we were in a cage with an open door.I went back to our room. I described to Vera what I learned from the housekeeper and told her that I am going to explore our surroundings. I put on my winter coat and went on a reconnaissance trip.

The weather was as gray, wet, unfriendly and cold as when we arrived. I now inspected everything better. Unquestionably our accommodation was in a very well kept suburb with lots of gardens. In our street, and in the neighboring streets, the villas were very similar to the one in which we were housed, each of them in a very big garden. A few cars were parked on the streets and some of them in the driveway of the houses. They were Mercedes and VW. I did not see anyone.

The area made a very good impression on me, but in Berlin I was promised that we will be settled in the city of

Frankfurt until we get our papers, where we could move around on buses, street cars, go to museums, movies. It is difficult with a child, whom we cannot keep in a room all day. In December we cannot even let her play in the garden. It bothered me also, that they housed us in a community housing, where we do not have a private life. When we talk on the telephone everybody can listen to it. I have to be in touch with American companies in case we receive a visa to the USA, so that I will have a job when we arrive. If not, we will move to Ulm, where I have already a job. The community telephone is not good to make all of the telephone calls needed for this.

Just when I got this far in my thoughts, I walked in front of a house where I saw the first people. A man, a woman and two small children came out of a house and went through the path in the garden to their car, a big white Mercedes.

I was thinking of my small Tatra, if that would be here, there would be no problem with distances. The question is, when are we going to be transported to Frankfurt to wait until we get our papers, where there is public transportation.

The problem is, shall I speak with somebody to request to go to Frankfurt forthwith, as we were promised, or should I say nothing, just wait. I thought it over that in Hungary one did not dare open his mouth, there for sure it would not have been advisable to say anything, but finally here in the "free West" I believed the reason they call it 'free' is because everybody can tell his or her opinion. If I cannot tell my opinion here, then why the hell did I leave Budapest?

I felt that was a deciding argument, and I should act accordingly. I went back to the villa, took off my winter coat, went to the telephone and dialed the number the housekeeper gave me. On the first ring the phone was picked up by a man who spoke German with a very strong accent. He gave me his name which suggested that he was American. He asked me who I am. I told him my name.

I did not change the discussion to English, because I thought it is better to discuss my problem in a language which is not a mother tong to either of us, so I continued the telephone conversation in German. I told him that this morning I arrived with my family from Berlin and at present, as far as I know, we are located in Bad Homburg.

"Excuse me for a minute." I heard that he was shuffling some papers.

"Mr. Varadi, very nice to talk to you. What is the problem you called me for?"

I told him briefly that I was told that we would receive an apartment in the city of Frankfurt until we get our papers, but we are not in Frankfurt ,and we would like to be in the city. My understanding is that only on Monday will somebody come with whom this could be discussed That is the reason I am calling him.

"Mr. Varadi, Bad Homburg is a very nice exterior part of the town."

"I do not know where Bad Homburg is, but for sure, it is not a city. It is specific for a city that the city blocks are surrounded by paved streets, and here the houses are surrounded by large gardens."

There was silence on the other end of the line. I assumed he was considering my definition of a city.

"I cannot do anything in connection with where you are going to stay."

"You know there are three of us, and one of us is a two and a half year old child, whom it would be very hard to keep in a room for a long time. To whom could I talk, who can act in this case?"

"Until Monday there is nobody here who could do anything to change your accommodation."

"Then I think the best would be if we move today to a hotel in Frankfurt."

Another silence on the other end of the line.

"As I said I cannot do anything with your relocation. Then how would you be able to move to a hotel in Frankfurt?"

"I would find a hotel in the telephone book. I will call them to reserve a room, call a taxi and that will take us to the hotel in Frankfurt. When we are checked in I am going to call you or whoever is on duty then and tell him where we are."

It looked like he must have been flabbergasted by this simple solution, because he answered with some delay.

"I am going to try to find the person who is dealing with Hungarian refugees. I am going to call you in a half hour."

In about ten minutes the phone was ringing. The housekeeper picked it up and motioned to me and gave me the phone. The same person was on the line.

"I was able to reach the gentleman responsible for the Hungarian issues. He asked me to call you and ask you to wait an hour, when he will be able to get in touch with you."

"Thank you. I am going to wait."

It was not even an hour when an American passenger car, a JEEP, stopped in front of the garden entrance of our building, and an American soldier got out. The bell rang and the housekeeper opened the door. A young soldier came in. The housekeeper said that he is looking for me.

I went to the soldier who handed me an envelope. He said he brought it for me. He saluted turned around and left.

I opened the envelope which contained a hand written Hungarian letter:

> Welcome to the Free World!
> I would like to ask you to be patient until tomorrow morning, when I am going to visit you. I am going to try to give you a satisfying answer on every question you have. Until then please rest, and for your own security and future do not leave the house until I arrive. I am going to take care of you while you are going to be our guests, and I hope that our relationship will be pleasant until then.
>
> Warmest regards
> Mr. Leslie

I read the letter twice and came to the conclusion that there is a real difference between the communist Hungary and as Mr. Leslie wrote it, the 'Free World'. If I would have opened my mouth in Budapest, then instead of the young soldier who brought the letter, I would have been visited by two State Security goons. I opened my mouth here, and the American fellow with whom I talked on the telephone, who was very casual at the beginning but took the matter seriously and, in spite of the weekend, found me Mr. Leslie who wrote me this very nice, but slightly threatening sounding letter and sent it immediately with a military courier.

I informed Vera about the events She also read the letter, and she remarked that Mr. Leslie must be literally inclined, because he used a few words which one reads only in the last century's novels. I suggested that we should walk and take Éva with us to look at this nice area.

Vera said that we should not go, because Mr. Leslie definitely said we should not leave this house.

My opinion was that Mr. Leslie's Hungarian is not perfect, and he only meant that we should not move to a hotel in Frankfurt, and not that we are in a house arrest. So all of us got dressed for winter and left. I told the housekeeper that we are going to take a walk.

In the evening the housekeeper, now again with a white apron, informed everybody that she is going to serve us dinner. We and our eight travel companions sat around the dining room table. Our housekeeper served us an excellent dinner, and we even had wine on the table. Our travel companions told the history of their lives. It was very hard to keep Éva at the table, because the conversation was in German, and she did not understand anything.

Next day was Sunday. In the morning the housekeeper came and said that Mr. Leslie called to say he will be here at 11 AM. Exactly at 11 AM, like a clock, a black automobile, same as what I have seen in Berlin used by the Americans, stopped in front our garden door. A moderately tall man in a winter coat and a briefcase in his hand came to the door of our villa. Our housekeeper let him in. By the time he was in the house, I was also at the door. I shook hands and introduced myself in Hungarian. Mr. Leslie, as he called himself, was probably over 50 years old. He took off his coat, and the housekeeper guided us to the dining room table. Before we sat down I told him I will get Vera and Éva to introduce them. Mr. Leslie was very friendly, smiled and said it was a good idea.

So I went to our room and asked them to join us. Mr. Leslie shook hands with Vera and Éva and told them in a very friendly tone, that he hoped we spent our first night in Frankfurt well.

Vera said that they will let us discuss matters, and when we finished they are going to join us again. Éva became very friendly. Because as it was in Hungarian, she understood what we were talking. They went back to our room. The housekeeper asked us if we would like to have coffee. We both said yes and thanked her and sat down. Mr. Leslie opened his briefcase and took out a dossier.

The housekeeper came with a tray which she put down on the table. She picked up two porcelain cups with coffee

and put it next to us. She also put on the table a larger porcelain pitcher with coffee, a smaller one with milk and a sugar bowl. We thanked her. Both of us pulled the coffee cup nearer to us. Mr. Leslie pulled the dossier in front of him and opened it.
"Dr. Váradi..."

"Please call me Ferenc."

"With pleasure, but then please call me György. We can agree on this, and I am pretty sure, that we are going to agree on everything else. But first let me tell you a few words about myself. My parents moved from Hungary to America around the turn of the century, because at that time the economic conditions there were very bad. With other Hungarians they settled in Cleveland, which became, after Budapest, the second city with the largest Hungarian population. My father worked in a factory. I received a law degree from Case Western University in Cleveland. After that I got a job with the American government. Because of the Hungarian Revolution many Hungarian refugees are arriving, and many of them speak only Hungarian. As I speak Hungarian, they sent me over to deal with the issues related to the Hungarian refugees. I have a family in Cleveland. My son is 20 and my daughter is 18 years old. The colleague on duty yesterday with whom you talked was very surprised because that part of the city where you were housed is one of the most prestigious and elegant "suburbs." A few blocks from here a very famous Casino is located. The officer on duty asked me to get in touch with you, because you sounded very upset and annoyed that you were not located in downtown Frankfurt. At the beginning I could not understand what your problem was, but shortly I realized that in some extent you are right that in this building you are the only one with a child, and you cannot go anywhere with a child around this location. In December you cannot even let her out in the garden. You would be in a very bad situation with a child if you would have to stay here until you received your papers, which, considering the time of the year, could take several weeks. It would be very hard to keep a child in a room for that long a time. After I realized this I investigated what could we do. I found a two bedroom nicely furnished apartment in downtown Frankfurt which is now available. I am going to arrange that you should be moved there. As today is a weekend, nothing can be done, but tomorrow it can be done, and I promise you that Tuesday before noon we are going to move you into that apartment, which is in 6 Leon Street on the first floor."

"György," I said, " You see our problem perfectly well. Thank you very much, that you were able to solve this so fast. I did not want to cause difficulty to anybody, but the officer on duty handled the matter with such a negative attitude that I became afraid if the administration of these cases is so negative, than we are going to have lots of problems. But you totally changed my opinion. Thank you very much that you took the trouble to immediately visit us, to tell me this in person, even on a Sunday. As you are here I would like to repeat what you probably have seen from my dossier that I was offered a job at Telefunken's Research Laboratory in Ulm, but we would rather go to the USA. Only if that will not happen for some or other reason, or would be dragged out for a long time, would we go to Ulm. Could you please tell me, what we should do or what is going to be done in our case."

"First I would like to give you spending money."

He opened his briefcase and took out an envelope and a sheet of paper.

"In the envelope is one hundred Mark. Please account for it the same way you did in Berlin. When it is running low, let me know and I am going to give you more. From your account in Berlin I can see that you are not wasting money, therefore I do not have to tell you what you can spend it on."

With this he gave me the paper which was in his hand.

"Please sign it, that you received the one hundred Mark."

I signed it and put a date under my name and gave it back to him.

"Thank you. As of what is going to happen? As I mentioned, I am going to arrange that a car will come here Tuesday morning to move you to Leon Street. A cleaning woman is going to wait for you there. She is going to go there every day to clean the apartment. The papers you signed are going to be submitted to the German authorities to issue you the identification cards for refugees. We are also going to submit your papers to the American Consulate to apply for the visa. Both of these require photographs, therefore after you moved in to Leon Street, during the afternoon or latest on Wednesday, a photographer will go to your apartment to make photographs of the three of you. As for your food, your wife can cook in the kitchen, or if you want you can go to a restaurant to eat. You can go wherever you want, because until you get the German ID card I am going to send you a temporary ID card. You will get it already tomorrow. You can use the money I gave you for buying clothing or anything else, but if you want to buy more, I can arrange to take you to the American military store, which is called PX where you can buy very good quality merchandise at a very low price."

"Thank you for all this information, but let me call my wife and daughter because maybe they have some questions."

"Good idea."

I asked Vera and Éva to join us. They came and sat at the table. I summarized our discussion. Éva noticeably enjoyed the situation that she finally understood what we are speaking. She immediately inquired about toy stores. György said that in a few days he will organize that we should go to a store called a PX, which is an American department store where one can buy everything, including toys. Vera inquired about movies, and she was told that from the money we have we can buy movie tickets. The program of the movie theatres can be found in the newspapers.

György repeated to Vera that a maid will come every day to clean the apartment and he also said that one can go from Bad Homburg to the city by bus. The station is a few blocks from where we are, but he recommended that tomorrow, on Monday, we should not go, rather we should look around where we are, because from Tuesday we are going to be in the middle of Frankfurt where we can easily go anywhere with trams and buses. He said that the next day he is going to call us by phone, and he is going to be there when we arrive to our apartment.

"I forgot to tell you that if you have any question or problems, do not hesitate to call me. I am going to give you my direct telephone number."

He wrote the number on a paper and gave it to me, he collected all of his papers, put them in his briefcase, and shook hands with the three of us. We went with him to the door. I noticed that some of our cohabitants were sitting around the fireplace reading newspapers. Our housekeeper seemed to be very happy that her dining room table became available and started to set the table for lunch.

36. Lorelei

On Tuesday, December 11, a soldier arrived in the usual black passenger car to pick us up. Our move to the first floor apartment at 6 Leon Street went very smoothly. We said good bye to our refugee colleagues, whoever was present and also to the housekeeper lady. In the Leon street apartment the cleaning woman waited for us and not much later György also arrived. The apartment as György described had two bedrooms and was simply but well furnished, including towels, bed linen and everything for the kitchen.

György informed us that we can find stores in the neighborhood to buy food for breakfast or for anything else if Vera wants to cook. If we want to buy clothing or other things we could buy that in the department stores downtown or we should tell him and he will arrange for us to go to the American military store the PX. He said daily a military vehicle will come and bring a variety of useful stuff. He also said that on the next or the following day a photographer will come to make pictures necessary for the documents to be submitted.

He mentioned that a few new Hungarian refugees arrived and some of them knew us well. We found out, these were Laci and Kitty, with whom I met a few weeks ago in East Germany after the conference in Leipzig, the other was Pista, who was my colleague at the University of Szeged.

I asked György if we can tell our address to our mothers, who live in Budapest and to other acquaintances. He said we certainly can.

I asked if we could use the telephone in the apartment. He said naturally we can use it. We can use it to call Budapest, or anybody else, for example Telefunken. But we should possibly use it for a minimum amount of time, because telephone is quite expensive.

We wrote a card to our mothers telling them where we are and giving them our address. We wrote a post card and not a letter, because the proper department in Hungary would anyhow open the letter to read it and would take longer than just reading a post card and therefore it would be delivered faster. In the evening we telephoned them. It was a big surprise. We told them briefly where we are and that we probably are going to be here until mid-January and that we wrote a postcard with our address where they can send letters and we are also going to write regularly. We did not speak much, because we were sure that the discussion is being listened to in Hungary but probably also in Frankfurt. They said they are OK, but said nothing else. They also talked only briefly, they knew that the telephone calls are listened in. Éva made noises that she wants also to talk with her grandmothers. So we had to hand her the receiver and she told them, that she was promised we are going to a big toy store tomorrow. After we were able to recover the phone from her, we promised to call them at least once a week.

Leon Street met my definition, I gave to the American officer at duty, that it was in the 'city'. The blocks were surrounded by paved streets it was also near tram and bus stations. By walking or by tram it was very close to the middle of Frankfurt, An der Hauptwache Square and from the river Main.

Our daily life started to shape up. About 10:00 o'clock in the morning an American JEEP stopped in front of the door of our building with two American soldiers. One of them was the driver the other was sitting next to him. They stopped the engine, the driver stayed in the car while the other soldier picked up a package from the car and came up to our apartment and rang the bell. We opened the door the soldier saluted, handed the package over, saluted again, we thanked him and he turned around and left. Whoever of us got the package put it on the dining room table. We stood around because we were curious what did they bring us that day, as every day was something else. Sometimes it was two pounds of coffee, another day writing paper with pencils, or toilet soap, or brushes for scrubbing dishes, etc. It was impossible to guess what is arriving at that day, where is coming from and who is sending it. We decided that it was intended to be a daily surprise package. After we received the package one of us went to the grocery store which was very close to buy some needed food and around noon we went to have lunch in one of the restaurants. Our favorite became the 'Löwenbrau' which was located on the Square 'An der Hauptwache'.

After lunch Vera usually went to see a movie. There were many movie houses in the area, so it was not difficult for her to find every day a different movie. When the movie's subject was also for children Éva went with her.

On the days when Vera did not go to a movie we went to see stores and after that we went home, after Laci and his wife and Pista arrived we started to play our daily card game. Dinner was either at our place or we went again to a restaurant.

This was our everyday routine, but then were days when something came up and we could not do it.

An exception to our schedule was right on the first day after we moved in a JEEP arrived with four young soldiers. They downloaded a great number of photographic equipment and carried them to our apartment. We let them in. They were very glad that we spoke English. They said they came to take pictures. We said it was excellent because we need the pictures. Éva inspected the equipment. The boys started to explain them to her, but when they found out that she does not speak English all four of them sat on the floor around Éva and started to teach her English. Éva was delighted to be the center of attention. One of the soldiers took a pack of cigarettes and matches from the upper pocket of his jacket to light it, but Vera advised him not to smoke in the apartment. The young soldier apologized and went out of the apartment, I assumed to the corridor. Awhile he came back and another guy did the same. In the meantime Éva progressed well in learning English.

Finally the soldiers got up, told Éva that they are going to continue the lessons at some other time and started to assemble their equipment. They put a chair in the middle of the room and around it they set up white reflectors. They mounted a camera, which was a quite large machine, on a tripod. By that time a little more than an hour passed, because they had some cigarette breaks when all four of them left the apartment for 5 – 10 minutes. They asked if we have some beer. As we had none they were satisfied with a glass of water.

Finally everything got ready and they asked Vera to sit on the chair. She sat down. They tried several settings at the end they said OK, one of them went to the camera clicked a button, big flash. They sat Vera in a new posture, flash again. They made at least ten pictures of Vera. They continued with Éva, for whom we brought some pillows to sit high up. Éva enjoyed it very much as they positioned her. They made again at least ten pictures. I came after that, they paid much less attention to the pictures about me and made only about six of them.

When they finished they said they will bring the pictures in a few days so we should be able to provide them for our ID certificates. I tried to convince them that they should give them to us the next day because we need those IDs urgently. They said they are going to try to get it ready. I called to their attention what I learned from the paper György gave me, that the pictures to be submitted have strict regulations. The size of the picture must be 5x5 cm. On the picture the size of the head must be from the jaw to the tip of the head exactly 3.125 cm.

That amused them they and said they know well the regulations, also that the picture has to be printed on thin paper, the background should be light and the person on the picture cannot wear a hat. They packed up their equipment and carried everything to their JEEP. It was past noon when they left. They spent two and a half hours photographing us.

Our daily program was also influenced when we had to go to some office because of the German refugee papers or the American visa. Mine and my friends program was changed when we were in contact with companies looking for job possibilities.

I had my job offer from Telefunken, called the personnel department in Ulm and told them that I am waiting for my German papers and I hope we are going to get them after the holidays. They asked me to visit them at the beginning of January.

Pista wanted to stay in Europe, in Germany or maybe in England, but he specifically wanted to get a position at a University. He got in contact only with German Universities and companies. On the other hand Laci was interested only in American companies, because they wanted to emigrate to America.

Two days after the photographing György visited us. I gave him an account of our money, because not much was left. He gave us some more. Said that the photographs did not turn out well and he is sending the next day, on a Saturday, another photographer to make the pictures.

On Saturday morning only two soldiers came to us with their photographic equipment. One was older maybe at least 40 years old the other was a young boy. After they introduced themselves, they immediately set up their equipment and finished the operation in less than a quarter hour. The 'older' soldier said that we are going to get the pictures on Monday. That is what happened, on Monday a soldier delivered the photographs. They turned out well.

On Monday György came to see us partially to give us sufficient amount of money for the holidays, partially to tell us the plans in connection with the German ID papers and the American visa. I complained that everything is progressing very slowly. His opinion was that our case is progressing surprisingly fast. We checked in at the American office in Berlin on December 4. On December 8 we arrived already in Frankfurt. Two weeks passed since during which time we submitted the German ID application and we are starting now the American visa process. In his opinion the problem will be that only a few days are left until Christmas and New Year. Between Christmas and New Year everything is coming to a grinding halt and he does not know if during that time anything will happen. At any rate because of our visa application, in a few days we have to go to the American Consulate. He is going to let us know the day and time when we are going to have an appointment. I admitted that things are progressing and probably I was impatient.

He informed me that on the next day, December 18 at 10 in the morning a civilian American official is going to visit me who wants to talk with me about my work in Hungary and other issues related to Hungary.

As I was working in Hungary in a military research laboratory and had there a responsible job, which meant that I must know about many things, I assumed the Americans will be interested to talk to me. I thought the matter over. It is obvious, that whatever they ask me, I have to tell the truth, because most likely they have most of the information and if I do not tell the truth I would cut my own throat.

Next morning at 10 o'clock the usual black Chevrolet stopped in front of our building and a man in a winter coat and wearing a hat, got out. He took a briefcase from the trunk, came into our building and rang our bell. I opened the door, shook hands and introduced ourselves. He said, that his name was Jack Smith he took a photo ID from his pocket, which had the American crest the name of some American office of which I could only read 'Central Agency'.

He took off his coat and I seated him at our dining room table. He put his briefcase on the table, opened it and took out a folder.

I asked him if he would like to have coffee or water. He said coffee would be excellent. I went into one of the bedrooms where Vera was entertaining Éva. Vera came out. I introduced her. Shortly Vera brought on a plate two cups with coffee, milk in a small pitcher and sugar in a bowl. She gave each of us a cup. He took the milk and poured a little in the coffee, but no sugar. I put sugar in my coffee, but no milk.

He opened the folder took out some papers and studied them. I told him, that I assume he is not speaking Hungarian, my German is about as bad as my English, for this reason we should talk in English.

He grinned, apparently he was happy about this.

"Thank you because my German is not the best. I see from the papers that you were the Head of one of the Chemical Department at the Research Institute for Telecommunication's Laboratory in Újpest."

"Yes. That is correct."

“The Research Institute for Telecommunication’s Laboratory in Újpest was split off from Tungsram’s Research Laboratory.”

”Yes, when I finished my University studies and received my diploma I started to work at Tungsram’s Research Laboratory, when the Research Institute for Telecommunication’s Laboratory in Újpest, abbreviated name is TKI was established I was transferred there.”

”I see that TKI as you call it abbreviated was a military research laboratory, where the work was the development of electron tubes.”

”Yes, that is true.”

”As you can imagine we are interested in very many things in connection with Hungary. Therefore I am very glad that I can talk with you and you are going to be able to give us information about issues of interest to us. What we are very interested and please think about it and tell me what you know about, where bauxite can be found in Hungary? As you know this mineral is the base material of the manufacturing of Aluminum.”

As I was working in a research laboratory where the projects were related to electron tubes used by the military, such as for example in radars, I expected questions related to that, but I did not expect a question where bauxite can be found in Hungary. I think I must have looked at him perplexed, because he repeated it.

“Hungary is blessed with one of the largest amount of bauxite mineral resources in the world. My question is what do you know about the location of these deposits and about its production."

I realized that Mr. Smith seriously asked this question, but I had no knowledge of this and therefore I could not answer the question. What shall I do about it? I cannot say that I know nothing about it, so I told the only thing I knew.

"At the University of Szeged, where I was studying, during the fall of 1946 the Mineralogical Department announced a competition to write an original essay on the "Mineralogical study of the Hungarian Bauxite". Mineralogy was an obligatory subject for students studying Chemistry, therefore I had also to take it. As we had a long winter vacation as there was not enough heating material, I was every day in the University's Library, because that was heated and decided if I am in the Library where I can find lots of information, I should be able to write an assay for that competition and decided to develop a theory of the genesis of the bauxite mineral. The rule was that on the envelope in which the essay was submitted one must not write the author's name that the professor evaluating it should not be influenced by the person who submitted it. There were several essays submitted for this competition, but the professor found mine to be the best. Naturally he did not know who wrote it. At the year's closing ceremony in June 1947, when he announced the title of the essay which won the competition and opened the envelope to find out who was the author, he announced my name. He was very surprised, because he did not know me in person, I was one of the many students who had to take Mineralogy as a mandatory subject. He gave me the diploma that I won the prize and immediately asked me to visit him in his office. When I visited him, he told me, that he found my essay excellent and he hoped I am going to continue in the future to study Mineralogy.

"He asked me if there is anything he could do for me. I said, that if he would please show me a piece of the bauxite mineral, because I never in my life saw one. He was a little bit annoyed, but he took me to a room, where minerals were displayed and picked up a piece of bauxite and put it in my hand. That was almost ten years ago I never since had anything to do with bauxite. I am sorry, but the only thing I can answer that according to my recollection the bauxite mineral sites are in Transdanubia, but that you can find in any Mineralogy textbook."

Mr. Smith was busily making notes when I started my story. Apparently he slowed down when I got so far that the professor invited me to his office and completely stopped taking notes when I told him that all that happened 10 years ago.

He continued and came back several times to the issue related to bauxite, but as I had absolutely no idea about this subject, he gave up, packed up his papers, put them in his briefcase.

"Thank you for the information, if we have further questions I hope you will be available."

I told him that I am going to be available for any questions they may have. I am still very surprised that nobody ever came and asked me any questions.
Shortly after Mr. Smith left, György arrived. I told him that on December 20 I am planning to go to Cologne to visit the Leybold Company, namely they are very interested in the

mass spectrometer of which I gave my presentation at the Conference in Leipzig and they invited me to visit them for a day. He said that is excellent and he would give me money for the trip. I thanked him, but told him, the person at Leybold who invited me said they are paying for all my expenses.

György started to tell me the plans for the next days. We do not have to do anything in connection with the German refugee papers. On the other hand in connection with the American visa we have an appointment on December 19 at 10 in the morning with a lady at the American Consulate and gave me her name.

György also said, that as I am going on December 20 to Cologne, he will make arrangement for a car to pick us up on December 21 to take us to the American military PX where we can buy everything very inexpensively. The person who is going to pick us up will pay for everything we are buying. He also mentioned, that after December 21 because of Christmas and New Year everything is going to stop except the stores and the movies, which are going to operate. He is also going on a vacation and will be back only on Wednesday, January 2, when he is going to see us again. He gave me more money and said if we need anything we should call the person on duty and he gave that telephone number. We wished each other Merry Christmas and Happy New Year and expressed our wishes, that 1957 should be a good year for all of us.

The lady at the American Consulate was very nice, she reviewed all of the papers we completed and said that she finds them perfectly good and asked for the pictures. She looked at them and said they are according to the rules.

She put all of that in an envelope and wrote my name on it. She made a telephone call and informed us that we will need a medical checkup and we should go on January 3 at 10 in the morning to the medical department at another building of the American Consulate.

On the next day, on December 20 I traveled to Cologne to visit the Leybold Company. The connection with Leybold actually started in Leipzig, where a person after our presentation came to Gábor Sebestyén and me and told us, that the Leybold Company is very intersted in the RF massspectrometer which we developed. He gave us his name and telephone number. Leybold was a world famous company in the development and manufacturing of vaacuumtechnical systems and components. We felt very honored that a company such as Leybold was interested in our work.

When we came to Frankfurt I called Leybold, or rather the person whom we met in Leipzig and told him, that Gábor Sebestyén is in London, but I am now in Frankfurt. He said that was very good and they would love to have me visiting them. He said I can go from Frankfurt by train in two hours and I could be back in Frankkfurt the same evening. He is going to talk with other people in his company to be available, becasue the subject we talked about in Leipzig is very interesting for them. When he called me back he told me, that December 20 would be the best for my visit. He immediately gave me the departure time of the train and told me to get off the train at the Bonn station because

the Leybold plant is between Bonn and Cologne. A car is going to wait for me at the Bonn station and drive me to their plant and in the afternoon will take me back to the

Bonn station that I should be able to catch the train going back to Frankfurt. Naturally they are going to cover my expenses.

So on December 20, on a cold but sunny day I went by train from Frankfurt to Bonn.The train somwhere around Maiz reaches the river Rhine and goes from there on the left bank of the river. The river Rhine and its surroundings from there until almost near Bonn is a spectacular view. The train was practically empty, so I sat at the right side of the car next to the window, looking ahead to admire this part of the Rhine which I only knew from books. On this sunny winter day the Rhine with its rocks, castles and fortifications presented a beautiful sight. I remembered Heinrich Heine's poem, 'Lorelei'88 which I learned in high school about a beautiful girl sitting on a cliff and because of whom the sailors do not watch out for the rocks and whirlpools and lose their ship in the stream,:

^ ^ ^

The train passed it already but I was still looking back at the peak of the 132 meter (433ft) high rock emerging from the water like the ancient boatman aboard his small skiff. I thought if this rock would have been in Hungary then Rákosi or one of his cronies would have pushed Lorelei off that cliff and he would have stood in her place and everybody had to look up to them and listen to their music. I considered myself drifting in a locked rusty cage on a dingy having a hole in its bottom which would crash on which would crash on a rock or pulled down in the deep by a whirlepool, I tought that would have been my fate from which I got out by a miracle and Rákosi and his cronies drifted to become only an old fable, unfortunately their memory remained and cannot be deleted from one's mind.

---

[88] See the next page (page 517)

LORELEI

Heinrich Heine[89]

Ich weiß nicht, was soll es bedeuten,
Daß ich so traurig bin,
Ein Märchen aus uralten Zeiten,
Das kommt mir nicht aus dem Sinn.

Die schönste Jungfrau sitzet
Dort oben wunderbar,
Sie kämmt ihr goldenes Haar,
Und singt ein Lied dabei;
Das hat eine wundersame,
Gewalt'ge Melodei.

Den Schiffer im kleinen Schiffe,
Ergreift es mit wildem Weh;
Er schaut nicht die Felsenriffe,
Er schaut nur hinauf in die Höh'.
Ich glaube, die Wellen verschlingen
Am Ende Schiffer und Kahn,
Und das hat mit ihrem Singen,
Die Lorelei getan.

I cannot determine the meaning
Of sorrow that fills my breast:
A fable of old, through it streaming,
Allows my mind no rest.

The loveliest maiden is sitting
Up there, so wondrously fair;
She combs her golden hair.
And sings a song, passing time.
It has a most wondrous, appealing
And pow'rful melodic rhyme.

The boatman aboard his small skiff, -
Enraptured with a wild ache,
Has no eye for the jagged cliff, -
His thoughts on the heights fear forsake.
I think that the waves will devour
Both boat and man, by and by,
And that, with her dulcet-voiced power
Was done by the Lorelei.

[89] A.Z. Foreman http://poemsintranslation.blogspot.com/p/credit-where-it-is-due.html

37. Year-end balance

On my return train ride from Bonn to Frankfurt, because of the winter's early darkness, the sights of the Rhine River were not visible and did not distract me from thinking over my visit to Leybold. It was a very interesting and informative day, not only from a technical and scientific point of view.

I had made up my mind in Berlin that I would emigrate from Hungary. Between Komarno and Bratislava I put this issue on a scale, and I came to the conclusion that more argument was in favor of leaving than staying in Hungary. But that decision was based mostly on my imagination about the western world compared to the real conditions in Hungary. This visit proved that my imagined ideas were consistent with the facts.

First of all, I had the opportunity to compare an individual's freedom of movement. Before 1956, during the soviet/communist dictatorship in Hungary, this was strongly curtailed. It was not easy to travel to another "socialist country" as a tourist or on a trip to attend a scientific conference. Examples were to get permission to attend the conference in Leipzig, East-Germany and our tourist trip to Zakopane, Poland. To make a tourist trip to a western country, not belonging to the soviet bloc, before 1956, was unimaginable, but in case one received permission, he/she could not take children or family with them on the trip. On this trip to Bonn I realized that in the West everybody goes where he or she wants, one does not have to ask any one and does not need any permit or signature to approve the trip. The Leybold Company invited me to visit them and despite that I only had a temporary ID without even my picture on it stating that Germany accepted me as a Refugee, I did not have to ask anybody to give me permission to go on this trip. I bought my ticket, got on the train and could return whenever I want. I did not have to be afraid that the police want to verify my identity, maybe detain me, and I could disappear for a shorter or longer time.

I also made a comparison of the 'vigilance' of which we were in Hungary continuously reminded. On "the road to socialism" in Hungary the 'vigilance' was our life's central issue, so that the 'enemy' should not be able to find out and utilize our 'leading' research results, for example. The 'vigilance' was a very wide concept. It was a part of the 'Secret Case Handling' (SCH), the locking up of typewriters, the secrecy of electron tubes used in radar equipment, photographing bridges, railroad stations, including the railroad operated for children, or important buildings and many other things. The severity of penalties for the breach of 'vigilance' depended on a variety of reasons. For an example, one of my colleagues at TKI walked with his girlfriend across the Danube on the Margaret Bridge and stopped in a small park at the Pest side. This little park was in front of the building which at that time was the Ministry of Interior. My colleague made a few pictures of the girl with the Buda castle on the other side of the river. In seconds several policemen arrived, arrested the pair and confiscated the camera. They were escorted to the Ministry and were locked up in a room until the police developed the film and verified that he had told the truth. The building was not on any of the pictures, and he had really made photos only of the girl. After a few hours they were told they can go. He never got his camera or film back. In other cases the breach of 'vigilance' was a good reason to jail a person who they wanted to get rid of for a longer period of time.

My reception at Leybold gave me the opportunity to make a very interesting comparison. First I met the colleague I got acquainted with at the conference in Leipzig. He proposed that he would show me the factory and their research laboratories first, to make me familiar with what they are manufacturing and how it is done, and also to show me which direction their research work is going. From catalogues I received in Hungary I was familiar with the products of this famous company, but because of the 'vigilance' which was indoctrinated in me, I could not even imagine to be able to escort a foreigner, especially one who is coming from an 'imperialist' country, through the TKI laboratories and the Tungsram production areas to show them and tell them what and how they are making things. My visit however started with exactly that program.
After my colleague showed me the production and the Research Laboratories and answered all of my questions, he indicated, that we are expected for lunch, which will be in the Company dining room's special section. It was exactly noon when we entered the special dining area where a few people were standing and talking to each other with a small glass of drink in their hands. I was introduced and, according to German custom, we shook hands. I was introduced first to the owner of Leybold, Dr. Manfred Dunkel, then to Professor K. Diels, who was the Director of Research and to Dr. Georg Nöller, who was the Department Head of vacuum technical measuring equipment. After I got a small glass of cherry brandy and was thanked for visiting them, we sat down for lunch.

After lunch Dr. Dunkel said good bye and left, and the rest of us went to the next room which was a conference room. They asked me to describe the topics which I gave at my presentation in Leipzig. As I did not bring any technical material from Hungary, that they should not discover them on the border and accuse me of violating the 'vigilance,' I had no slides to project the pictures. Therefore I sketched what was needed on the blackboard with a chalk. They asked me many interesting questions and discussed some of it between themselves. Finally they came to the conclusion that the RF mass spectrometer, the research on which I was working and which was only a minor incidental topic at TKI, is a very important and needed instrument to detect, identify and measure residual gases in vacuum systems. They decided there and then that they would develop and manufacture it by the end of next year, in 1957. I suggested they should call it 'Topatron.'

For me it was an unbelievable idea that the research leaders of a company can decide in one meeting what they are going to manufacture and market in the following year[90]. They did not have to send for approval to upper levels, e.g. to a Ministry. The decisions did not come from above like in the soviet/communist system, but every company or institution, and even every person, decided what they do and what they are not going to do.

But finally, such are the decisions which are advancing the technology, development, and evolution. In the soviet style Hungary, I well knew I would have lived in stagnation, copying what was developed and was already very

[90] The measuring instrument, which I called "Topatron," Leybold started to produce and market as decided and was in production for 15 years.

successful in the West. Nobody dared to start something new.

Topatron advertisement by Leybold in a French Magazine – 1972

I was considering another interesting difference. While in Hungary the "house wardens" and the "party functionary" were the dreadful ringleaders. In the evaluation of those who did not belong to that clique, it was immaterial what they achieved and what results they had in their work. Here in the West, during my visit, I experienced that people are appreciated because of what they did, and their origin did not matter or who their parents were, whether owners of land, real estate, shop or factory or if they were rich or poor. I realized that when they inquired about my work and asked for details, they did not want to steal my knowledge, but recognizing my knowledge, immediately offered me a high position job in their Research Laboratory. Similarly to Telefunken where I got my job offer for my work and capability, they never asked about my origin, or my parents or which class we belonged to.

The train arrived to the suburbs of Frankfurt, and I saw the illuminated car dealerships. I remembered my Tatra, which I had left in Berlin, and the question arose in me, how is it possible that ten years after the war that totally destroyed and defeated Germany, which is still under occupation, anybody can go into an automobile shop and buy a car. While in Hungary, which was not much destroyed by the war, I needed five recommendations and the permission of two Ministers to go to a junkyard to buy a junk car which I could reconstruct. My thoughts went back to my Tatra, about which I had not heard anything yet, what I would be able to do with it if the Americans would really keep their promise and send it to Frankfurt.

The next day, our friend György arranged that we were taken to the PX, where the abundance of goods was incredible for us. We bought a lot. From that evening on everything stopped, everybody went on Christmas vacation. Until the New Year started we saw lots of movies, played lots of cards and discussed what happened to us in 1956 and what is going to happen the next year.

38. Simplified choice

At the beginning of the New Year events followed each other very fast. György visited us already on January 2 before noon. I gave him the account of our spending, and he gave me more money for our expenses. He inquired about my trip to Cologne and was very pleased that my visit to the Leybold Company went so well. He reminded me that we have the medical visit scheduled at the American Consulate for the next day, and he also said that in his opinion we are going to get our German papers within a week.

On the next day, on January 3, we went to the American Consulate for our medical checkup, which was needed to obtain a visa. The basis for the medical checkup to obtain an immigration visa is an 1891 law which prohibits immigration to the USA for those who have a 'loathsome or contagious disease.' Tuberculosis falls into this category. They took blood for blood tests, made X-rays, and some other examinations. They also fingerprinted us, except Éva because according to American law there is no need to fingerprint children less than 14 years of age. They told us to come back a week later, by which time the results will be ready and we can submit our visa applications.

György called us to tell us that on January 10 we should go to a German office where we are going to get our German refugee passports. For us, used to the traumatic experiences of the issuance of Hungarian passports, the process to receive the German refugee passport was amazing. We visited the official, we told him our name, and he pulled the passports from his drawer. He opened them and looked at our pictures. He looked at us that we are the same as the picture, then simply handed them to us and asked us to sign under our picture. Then he asked us to sign a paper that we received them. After we signed the paper he said good bye, and we simply walked out of the office with our passports in hand valid for two years for Germany and abroad.

The same day I called Telefunken's Research Laboratory in Ulm and talked with Mr. Logier, the Head of the Personnel Department. I told him that we had just received our German permanent residence permits, and I would like to go to Ulm to introduce myself and to select an apartment. Mr. Logier asked me to call him back the next day to discuss the details. The following day, we agreed on the date of my visit, and he asked me to stay there for two days.

As we had now received our German refugee passports, this brought us to the next step, to make a decision what direction we should go. Our choice was to stay in Germany or to go to America. I kept the door open to stay in Germany when I called Mr. Logier. The other choice, to obtain the American visa was also in progress. György informed us that we have all the papers necessary to apply for the American visa, and we have an appointment at the American Consulate for January 15.

The choice whether we should stay in Germany or go to America was decided with unexpected speed on January 15. That was the day we had an appointment with an American official who was conducting an interview with us, and we were presenting to him all of our papers, including the medical reports.

The American official at the Consulate greeted us very friendly, seated us and reviewed all of our papers. After he finished he looked at us:

"I am sorry, but I cannot give you a visa, because according to the present American regulations you are not refugees. Or rather you are refugees, but you are in Frankfurt and not in Austria."

I assume that this official must have found this out only that day when he reviewed our file, and György must not have known about this at all, since he was pursuing our visa and organized the appointments, including the medical exam. I must have looked at him quite perplexed, because he immediately started to explane that immigration to America is based on a quota system. This means that yearly from every country only so many people can immigrate to America, as many as the percentage of people from that country who lived in America in 1920. In 1957, this quota would be about 2,000 for Hungarians.

“The flood of Hungarian refugees to Austria caught everybody by surprise. The number of Hungarian refugees in Austria and in Yugoslavia was about 200,000. Many countries teamed up and announced that each are willing to accept a certain number of Hungarian refugees.

“The President of the USA, Mr. Eisenhower, had announced already on November 8 that America will also accept Hungarian refugees. Naturally, in a few days it would have been impossible to change the quota law so that the refugee freedom fighters should be able to get an immigration visa.

“The American State Department established that according to the existing law only 6,130 immigration visas can be issued for Hungarians. By December 1 that quota was exhausted, and all of those people were transported by American military airplanes to the USA. Mr. J.M. Swing,[91] High Commissioner of the Immigration and Naturalization Service of the USA, arrived on November 10 in Vienna. Mr. Swing’s assignment was to organize the admission of large numbers of Hungarian refugees to enter the USA without visa, but on parole. Those who were

---

[91] J.M. Swing: Hungarian Escape Program. I&N Reporter Volume 6, number 4(April 1958), page 43

entering the USA on parole[92] would not have a permanent residence and would not have the rights of a citizen until the American Congress enacted a law. [93]

"At this time", continued the official, "the refugees who can enter the USA on 'parole' are those who left Hungary through the Hungarian – Austrian border and are now in refugee camps. [94] Because of this you and your family, who did not cross the Hungarian - Austrian border and are not in refugee camp, do not qualify under the 'parole' plan, and because all of the Hungarian quota has been used for the first batch of Hungarian refugees; therefore, in this year's quota there is no possibility for any Hungarian to get an immigration visa.

"The only possibility to go to America is if you could get a 'preferential' immigration visa. In the present law there is for this category of applicants a large quota available, which cannot be used for any other purpose without the changing of the law. This would be immediately available for you if an American company would have a need for a specialist like you and would ask that a visa be provided to you. As you have a good name in the scientific world, I would suggest that you should get in touch with companies

---

[92] The English word 'parole' in the Immigration law is defined: A person who does not meet the technical requirements for a visa may be allowed to enter the U.S. for humanitarian purposes. Persons who are allowed to enter the U.S. in this manner are known as *parolees*. (Wikipedia)

[93] It is typical of the speed of the law making in the USA that the permanent residence permit and the legal immigrant status of those Hungarians admitted on 'parole' without any rights to the USA, was voted on July 25. 1958 to become law and give these rights retroactively.

[94] Until December 31, 1957 a total of 31,738 Hungarian refugees were admitted to the USA on 'parole' (J.P. Swing: Hungarian Escape Program. I&N Reporter Volume 6, number 4(April 1958), page 45.

in your field, and if they have a need they should ask that a visa be issued for you. You would get a preferential visa immediately. I assume this will happen sooner or later; therefore I am not going to reject your visa application. I am going to keep your entire file, including the medical reports, pending so when an American company or University would request a visa for you, then you should not have to start everything from the beginning, and you will be able to get a visa immediately.

“Concerning your requirements, food, housing etc. we are going to provide them indefinitely, so you should be able to contact American companies.”

On our afternoon card game I told this turn of events to Laci, Kitty and Pista and told them that soon we are going to move to Ulm. I found the job offer from Telefunken good, and I thought that I am not going to chase after American companies. If in the future an American company offers me a suitable job, I am going to accept it, but until then I am going to continue my research work, because I know that in Telefunken’s Research Laboratory the level of work is world class, and their research staff is excellent.

As I agreed with Mr. Logier, on the second of January I went by train to Ulm and from the train station went to Telefunken’s plant in Söflinger Street. At the Research Laboratories, Mr. Logier assembled for me a very complete program. First I had to be introduced to the management of the Laboratory, following this came the selection of my apartment combined with some sightseeing of the city of Ulm.

First we went to the office of Dr. Dahlke. His secretary Ms. Eiselei, when we entered, was talking on the telephone in a language which I did not know. I found out later that this language was actually German. It was the ‘Schwab’ dialect. The city of Ulm is a city on the Danube, and it is in two German states. On the north side of the Danube is the city of Ulm, and it is in the German state of Baden-Würtenberg. While the part of the city which is on the south bank of the River, Neu Ulm (New Ulm), is in the German state of Bavaria, where they speak the 'Schwab' dialect. When Mrs. Eisele saw us enter, she hung up the phone, got up from her desk and, with a broad smile, came to us and shook hands. With the most understandable German, which is called 'Hoch Deutsch' (High German), she greeted us and said that Dr. Dahlke is waiting for me.

When we entered his office, Dr. Dahlke came to me, shook hands and invited me to sit at his conference table. We both said how happy we were that we can work together. Mr. Logier departed and Mrs. Eisele brought in coffee. Dr. Dahlke picked up two sheets from his desk. On the first one he showed me, I saw the printed organization chart of Telefunken Research Laboratory, its Departments and Groups. He showed how his Department fits into the structure of the Laboratory. He picked up the second sheet on which his Department's organization structure was shown, who is in which group and where my group is and what will be my duty there. I had not seen such a detailed organizational chart before, it would have been unimaginable at TKI to put something like this on paper because of the great 'vigilance.' To print it would have been probably a major crime.

Telefunken's Laboratory in Ulm was engaged in research in connection with electron tubes, and as I worked in the same field, it was very easy to discuss all the issues. ahlke was obviously interested in my opinion. After we iscussed the work I was going to do, he suggested that he will give me a tour of his laboratories to meet my colleagues and also to show me which will be the laboratory I am going to direct.

First we went to Dr. Lothar Brück's office to introduce me to him. He was the director of Telefunken Research Laboratory in Ulm, and also he was the boss of Dr. Dahlke.

After that we went to several laboratories to meet many of my colleagues. Finally we went to an office which Dr. Dahlke said will be my office. In the office were two desks facing each other. At one of the desks a tall, balding, very likeable young fellow was sitting. He got up and introduced himself as Dr. Hans Jürgen Schütze. I introduced myself. Dahlke said that Dr. Schütze obtained his doctorate in physics at the University in Kiel, and after that he started to work in the laboratory in Ulm. Dahlke pointed to the other desk and said that will be mine. Dr. Dahlke motioned that I should sit at my desk to discuss the program.

Dr. Hans Jürgen Schütze amd Prof. Dr. Walter Dahlke

After our discussion most of the afternoon was gone. They suggested that Dr. Schütze take me to my hotel, and we will have dinner together. Next morning Dr. Schütze will pick me up, will show me the city and hand me over to somebody at the Personnel Department who is going to take me to look at several apartments from which I could choose. The details I should discuss with the Head of the Personnel Department, and before I go to the train station Dr. Dahlke would like to meet me again.

Next morning Dr. Schütze picked me up in the hotel and showed me the sights of Ulm. The first was the Cathedral. This beautiful church is the tallest in Europe, its spire is 161 meter and 53 cm (529.95 ft) high. During World War II the city of Ulm was bombed. It was a miracle that the cathedral was not damaged at all. They started to build it in 1377, but it was completed only in 1890. The dimensions of the cathedral are impressive, its capacity is 30,000 people.

From there we went to the Danube, which here is only a narrow river. I calculated in my head that if I would throw a message in a bottle in the water it would need at least 15 days to reach Budapest. From there we went through this very nice little town to Telefunken's facility. Dr. Schütze mentioned that Albert Einstein was born in this city but could not tell me in which house.
When we arrived to Telefunken, he escorted me to the personnel department, to Mr. Logier, and said that in the afternoon, before I go back to Frankfurt, we are going to meet again. Mr. Logier informed me that one of the secretaries, Mrs. Nickel, is going to drive me to show me the apartments from which I can choose. A young blond girl got up from her desk, took her winter coat from a rack and after the customary handshake and exchanging of our names, invited me to go with her. We drove about 3 km (2 miles) to the top of a hill where I saw a new settlement, including three 16 story apartment buildings. She said that the name of this area is 'Eselsberg' (Donkey's mountain) and continued:

"Ulm was very much destroyed during the war. Therefore now there is a big need of apartments. It is desired that factories and companies should move to the city. That is only feasible if they can get a suitable work force, but they need to provide them with suitable housing. These three 16 story apartment buildings and the several other lower buildings were recently built so companies moving to this area, which included Telefunken, should be able to provide accommodation for the employees they need. Dr. Varadi you belong to this category and you are lucky because these buildings were just completed and therefore there are still several empty ones, so you can choose from them."

When we arrived to the building complex consisting of these three tall buildings, Mrs. Nickel went to find the caretaker. After the obligatory introductions, he said that there are three different types of apartments available. Three, four and five room types. I told him, that I am interested in the four room apartment, because that was the type which had two bedrooms. He said there is one with a beautiful location. It is in Burgunder Street 10 on the 10th floor.

When we entered the building I was very much impressed. I was used to the communist Hungary and for a short time to the soviet zone of Berlin, where everything was in rundown condition, and the new buildings in Budapest, built by the Rákosi era, were especially horrible. When I entered this new apartment building I saw that everything was in spotless condition, everything was built simple but very tasteful. I was used to the elevators in Budapest which survived a war and had not been maintained for a decade or more. So I was surprised when we got into this one, which was elegant, even with a mirror in it. We went to the 10th floor, and he opened the apartment he had mentioned. It was a beautiful apartment. I inspected every room. The bathroom and the kitchen were well equipped. I was again thinking of Budapest, the housing of the Rákosi era, the horrible buildings where the bathtub did not fit into the bathroom, and they had to stick it through the bathroom wall, and where the walls were not straight. How is it possible that here in West Germany, where 12 years ago were only ruins, whatever they build is of high quality and very useful, and in spite of this is not expensive?

The apartment had a balcony looking south. We went out to the balcony, because the caretaker suggested that I should see the view from there. It was a crystal clear, sunny, cold winter day. From the balcony I could see snow covered mountain peaks very far away. The caretaker said that those are the Alps in Switzerland. They were about 250 – 300 km (150 – 190 miles) from us, but in clear, low humidity days one can see the 4000 meter (13,000 ft.) peaks such as the 'Jungfrau', 'Mönch' and 'Eiger.'

He told me the rent, which I could easily pay from the salary I was going to get. So I told him that I am going to rent this apartment. We went to the caretaker's office. He completed the agreement and gave it to Mrs. Nickel and said that after I signed and Telefunken signed, guaranteeing the payment, she should send it back to him. When we returned to Telefunken, Mrs. Nickel escorted me to Mr. Logier's office. She briefly summarized what had happened, gave him the rental agreement and left the office. Logier reviewed the agreement and told me that it is OK, I can sign it. He gave me another paper, which I realized was my employment agreement, saying that I am starting to work there on February 1, 1957. I thanked him. He said that I should sign that, too. I did and gave it to him. He looked at it for a second, then opened his drawer took out an envelope and gave it to me.

"We thought that as you are refugees, therefore you have no money for furnishing you home. For this reason the management decided that we are going to give you an advance, which will be deducted from your salary for three years. I hope that the amount in the envelope will be sufficient, so you are able to start your life here. Please count the money in the envelope and sign the receipt."

He put a paper on the table in front of me. I took the envelope and the paper, which I signed immediately, and gave it back to him. I put the envelope in the inner pocket of my jacket.

"Thanks for this extraordinary attentiveness. We were not used to such things in Hungary."

He took the signed paper. “You did not count the money and signed the paper?”

“Yes I know the amount is exactly what was on the paper I signed. I would like to thank you again. We were thinking of how are we going to furnish our apartment, but we were not even dreaming about such a generosity.”

Before I left I shook hands with Dahlke and Schütze. Mrs. Eisele asked if I am going to work there very soon. I said yes and asked her what time in the morning one has to be in the office?
“The working hours start at 7:10 in the morning, but the Messrs. arrive around eight thirty.”

I assumed that ‘the Messrs.’ meant the ‘Herr Doctors.’ I was one of them. For a second I remembered the ‘Shame-board’ at TKI and Andris Dallos, who introduced TKI’s own time zone to avoid that his coworkers, should be punished by some disciplinary action. There and then the ‘Shame-board’ was winning.

We moved to Ulm, and on February 1, 1957, I started work at Telefunken’s Research Laboratory in Ulm, West Germany.

Epilogue

Sic transit gloria mundi

The contents of the envelope I received from Mr. Logier of Telefunken as an advance on my salary proved to be sufficient to furnish our apartment on the 10th floor of 10 Burgunder Weg in Ulm. The first big event in our apartment, at the end of March, was Éva's 3rd birthday. Éva's friends the Merkel children, Uli a boy younger than Éva, Barbara a little older and Heidi, the oldest, lived in the building and were at the party. As I noticed during the birthday party, Éva was speaking fluent German with the kids. Naturally we all spoke Hungarian at home.

My Hungarian driver's license was accepted, and I received my German driver's license on March 7, 1957. A few days later on April 1, I became the owner of a black VW Beatle with a license plate: ULL 138. The reason for this was that in spite of promises, my Tatra which I left in Berlin was never sent over to me, and after spending three months in West Germany, I realized that my 20 year old automobile which was rebuilt from a wreck and for which I was the object of much envy in Hungary, here in Germany would be considered strange and eccentric. If it would come to repairs, to obtain replacement parts would be an insoluble problem. Therefore, I decided to buy a used car.

One of my colleagues who wanted to replace his car suggested that we go during the weekend to Stuttgart, which is about a one hour drive from Ulm, to look at the once a year organized incredibly large used car market. So we went to Stuttgart. In Budapest when I went to the junkyard to select "my junk," I fell in love with an age-old Rolls-Royce. The same way in Stuttgart, not an age-old, but at least a 10 year old beautiful Mercedes, became my favorite. Naturally I was able to talk myself out of this, and at the end of our one day excursion, I decided that because of my financial situation, it would be best to buy a used VW in Ulm. Here I did not need letters of recommendations and two Minister's signatures, I only needed money, and I could buy a used VW on the next day. To buy a car so simply was a big letdown for me. When I bought my car in Hungary in 1953, I was one of only one thousand people who owned a car. In 1957 in West Germany, with a population 5.5 times bigger than Hungary, I became only one of the five million car owners.

In 1957, Easter Sunday was on April 21 and we used the four day holiday to try the car on a long trip and drove to Paris. When we returned, I wrote to my mother about our trip. In her return letter she mentioned that she is worried about us going on such a long trip at night on those empty roads. I wrote her back that the problem is not the emptiness of the roads, but the traffic jams. When I tried to write it, I realized that in Hungary there are so few cars on the road that the word for traffic jam does not even exist.

After the Easter holidays Ms. Nickel of the Personnel Department came to my office and gave me a letter which had arrived to Telefunken for me from the Berlin police department. My colleague Schütze was sitting opposite me at his desk when I opened the letter and read it. I started to swear furiously but eloquently in Hungarian. My colleague, over a large stack of papers, magazines, miscellaneous papers and literature which was on his desk, in his normal calm manner inquired:

“Was ist loss?” (What happened?)

That was the time when I realized that in unexpected moments my brain automatically switches to Hungarian, my native language, because the Hungarian language is much more colorful to describe the situation than the simple German language. Still looking at the paper I told Schütze the essence of the letter. He knew from our previous discussions that I went from Budapest by car to Berlin, and that the car was left there in the care of an

American organization which had promised to send it over as soon as they found space on one of their airplanes. He also knew that the car had not arrived yet and based on the age and condition of the car, the Tatra was really not a big loss for me, as I would do better with the VW which I purchased. I summarized this for him, to remind him about the story, as we had not discussed this for some time. When I completed this story, I told him that now I am going to read to him the letter from the Berlin police, brought a few minutes ago by Ms. Nickel.

“The essence of the letter was that in December I left my car in the custody of the Berlin police and since that time I did not pick it up. Therefore, they are charging me a storage fee which, at the date of the letter, was for 115 days. They are notifying me to remove the car within 2 weeks. Until then the storage fee would remain the same, but if I do not remove it within 2 weeks, they are going to charge me an additional penalty.”

Schütze almost fell off his chair laughing and asked, "Now what are you going to do?"

I got upset that he was laughing at this unbelievably absurd situation. "It would be good if you would remove this amount of piled up paper and magazines from your desk, because I cannot even see you anymore!"

Namely his habit was that he did not throw out any paper. When he finished a magazine he put it on his desk, the pile of which increased every day. If the pile became so high that we could not see each other, then he picked up the whole thing and put it into a tall steel cabinet. If one got filled up he ordered a new one and started to fill that one too. On my complaint he straightened up so we could now see each other.

“This was a lousy thing the Americans did.” - I said, - “Because they could not transport the car over by airplane they gave it to the police in Berlin, but they did not notify me about that. I think I should write a letter to the Consulate in Frankfurt. They should settle the matter with the police in Berlin. It was not my fault if the car wound up there."

"I think this is a good idea. Write it, and as your wife invited me for dinner, I'll see you in the evening and review it. Mrs. Eisele could type it tomorrow."

"Thank you."

"As to the pile of papers on my desk, you are right."

He got up opened the door of the metal cabinet. I could see that, except for the top shelf, the cabinet was full of papers. He went to his desk and gathered the pile. As he was a very tall fellow, he was able to put everything on the top shelf.

By the evening I thought the matter over and decided to do what I had told Schütze. I would ask the American Consulate in Frankfurt to straighten out this matter. I sat down and drafted a polite but very firm letter in which I wrote how and why the car was left in Berlin, and that I do not even have a key to it, because that was also left with the American Refugee Center there. I asked them to settle the matter with the Berlin police.

When Schütze came for dinner, he reviewed the draft of my letter and said that in his opinion the letter is perfect. At that point we both started to laugh about the whole thing. It was really funny, and Schütze told me that he would like to learn swearing in Hungarian. He did not understand what I said when I read the letter from the Berlin police, but it sounded very colorful and convincing. I told him that, in my opinion, the quality of swearing in Hungarian is at the top and English is at the bottom, the German language is somewhere in between.

Next morning I gave the draft to Mrs. Eisele. I asked her to type it and find the address of the American Consulate in Frankfurt, and I will mail it. The letter was mailed that day. Two weeks later I received a letter from the Berlin police. It seems that the American Consulate was in touch with them, because the letter arrived not to Telefunken but to my home address, which I provided to the Consulate. The letter's tone was quite different from the first one. In this, they informed me where the car is stored, and that if possible, I should remove it in two weeks. I do not have to pay anything.

I called Michael Oppert in Berlin with whom I had talked a few times since we came to Ulm. Therefore he knew about our life and where we are. I told him that the Americans had not yet transported my car as promised, and now I received a letter from the Berlin police that they have my car. I would like to ask as a favor from him to go to the police and try to somehow arrange that the car should be removed from the police storage and sold, as I am not going to need it. In the meantime I had bought a used VW. He said that he will be glad to do all that.

I told him that I am going to send him the letter from the police and an authorization that he has the right to act for me in connection with the car. I am going to get it also signed by Telefunken so he should have no problems. I mailed everything to him the next day.

He called me a week later and told me that everything was settled. He found a junkyard which bought the car. The car by itself had no value, but he got a little money, because the tires were in good condition and they had some value. Also, they transported the car from the police storage free of charge. He said he is sending me a picture which they made of my car when it was sold.

Mr. Michael Oppert and Tatra 57A when it was sold in Berlin in 1957.

He mentioned one interesting thing. All the seats were cut open with a knife, and the inner walls of the car also were opened. One could assume that the car was searched before it was transferred to the police.

The poor little Tatra. Its acquisition, on the road towards communism, needed five letters of recommendation and two Minister's signatures, and behind the iron curtain, I was admired by everyone. On the other side of the iron curtain it was worth only as much as the tires on its wheels. However, independent of how much the little Tatra 57A was worth, for me it will always remain my dream car.

ACKNOWLEDGEMENTS

The story in this book which took place between 1948 and 1957 is based not only on my memory, documents, writings, diaries, pictures, but also on those people's, whom I would like to thank to help me to assemble all the facts by providing their memories, documents, writings, pictures etc.

The entire team of the Tungsram Research Institute and the Research Laboratory for Telecommunication's branch in Újpest (TKI-2) was among the bests for their technical knowledge, diligence, humanity and solidarity. The same can be said about the people at the Headquarter of TKI at the Rózsadomb location, who were the superiors of TKI-2. I feel honored and proud that I was a member of the team at Tungsram Research Institute as well as at TKI-2.

The individuals mentioned in this book are those with whom I worked closely together, but I would like to thank those colleagues and coworkers also, who are not mentioned by their name. I would like to thank those, who provided their memories or work that I was able to write this story:

Dr. András Dallos (Boston, MA). I would like and also those colleagues I had contact when I wrote this book would also like to express thanks to "Andris" who at the time of this story was the Head and "lightning arrestor" of TKI-2 Laboratory. Andris managed to create in the midst of the communist inferno, which was engulfing us, a civilized island, where nobody suffered any indignity or was harmed. I would like to thank him telling me what he remembered, conducted some research for this book and gave me some pictures to make the content of this book accurate and more interesting.

András Dallos – Zsuzsi Dallos – János Ádám (1995)

Károly Ducza (Melbourne, Australia) had an Engineering Degree from the Technical University of Budapest, but he had at that time the position of liaison officer of TKI-2 to the military. He did a lot for us in administrative matters, and he did everything to avert any danger which could be harmful to us, so we should be able to live a civilized life. "Karcsi" and his wife Éva told me their memories on the telephone and provided me with their pictures.

My colleagues, Dr. János Ádám (Budapest), Dr. György Gergely (Budapest), Dr. Gábor Sebestyén (London) and Dr. Lajos Takács (Cleveland, USA) with whom I worked in many research projects, wrote as well as told me their memories, read several chapters and suggested also some corrections. I specially would like to mention Dr. János Ádám who became the director of TKI-2 and continued in that position even after it was renamed again to Tungsram Research Laboratory, to thank him for his outstanding help for reviewing my information, making corrections, conducting research and with all this helped me very much to assure the accuracy of this book.

Vera Bettelheim (Rockville, MD, USA) was for many years my wife. She preserved a largecollection of papers, documents, diaries and pictures and spent lots of time to review all of that and to select for me the proper and suitable ones which were applicable for this book.

Dr. Valéria Széll (Budapest) I would like to thank her for her very valuable research work that she would review chapters of the book and give advice that helped to write it.

Dr. Ildiko Petri (Budapest) I would like to express my thanks for reviewing most of the chapters of this book and not only advising me, but also for her encouragement to write this book.

Metta Kolozs (Mrs. János Horvath – Budapest) I am thanking her for the information she provided me in connection with Szeged.

This book was first published in 2010 in Hungarian by Móra, one of Hungary's major publishing Company. I would like to thank Mr. János Janikovszky, President of Móra for his help and also Mrs. Anna Balassa who was the Editor of this book. In reality, the author creates the book like a big garden. The Editor is the chief gardener, kills the weeds, removes the wilted flowers, forms the bushes and trees. The Editor of a book is not appreciated by the public reading the book, because the visitor of the garden, the reader believes that everything was created by the writer.

In connection with the English language version of this book, which I translated I would like to express my special thanks to people, without whose help the book would not have been completed:

Helene Ramo (Chevy Chase, MD, USA), very much encouraged me to prepare the English translation and spent much time to proofread and make corrections, and offered advice for every chapter of the book.

Richard Kay (Switzerland), with whom I worked for many years in the quality issues related to solar energy. Richard being the master of the English language, I am very thankful that he gave advice and offered also his lifelong experience that in the first half of the book every t should be crossed and every i dotted.

My daughter, Mrs. Tom Bornstein (Éva) (Juneau, Alaska, USA), reviewing, correcting and approving the chapters she is mentioned in.

Table of Contents

Made in the USA
Charleston, SC
24 May 2012